AMERICA'S BYWAYS™
ALL-AMERICAN ROADS

come **CLOSER** *to* the heart and soul of *your* AMERICA

America's Byways Series | MOBIL TRAVEL GUIDE

We gratefully acknowledge our inspection team for their efficient and perceptive evaluations of the establishments listed in this book and the establishments for their cooperation in showing their facilities and providing information about them.

Thanks also go to the National Scenic Byways Program and the coordinators of the individual Byways for all their help and support in the coordination of this project.

VICE PRESIDENT, PUBLICATIONS: **Kevin Bristow**
MANAGING EDITOR: **Pam Mourouzis**
MANAGER OF PUBLISHING PRODUCTION SERVICES: **Ellen Tobler**
CONCEPT AND COVER DESIGN: **ABS Graphics, Inc. Design Group**
EDITOR: **Tere Drenth**
PRINTING ACKNOWLEDGEMENT: **North American Corporation of Illinois**

Copyright © 2004 EMTG, LLC. All rights reserved. Except for copies made by individuals for personal use, this publication may not be reproduced in whole or in part by any means whatsoever without prior written permission from Mobil Travel Guide, 1460 Renaissance Drive, Suite 401, Park Ridge, IL 60068; 847/795-6700; info@mobiltravelguide.com.

Mobil, Exxon, and Mobil Travel Guide are trademarks of Exxon Mobil Corporation or one of its subsidiaries. All rights reserved. Reproduction by any means, including, but not limited to, photography, electrostatic copying devices, or electronic data processing is prohibited. Use of information contained herein for solicitation of advertising or listing in any other publication is expressly prohibited without prior written permission from Exxon Mobil Corporation. Violations of reserved rights are subject to prosecution.

The information contained herein is derived from a variety of third-party sources. Although every effort has been made to verify the information obtained from such sources, the publisher assumes no responsibility for inconsistencies or inaccuracies in the data or liability for any damage of any type arising from errors or omissions.

Neither the editors nor the publisher assumes responsibility for the services provided by any business listed in this guide or for any loss, damage, or disruption in your travel for any reason.

ISBN: 0-9727-0226-1

Manufactured in the United States of America.

10 9 8 7 6 5 4 3 2 1

America's Byways Series | MOBIL TRAVEL GUIDE

Table of Contents

America's Byways All-American Roads

MAPS

Alabama
Natchez Trace Parkway A5
Selma to Montgomery March Byway A6

Alaska The Seward Highway A7

California
Big Sur Coast Highway—Route 1 .... A8
San Luis Obispo North Coast Byway—Route 1 .... A9
Volcanic Legacy Scenic Byway A10

Colorado
San Juan Skyway A11
Trail Ridge Road/Beaver Meadow Road A12

Illinois The Historic National Road A13

Louisiana Creole Nature Trail A14

Maine Acadia Byway A15

Minnesota North Shore Scenic Drive A16

Montana Beartooth Highway A17

Nevada Las Vegas Strip A18

New York Lakes to Locks Passage: The Great Northeast Journey A19

North Carolina Blue Ridge Parkway A20

Oregon
Hells Canyon Scenic Byway A21
Historic Columbia River Highway A22
Pacific Coast Scenic Byway A23

Utah A Journey Through Time Scenic Byway—Highway 12 .... A24

Washington Chinook Scenic Byway A25

FEATURED BYWAYS A26

A WORD TO OUR READERS A33

OVERVIEW OF THE NATIONAL SCENIC BYWAYS PROGRAM A35

INTRODUCTION A37

continued on next page

America's Byways Series | MOBIL TRAVEL GUIDE
Table of Contents

ALL-AMERICAN ROADS

Alabama
Natchez Trace Parkway 1
Selma to Montgomery March Byway 7

Alaska The Seward Highway 13

California
Big Sur Coast Highway—Route 1 21
San Luis Obispo North Coast Byway—Route 1 33
Volcanic Legacy Scenic Byway 41

Colorado
San Juan Skyway 49
Trail Ridge Road/Beaver Meadow Road 59

Illinois The Historic National Road 65

Indiana The Historic National Road 71

Louisiana Creole Nature Trail 83

Maine Acadia Byway 91

Maryland The Historic National Road 99

Minnesota North Shore Scenic Drive 111

Mississippi Natchez Trace Parkway 121

Montana Beartooth Highway 131

Nevada Las Vegas Strip 137

New York Lakes to Locks Passage: The Great Northeast Journey 149

North Carolina Blue Ridge Parkway 157

Ohio The Historic National Road 167

Oregon
Hells Canyon Scenic Byway 173
Historic Columbia River Highway 179
Pacific Coast Scenic Byway 185
Volcanic Legacy Scenic Byway 197

Pennsylvania The Historic National Road 203

Tennessee Natchez Trace Parkway 209

Utah A Journey Through Time Scenic Byway—Highway 12 217

Washington Chinook Scenic Byway 223

West Virginia The Historic National Road 229

Wyoming Beartooth Scenic Byway 233

Natchez Trace Parkway
also covers MS • TN • AL

ALL-AMERICAN ROADS A5

AL Selma to Montgomery March Byway

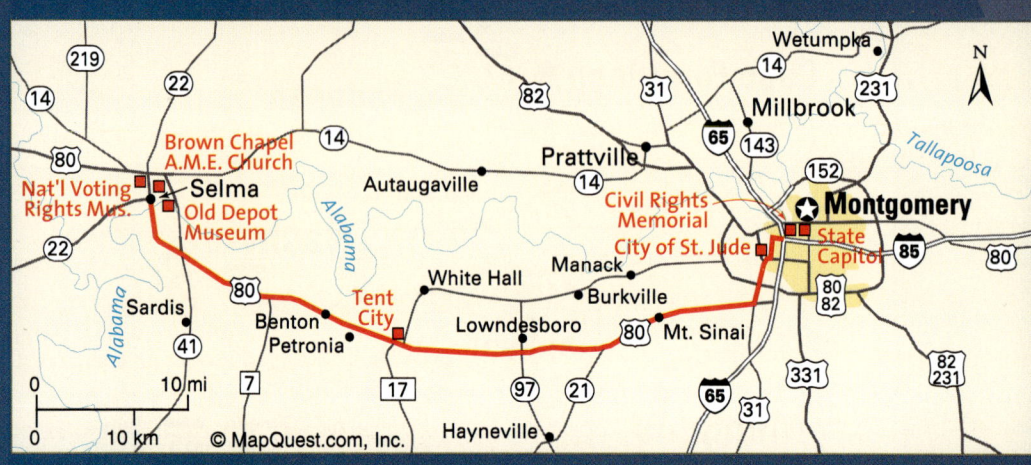

The Seward Highway AK

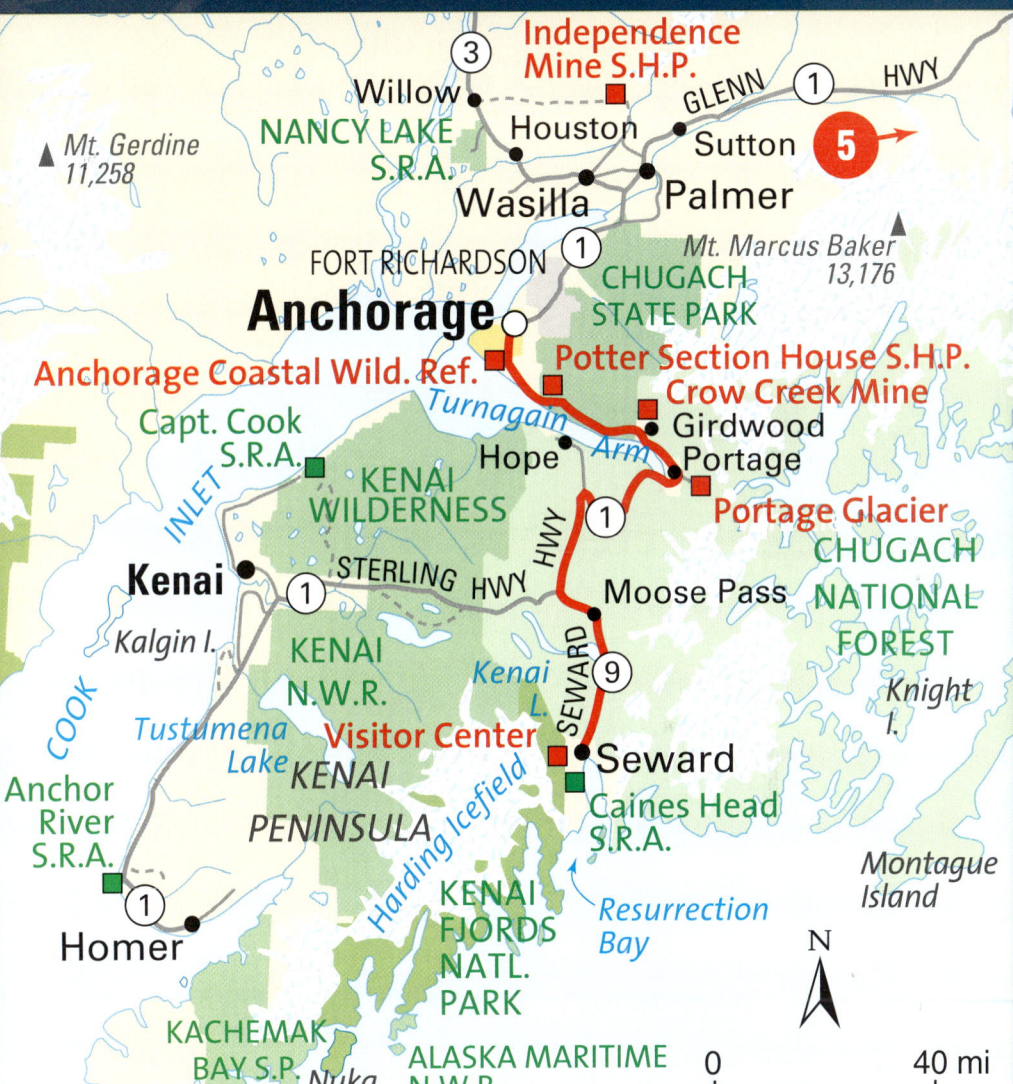

ALL-AMERICAN ROADS

CA Big Sur Coast Highway—Route 1

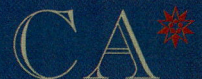

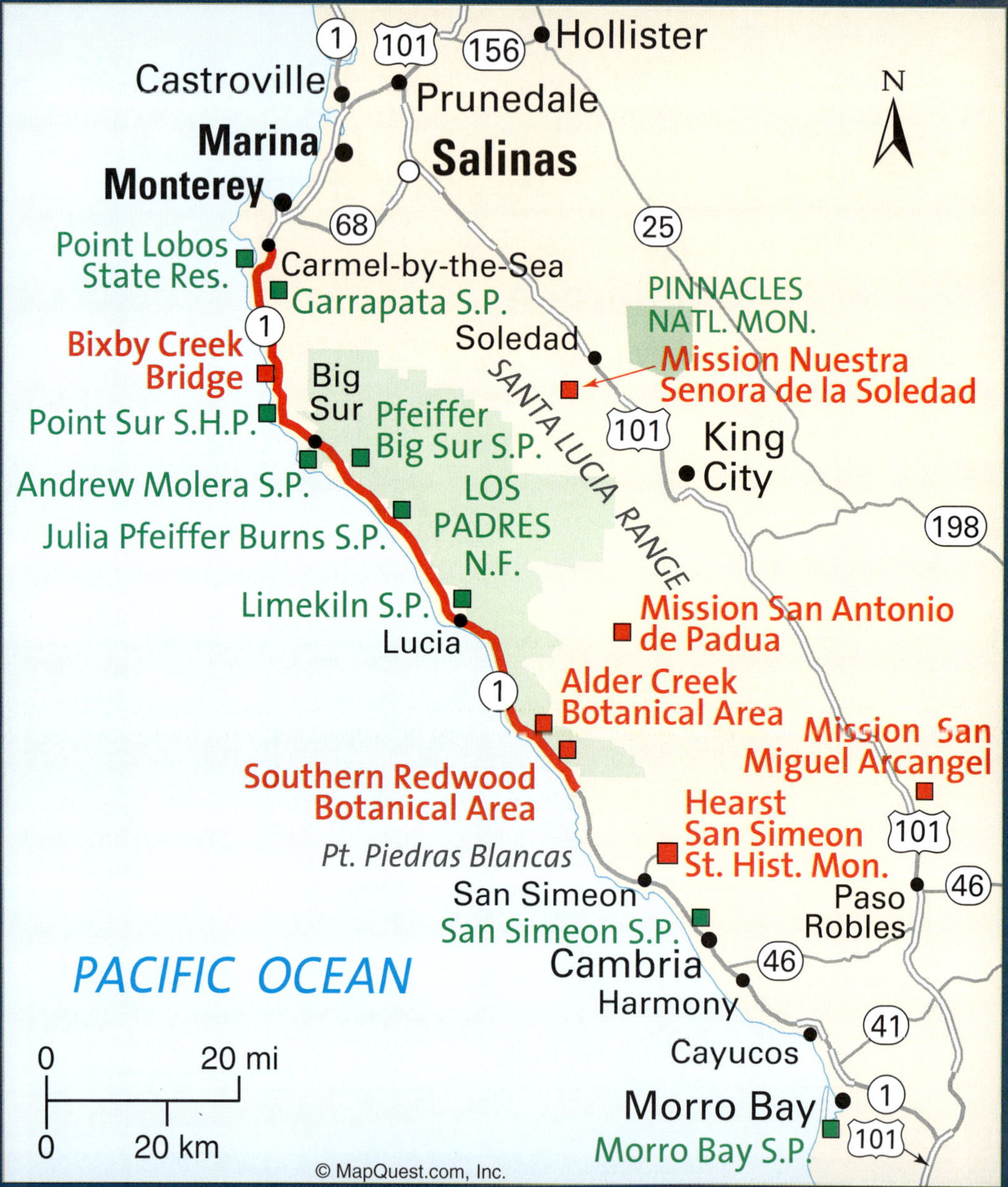

San Luis Obispo North Coast Byway—Route 1

CA

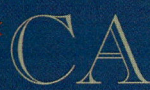

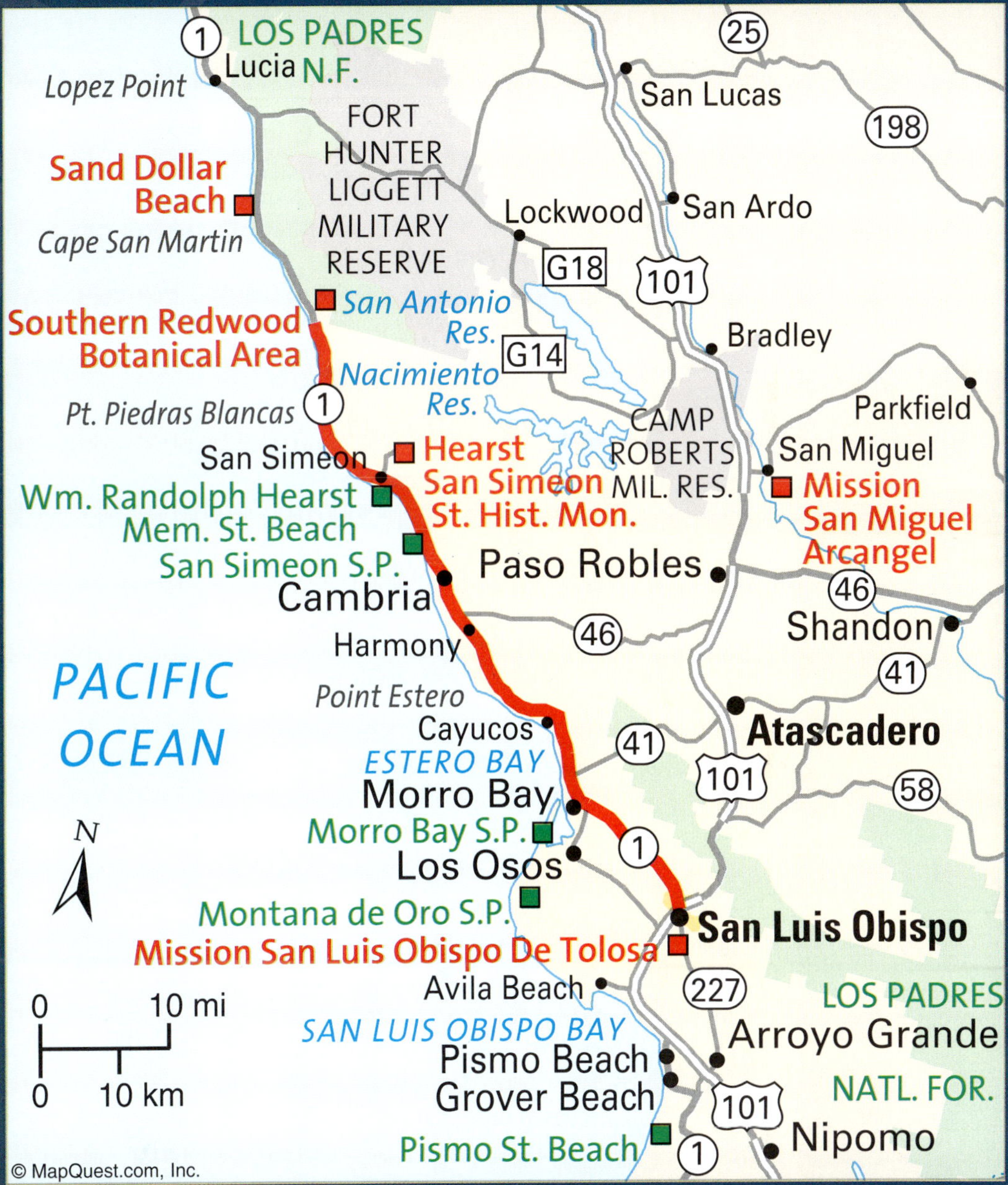

CA Volcanic Legacy Scenic Byway

also covers OR

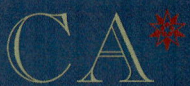

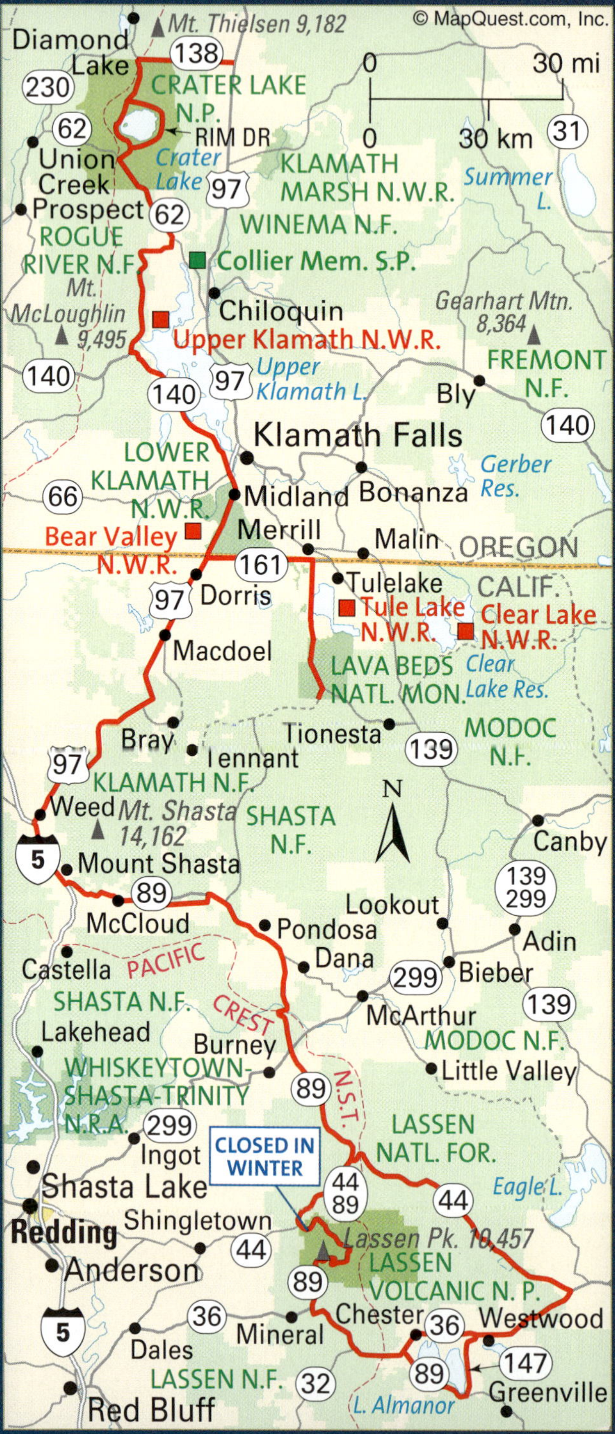

Trail Ridge Road/Beaver Meadow Road

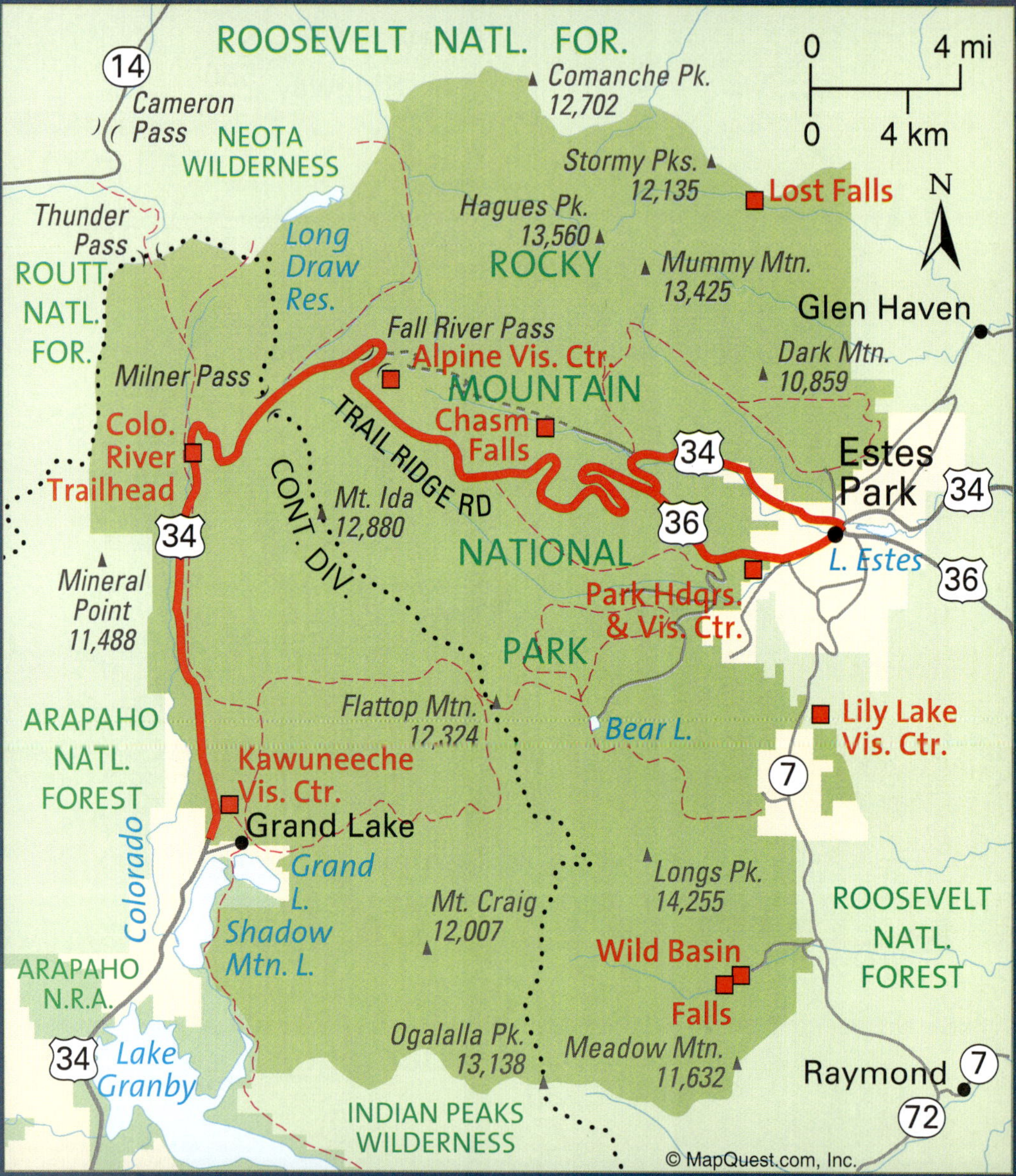

The Historic National Road ✳ IL

also covers IN ✳ MD ✳ OH ✳ PA ✳ WV

ALL-AMERICAN ROADS A13

LA Creole Nature Trail

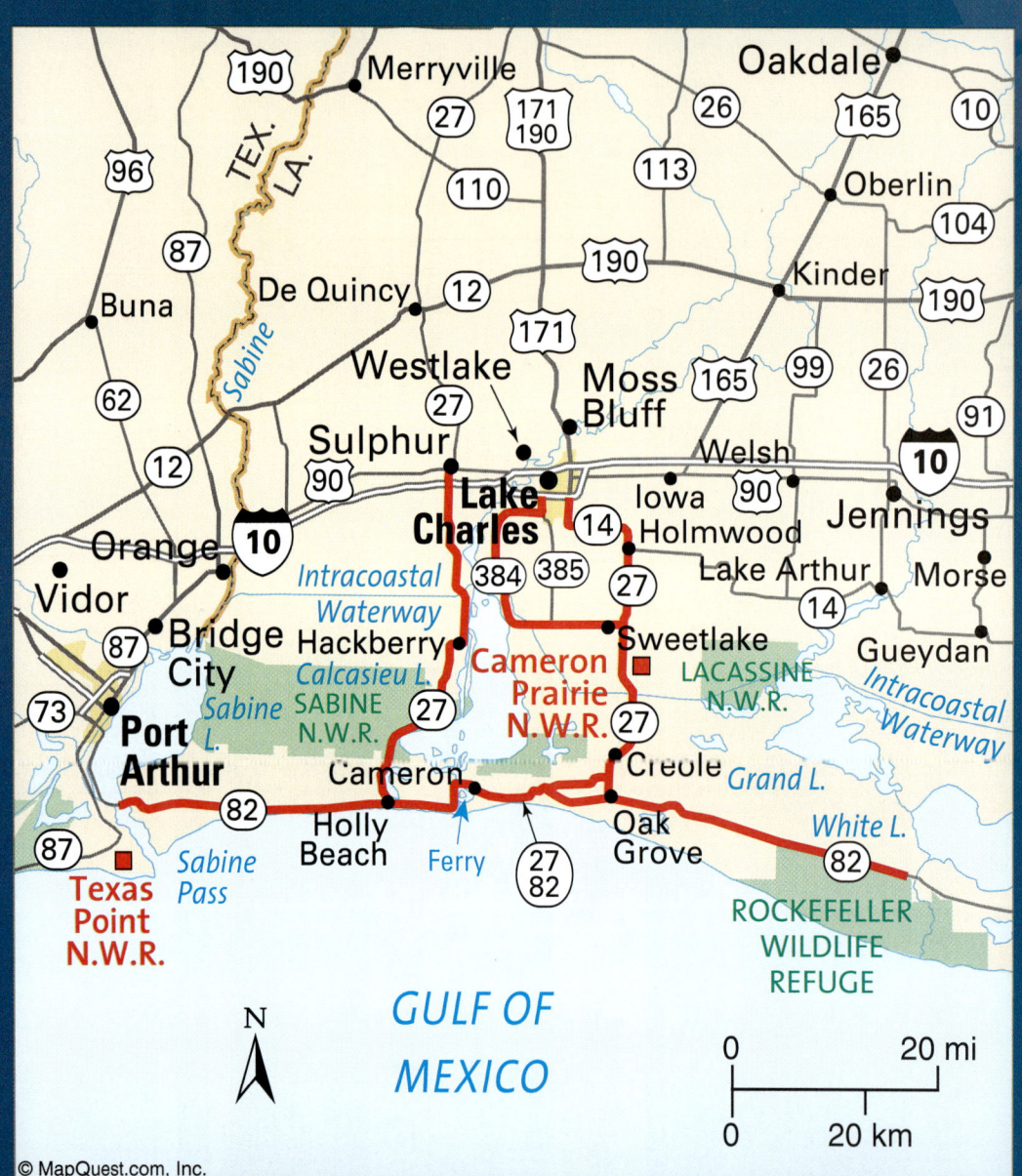

Acadia Byway ME

ALL-AMERICAN ROADS A15

MN North Shore Scenic Drive

Beartooth Highway

also covers WY

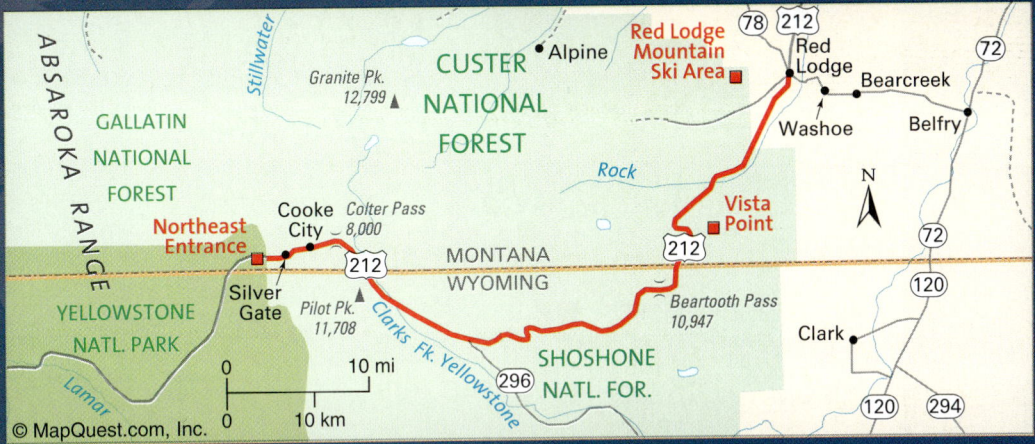

Lakes to Locks Passage: The Great Northeast Journey **NY**

NC Blue Ridge Parkway

Hells Canyon Scenic Byway

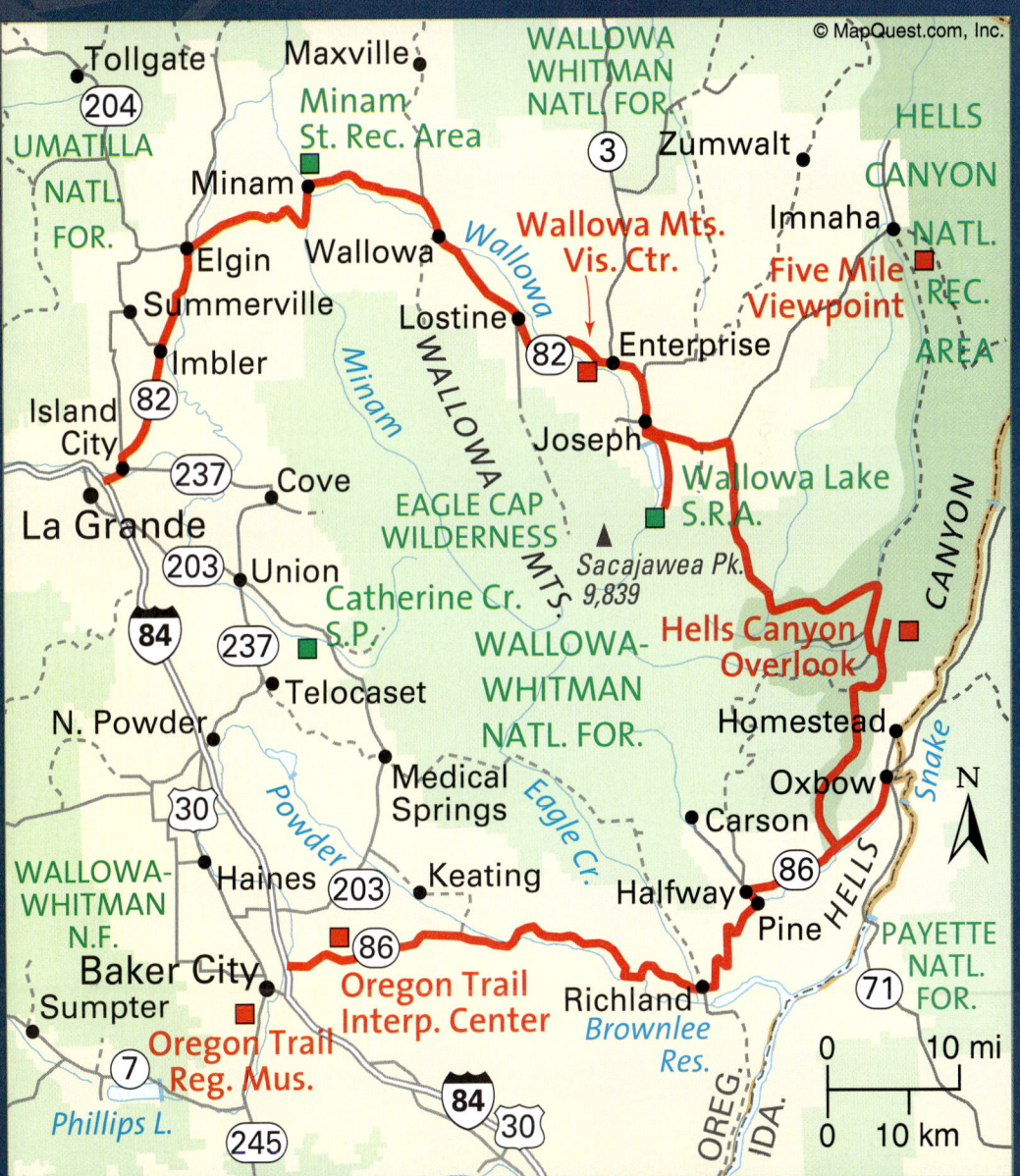

OR — Historic Columbia River Highway

Pacific Coast Scenic Byway

UT — A Journey Through Time Scenic Byway—Highway 12

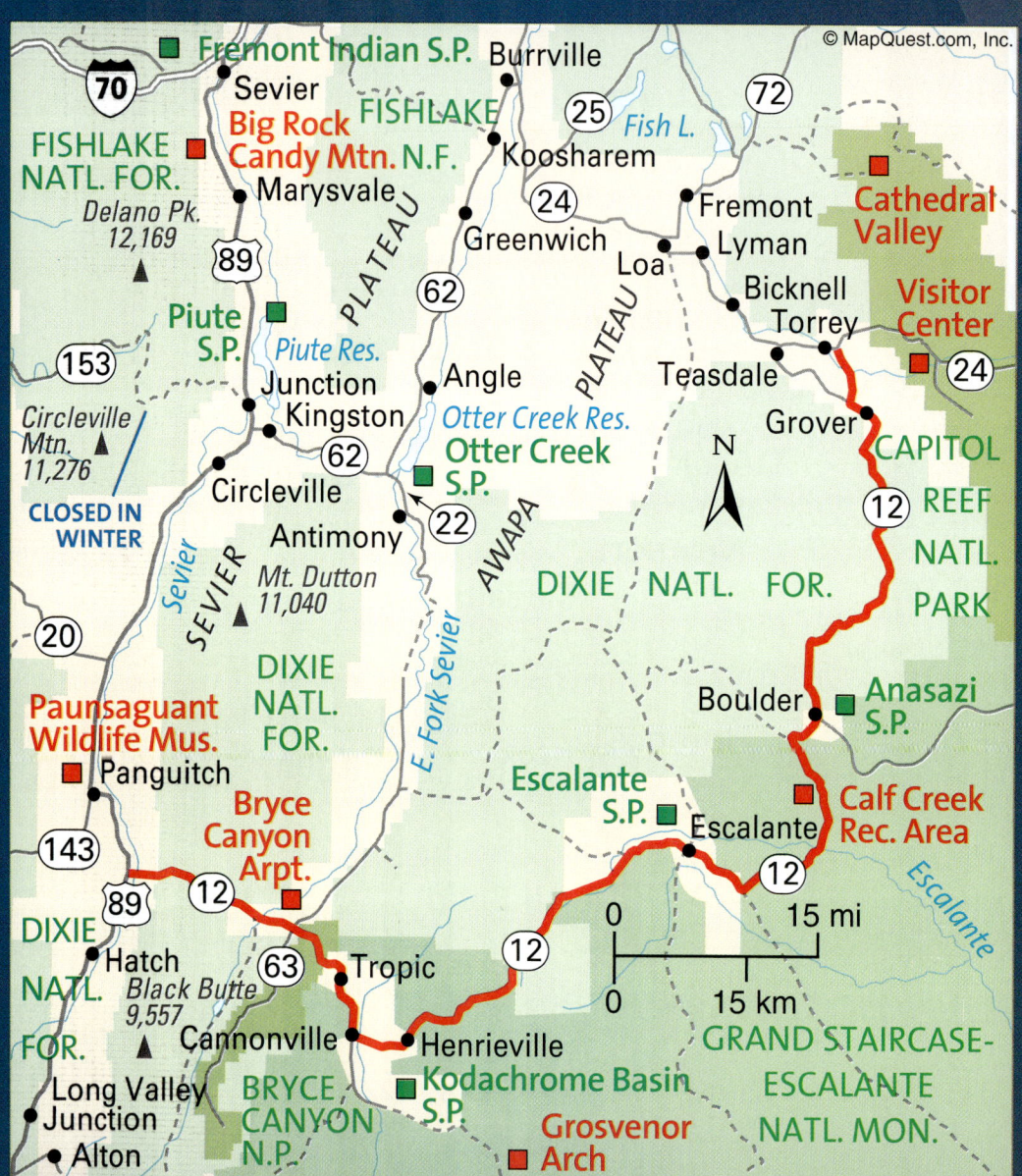

Chinook Scenic Byway

come CLOSER to the heart and soul of your AMERICA

America's Byways are a distinctive collection of American roads, their stories and treasured places. They are roads to the heart and soul of America. Each and every Byway has unique qualities that make it special, whether it is a coastal highway known for its striking scenery or a historic route that takes travelers on a path through the country's past. The images on these pages give you only a taste of what the Byways in this region have to offer. For more photos, see the individual Byways.

The Seward Highway

Lily pads in Kenai Lake

Kenai Lake, one of the spectacular views along The Seward Highway, was created by meltwater from surrounding glaciers. Colorful lily pads in the milky-blue water, framed by forests and mountains in the distance, create a breathtaking scene.

Alaska

Big Sur Coast Highway

Aerial view of the Big Sur coastline

Although Route 1 hugs the Pacific Ocean's beautiful shoreline, this Byway offers more than coastal views. The Byways winds through rugged mountains and majestic forests that harbor bountiful wildlife.

California

Acadia Byway

Lobstering in Acadia

Lobster boats, which have been trolling the waters of the Atlantic Ocean for over 150 years, are a picturesque sight along the Acadia Byway. Lobstermen mark their traps with colorful buoys.

Maine

North Shore Scenic Drive

Grand Portage National Monument

The Grand Portage National Monument, located along the North Shore Scenic Drive, preserves the history of both Ojibwe Indians and the fur trade that thrived here during the 18th, 19th, and 20th centuries.

Minnesota

Las Vegas Strip

Dusk falls over the Las Vegas Strip

The Las Vegas Strip dazzles Byway visitors with four and a half miles of luxury hotels, fine restaurants, and first-class entertainment. While on the Strip, be sure to try your luck at any of the world-renowned casinos found here.

Nevada

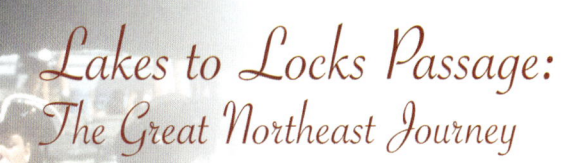

Lakes to Locks Passage:
The Great Northeast Journey

Fort Ticonderoga Fife & Drum Corps

The Fife & Drum Corps performs daily at Fort Ticonderoga, site of the first colonial victory of the Revolutionary War. The fort and other attractions along the Byway highlight the deep historical roots of the area.

New York

Blue Ridge Parkway

Flowers in bloom along the Blue Ridge Parkway

From early spring wildflowers to brilliant fall foliage to snow-colored mountain peaks in winter, changing seasons along the Blue Ridge drench the Byway in color and grandeur throughout the year.

North Carolina

ALL-AMERICAN ROADS **A29**

Hells Canyon Scenic Byway

The snowy peaks of the Wallowa Mountains

At nearly 10,000 feet in elevation, the Wallowa Mountains are visible from most of the Hells Canyon Scenic Byway. The jagged peaks retain pockets of snow throughout the summer.

Oregon

Natchez Trace Parkway

Autumn foliage on the Natchez Trace

While all seasons are beautiful on the Natchez Trace Parkway, in autumn, trees that surround the Byway put on a stunning array of colors, ranging from red and maroon to orange and gold.

Tennessee

A Journey Through Time
Scenic Byway—Highway 12

Fossilized Rock Formations

Along Highway 12, the stone towers, pinnacles, and arches—formed by water and wind over millions of years—present an artistic masterpiece to travelers. Vivid colors and irregular shapes beckon you to look closer.

Utah

Chinook Scenic Byway

Mount Rainier

Mount Rainier, "the shining jewel of the Northwest," rises in the background as a deer grazes nearby. The mountain is best viewed by driving the Chinook Scenic Byway.

Washington

ALL-AMERICAN ROADS A31

The Historic National Road

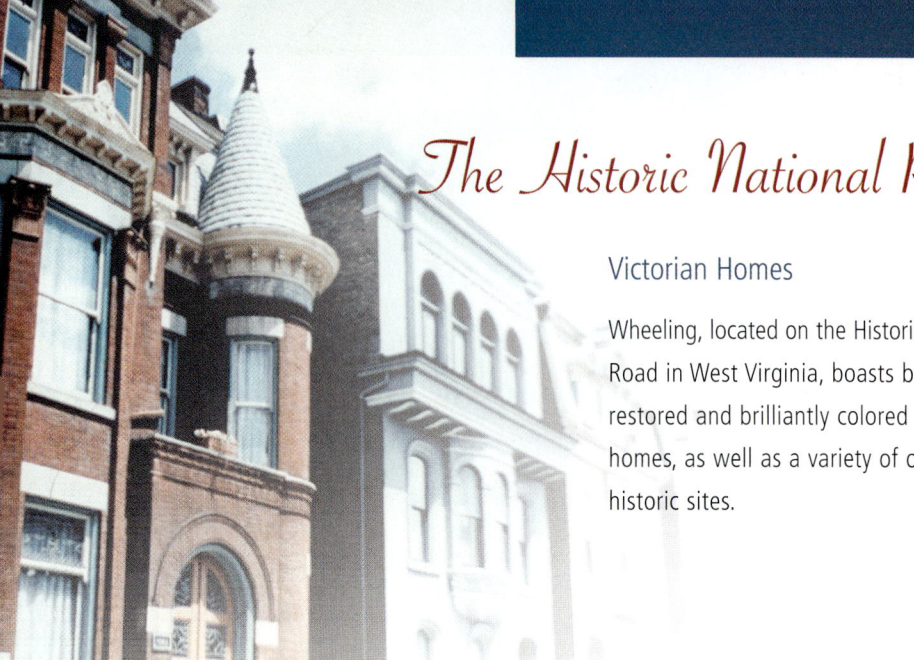

Victorian Homes

Wheeling, located on the Historic National Road in West Virginia, boasts beautifully restored and brilliantly colored Victorian homes, as well as a variety of other historic sites.

West Virginia

Beartooth Scenic Byway

Fisherman in Clarks Fork of Yellowstone River

The area surrounding the Beartooth Scenic Byway offers a wealth of recreational opportunities, including trout-fishing. Visitors also enjoy hiking, cross-country skiing, and riding horseback on the area's many trails; watching and photographing wildlife; and camping in any of the 12 national forests along the way..

Wyoming

America's Byways Series | MOBIL TRAVEL GUIDE

A Word to Our Readers

Travelers are on the roads in great numbers these days. They're exploring the country on day trips, weekend getaways, business trips, and extended family vacations, visiting major cities and small towns along the way. Because time is precious and the travel industry is ever-changing, having accurate, reliable travel information at your fingertips is critical. Mobil Travel Guide has been providing invaluable insight to travelers for more than 45 years, and we are committed to continuing this service well into the future.

The Mobil Corporation (known as Exxon Mobil Corporation since a 1999 merger) began producing the Mobil Travel Guide books in 1958, following the introduction of the US highway system in 1956. The first edition covered only five southwestern states. Since then, our books have become the premier travel guides in North America, covering the 48 contiguous states and Canada. Now, Mobil Travel Guide presents a brand-new series in partnership with the National Scenic Byways Program. We also recently introduced road atlases and specialty publications; a robust new Web site; as well as the first fully integrated, road-centric travel support program called MobilCompanion, the driving force in travel.

Since its founding, Mobil Travel Guide has served as an advocate for travelers seeking knowledge about hotels, restaurants, and places to visit. Based on an objective process, we make recommendations to our customers that we believe will enhance the quality and value of their travel experiences. Our trusted Mobil One- to Five-Star rating system is the oldest and most respected lodging and restaurant inspection and rating program in North America. Most hoteliers, restaurateurs, and industry observers favorably regard the rigor of our inspection program and understand the prestige and benefits that come with receiving a Mobil star rating.

The Mobil Travel Guide process of rating each establishment includes:

- Unannounced facility inspections
- Incognito service evaluations for Mobil Four- and Five-Star properties
- A review of unsolicited comments from the general public
- Senior management oversight

For each property, more than 450 attributes, including cleanliness, physical facilities, employee attitude, and courtesy, are measured and evaluated to produce a mathematically derived score, which is then blended with the other elements to form an overall score. These quantifiable scores allow comparative analysis among properties and form the basis that Mobil Travel Guide uses to assign its Mobil One- to Five-Star ratings.

This process focuses largely on guest expectations, guest experience, and consistency of service, not just physical facilities and amenities. It is fundamentally a relative rating system that rewards those properties that continually strive for and achieve excellence each year. Indeed, the very best properties are consistently raising the bar for those that wish to compete with them. These properties proactively respond to consumers' needs even in today's uncertain times.

Only facilities that meet Mobil Travel Guide's standards earn the privilege of being listed in our books. Deteriorating, poorly managed establishments are deleted. A Mobil Travel Guide listing constitutes a positive quality

A WORD TO OUR READERS

recommendation; every listing is an accolade, a recognition of achievement. Our Mobil One- to Five-Star rating system highlights its level of service. Extensive in-house research is constantly underway to determine new additions to our lists.

- The **Mobil Five-Star Award** indicates that a property is one of the very best in the country and consistently provides gracious and courteous service, superlative quality in its facility, and a unique ambience. The lodgings and restaurants at the Mobil Five-Star level consistently and proactively respond to consumers' needs and continue their commitment to excellence, doing so with grace and perseverance.

- Also highly regarded is the **Mobil Four-Star Award**, which honors properties for outstanding achievement in overall facility and for providing very strong service levels in all areas. These award-winners provide a distinctive experience for the ever-demanding and sophisticated consumer.

- The **Mobil Three-Star Award** recognizes an excellent property that provides full services and amenities. This category ranges from exceptional hotels with limited services to elegant restaurants with a less-formal atmosphere.

- A **Mobil Two-Star property** is a clean and comfortable establishment that has expanded amenities or a distinctive environment. A Mobil Two-Star property is an excellent place to stay or dine.

- A **Mobil One-Star property** is limited in its amenities and services but focuses on providing a value experience while meeting travelers' expectations. The property can be expected to be clean, comfortable, and convenient.

Allow us to emphasize that we do not charge establishments for inclusion in our guides. We have no relationship with any of the businesses and attractions we list and act only as a consumer advocate. In essence, we do the investigative legwork so that you won't have to.

Keep in mind, too, that the hospitality business is ever-changing. Restaurants and lodgings—particularly small chains and standalone establishments—change management or even go out of business with surprising quickness. Although we make every effort to double-check information during our annual updates, we nevertheless recommend that you call ahead to make sure the place you've selected is still open and offers all the amenities you're looking for. We've provided phone numbers; when available, we also list Web site addresses.

We hope that your travels are enjoyable and relaxing and that our books help you get the most out of every trip you take. If any aspect of your accommodation, dining, or sightseeing experience motivates you to comment, please drop us a line. We depend a great deal on our readers' remarks, so you can be assured that we will read your comments and assimilate them into our research. General comments about our books are also welcome. You can write to us at Mobil Travel Guide, 1460 Renaissance Drive, Suite 401, Park Ridge, IL 60068, or send an e-mail to info@mobiltravelguide.com.

Take your Mobil Travel Guide books along on every trip you take. We're confident that you'll be pleased with their convenience, ease of use, and breadth of dependable coverage.

Happy travels!

Overview of the National Scenic Byways Program

WHAT ARE AMERICA'S BYWAYS™?

Under the National Scenic Byways Program, the US Secretary of Transportation recognizes certain roads as National Scenic Byways or All-American Roads based on their archaeological, cultural, historic, natural, recreational, and scenic qualities. There are 96 such designated Byways in 39 states. The Federal Highway Administration promotes the collection as America's Byways™.

America's Byways™ are a distinctive collection of American roads, their stories and treasured places. They are roads to the heart and soul of America. Byways are exclusive because of their outstanding qualities, not because Byways are confined to a select group of people.

Managing the intrinsic qualities that shape the Byway's story and interpreting the story are equally important in improving the quality of the visitors' experience. The National Scenic Byways Program is founded upon the strength of the leaders for individual Byways. It is a voluntary, grassroots program. It recognizes and supports outstanding roads. It provides resources to help manage the intrinsic qualities within the broader Byway corridor to be treasured and shared. Perhaps one of the underlying principles for the program has been articulated best by the Byway leader who said, "The program is about recognition, not regulation."

WHAT DEFINES A NATIONAL SCENIC BYWAY AND AN ALL-AMERICAN ROAD?

To be designated as a National Scenic Byway, a road must possess at least one of the six intrinsic qualities described below. To receive an All-American Road designation, a road must possess multiple intrinsic qualities that are nationally significant and contain one-of-a-kind features that do not exist elsewhere. The road or highway must also be considered a destination unto itself. That is, the road must provide an exceptional traveling experience so recognized by travelers that they would make a drive along the highway a primary reason for their trip.

Anyone may nominate a road for possible designation by the US Secretary of Transportation, but the nomination must be submitted through a state's official scenic byway agency and include a corridor management plan designed to preserve and enhance the unique qualities of the Byway.

The Byways themselves typically are supported through a network of individuals who volunteer their time and effort. It is a bottom-up, grassroots-oriented program. Local citizens and communities create the vision for their Byway, identify the resources comprising the intrinsic qualities, and form the theme or story that stirs the interest and imagination of visitors about the Byway and its resources. Local citizens and communities decide how best to balance goals, strategies, and actions for promoting the Byway and preserving its intrinsic qualities. The vision, goals, strategies, and actions for the Byway are laid out in the required corridor management plan.

Nomination is not about filling out an application. It's all about telling the Byway's story. That's the premise that is driving the FHWA's work on requesting nominations for possible national designation. Nominees might want to think of their Byway's nomination as a combination of the community's guide and a visitor's guide for the Byway.

OVERVIEW OF THE NATIONAL SCENIC BYWAYS PROGRAM

WHAT ARE INTRINSIC QUALITIES?

An intrinsic quality is a scenic, historic, recreational, cultural, archaeological, or natural feature that is considered representative, unique, irreplaceable, or distinctly characteristic of an area. The National Scenic Byways Program provides resources to the Byway community and enhances local quality of life through efforts to preserve, protect, interpret, and promote the intrinsic qualities of designated Byways.

- **Archaeological quality** involves those characteristics of the Byway corridor that are physical evidence of historic or prehistoric life that is visible and capable of being inventoried and interpreted.

- **Cultural quality** is evidence and expressions of the customs or traditions of a distinct group of people. Cultural features include, but are not limited to, crafts, music, dance, rituals, festivals, speech, food, special events, and vernacular architecture that are currently practiced.

- **Historic quality** encompasses legacies of the past that are distinctly associated with physical elements of the landscape, whether natural or man-made, that are of such historic significance that they educate the viewer and stir an appreciation of the past.

- **Natural quality** applies to those features in the visual environment that are in a relatively undisturbed state. These features predate the arrival of human populations and may include geological formations, fossils, landforms, water bodies, vegetation, and wildlife.

- **Recreational quality** involves outdoor recreational activities directly associated with, and dependent upon, the natural and cultural elements of the corridor's landscape.

- **Scenic quality** is the heightened visual experience derived from the view of natural and man-made elements of the visual environment.

For more information about the National Scenic Byways Program, call 800/4BYWAYS or visit the Web site www.byways.org.

America's Byways Series | MOBIL TRAVEL GUIDE

Introduction

America's Byways™ are a distinctive collection of American roads, their stories, and treasured places. They are the roads to the heart and soul of America. This book showcases a select group of nationally designated Byways and organizes them by state, and within each state, alphabetically by Byway. Information in this book is collected from two sources:

- The National Scenic Byways Program (NSBP) provides content about the Byways themselves—quick facts, the Byway story, and highlights. NSBP's information contributors include federal, regional, and state organizations, as well as private groups and individuals. These parties have been recognized as experts in Byways and are an authoritative source for the Byways information that appears in this book.

- Information in this book about lodgings, restaurants, and most sights and attractions along the Byways comes from Mobil Travel Guide, which has served as a trusted aid to auto travelers in search of value in lodging, dining, and destinations since its inception in 1958. The Mobil One- to Five-Star rating system is the oldest and most respected lodging and restaurant inspection and rating program in North America. This trusted, well-established tool directs you to satisfying places to eat and stay, as well as to interesting events and attractions in thousands of locations.

The following sections explain the wealth of information you'll find about the Byways that appear in this book: information about the Byway, things to see and do along the way, and places to stay and eat.

Quick Facts

This section gives you an overview of each Byway, including the following quick facts:

LENGTH: The number of miles from one end of the Byway to the other.

TIME TO ALLOW: How much time to allow to drive the entire length. For some Byways, the suggested time is several days because of the length or the number of attractions on or near the Byway; for others, the time is listed in hours.

BEST TIME TO DRIVE: The season(s) in which the Byway is most appealing. For some Byways, you also discover the peak season, which you may want to avoid if you're looking for a peaceful, uncrowded drive.

BYWAY TRAVEL INFORMATION: Telephone numbers and Web sites for the Byway organization and any local travel and tourism centers.

SPECIAL CONSIDERATIONS: Words of advice that range from the type of clothing you'll want to bring to winter-weather advisories.

RESTRICTIONS: Closings or other cautionary tips.

BICYCLE/PEDESTRIAN FACILITIES: Explains whether the Byway is safe and pleasant for bicycling and/or walking.

INTRODUCTION

THE BYWAY STORY

As explained in the preceding section titled "Overview of the National Scenic Byways Program," a road must possess intrinsic qualities and one-of-a-kind features to receive a National Scenic Byway or All-American Road designation. An All-American Road must also be considered a destination unto itself. This section describes the unique qualities of each Byway, with a separate section for each of its intrinsic qualities. Here you'll find information about the history and culture of the roadway, the wildlife and other natural features found along the Byway, and the recreational opportunities that are available to visitors to the area.

HIGHLIGHTS

Some local Byway organizations suggest tours or itineraries that cover all or part of the Byway. Where these itineraries are available, they're included in this book under the heading "Highlights."

THINGS TO SEE AND DO

Mobil Travel Guide offers information about nearly 20,000 museums, art galleries, amusement parks, historic sites, national and state parks, ski areas, and many other types of attractions. A white star on a black background ★ signals that the attraction is a must-see—one of the best in the area. Because municipal parks, public tennis courts, swimming pools, and small educational institutions are common to most towns, they generally are not mentioned.

When a Byway goes through or comes quite close to a particular town, city, or national park, attractions in those towns or parks are included. Otherwise, attractions are limited to those along the Byway.

Attractions for the entire Byway are listed alphabetically by name. Following an attraction's description, you'll find the months, days, and, in some cases, hours of operation; the address/directions, telephone number, and Web site (if there is one); and the admission price category. The following are the ranges we use for admission fees:

- **FREE**
- **DONATION**
- $ = Up to $5
- $$ = $5.01-$10
- $$$ = $10.01-$15
- $$$$ = $15.01 and up

PLACES TO STAY

For each Byway, recommended lodgings are listed in alphabetical order, based on the cities in which they're located. In general, only lodgings that are close to or located right on the Byway are listed.

Each lodging listing gives the name, address/location (when no street address is available), neighborhood and/or directions from downtown (in major cities), phone number(s), Web site (if available), total number of guest rooms, and seasons open (if not year-round). Also included are details on business, luxury, recreational, and dining facilities on the property or nearby. A key to the symbols at the end of each listing can be found in the "Terms, Abbreviations, and Symbols in Listings" section of this Introduction.

Because most lodgings offer the following features and services, information about them does not appear in the listings unless exceptions exist:

- Year-round operation with a single rate structure
- Major credit cards accepted (note that Exxon or Mobil Corporation credit cards cannot be used to pay for room or other charges)
- Air-conditioning and heat, often with individual room controls
- Bathroom with tub and/or shower in each room
- Cots and cribs available

- Daily maid service
- Elevators
- In-room telephones

For every property, we also provide pricing information. Because lodging rates change frequently, we list a pricing category rather than specific prices. The pricing categories break down as follows:

- ¢ = Up to $90
- $ = $91-$150
- $$ = $151-$250
- $$$ = $251-$350
- $$$$ = $351 and up

All prices quoted are in effect at the time of publication; however, prices cannot be guaranteed. Note that in some locations, short-term price variations may exist because of special events or holidays. Certain resorts have complicated rate structures that vary with the time of year; always confirm rates when making your plans.

All listed establishments have been inspected by experienced field representatives and/or evaluated by a senior staff member. Our ratings are based on detailed inspection reports of the individual properties, on written evaluations of staff members who stay and dine anonymously, and on an extensive review of reader comments. Rating categories reflect both the features a property offers and its quality in relation to similar establishments.

Here are the definitions for the star ratings for lodgings:

- ★★★★★: A Mobil Five-Star lodging provides consistently superlative service in an exceptionally distinctive luxury environment, with expanded services. Attention to detail is evident throughout the hotel, resort, or inn, from bed linens to staff uniforms.
- ★★★★: A Mobil Four-Star lodging provides a luxury experience with expanded amenities in a distinctive environment. Services may include, but are not limited to, automatic turndown service, 24-hour room service, and valet parking.
- ★★★: A Mobil Three-Star lodging is well appointed, with a full-service restaurant and expanded amenities, such as a fitness center, golf course, tennis courts, 24-hour room service, and optional turndown service.
- ★★: A Mobil Two-Star lodging is considered a clean, comfortable, and reliable establishment that has expanded amenities, such as a full-service restaurant on the premises.
- ★: A Mobil One-Star lodging is a limited-service hotel, motel, or inn that is considered a clean, comfortable, and reliable establishment.

PLACES TO EAT

For each Byway, dining establishments are listed in alphabetical order, based on the cities in which they're located. These restaurants and other eateries are either right on or close to the Byway chapter in which they're listed. All establishments listed have a full kitchen and offer table service and a complete menu. Parking on or near the premises, in a lot or garage, is assumed.

Each listing also gives the cuisine type, address (or directions if no street address is available), neighborhood and/or directions from downtown (in major cities), phone number, Web site (if available), meals served, days of operation (if not open daily year-round), reservation policy, and pricing category. We also indicate whether a children's menu is offered. The pricing categories are defined as follows per diner and assume that you order an appetizer, entrée, and one drink:

- $ = Up to $15
- $$ = $16-$35
- $$$ = $36-$85
- $$$$ = $86 and up

All listed establishments have been inspected by experienced field representatives and/or evaluated by a senior staff member. Our ratings are based on detailed inspection reports of the individual properties, on written evaluations of staff members who stay and dine anonymously, and on an extensive review of reader comments. Rating categories reflect both the

INTRODUCTION

features a property offers and its quality in relation to similar establishments.

The Mobil star ratings for restaurants are defined as follows:

- ★★★★★: A Mobil Five-Star restaurant offers one of few flawless dining experiences in the country. These establishments consistently provide their guests with exceptional food, superlative service, elegant décor, and exquisite presentations of each detail surrounding a meal.
- ★★★★: A Mobil Four-Star restaurant provides professional service, distinctive presentations, and wonderful food.
- ★★★: A Mobil Three-Star restaurant has good food, warm and skillful service, and enjoyable décor.
- ★★: A Mobil Two-Star restaurant serves fresh food in a clean setting with efficient service. Value is considered in this category, as is family friendliness.
- ★: A Mobil One-Star restaurant provides a distinctive experience through culinary specialty, local flair, or individual atmosphere.

TERMS, ABBREVIATIONS, AND SYMBOLS IN LISTINGS

The following terms, abbreviations, and symbols are used throughout the Mobil Travel Guide lodging and restaurant listings to indicate which amenities and services are available at each establishment. We've done our best to provide accurate and up-to-date information, but things do change, so if a particular feature is essential to you, please contact the establishment directly to make sure that it is available.

Continental breakfast: Usually coffee and a roll or doughnut.

In-room modem link: Every guest room has a connection for a modem that's separate from the main phone line.

Laundry service: Either coin-operated laundry facilities or overnight valet service is available.

Luxury level: A special section of a lodging, spanning at least an entire floor, that offers

Locals recommend

Byway experts from around the country recommend special restaurants and/or lodgings along their particular Byways that can make your trip even more pleasant. You'll see these special recommendations throughout this book. Look for this symbol next to the hotel or restaurant name:

increased luxury accommodations. Management must provide no less than three of these four services: separate check-in and check-out, concierge, private lounge, and private elevator service (with key access). Complimentary breakfast and snacks are commonly offered.

MAP: Modified American plan (lodging plus two meals).

Movies: Prerecorded videos are available for rental or check-out.

Prix fixe: A full, multicourse meal for a stated price; usually available at finer restaurants.

Valet parking: An attendant is available to park and retrieve your car.

VCR: VCRs are present in all guest rooms.

VCR available: VCRs are available for hookup in guest rooms.

- Pet allowed
- Fishing
- Horseback riding
- Snow skiing nearby
- Golf, nine-hole minimum, on premises
- Tennis court(s) on premises
- Swimming
- In-house fitness room
- Jogging
- Major commercial airport within 10 miles
- Nonsmoking guest rooms
- SC Senior citizen rates
- Business center

SPECIAL INFORMATION FOR TRAVELERS WITH DISABILITIES

The Mobil Travel Guide [D] symbol indicates establishments that are at least partially accessible to people with mobility problems. Our criteria for accessibility are unique to our publications. Please do not confuse them with the universal symbol for wheelchair accessibility.

When the [D] symbol follows a listing, the establishment is equipped with facilities to accommodate people using wheelchairs or crutches or otherwise needing easy access to doorways and rest rooms. Travelers with severe mobility problems or with hearing or visual impairments may or may not find the facilities they need. Always phone ahead to make sure that an establishment can meet your needs.

All lodgings bearing our [D] symbol have the following facilities:

- ISA-designated parking near access ramps
- Level or ramped entryways to buildings
- Swinging building entryway doors a minimum of 39 inches wide
- Public rest rooms on the main level with space to operate a wheelchair and handrails at commode areas
- Elevator(s) equipped with grab bars and lowered control buttons
- Restaurant(s) with accessible doorway(s), rest rooms with space to operate a wheelchair, and handrails at commode areas
- Guest room entryways that are at least 39 inches wide
- Low-pile carpet in rooms
- Telephones at bedside and in the bathroom
- Beds placed at wheelchair height
- Bathrooms with a minimum doorway width of 3 feet
- Bath with an open sink (no cabinet) and room to operate a wheelchair
- Handrails at commode areas and in the tub
- Wheelchair-accessible peepholes in room entry door
- Wheelchair-accessible closet rods and shelves

All restaurants bearing our [D] symbol offer the following facilities:

- ISA-designated parking beside access ramps
- Level or ramped front entryways to the building
- Tables that accommodate wheelchairs
- Main-floor rest rooms with an entryway that's at least 3 feet wide
- Rest rooms with space to operate a wheelchair and handrails at commode areas

Natchez Trace Parkway
✤ ALABAMA
Part of a multistate Byway; see also MS, TN.

The Natchez Trace Parkway tells the story of people on the move, of the age-old need to get from one place to another. It is a story of Natchez, Chickasaw, and Choctaw Indians following traditional ways of life; of French and Spanish people venturing into a new world; and of people building a new nation.

At first, the Natchez Trace was probably a series of hunters' paths that slowly came together to form a trail that led from the Mississippi River over the low hills into the Tennessee Valley. By 1785, Ohio River Valley farmers searching for markets had begun floating their crops and products down the rivers to Natchez or New Orleans. Because they sold their flatboats for lumber, returning home meant either riding or walking. The trail from Natchez offered the most direct route for them to follow.

The parklands along the Natchez Trace preserve important examples of the nation's natural and cultural heritage. Since the late 1930s, the National Park Service has been constructing a modern parkway that closely follows the course of the original trace. Today, the parkway gives travelers an unhurried route from Natchez, Mississippi, to Nashville, Tennessee. It is a subtle driving experience. Motorists and bicyclists alike enjoy the scenery, from the rock-studded hills of Tennessee, past the cotton fields of Alabama, to the flat and meandering southern extremes shaded by trees and Spanish moss. The Natchez Trace Parkway winds along 445 scenic miles through three states, including Alabama, Mississippi, and Tennessee.

The Alabama segment of the Natchez Trace Parkway is the middle leg of a Byway that covers the entire length of the Natchez Trace. The Old Trace is still closely followed by the parkway, which is preserved and administered

Quick Facts

LENGTH: 31 miles.

TIME TO ALLOW: 1 hour.

BEST TIME TO DRIVE: Summer is best to see the lush vegetation along the Byway. Late March and April bring spring flowers, and September and October bring fall colors. However, the Natchez Pilgrimage during March-October is an excellent time to visit many of Natchez's antebellum homes. High season is during March and April.

BYWAY TRAVEL INFORMATION: Natchez Trace Parkway: 800/305-7417; Byway local Web site: www.nps.gov/natr.

SPECIAL CONSIDERATIONS: Be alert for animals on the parkway, as well as copperheads, cottonmouths, and rattlesnakes. Fire ants can inflict painful bites, so do not disturb their mounds. Poison ivy grows throughout the area. All natural, historical, and archaeological objects must be left undisturbed. Also, the Natchez Trace Parkway is a designated bike route, so please watch for bikers. Gas, food, and lodging are available in the communities near the parkway. Plan ahead for these amenities because of the relatively rural setting of most of the parkway. Also, the roadway is not illuminated.

RESTRICTIONS: The speed limit along this Byway is 50 mph. Commercial trucking is not allowed, and tent and trailer camping is allowed at designated campgrounds only.

BICYCLE/PEDESTRIAN FACILITIES: The Natchez Trace Parkway is popular with bicyclists—both for distance touring and for local riders out for a day of fresh air. Pedestrian facilities along the parkway consist of separate hiking, nature, and horse trails.

Alabama

✳ Natchez Trace Parkway

by the National Park Service. A lovely tree-lined drive through woods and fields, the Byway offers a wealth of early pioneer history at well-maintained historic sites like Colbert Ferry Park, Freedom Hills, and Buzzard Roost Springs. Views are particularly pretty on crossing the Tennessee River midway through Alabama.

THE BYWAY STORY

The Natchez Trace Parkway tells archaeological, cultural, historical, natural, recreational, and scenic stories that make it a unique and treasured Byway.

Archaeological

Archaeological sites on the Natchez Trace date from the Paleo-Indian period (12,000 BC–8,000 BC) through historic Natchez, Choctaw, and Chickasaw Indian settlements (AD 1540–1837). Campsites, village sites, stone quarry sites, rock shelters, shell heaps, and burial sites are among the archaeological treasures along the Natchez Trace. The most visually obvious are burial and ceremonial earthen mounds associated with the Woodland and Mississippian periods. The Mississippians were highly skilled farmers and artists who may have traded with people from as far away as Mexico and Central America. They established elaborate political systems, and they lived in large permanent towns that were often fortified with stockades.

Cultural

The cultural aspects of the Natchez Trace can be seen in its heritage. From rough frontier towns on the edge of Indian Territory to the rise of Southern comforts, the people who live along the Natchez Trace embody its rich culture. Southern traditions and hospitality are apparent as you meander through the heart of Dixie. From Natchez to Memphis, you'll enjoy the people you meet along the Natchez Trace.

Because the Natchez Trace is a long Byway, take an extra day or two to fully appreciate Southern living. On your extended stay, take in one of the many opportunities for cultural entertainment. These range from concerts by community bands to performances by small stage theater troupes. Spend a night at the opera or attend some of the special events on the Byway. Just be sure to keep your camera handy for some good ol' Southern memories.

Historical

The Natchez Trace Parkway was established to commemorate the historical significance of the Old Natchez Trace as a primitive trail that stretched some 500 miles through the wilderness from Natchez, Mississippi, to Nashville, Tennessee. Although generally thought of as one trail, the Old Natchez Trace was actually a number of closely parallel routes. The Natchez Trace probably evolved from the repeated use of meandering game trails by the earliest human inhabitants. Over time, these paths were gradually linked and used for transportation, communication, and trade, first by Native Americans and later by European explorers, American traders, and others.

History has witnessed several phases in the development of the Natchez Trace, each with a distinct origin and purpose. The first phase was an Indian trail, actually known as the Chickasaw Trace by residents of Fort Nashborough (present-day Nashville, Tennessee). Heading to the southwest from Nashville, the Chickasaw Trace led to the Chickasaw Nation, near present-day Tupelo, Mississippi. From there, other trails led southwest through country controlled by the Choctaw Nation and onward to Natchez. The southern portion of this trail appeared on 18th-century British maps as the "Path to the Choctaw Nation."

Word spread among the early white settlers that it was possible to travel by foot between Nashville and Natchez through the Indian nations. Traffic increased along this "Boatman's Trail," with men returning home to the north after selling cargo and flatboats at Natchez or New Orleans. Added usage caused discontent to grow due to the harsh conditions of this new route. In 1806, Thomas Jefferson directed the Postmaster General to oversee a route improvement project. Unfortunately, funds for maintenance weren't included in the appropriation. Complaints concerning conditions on the rugged wilderness trail flooded in as river trade boomed along with the increasing population.

However, before improvements were ever made, the need for them diminished. After his victory at the Battle of New Orleans in 1815, Andrew Jackson marched his troops home along the Natchez Trace—an event that signaled not only the war's end, but also the decline of the Natchez Trace's importance as a transportation corridor. By 1820, steamboats were common on the Mississippi River, making upriver travel easy. Boatmen now chose to return home by water rather than by the overland route.

Not until the years following 1820, when much of the route fell into disuse, was it referred to as the "Natchez Trace." Speculation is that those who had experienced hardships and adventure on the Natchez Road spoke of it more glamorously as the "Natchez Trace" when reminiscing about it. By the 1830s, this term had replaced "Natchez Road."

Natural

The Natchez Trace Parkway encompasses a diversity of natural resources. From Natchez, Mississippi, to Nashville, Tennessee, the motor road cuts through six major forest types and eight major watersheds. The park ranges from 70 to 1,100 feet in elevation and covers a distance of 445 miles, resulting in a variety of habitats.

Within the park, approximately 800 species of plants help to support 57 species of mammals, 216 species of birds, 57 species of reptiles, 36 species of amphibians, and a variety of other vertebrates and invertebrates. Three of these species are classified as endangered and include the southern bald eagle, the red-cockaded woodpecker, and the gray bat; three more are classified as threatened and include the Bayou darter, the slackwater darter, and the ringed sawback turtle.

see page A5 for color map

North of Tupelo, Mississippi, the parkway cuts through a mixture of pine and hardwood forests in the hills above the Tombigbee River. The parkway then makes its way up onto Alabama's Cumberland Plateau—actually the westernmost extension of the legendary Appalachian Mountain range. The parkway drops from the plateau into the Tennessee River Valley of northeastern Alabama with its red clay soils, excellent for the growing of cotton.

The more fertile farm lands along the parkway are devoted to the production of milo, soybeans, corn, wheat, and cotton, while the marginal agricultural lands are used primarily for the grazing of cattle and horses. Some of the more common wildlife along the entire length of the parkway includes white-tailed deer, turkeys, bobcats, raccoons, opossums, foxes, coyotes, and field and forest dwelling songbirds.

Alabama

✻ *Natchez Trace Parkway*

Recreational

You can find numerous opportunities for recreation along the Natchez Trace Parkway. By far the most popular is simply enjoying the historic and natural beauty, which abounds all along the parkway. Take in one of the many museums located throughout the Byway or take a walk among the dogwoods. The Byway has many historic battlefields, allowing you the chance to stretch your legs and reminisce about the past. Pack a picnic and see the many Southern mansions along the route or hunt for souvenirs in one of the many quaint shops along the way.

At least ten months of fine weather each year and a combination of natural resources, including lakes, woodlands, and wildlife, make outdoor recreation along the Natchez Trace favorable. Hunting is excellent, as are golfing, bicycling, jogging, swimming, tennis, baseball, football, soccer, and other sports. If you're a fisherman, take advantage of the many rivers located throughout the Byway and wet your line.

Scenic

As the interstate highway of its time, the Natchez Trace entertained travelers along its well-trod path with its picturesque views of the surrounding countryside. You can enjoy these same wonders today. From blossoming flowers and trees to historical Native American earthen mounds, the Natchez Trace offers scenic vistas at every turn. By winding through six major forest types and eight major watersheds, you are afforded the opportunity to see a variety of habitats and wildlife; the changing seasons enhance the scenic qualities of the Natchez Trace.

THINGS TO SEE AND DO

Driving along the Natchez Trace Parkway will certainly keep your senses engaged, but if you yearn to get out of the car and stretch your legs, or if you'd like to make a mini-vacation out of your trip, check out these attractions along the route.

COLBERT FERRY. George Colbert, a leading Chickasaw of the area, operated a stand and ferry here and reportedly charged Andrew Jackson $75,000 to ferry his army across the river. Open daily dawn-dusk.

FREEDOM HILLS OVERLOOK. A steep, 1/4-mile trail leads to Alabama's highest point on the parkway, at 800 feet. Open daily dawn-dusk. **FREE**

ROCK SPRING TRAIL. This self-guided trail along Colbert Creek takes 20 minutes to walk. Interpretive trail markers are located at points of special interest. Open daily. **FREE**

PLACES TO STAY

If you choose to include an overnight stay in your trip along this All-American Road, Mobil Travel Guide recommends the following lodgings.

★ **HOMESTEAD EXECUTIVE INN.** *505 S Court St, Florence (35630). Phone 256/766-2331; toll-free 800/248-5336.* 120 rooms, 2 story. Pet accepted, some restrictions. Check-out noon. TV; cable (premium), VCR available (movies). Coin laundry. Restaurant, bar. Room service. Pool, poolside service. ¢

★ **DAYS INN.** *2700 Woodward Ave, Muscle Shoals (35661). Phone 256/383-3000; toll-free 800/329-7466. www.daysinn.com.* 77 rooms, 2 story. Complimentary continental breakfast. Check-out noon. TV; cable (premium). Pool. Restaurant, bar. ¢

★★ **JOE WHEELER STATE RESORT LODGE.** *4401 McLain Dr, Rogersville (35652). Phone 256/247-5461; toll-free 800/544-5639.* 75 rooms, 3 story. Check-out 11 am, check-in 3 pm. TV; VCR available. Private patios, balconies. Some refrigerators. Coin laundry. Dining room. Playground. Pool, wading pool. 18-hole golf, pro, putting green, driving range. Lighted tennis. Picnic tables. Private beach, marina, boat rentals. Hiking trails. Meeting rooms, business services. Sundries. State-owned; facilities of park available. ¢

Selma to Montgomery March Byway

✤ ALABAMA

Quick Facts

LENGTH: 43 miles.

TIME TO ALLOW: 1 hour.

BEST TIME TO DRIVE: Year-round. Due to the focus of the Byway, Martin Luther King, Jr. Day (the third Monday in January) tends to be the busiest.

BYWAY TRAVEL INFORMATION: State of Alabama Department of Tourism: 334/242-4144; Selma-Dallas County Chamber of Commerce: 334/875-7241.

SPECIAL CONSIDERATIONS: Martin Luther King, Jr. Day is an excellent time to visit the Byway, with all of the associated activities.

BICYCLE/PEDESTRIAN FACILITIES: At either end of the Byway, portions of the route wind through the city streets of Selma and Montgomery, Alabama. The remainder of the route consists of a four-lane highway between the two cities. Pedestrian and bicycle travel on this highway is limited.

As you travel this All-American Road that winds its way from the streets of Selma, Alabama, through the gentle rolling hills of Lowndes County, and into the state's capital city of Montgomery, you'll find yourself transfixed in history. Also designated as a National Historic Trail, this Byway has known many facets of history in its years of existence. However, it wasn't until Dr. Martin Luther King, Jr. began leading voting rights demonstrations in Selma early in 1965, culminating with the historic Selma to Montgomery March, that the route became internationally known.

After a failed attempt just three weeks earlier, Dr. King marshaled a group of protesters who made their way 43 miles from the Edmund Pettus Bridge in Selma to Montgomery, giving birth to the most important piece of social legislation of the 20th century. This march helped bring access to the ballot box for many African Americans in Southern states. On this Byway, for the first time in US history, you can reach out and touch live persons who were a part of making this a Scenic Byway and Historic Trail.

THE BYWAY STORY

The Selma to Montgomery March Byway tells cultural and historical stories that make it a unique and treasured Byway.

Cultural

Dr. Martin Luther King, Jr. stood on the platform in front of the stark white state capitol in Montgomery, Alabama, and gazed out at the crowd of 10,000 people. The largest civil rights march ever to take place in the South had finally reached its destination after weeks of

Alabama

✹ Selma to Montgomery March Byway

uncertainty and danger. Two blocks down the street, at the edge of the vast assemblage, was Dexter Avenue Baptist Church, from whose pulpit King had inspired black bus boycotters a decade earlier. Their year-long display of nonviolence and courage had not only earned blacks the right to sit where they wanted on the buses; it had also started a fire in the hearts of many Americans.

In the ten years since then, King and his fellow travelers had seen that fire burn in all its glory and its pain—through victories in Little Rock, Jackson, and Birmingham; through beatings, burnings, and bombings; and most recently, through the murders of Jimmie Lee Jackson and James Reeb. Now, here they stood, 10,000 strong, supported by countless other Americans who believed in their cause.

King did not refer directly to the brutal attack by state troopers upon the marchers just 18 days earlier. However, that attack, seen on national television, drew the attention of the world to this moment. "Selma, Alabama," King declared, "became a shining moment in the conscious of man . . . . Confrontation of good and evil compressed in the tiny community of Selma generated the massive power to turn the whole nation to a new course."

King warned the marchers that although this march was finished, the struggle for civil rights was not yet won. However, it would be won, he said, and it wouldn't be long. "How long? Not long. Because no lie can live forever . . . . How long? Not long. Because the arm of the moral universe is long but it bends toward justice."

Less than five months later, the 1965 Voting Rights Act was signed, and blacks throughout the South streamed into courthouses to register as voters. They were at last exercising a fundamental promise of democracy, a promise that took our nation 178 years to fulfill.

Historical

While black voters were struggling for representation in Mississippi and other areas of the country, a similar struggle was going on in Dallas County, Alabama, and its county seat, Selma. Blacks there formed the Dallas County Voters League (DCVL) under the leadership of Samuel W. Boynton, a local agricultural extension agent and former president of the local chapter of the National Association for the Advancement of Colored People (NAACP).

Despite stiff resistance from white officials, local activists persisted. Their courage attracted the attention of other African-American leaders. In early 1963, Bernard and Colia Lafayette of the Student Nonviolent Coordinating Committee (SNCC) went to Selma to help the DCVL register African-American voters. Marie Foster, a steering committee member of the DCVL, began teaching classes on the complicated registration forms required by the state of Alabama.

The Selma activists quickly found themselves battling not only bureaucratic resistance, but also the intimidation tactics of Sheriff Jim Clark and his deputized posse. In 1961, the US Justice Department filed a voter discrimination lawsuit against the County Board of Registrars and, two years later, sued Clark directly for the harassment of blacks attempting to register.

Fearful that more "outside agitators" would target Selma, State Circuit Judge James Hare on July 9, 1964, enjoined any group of more than three people from meeting in Dallas County. As protests and meetings came to a virtual halt, local activists Amelia Platts Boynton and J. L. Chestnut asked Southern Christian Leadership Conference (SCLC) officials for help. SCLC leaders, following their hard-won victory in Birmingham, had already declared that their next push would be for a strong national voting rights law. Selma offered the perfect opportunity.

On January 2, 1965, Dr. Martin Luther King, Jr. defied Judge Hare's injunction and led a rally at Brown Chapel African Methodist Episcopal (AME) Church, promising demonstrations and even another march on Washington if voting rights were not guaranteed for African-

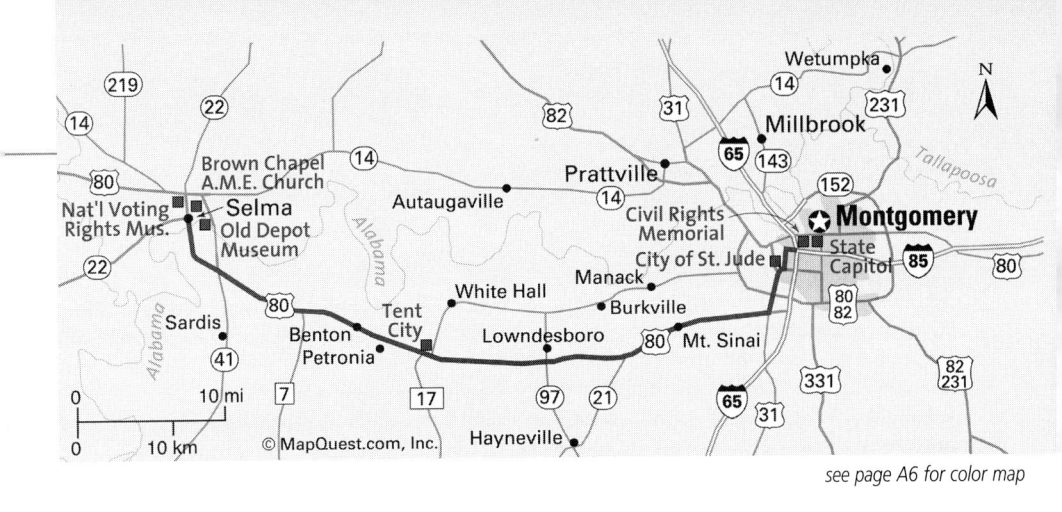

Americans in the South. Immediately, a series of mass meetings and protest marches began with renewed momentum in Selma and nearby Marion, the seat of Perry County.

Then, on February 18, a nighttime march in Marion ended in violence and death. Alabama State Troopers attacked African Americans leaving a mass meeting at Zion Methodist Church. Several people, including Viola Jackson and her son Jimmie Lee, sought refuge in a small café, but troopers soon found them. An officer moved to strike Viola Jackson, then turned on Jimmie Lee when he tried to protect her. Two troopers assaulted Jackson, shooting him at point blank range. On February 25, Jimmie Lee Jackson died in Selma from an infection caused by the shooting.

Jackson's death angered activists. Lucy Foster, a leader in Marion, bitterly proposed that residents take Jackson's body to the Alabama Capitol to gain the attention of Governor George Wallace—a proposal repeated later by SCLC's James Bevel. Bevel and others realized that some mass nonviolent action was necessary, not only to win the attention of political leaders, but also to vent the anger and frustration of the activists.

Even as Jackson was buried, the idea for a Selma to Montgomery march was growing. By March 2, plans were confirmed that Dr. King would lead a march from Selma to Montgomery beginning on Sunday, March 7, 1965.

The danger of such a march was apparent, and SCLC leaders debated whether to march without a court order restraining Governor Wallace, Sheriff Clark, and the Alabama troopers. The decision was made on Sunday, when more than 500 people arrived at Brown Chapel AME Church in Selma, determined to march. Perhaps 300 or more were from Marion. SCLC staffers contacted King and Ralph Abernathy in Atlanta, received the authorization to march, and immediately began to brief the crowd on march procedures and the techniques of nonviolence.

HIGHLIGHTS

The following tour encompasses the first section of the Byway beginning on the corner of Martin Luther King, Jr. Street and Jeff Davis Avenue and passes the George Washington Carver Home, historic landmark Brown AME Church, and the Martin Luther King, Jr. monument. Through the written word and vivid historic photographs, each of the 20 memorials along the route tells the story of the individuals, known and unknown, rich and poor, black and white, who came together for a common cause.

- On the Byway, the first point of interest is the **Cecil C. Jackson, Jr. Public Safety Building,** which was once the old Selma city hall. This building served as the city and county jail in which Dr. King and other protesters were imprisoned in 1965.

- Farther on is the **Dallas County Courthouse,** the destination of most protest marches in an effort to register to vote.

- Just before the Alabama River is the **National Voting Rights Museum and Institute,** dedicated to honoring the attainment of voting rights.

- Crossing the Alabama River is the **Edmund Pettus Bridge,** the famous landmark were "Bloody Sunday" took place on March 7, 1965.

Alabama

✺ *Selma to Montgomery March Byway*

- From here, the Byway travels along Highway 80 to the **city of Montgomery,** passing numerous campsites that were used by marchers during the historic event. Between the cities of Petronia and Whitehall stands the **memorial to Viola Liuzzo,** who was murdered while supporting the civil rights movement.
- The final destination of the Selma to Montgomery march is the **Alabama State Capitol** in Montgomery. On the steps of this great building, Dr. Martin Luther King, Jr. told marchers that the journey was through, but the struggle for civil rights was far from over. But it would be won, he said, and it wouldn't be long.

THINGS TO SEE AND DO

Driving along the Selma to Montgomery March Byway will certainly keep your senses engaged, but if you yearn to get out of the car and stretch your legs, or if you'd like to make a mini-vacation out of your trip, check out these attractions along the route.

BLACK HERITAGE TOUR. *513 Lauderdale St, Selma (36701). Phone 334/875-7241.* Visit Brown Chapel AME Church (also a part of the Martin Luther King, Jr. self-guided Street Walking Tour), the Edmund Pettus Bridge, the National Voting Rights Museum, Selma University, the Dallas County Courthouse, and the Wilson Building. **FREE-$$$**

✺ **CIVIL RIGHTS MEMORIAL.** *400 Washington St, Montgomery (36104).* Designed by Vietnam Veterans' Memorial artist Maya Lin to commemorate the Civil Rights Movement. **FREE**

✺ **DEXTER AVENUE KING MEMORIAL BAPTIST CHURCH.** *454 Dexter Ave, Montgomery (36104). Phone 334/263-3970.* The Reverend Dr. Martin Luther King, Jr. was a pastor from 1954-1960; from the church he directed the Montgomery bus boycott, which sparked the modern civil rights movement. Mural and original painting "The Beginning of a Dream." Mon-Sat, by appointment; closed holidays. **$**

✺ **NATIONAL VOTING RIGHTS MUSEUM AND INSTITUTE.** *1012 Water Ave, Selma (36702). Phone 334/418-0800. www.voterights.org.* Located near the foot of Edmund Pettus Bridge, this museum offers a pictorial history of the voting rights struggle. It displays an exceptional record of events and participants, including Viola Liuzzo and Marie Foster, who made voting rights history. Open 24 hours. **FREE**

OLD DEPOT MUSEUM. *4 Martin Luther King St, Selma (36701). Phone 334/874-2197. www.selmalabama.com/olddepot.htm.* Interpretive history museum with artifacts of Selma. Open Mon-Sat 10 am-4 pm; other times by appointment; closed holidays. **$$**

PLACES TO STAY

If you choose to include an overnight stay in your trip along this All-American Road, Mobil Travel Guide recommends the following lodgings.

Montgomery

★ **COMFORT SUITES.** *5924 Monticello Dr, Montgomery (36117). Phone 334/272-1013; toll-free 800/517-4000. www.choicehotels.com.* 49 suites, 3 story. Complimentary continental breakfast. Check-out noon. TV; cable (premium). In-room modem link. Exercise room. Pool. ¢
D ⛔ SC ≈ 𝍎

★★ **COURTYARD BY MARRIOTT.** *5555 Carmichael Rd, Montgomery (36117). Phone 334/272-5533; toll-free 800/321-2211. www.courtyard.com.* 146 units, 3 story. Check-out noon. TV. Pool; whirlpool. Bar. Guest laundry. In-room modem link. Exercise equipment. Refrigerators available. Some private patios, balconies. **$**
𝍎 D ⛔ ≈

★ **LATTICE INN.** *1414 S Hull St, Montgomery (36104). Phone 334/832-9931.* 4 rooms, 2 story. Located in the historic Garden District, this home was built in 1906 and is furnished with antiques and family pieces. A large Southern breakfast is served each morning. ¢

★★ **RAMADA INN STATEHOUSE.** *924 Madison Ave, Montgomery (36104). Phone 334/265-0741; toll-free 800/552-7099. www.ramada.com.* 162 rooms, 6 story. Check-out noon. TV. Restaurant, bar. Exercise room. Pool, wading pool. ¢

★ **RED BLUFF COTTAGE BED & BREAKFAST.** *551 Clay St, Montgomery (36101). Phone 334/264-0056; toll-free 888/551-CLAY. www.redbluffcottage.com.* 6 rooms, 3 story. 19th-century Victorian cottage located in downtown Montgomery featuring a large Southern breakfast. $

★ **WYNFIELD INN.** *1110 East Blvd, Montgomery (36117). Phone 334/272-8880.* 64 rooms, 2 story. Complimentary continental breakfast. Check-out 11 am. TV. Pool. Coin laundry. In-room modem link. Private patios, balconies. ¢

Selma

★ **BRIDGE TENDERS HOUSE.** *2 Lafayette Park, Selma (36701). Phone 334/875-5517.* 2 rooms, 2 story. This small cottage sits in the shadow of Pettus Bridge on the Alabama River. Each suite is private with a full kitchen, living room, bedroom, and bath. ¢

★★ **HOLIDAY INN.** *US Hwy 80 W, Selma (36701). Phone 334/872-0461; toll-free 800/465-4329. www.holiday-inn.com.* 165 rooms, 2 story. Pet accepted. Check-out noon. TV. Pool; wading pool. Restaurant, bar. Room service. In-room modem link. Valet service. ¢

PLACES TO EAT

A long day of driving is sure to make you hungry. At the end of your journey, take a table at one of the following restaurants.

Montgomery

★★ **ALA THAI.** *1361 Federal Dr, Montgomery (36114). Phone 334/262-5830.* Thai menu. Lunch, dinner. Authentic Thai cuisine with an emphasis on noodle dishes in a romantic environment. $

★ **MARTHA'S PLACE.** *458 Sayre St, Montgomery (36104). Phone 334/263-9135.* Southern/Soul menu. Closed Sat-Sun. Breakfast, lunch. Classic soul food restaurant in a homelike setting. Famous for fried chicken. $

Alabama

❋ *Selma to Montgomery March Byway*

★★ **SAHARA.** *511 E Edgemont Ave, Montgomery (36111). Phone 334/262-1215.* Specializes in fresh seafood, steak. Closed Sun, most major holidays. Lunch, dinner. Bar. $$
[D]

★★★ **VINTAGE YEAR.** *405 Cloverdale Rd, Montgomery (36106). Phone 334/264-8463. www.vintageyearonline.com.* Located in Montgomery's historic Cloverdale District, this restaurant serves unique appetizers and desserts. Modern décor with intimate lighting makes it a great spot for a romantic dinner. Specializes in chicken, seafood. Closed Sun, Mon; major holidays. Dinner. Bar. Wine list. $$
[D]

Selma

★ **MAC'S FISH CAMP.** *4407 County Road 17, Selma (36701). Phone 334/-874-4087. www.outdoorsusa.com/macs/index.htm.* American menu. Open Fri, Sat, Sun. Dinner. Famous for Southern fried catfish and very popular locally. $

★★ **MAJOR GRUMBLES.** *1300 Water Ave, Selma (36702). Phone 334/872-2006.* Specializes in charbroiled chicken and steak, seafood. Closed Sun, most major holidays. Reservations accepted Mon-Fri. Lunch, dinner. Bar. Located on the river in a former cotton warehouse (1850). $$
[D]

★★ **TALLY-HO.** *509 Mangum Ave, Selma (36701). Phone 334/872-1390.* Specializes in seafood, steak. Closed Sun, major holidays. Reservations accepted. Dinner. Bar. Children's menu. Own baking. Entrance and waiting area in an old log cabin. $$
[D]

The Seward Highway
❊ ALASKA

Quick Facts

LENGTH: 127 miles.

TIME TO ALLOW: 3 to 5 hours.

BEST TIME TO DRIVE: From May to mid-October, salmon fishing is at its peak, and you can see whales along the shore and sheep on the mountainsides. The off-season consists of winter and spring. Avalanches may cause the road to be closed for short periods of time throughout the winter.

BYWAY TRAVEL INFORMATION: Alaska Public Lands Information Center: 907/271-2737; Alaska Deptartment of Transportation and Public Facilities: 907/465-6975; Chugach National Forest: 907/743-9500; Byway local Web site: www.dot.state.ak.us/stwdplng/scenic/bsewardhwy.html.

SPECIAL CONSIDERATIONS: The only significant seasonal problem facing the Seward Highway is adverse winter conditions. The Alaska Department of Transportation and Public Facilities has made a serious and effective commitment to keeping the Seward Highway passable during the winter months, however, because it is the principal highway serving the Kenai Peninsula.

RESTRICTIONS: Due to extreme conditions during the winter, the road is closed by avalanches an average of five times a year for approximately four hours.

BICYCLE/PEDESTRIAN FACILITIES: Bicyclists can take advantage of existing wide shoulders and many miles of separated bike paths. Pedestrians are accommodated at most of the highway's pullouts and along many of the trails paralleling the route.

The Seward Highway, linking Anchorage with Seward, passes through some of the most spectacular scenery in the country. The landscape varies from the muddy waters of Turnagain Arm to the icy blue glaciers that hang almost to the sea. Wildflowers and waterfalls brighten every corner of the road as it glides below rough mountains that pierce thick, heavy clouds. Only Alaska's Seward Highway can offer this particular mix created by climate, geography, and geology.

The Seward Highway is located in a richly varied and highly diverse corridor. Its character changes over the course of its length. Roadside topography, the proximity of water, the types of views, the levels and types of development, and the width and character of the road are some of the ways in which the Seward Highway expresses different moods and landscapes between Anchorage and Seward. Each of these distinctive landscapes is uniquely spectacular.

For 127 miles, the road winds through a land of remarkable beauty, a land of saltwater bays, frigid-blue glaciers, knife-edged ridges, and alpine valleys. From the reflective waters of Turnagain Arm, you rapidly ascend 1,000 feet above sea level to an alpine meadow. Within the hour, you find yourself back at sea level surrounded by fjords, having just passed through a district of rivers and lakes.

Whether you drive for pleasure or you fish, hunt, backpack, camp, or ski, the Seward Highway can take you there. And it's all against a backdrop of spruce forests, wildflowers, and extraordinary wildlife.

Alaska

❋ The Seward Highway

THE BYWAY STORY

The Seward Highway tells historical, natural, recreational, and scenic stories that make it a unique and treasured Byway.

Historical

Far removed from the rest of the world sits Alaska, perched above the fast-paced industry of the world below. The route from Resurrection Bay to Alaska's interior has been in existence for thousands of years; even Russian explorers searched the area for gold and fur in the 1700s. Following the same early routes used by native Alaskans, sled dogs, miners, and trains, the Seward Highway has evolved into a modern transportation system.

Natives first used an area along the Seward Highway 9,000 years ago as a hunting camp. In this area, now known as Beluga Point on Turnagain Arm, Tanaina Indians also discovered abundant game in the region over 8,000 years after the first natives inhabited the area. The region finally received its name in 1778 when Captain Cook sailed along the coast in his quest for the Northwest Passage. When shallow water forced him to turn around, he christened the sound Turnagain River. South of Anchorage, Highway 1 now follows the shore of Turnagain Arm.

In 1895, prospectors discovered gold in Hope, Alaska, in the Kenai Peninsula, and the rush began. One miner panned 385 ounces of gold from the river in one day. (Now, fishermen line the stream with hopes of catching salmon.) This gold rush of the late 1800s brought several thousand gold seekers to the area. Suddenly, the tiny towns of Hope and Sunrise grew into booming gold mining towns. Sunrise became the largest town in the Cook Inlet area and was even considered as a potential state capital. Scattered findings of gold all over the Kenai Mountains established the need for improved transportation routes from the ice-free port of Seward to Turnagain Arm.

Today's Byway traces several historic routes that miners used to cross the Kenai Mountains. The route from Seward to Snow River was used by hikers, dog teams, and horse parties. These travelers crossed Kenai Lake and landed at Cooper Landing, or they continued on to Moose Pass. The route from Moose Pass to Tern Lake and Cooper Landing was used when Kenai Lake was impassable, and it was used by northbound travelers from Kenai and Cooper Landing. Johnson Pass was the route of choice from Moose Pass to Sunrise and Hope. The Trail Creek to Placer River route was a direct path from Moose Pass to Portage Valley. This route was later chosen for the Alaska Central Railroad, which was in use by 1909.

By 1910, most miners had left the area in order to follow prospects of gold farther north. Sunrise dwindled into nothing more than a few residences, and mining activity in Hope came almost to a standstill. However, Cooper Landing's economy was soon influenced not by mining but by interest in big game hunting and fishing.

Today, the mining legacy of the Kenai Peninsula lives on through stories, museum photos, and weathered wood remains scattered throughout the Kenai Mountains. The privately owned townsite of Sunrise is a historic archaeological district. The Hope Historical Society operates a small museum that includes photographs, journals, mine buildings, and equipment from the gold rush.

Natural

As you travel the Seward Highway, watch for wildlife along the highway. You may hear the honking of Canadian geese in the wetlands, the whistle of hoary marmots in the alpine valleys, and the cry of bald eagles in the dense coastal forests. Just south of Anchorage, Potter's Marsh Wildlife Viewing Area offers a temporary home to ducks, geese, and other nesting water birds as they raise their young. Along Turnagain Arm, you may spot Dall sheep as they scale rugged mountainsides or bring their young near the highway to forage. Bald eagles, moose, bears, mountain goats, salmon, and a variety of birds thrive along the highway as well. Many species of wildflowers help beautify the road corridor. Two of the most common and colorful are the blue-purple arctic lupine and the pink-red fireweed.

Spotting Alaska's wildlife isn't always easy. Catching a glimpse of wildlife usually means being in the right place at the right time, but you can increase your chances by taking time to stop and scan hillsides and valleys, using binoculars to search for movement. Knowing where and why animals frequent can increase your chances of seeing them.

Recreational

From the beginning of human habitation in Alaska, people have been aware of the great natural resources of the land. In more recent years, people have come to discover another resource besides good hunting and gold mining: recreation. Although the activities offered on the Byway are unique and diverse, you will find camping, hiking, and picnicking spots in abundance all along the highway.

The section of the Seward Highway adjacent to Turnagain Arm provides scenic vistas across the Arm to the Kenai Mountains. Most of the lands above the highway are within Chugach State Park and provide you with a collection of things to see and ways to see them: windsurfing on the Arm, rock climbing on roadside rock cuts, rafting or canoeing on the Russian River, kite-flying at Beluga Point, angling at Bird Creek, and bicycling the highway. Two hundred miles of trails are in the forest alone.

Once a mining town, Girdwood is now home to a world-famous ski resort that offers excellent scenery and plenty of challenges. This town combines the best of today's recreation with classic activities of the past, like panning for gold—try your luck! During the summer, the community celebrates a Forest Fair with arts, crafts, food, and entertainment. Other Byway towns like Hope and Cooper Landing offer havens for fishing. In Anchorage, you can stroll the streets and browse in shops or visitor centers.

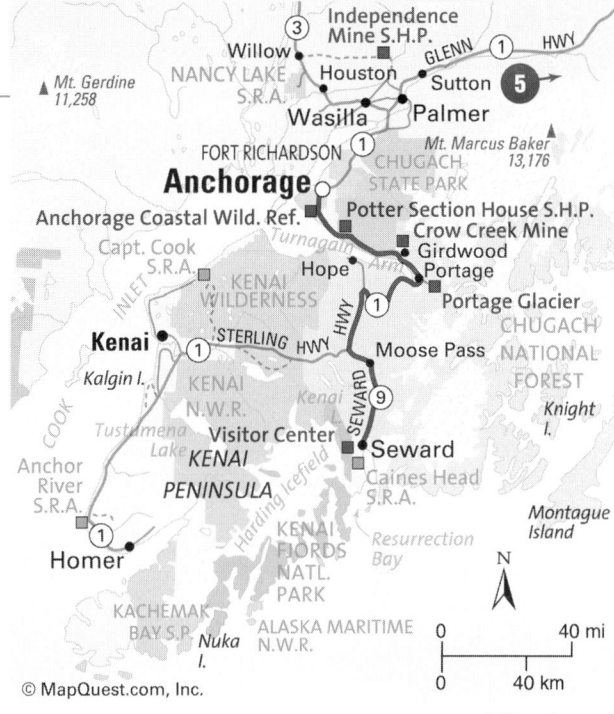

Scenic

The trip from Anchorage to Seward is one of the most scenic 127-mile drives you can take. Frequent pullouts offer vistas of snow-capped mountains, glaciers, wildlife, and wildflowers at almost every turn, and side trips and hiking trails beckon adventurous explorers. With such an impressive "menu" of vacation selections, you don't want to rush between appetizer and dessert.

The road up Portage Valley leads into the 5.8-million-acre Chugach National Forest and past three "hanging" glaciers that are perched in the cleavage of mountain canyons. Portage Glacier pokes its nose through the mountains at the head of a valley that it cut a long time ago. Since 1890, it has receded 1 mile and will be out of view by 2020, so don't procrastinate

Alaska

❋ The Seward Highway

taking a trip to see it. Last year, the glacier finally withdrew from the lake and stopped calving. Now, only a few bergs float in water that was once brimming with ice. The visitor center offers excellent descriptive displays of glaciers and the best chance to see ice worms, pin-sized critters that burrow into glaciers and eat algae. Temperatures above freezing kill them.

If the many sights along the road to Seward make up the appetizer and main course, a boat trip along the rugged coast of Kenai Fjords National Park offers a high-calorie dessert. You can take a day cruise to see wildlife and tidewater glaciers that calve into the sea. Along the way, you may see orcas breach at boatside or a humpback whale with young swimming placidly along. At Chiswall Islands, thousands of puffins and kittywakes circle the boat. Just when you think you've seen the best, the boat stops at the foot of Holgate Glacier. With the engines cut, the cracking and popping of the 500-foot wall of aquamarine ice thunders through the frigid air like cannons firing. A slab of ice silently slips from the face of the glacier and crashes into the water. Seconds later, the blast reaches your ears. This is no dainty wildflower beside a trickling stream; you're witnessing the raw power of nature that carves valleys through mountains and determines the weather of the entire planet.

HIGHLIGHTS

The Seward Highway is in a richly varied and highly diverse area of Alaska. Over the length of its route, the character of the Byway continually changes with its proximity to water, mountains, and towns. The Seward Highway begins in the town of Seward nestled among the fjords surrounding Resurrection Bay. Nearby Kenai Fjords National Park offers the chance to see puffins, otters, eagles, arctic terns, whales, seals, and other marine life.

- As you travel north, the landscape surrounding the Byway becomes one of alpine meadows dotted with rivers and lakes. During late July and early August, **Ptarmigan Creek Recreation Site,** 23 miles from Seward, is an excellent place to stop and watch the incredible salmon run when thousands of red salmon can be seen in this creek heading upstream to spawn.

- Farther north, approximately 75 miles from Seward, is **Twentymile Flats,** an expanse of lowlands and intertidal mudflats where three river valleys empty their silt-laden waters into Turnagain Arm and provide unobstructed views of the surrounding mountain peaks and glaciers. The view here is breathtaking, definitely worth stopping and taking in for a few minutes at the very least.

- Another 5 miles along the Byway is **Portage Lake.** Portage Glacier, located on the far side of Portage Lake, is rapidly receding out of the lake and provides an incredible opportunity to watch glacial action on fast-forward. One-hour boat tours are available to better witness the action.

- The remaining portion of the Seward Highway travels along the **Turnagain Arm** and offers you a plethora of things to see, both on and off the water. Turnagain Arm experiences the second highest tides in the world, often up to a 38-foot change in water level. Bore tides, a rare natural phenomenon in which the front of an incoming tide is a moving wall of water from 3 to 5 feet high, can be witnessed during extremely low tides in Turnagain Arm.

- The city of **Anchorage** is located at the northern terminus of the Seward Highway. With its rich history as a city on the edge of one of the final frontiers, Anchorage offers a wealth of historic and cultural sites that you can enjoy, whether you have an hour or a day to spend.

THINGS TO SEE AND DO

Driving along the Seward Highway will certainly keep your senses engaged, but if you yearn to get out of the car and stretch your legs, or if you'd like to make a mini-vacation out of your trip, check out these attractions along the route.

ALL-AMERICAN ROADS

ALASKA SEALIFE CENTER. *301 Railway Ave, Seward (99664). Phone 907/224-6300; toll-free 800/224-2525. www.alaskasealife.org.* The Alaska SeaLife Center offers an unrivaled up-close and personal experience with Gulf of Alaska marine wildlife. Witness 1,500-pound Steller sea lions gliding past underwater viewing windows, puffins diving in a carefully crafted naturalistic habitat, and harbor seals hauled out on rocky beaches. Alaskan king crabs, sea stars, and Pacific octopi also await you, as well as a variety of intertidal creatures and deep-sea fishes. Open daily; closed Thanksgiving, Dec 25. **$$$**

CHUGACH NATIONAL FOREST. *3301 C St, Anchorage (99503). Phone 907/743-9500. www.fs.fed.us/r10/chugach/.* The Chugach National Forest is the second largest forest in the National Forest System. Roughly the same size as the states of Massachusetts and Rhode Island combined, the Chugach (pronounced CHEW-gatch) is the most northern of national forests, only 500 miles south of the Arctic Circle. One-third of the Chugach is composed of rocks and moving ice. The remainder is a diverse and majestic tapestry of land, water, plants, and animals. The mountains, lakes, and rivers of the Kenai Peninsula, the islands and glaciers of Prince William Sound, and the copious wetlands and birds of the Copper River Delta make this national forest a mecca for adventurers.

CHUGACH STATE PARK. *Mile 115 Seward Hwy, Anchorage. Phone 907/345-5014. www.dnr.state.ak.us/parks/.* Chugach State Park is an accessible wilderness in the backyard of Anchorage. Wildlife viewing and mountain scenery are year-round pleasures, and campers can choose developed campgrounds or secluded backcountry valleys. Nearly 30 trails take hikers throughout the park to see some of its most enchanting views. Many visitors stop at the Eagle River Nature Center for a guided tour or interpretive program. Travelers may want to explore a few of the park's 50 glaciers on their own. And for extreme adventure, try climbing a mountainside or plunging through river rapids. The 495,000-acre park offers a wide variety of activities in all seasons. **$**

★ **KENAI FJORDS NATIONAL PARK.** *Seward (99664). Phone 907/224-2132. www.nps.gov/kefj/.* Kenai Fjords National Park includes one of the four major ice caps in the United States, the 300-square-mile Harding Icefield, and coastal fjords. Located on the southeastern Kenai Peninsula, the national park is a pristine and rugged land supporting many unaltered natural environments and ecosystems. Here, a rich, varied rain forest is home to tens of thousands of breeding birds, and adjoining marine waters support a multitude of sea lions, sea otters, and seals. The most popular visitor activity at Kenai Fjords is viewing the park from a tour boat. The boats are privately owned, and the many operators offer tours of varying lengths and features. Authorized commercial guides provide camping, fishing, and kayaking services. Air charters fly over the coast for flight seeing and access to the fjords. Boat tours and charters are available from Seward. In summer, boat tours ply the coast, observing calving glaciers, sea birds, and marine mammals.

Alaska

❊ The Seward Highway

PORTAGE GLACIER. *Portage. Phone 907/783-3242 or -2326. www.fs.fed.us/r10/chugach/chugach_pages/bbvc.html.* Many of the world's glaciers are receding. This phenomenon is strikingly evident at Portage Glacier. At Portage, the **Begich-Boggs Visitor Center** used to squarely face the massive blue Portage Glacier directly in front of it. But only a few years after the Forest Service built the visitor facility, Portage Glacier receded—around a corner of Portage Lake and out of view. Now, tourists must view the glacier's face from a tour boat. Visitor center open daily 9 am-6 pm Memorial Day-Labor Day, Sat-Sun 10 am-5 pm the rest of the year.

✥ TURNAGAIN PASS. The drive through Turnagain Pass may be one of the most scenic on the Byway. This is the highest point on the Byway, and wildlife spotting occurs regularly here. Turnagain Pass is located in the south beyond Turnagain Arm. Two large pullouts are easily accessible from the only section of divided highway outside of the Anchorage bowl. Views from the highway here show off the distinctive U-shaped valley created by retreating glaciers. Northbound travelers are treated to spectacular views of Turnagain Arm and Twentymile glaciers as they head down from this 900-foot pass to sea level. This area is especially popular in the winter for skiing and snowmobiling, and in mid-summer for its wildflower displays.

PLACES TO STAY

If you choose to include an overnight stay in your trip along this All-American Road, Mobil Travel Guide recommends the following lodgings.

★★ ALASKAN LEOPARD BED & BREAKFAST. *16136 Sandpiper Dr, Anchorage (99501). Phone 907/868-1594; toll-free 877/277-7118. www.alaskanleopard.com.* 4 rooms, 2 story. Hillside chalet with spectacular views of the Anchorage Bowl, Cook Inlet, Mount McKinley, the Kenai Peninsula, and the volcanoes of the Alaska Range. Known for extraordinary breakfasts. $

★★★ FIFTEEN CHANDELIERS B&B INN. *14020 Sabine St, Anchorage (99511). Phone 907/345-3032.* 5 rooms, 3 story. European-style Georgian mansion set in a botanical garden. Breakfast is served in a formal dining room with fine china and stemware. $$

★★ K STREET BED & BREAKFAST. *1433 K St, Anchorage (99501). Phone 907/279-1443; toll-free 888/KST-BANB. www.cruising-america.com/kstreetbb/kst.html.* 3 rooms, 2 story. Contemporary cedar-sided home in a residential neighborhood with a garden and solarium. Features homemade breakfasts and original Alaskan art. $

★★ A LOON'S NEST BED & BREAKFAST. *1455 Hillcrest Dr, Anchorage (99503). Phone 907/279-9884; toll-free, 800/786-9884. www.aloonsnest.com.* 2 rooms, 2 story. Frank Lloyd Wright-designed house poised on a bluff overlooking Westchester Lagoon featuring Shaker-style furniture and whirlpool tubs. $ Ⓓ

★★★ THE OSCAR GILL HISTORIC BED & BREAKFAST. *1344 W 10th Ave, Anchorage (99501). Phone 907/279-1344. www.oscargill.com.* 3 rooms, 2 story. 1913 home located in Delaney Park, bordering the Cook Inlet, with views of Denali and Sleeping Lady. Cited as one of Alaska's best lodgings. ¢

★ **PLANET ANCHORAGE BED & BREAKFAST.** *1025 H St, Anchorage (99501). Phone 907/770-6742. www.planetanchoragebb.com.* 3 rooms, 2 story. 1950s-style home five minutes from downtown Anchorage. Fresh homemade breakfasts made with local ingredients. **$**

★ **SUSITNA SUNSETS BED & BREAKFAST.** *9901 Conifer St, Anchorage (99507). Phone 907/346-1067. www.susitnasunsets.com.* 3 rooms, 3 story. Children 10 and over only. Features views of Mount McKinley with breakfast served in your room or on one of the decks. **$**

PLACES TO EAT

A long day of driving is sure to make you hungry. At the end of your journey, take a table at one of the following restaurants.

★ **ALPINE BAKERY.** *1 Alyeska Hwy, Girdwood (99587). Phone 907/783-2550.* American menu. Breakfast, lunch, dinner. American- and European-style baked goods and light dinners. **$**

★ **THE BAKE SHOP.** *The Old Hotel on Olympic Circle, Girdwood (99587). Phone 907/783-2831. www.thebakeshop.com.* American menu. Breakfast, lunch, dinner. Homemade bakery items and desserts. Famous for sourdough pancakes. **$**

★ **THE DOUBLE MUSKIE INN.** *1 Crow Creek Rd, Girdwood (99587). Phone 907/783-2822.* Cajun menu. Closed Sun. Lunch, dinner. Renowned local restaurant serving Cajun preparations of local ingredients. **$$**

★ **SUMMIT LAKE LODGE.** *Seward Hwy mile 45.5, Moose Pass (99631). Phone 907/244-2031. www.summitlakelodge.com.* American menu. Closed Oct-Apr. Breakfast, lunch, dinner. Family-oriented restaurant with amazing views. **$$**

★ **RESURRECTION ROADHOUSE.** *1/2 mile exit Glacier Rd, Seward (99503). Phone 907/224-7116. www.sewardwindsong.com.* American menu. Closed mid-Oct-mid-Apr. Lunch, dinner. Known for authentic local specialties. **$$**

Big Sur Coast Highway
ROUTE 1 ❋ CALIFORNIA

Quick Facts

LENGTH: 72 miles.

TIME TO ALLOW: 3 to 5 hours.

BEST TIME TO DRIVE: Spring, summer, and fall. High season is during June, July, and August.

BYWAY TRAVEL INFORMATION: Monterey Travel and Tourism Alliance: 831/626-1424; Monterey Peninsula Visitor and Convention Bureau: 831/372-9323.

SPECIAL CONSIDERATIONS: Fill your gas tank in Carmel before heading south or in San Simeon before heading north on Route 1, because you'll encounter few gas stations along the way. The road is narrow and curvy, and in some places it has narrow shoulders and sharp drop-offs to the ocean far below. Large, long vehicles may have trouble with this winding road. Drive with care and watch for pedestrians and bicyclists.

RESTRICTIONS: The road is open all year, except for occasional mudslides during severe rainstorms.

BICYCLE/PEDESTRIAN FACILITIES: This Byway is a major attraction to pedestrians and cyclists. You'll find many shoulders along the way (although in some areas, they're narrow with sharp drop-offs) and plenty of room where all can share.

Route 1 from Carmel south to the San Luis Obispo County line follows some of the most spectacular and highly scenic shoreline found along California's coast. Views include rugged canyons and steep sea cliffs, granite shorelines, sea lions and other marine life, windswept cypress trees, and majestic redwood forests.

This Byway also provides you with a lesson in California's rich Mission-era and natural history. The primary goal of the Byway is to preserve California's delicate and pristine coastal ecosystem for its natives, visitors, and future generations, while still providing opportunities to experience its wonder.

Travel the route that hugs the California coast, providing access to austere, windswept cypress trees, fog-shrouded cliffs, and the crashing surf of the Pacific Ocean.

THE BYWAY STORY

The Big Sur Coast Highway tells cultural, historical, natural, recreational, and scenic stories that make it a unique and treasured Byway.

Cultural

The Big Sur is an area whose culture is largely shaped by the region's geography. The awe-inspiring scenic beauty of the Big Sur has lured and inspired countless artists, authors, and poets. The literary works of Henry Miller are filled with vivid descriptions of the Big Sur, while the artwork of Emil White and others attempts to portray the breathtaking scenery of the Big Sur's rocky coast and coastal mountains.

California

ROUTE 1 ❋ Big Sur Coast Highway

The Carmel area and the Salinas valley, less rugged but no less scenic or inspiring, also have played a vital role in the area's culture. The region has been home to many artists, none more famous than John Steinbeck, whose novels vividly describe life in the fertile Salinas valley. Although Steinbeck is the most famous, the area has also been home to actor Clint Eastwood, photographer Ansel Adams, and poet Robinson Jeffers.

Historical

Written histories regarding the region now known as the Big Sur began to appear in the mid-1500s, when a Portuguese ship passed by the area's coastline. New groups of European explorers approached the area throughout the late 1500s and early 1600s, many anchoring for a time in Monterey Bay. However, it wasn't until 1770 that the first permanent settlement was established, when a Spanish group started a mission in Carmel. The Spaniards first called the area south of the Carmel settlement El Pais Grande del Sur, or "the Big Country of the South." These same Spanish settlers were quick to introduce themselves and their culture to the area natives, who had lived in the region for centuries.

For centuries before the Europeans discovered the Big Sur, the Esselen Indians had thrived in the area as hunters and gatherers, using land and sea animals and plants in the woodlands and coastal plains between Point Sur and Lopez Point. By the early 18th century, other Spanish missions followed the Carmel Mission. The missions had the dual purpose of claiming the land for Spain and teaching the natives the Europeans' message of Christianity. In the late 1700s, the Spanish missionaries and soldiers forced many of the Esselen and other native peoples to leave their villages and move into the missions. Smallpox, cholera, and other European diseases almost completely wiped out the Esselen people when they came in contact with the foreign settlers. Those who were left mixed with the other natives in the missions so that they ceased to maintain a separate existence. As a result, very little is known today about their way of life.

A colorful variety of settlers of various nationalities began to take notice of the scenic Big Sur area and its inviting foothills. The Spanish and Mexican history also heavily influenced the culture and history of the area. Monterey was soon an important port, bringing even more people to the area.

Until the late 1800s, a small, rough trail served as the best overland route to Monterey from the Big Sur. Eventually, the trail widened into a road of sorts, which was still frequently lost in landslides. This widening allowed the journey to Monterey to be made in just 11 hours, as opposed to the three or four days it had taken previously. After many years of difficult passage over poor roads between Big Sur and the rest of central California, Route 1 was completed in 1937. By its completion, 15 years of labor and $9 million had been expended.

Natural

The allure of the Big Sur Coast Highway comes not just from the sea and the mountains, but also from the convergence of the sea with the mountains. Many other destinations around the country feature beautiful mountains, and countless others offer beaches from which to enjoy the ocean. The Big Sur, however, is one of the few places in America where these two dominant features converge so dramatically. Travelers from around the world visit the Big Sur to experience its breathtaking scenery.

The Byway enables you to experience the Pacific Ocean in its most natural, prehistoric state. The endless blue horizon, as seen from the Byway, is most often void of any man-made floating vessels, unlike most other coastlines. Travelers are more likely, in fact, to witness a massive whale surfacing for air or some sea otters playing than to see a freighter waiting to port. Additionally, the Big Sur offers you the unique experience of enjoying the enchanting sounds of the sea, unhindered by any other noise. Many people find that time escapes them as they park on one of the many turnouts and take in the sounds of the sea.

The San Lucia coastal mountain range offers the other side of the Big Sur's natural beauty. The range is a natural paradise of cypress and redwood forests, waterfalls, and meadows full of colorful wildflowers, such as lupines and poppies. The mountains also host one of the Byway's most unique natural elements: the giant redwood tree. The redwoods stretch along a narrow strip of land from the Big Sur area to the southwest corner of Oregon; redwood trees thrive in the specific climate along this area and are not native to any other region in the world. Many of the oldest of the trees are around 2,000 years old. The tallest redwoods have reached heights of about 350 feet. Most redwoods average 50 to 250 feet in height. Such heights require solid foundations, with many of the giant trees' diameters spanning 10 to 15 feet.

The convergence of the Pacific Ocean with the San Lucia Mountains of the Big Sur coastline is the source of the inviting, often overwhelming scenery of the Big Sur. The ocean has helped to carve out the tantalizing craggy rock inlets along the corridor. The highway hugs steep, rocky cliffs on the east side of the road, while blunt drops to the west fall straight to the sea. The solid land mass of the shoreline holds strong as waves of the mighty Pacific push against its cliffs and crash against its rocks. The Big Sur offers a fulfilling blend of natural sights and sounds unlike anywhere else.

Recreational

While Big Sur's beaches hardly resemble the vast stretches of sun-baked sand that dot southern California's coastline, they do offer a wide variety of recreational possibilities.

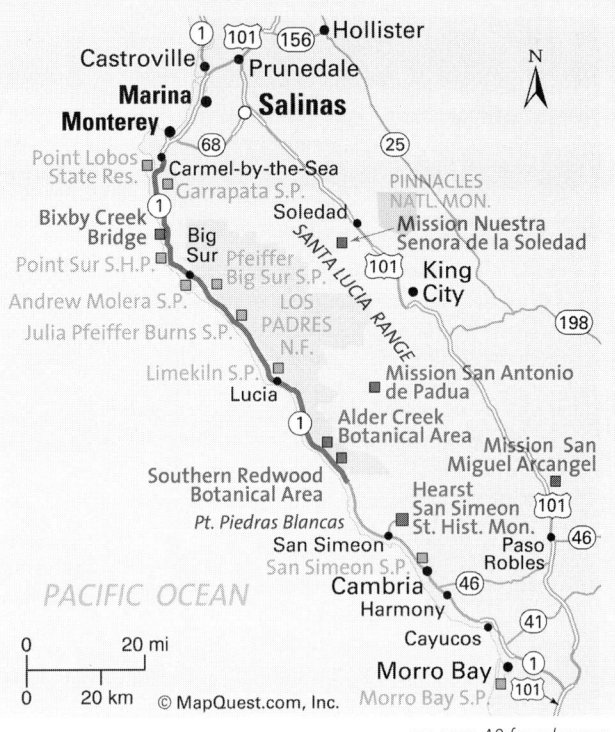

see page A8 for color map

Even during the summer, Big Sur's beaches are subject to generally cool weather. Sunny days are sporadic because a blanket of seasonal fog often hugs the coastline, lowering the temperature in the process. To be prepared, bring a change of warm clothes. Also, bring a pair of sturdy shoes—getting to Big Sur's beaches requires at least a short hike.

Private property and Big Sur's steep terrain make most of its coastline inaccessible to the public. Fortunately, however, several state park and US Forest Service beaches are open to the public all year. These beaches are recommended due to easy access and breathtaking scenery. Located 23 miles south of Carmel, **Andrew Molera State Park** is the largest state park on the Big Sur coast. A wide, scenic, mile-long path leads to a sandy beach that's sheltered from the wind by a large bluff to the north. The path itself is as much a delight as the beach, taking you through a meadow filled with wildflowers and sycamore trees and offering fine views of the coastal mountain range to the east. The path parallels the Big Sur River, which enters the sea adjacent to Molera's beach.

Although **Pfeiffer Beach** is Big Sur's most popular coastal access point, this beach is hard to find if you've never been to it before. The

California

ROUTE 1 ❋ Big Sur Coast Highway

trick is locating unmarked Sycamore Canyon Road. Here's a tip: Sycamore Canyon Road is the only paved, ungated road west of Route 1 between the Big Sur post office and Pfeiffer Big Sur State Park. After you find the turnout, make a very sharp turn and follow the road for about 2 miles until it ends. Drive carefully—this road is narrow and winding and is unsuitable for trailer traffic. From a large parking area at the end of the road, a short, well-marked path leads to the beach. Cliffs tower above this breathtaking stretch of sand, and a large arch-shaped rock formation just offshore makes for some dazzling sunsets.

Just a mile south of the US Forest Service Station in Pacific Valley and 14 miles north of the San Luis Obispo County line lies **Sand Dollar Beach.** From a large parking lot across Route 1 from Plaskett Creek Campground, a well-built stairway leads to a crescent-shaped beach that's protected from the wind by bluffs. Sand Dollar offers visitors the widest expanse of sand along the Big Sur Coast and, possibly, the mildest weather. Standing on the beach looking northeast, towering 5,155-foot **Cone Peak** is visible. For an interesting side trip, visit **Jade Cove,** which is located 2 miles south of Sand Dollar Beach. Big Sur's south coast is famous for its jade reserves, and Jade Cove is a popular spot for beachcombers and rock hounds.

Scenic

The Big Sur Coast Highway affords fantastic views of one of the nation's most scenic coastlines. (Keep in mind that the scenery can be overwhelming, and you may struggle to keep your eyes on the narrow, winding road.) At certain points along the Byway, the only way to get any closer to the Pacific is to get in it! Traveling Route 1 offers ample opportunity for experiencing the mighty ocean pounding against the pristine coastline, with waves crashing against the rocks and cliffs. Scenic overlooks are plentiful along the Byway, providing you with breathtaking views from safe turnouts.

If the vast blue waters of the Pacific aren't enough for you, direct your eyes inland, taking in the beautiful coastal hills and mountains. The inland side delights the eye with its cypress and redwood forests, impressive trees towering over the road. Other areas feature mountain meadows ablaze in colorful wildflowers.

Each season offers a unique scenic experience. The spring months are a wonderful time to experience the Big Sur's deep green colors and colorful wildflowers that brighten the grassy hillsides. Autumn in Big Sur country brings with it new fall colors. The sycamores, cottonwoods, and maples display golden yellows and oranges, while the leaves of the poison oak turn a deep red. The winter months of December through March are the best time to spot gray whales migrating to and from the warm waters of Baja. Whenever the season, the Big Sur showcases nature at its best.

HIGHLIGHTS

The Big Sur Coast Highway runs along Route 1 from north of San Simeon to Carmel. If you're traveling the opposite direction, simply follow this list from bottom up.

- **Ragged Point** marks the official entrance to the Big Sur Coast Highway. Ragged Point has incredible views in every direction and features a restaurant, gas station, and hotel.

- Not far after Ragged Point, the Byway enters **Los Padres National Forest.**

- Continuing north, the Byway travels past the **Southern Redwood Botanical Area** and then the **Alder Creek Botanical Area.**

- **Lucia,** consisting of a restaurant and a small motel, is the next major point of interest along the corridor.

- From Lucia, the Byway passes several state parks, including **Limekiln** and **Julia Pfeiffer Burns state parks.**

- Following Julia Pfeiffer Burns State Park, the corridor soon enters the expansive **Big Sur area**. This area consists of several inns, restaurants, and shops scattered along the corridor.
- An important point of interest near the Big Sur area is the **Point Sur State Historic Park**, home to the historic Point Sur Lighthouse.
- Historic **Bixby Bridge** lies farther north of Point Sur.
- From Bixby Bridge, the Byway continues north to its ending point in **Carmel**, known for its pristine beaches and charming shops, as well as its cozy cottages and extravagant mansions.

THINGS TO SEE AND DO

Driving along the Big Sur Coast Highway will certainly keep your senses engaged, but if you yearn to get out of the car and stretch your legs, or if you'd like to make a mini-vacation out of your trip, check out these attractions along the route.

BIXBY BRIDGE. *18 miles south of Carmel.* The Bixby Bridge, completed in 1932, is a marvel of engineering and one of the ten highest single-span bridges in the world. The bridge spans a large canyon along the Big Sur coastline. The weather conditions can have a noticeable impact on the bridge's appearance: clouds may partially hide it, or the sun may reflect off of the gleaming white structural supports. That quality, combined with the massive appearance of the bridge, brings countless people to photograph the bridge. **FREE**

CARMEL MISSION AND BASILICA. *3080 Rio Rd, Carmel (93923). Phone 831/624-1271. www.carmelmission.org.* The Carmel Mission, located on Rio Road off of Route 1, was the second of California's historical missions, built in 1771. At that time, Father Junipero Serra founded the Basilica of Mission San Carlos Borromeo de Carmelo, one of only two basilicas on the West Coast. It is considered the jewel of California missions, and it was Father Serra's favorite. He is buried near the altar. Mission San Carlos Borromeo de Carmelo has been a haven for artists and writers for over a century. Open Mon-Sat 9:30 am-4:30 pm, Sun 10:30 am-4:30 pm. **$**

★ **JULIA PFEIFFER BURNS STATE PARK.** *Big Sur Station #1, Big Sur (93920). Phone 831/667-2315. www.parks.ca.gov.* This state park stretches from the Big Sur coastline into nearby 3,000-foot ridges. The park features redwood, tan oak, madrone, chaparral, and an 80-foot waterfall that drops from granite cliffs into the ocean from the Overlook Trail. A panoramic view of the ocean and miles of rugged coastline are accessible from the higher elevations along the trails east of Route 1. The park also has a 1,680-acre underwater reserve that protects a spectacular assortment of marine life. Special-use permits allow experienced scuba divers to explore the reserve. Seals, sea lions, and sea otters can be seen in the park's cove. Hikers can discover the park's backcountry via several trail systems. Open daily dawn-dusk. **$$**

California

ROUTE 1 ✤ *Big Sur Coast Highway*

◼ **MONTEREY BAY AQUARIUM.** *886 Cannery Row, Monterey (93290). Phone 831/648-4888. www.mbayaq.org.* The Monterey Bay Aquarium contains more than 100 galleries and exhibits, each re-creating some of the bay's many habitats. The world-class aquarium contains some 6,500 live creatures, such as jellyfish, sharks, octopus, and giant ocean sunfish. Many exhibits enable visitors to interact with and even touch the sea creatures. The aquarium includes a towering three-story kelp forest, hands-on touch pools, a walk-through aviary, and an enchanting exhibit of playful sea otters. The outer Bay Wing features a depiction of life in the open ocean, while the "Mysteries of the Deep" exhibit offers a peek into the deepest of the undersea Monterey Canyon. Videos, special programs, and a host of hands-on activities bring the entire family closer to sea life than ever before. Open daily 9:30 am-6 pm Memorial Day-Labor Day; 10 am-6 pm the rest of the year; closed Dec 25. $$$$

POINT LOBOS STATE RESERVE. *Hwy 1, Carmel (93921). Phone 831/624-4909. pt-lobos.parks.ca.gov.* Deriving its name from the offshore rocks at Punta de los Lobos Marinos (Point of the Sea Wolves), where the sound of the sea lions carries inland, this reserve has often been called the crown jewel of the state park system. Point Lobos offers outstanding recreational opportunities, such as sightseeing, photography, painting, nature study, picnicking, and scuba diving. In addition to the spectacular beauty, nearly every aspect of its resources is of scientific interest. You'll see rare plant communities, endangered archeological sites, unique geological formations, and incredibly rich flora and fauna of both land and sea. The reserve contains headlands, coves, and rolling meadows. The offshore area forms one of the richest underwater habitats in the world, popular with divers. Wildlife includes seals, sea lions, sea otters, and migrating gray whales (December to May). Thousands of seabirds also make the reserve their home. Hiking trails follow the shoreline and lead to hidden coves. The area used to be the home of a turn-of-the-century whaling and abalone industry. A small cabin from that era still remains on Whaler's Cove, near Carmel. Open 9 am-5 pm, with longer hours during the summer. $$

POINT SUR STATE HISTORIC PARK AND LIGHTHOUSE. *On Hwy 1, 15 miles south of Carmel. Phone 831/625-4419. www.pointsur.org.* This park is the home of the historic Point Sur Light Station and an active US Coast Guard light station. The park sits 361 feet above the surf on a large volcanic rock. Point Sur has been a navigational landmark throughout history, and the nearby coastline has been the site of several notable shipwrecks, both before and after the installation of the lighthouse. Point Sur is on the National Register of Historic Places and is a California State Historic Landmark. From the highway, you can see the majestic stone buildings of the Point Sur Light Station that have been part of the Big Sur coast for more than 100 years. The facilities were established for the safety of seagoing vessels moving up and down the Big Sur coast. First lit on August 1, 1889, it has remained in continuous operation. Four lighthouse keepers and their families lived at the site until 1974, when the light station was automated. Call for specific hours and tour times. $-$$

PLACES TO STAY

If you choose to include an overnight stay in your trip along this All-American Road, Mobil Travel Guide recommends the following lodgings.

Big Sur

★★★★ **POST RANCH INN.** *Hwy 1, Big Sur (93920). Phone 831/667-2200; toll-free 800/527-2200. www.postranchinn.com.* Perched on the tip of a cliff overlooking the dramatic coastline of Big Sur, the Post Ranch Inn brings new meaning to living on the edge. This unique hideaway offers an experience far from the ordinary. Designed to live in harmony with the majestic natural setting, the architecture resembles a collection of sophisticated treehouses. Clean lines and simple interiors create an uncluttered appearance and state of mind. Floor-to-ceiling windows open to awe-inspiring views and enhance the subtle beauty of the accommodations, while two-sided fireplaces are the ultimate luxury, allowing guests to enjoy the warm glow from the bed or the bath. No televisions or alarm clocks disrupt the gentle rhythm of this place, where yoga and tai chi reawaken the soul and the spa soothes the spirit. The Sierra Mar restaurant is a triumph of California cuisine, and the extensive wine list is a perfect accompaniment to the superb dishes. 30 rooms, 2 story. Adults only. Complimentary continental breakfast. Check-out 1 pm, check-in 4 pm. Fireplaces. Restaurant. Spa, massage. Outdoor pool, whirlpool. Free wine tasting Sat. $$$$

★★★ **VENTANA INN & SPA.** *Hwy 1, Big Sur (93920). Phone 831/667-2331; toll-free 800/628-6500. www.ventanainn.com.* The views are breathtaking at this inn overlooking the Pacific's dramatic cliffs. The rooms and suites are divided among 12 buildings tucked into the 240-acre landscape. The Allegria Spa reconnects guests with nature and offers classes and guided hikes. 60 rooms, 1-2 story. Complimentary continental breakfast; afternoon refreshments. Check-out noon, check-in 4 pm. TV, VCR (movies). Heated pool, whirlpool, poolside service (in summer). Dining room. Picnics. Bar noon-midnight. In-room modem link. Luggage handling. Concierge. Exercise room; sauna. Massage. Hiking. Horseback riding. Refrigerators, wet bars; many fireplaces; some whirlpools. Balconies. Sun deck. $$$$

Carmel

★★ **CANDLE LIGHT INN.** *San Carlos, between 4th and 5th aves, Carmel (93921). Phone 831/624-6451; toll-free 800/433-4732. www.innsbythesea.com.* 20 rooms, 4 kitchen units, 2 story. No A/C. June-Oct, weekends 2-day minimum. Complimentary continental breakfast. Check-out noon. TV. Whirlpool. Business services available. Refrigerators; some fireplaces; microwaves available. Totally nonsmoking. $

★★★ **CARRIAGE HOUSE INN.** *Junipero between 7th and 8th aves, Carmel (93921). Phone 831/625-2585; toll-free 800/433-4372. www.innsbythesea.com.* Village restaurants, galleries, and shops are a short walk from this inn. 13 rooms, 2 story. No A/C. Complimentary continental breakfast; evening refreshments. Check-out noon, check-in 3 pm. TV; cable (premium), VCR (movies). In-room modem link. Refrigerators, wet bars, fireplaces; some in-room whirlpools. Antique furnishings. Totally nonsmoking. $$

★ **LOBOS LODGE.** *Ocean Ave and Monteverde St, Carmel (93921). Phone 831/624-3874. www.loboslodge.com.* The beach is four blocks away from this quaint lodge. 28 rooms, 2 suites, 1-3 story. Complimentary continental breakfast. Check-out noon. TV; cable (premium). In-room modem link. Fireplaces. $

★★ **NORMANDY INN.** *124 E Bearskin Rd, Carmel (93921). Phone 831/624-3825; toll-free 800/343-3825. www.normandyinncarmel.com.* 41 rooms, 2 story. Complimentary continental breakfast. Check-out 11 am, check-in 3 pm. TV. Refrigerators available. Heated pool. $

California

ROUTE 1 ❋ Big Sur Coast Highway

★★★★ **QUAIL LODGE RESORT AND GOLF COURSE.** 8205 Valley Greens Dr, Carmel (93923). Phone 831/624-2888; toll-free 888/828-8787. www.quaillodge.com. Quail Lodge Resort and Golf Club is a magnet for active travelers seeking the total resort experience. Set on 850 acres on the sunny side of the Carmel Valley, the grounds are a lovely mix of rolling hills, lakes, and gardens. It is no wonder that golf is a favorite pursuit here, with a fantastic 18-hole course designed by Robert Muir-Graves and a 7-acre driving range. The Carmel River gently snakes along the course, making it a particularly scenic round. Four tennis courts and two outdoor pools tempt others, while the spa alleviates aches and pains with its wonderful assortment of facials, massages, and hydrotherapy with Vichy showers. The rooms and suites are attractively appointed and cradle guests in comfort. All preferences are suited at the three restaurants, and The Covey stands out for its charming lakeside setting, gourmet cuisine, and extensive wine list. 97 units, 2 story. Summer weekends 2-day minimum; golf plan Sun-Thurs. Resort fee $15 per day. Pet accepted, $100. Complimentary continental breakfast. Check-out noon. TV; cable (premium), VCR available. Two heated pools; whirlpool, poolside service. Restaurants. Bars; entertainment. Room service. Meeting rooms. Business services available. In-room modem link. Bellhops. Concierge. Gift shop. Airport transportation. Shopping arcade. Tennis, pro. 18-hole golf, greens fee $140-$175, putting green, driving range. Valet service. In-house fitness room; steam room. Spa. Massage. Some fireplaces, wet bars. Refrigerators. Private patios, balconies. Hiking, bicycling. $$$

Monterey

★★★ **DOUBLETREE HOTEL.** 2 Portola Plaza, Monterey (93940). Phone 831/649-4511; toll-free 800/222-8733. www.doubletree.com. This hotel is a short drive from Pebble Beach, great golf courses, fine restaurants, and many shops and galleries. 380 rooms, 10 suites, 7 story. No A/C. Check-out noon, check-in 3 pm. TV; cable (premium). In-room modem link. Restaurant, bar. Room service. Babysitting services available. In-house fitness room, massage, steam room. Outdoor pool, whirlpool. Valet, self-parking. Business center. Concierge. $$

★★★ **HOTEL PACIFIC.** 300 Pacific St, Monterey (93940). Phone 831/373-5700; toll-free 800/232-4141. www.hotelpacific.com. Enjoy modern interiors, fountains, and gardens, all done in a Spanish-style motif. 105 suites, 2-3 story. Complimentary continental breakfast; evening refreshments. Check-out noon, check-in 4 pm. TV; cable (premium), VCR (movies). Refrigerators, fireplaces, wet bars. Whirlpool. Valet parking available. Concierge. Totally nonsmoking. $$

★★★ **JABBERWOCK BED AND BREAKFAST.** 598 Laine St, Monterey (93940). Phone 831/372-4777; toll-free 888/428-7253. www.jabberwockinn.com. This quiet bed-and-breakfast, a former convent, is only four blocks from Cannery Row, six blocks from the aquarium, and a 20-minute walk from Fisherman's Wharf. Half an acre of gardens and waterfalls create a tranquil atmosphere. 7 rooms, 2 share bath, 3 story. No A/C, no room phones. Closed Dec 24-25. Complimentary breakfast. Check-out noon, check-in 3 pm. Some fireplaces. Whirlpool. Totally nonsmoking. $$

★★★ **OLD MONTEREY INN.** 500 Martin St, Monterey (93940). Phone 831/375-8284; toll-free 800/350-2344. www.oldmontereyinn.com. Perfect for golfers visiting nearby courses or those wanting a romantic escape, this historic inn is set amidst striking gardens. Extra in-room comforts, such as feather beds, down comforters, terry robes, and candles, abound.

A pleasant breakfast and sunset wine hour make this a first-rate escape. 10 rooms. No A/C. Complimentary continental breakfast. Check-out noon, check-in 3 pm. TV; cable (premium), VCR (movies). In-room modem link. Many fireplaces; Totally nonsmoking. $$$

★★ **SAND DOLLAR INN.** *755 Abrego St, Monterey (93940). Phone 831/372-7551; toll-free 800/982-1986. www.sanddollarinn.com.* 63 rooms, 3 story. Complimentary continental breakfast. Check-out noon, check-in 3 pm. TV; cable (premium). In-room modem link. Laundry services. Outdoor pool, whirlpool. $

PLACES TO EAT

A long day of driving is sure to make you hungry. At the end of your journey, take a table at one of the following restaurants.

Big Sur

★★★★ **CIELO BIG SUR.** *Hwy 1, Big Sur (93920). Phone 831/667-4242; toll-free 800/628-6500. www.ventanainn.com.* Cielo is a magical place. Set on the cliffs of Route 1, the restaurant affords breathtaking mountain views and heart-stopping peeks at the white-capped, deep-blue ocean below. With nature's bounty on such magnificent display, outdoor seating on the wide, rustic, elegant patio is the way to go. If seats outside aren't available, the dining room is warm and cozy, with tall windows, a large stone fireplace, wood-beamed ceilings, and a bird's-eye view of the sparkling new exhibition kitchen, where you'll witness pristine California ingredients being transformed into sumptuous plates. California menu. Lunch, dinner. Bar. Reservations accepted (dinner). Outdoor seating (lunch). Totally nonsmoking. $$$

★★ **NEPENTHE.** *Hwy 1, Big Sur (93920). Phone 831/667-2345. www.nepenthebigsur.com.* A 40-mile view of the Pacific coastline is only one of the highlights at this longstanding family-owned restaurant that specializes in Ambrosia Burgers and homemade desserts. American, California menu. Lunch, dinner. Bar. Outdoor seating. $$$

★★★★ **SIERRA MAR RESTAURANT.** *Hwy 1, Big Sur (93920). Phone 831/667-2800. www.postranchinn.com.* Perched high over the Pacific Ocean is the highly acclaimed Sierra Mar restaurant, an elegant but comfortable space appointed with wood and chrome and, of course, surrounded by magnificent views of cliffs, mountains, and the wide ocean below. It's tough to compete with such incredible natural beauty, but the food at Sierra Mar does a winning job of it. Innovative and modern but grounded in precise French technique, the four-course prix fixe menu changes daily and utilizes seasonal organic products. You'll find seafood, lamb, and beef alongside luxurious ingredients like oysters, truffles, foie gras, and caviar. The restaurant has one of the most extensive wine cellars in North America, giving you many options for glass-clinking toasts. Eclectic California cuisine. Menu changes daily. Lunch, dinner. Bar. Reservations accepted. Outdoor seating (lunch). Totally nonsmoking. $$$

Carmel

★★★ **ABALONETTI SEAFOOD TRATTORIA.** *57 Fisherman's Wharf, Carmel (93921). Phone 831/373-1851. www.pisto.com.* Seafood menu. Closed Dec 25. Lunch, dinner. Bar. Children's menu. Casual attire. Outdoor seating. Exhibition kitchen. Harbor view. Totally nonsmoking. $$

California

ROUTE 1 ✱ Big Sur Coast Highway

★★★ **ANTON AND MICHEL.** *Mission St, Carmel (93921). Phone 831/624-2406; toll-free 866/244-0645. www.carmelsbest.com.* Continental menu. Specialties: rack of lamb, chateaubriand. Closed the first week of Jan. Lunch, dinner. Bar. Casual attire. Reservations required. Garden view from the main dining room. Outdoor seating. Totally nonsmoking. $$$
D

★★★ **CASANOVA.** *5th Ave and Mission, Carmel (93921). Phone 831/625-0501. www.casanovarestaurant.com.* Southern French, northern Italian menu. Closed Dec 25. Lunch, dinner, Sun brunch. Bar. Reservations accepted. Outdoor seating. Totally nonsmoking. $$$
D

★ **COTTAGE RESTAURANT.** *Lincoln St, Carmel (93921). Phone 831/625-6260. www.cottagerestaurant.com.* American menu. Closed Dec 25. Breakfast, lunch, dinner (Thurs-Sun). Children's menu. Casual attire. Reservations accepted. Totally nonsmoking. $$
D

★★ **FLYING FISH GRILL.** *Carmel Plz, Carmel (93921). Phone 831/625-1962.* Pacific Rim/Pan-Asian menu. Closed Tues; July 4, Thanksgiving, Dec 25. Dinner. Casual attire. Pacific Rim décor; fish motif includes artwork and papier mâché flying fish decorations. $$

★★ **MISSION RANCH.** *26270 Dolores, Carmel (93923). Phone 831/625-9040. www.missionranchcarmel.com.* American menu. Closed Dec 25. Dinner, Sun brunch. Bar. Piano. Children's menu. Casual attire. Outdoor seating. Totally nonsmoking. $$$
D

★★ **ROCKY POINT.** *Hwy 1, Carmel (93922). Phone 831/624-2933. www.rocky-point.com.* American, seafood, steak menu. Breakfast, lunch, dinner. Bar. Casual attire. Spectacular views from every table with outdoor seating available. A famous point for whale-watching. Totally nonsmoking. $$

Monterey

★★★ **CIBO RISTORANTE ITALIANO.** *301 Alvarado St, Monterey (93940). Phone 831/649-8151. www.cibo.com.* This simple yet elegant California-style restaurant offers a perfect setting for innovative interpretations of classical Sicilian cooking. Considered one of the best places for live jazz on the Monterey Bay, Cibo is located in the heart of historic downtown Monterey. Italian menu. Closed Thanksgiving, Dec 25. Dinner. Bar. Entertainment. Casual attire. Totally nonsmoking. $$$
D

★★★ **FRESH CREAM.** *99 Pacific St, Bldg 100C, Monterey (93940). Phone 831/375-9798. www.freshcream.com.* This restaurant overlooks Monterey Harbor. Stunning views, elegant décor, and impeccable service set the mood for romantic dining. French menu. Closed Easter, Dec 25. Dinner. Bar. Casual attire. Reservations accepted; required weekends. Totally nonsmoking. $$
D

★★★ **MONTRIO BISTRO.** *414 Calle Principal, Monterey (93940). Phone 831/648-8880. www.montrio.com.* This restaurant, set in a former firehouse dating to 1910, features eclectic décor and an open kitchen with a wood-burning rotisserie. Mediterranean menu. Closed July 4, Thanksgiving, Dec 25. Dinner. Bar. Children's menu. Casual attire. Totally nonsmoking. $$
D

★★ **RAPPA'S SEAFOOD.** *101 Fisherman's Wharf, Monterey (93940). Phone 831/372-7562. www.rappas.com.* This end-of-the-wharf spot, owned by the Rappa family since 1952, offers scenic views of the bay and, often, the sea lions that call it home. Seafood menu. Closed Thanksgiving, Dec 25. Lunch, dinner. Bar. Children's menu. Casual attire. Totally nonsmoking. **$$$**

★★★ **TARPY'S ROADHOUSE.** *2999 Monterey-Salinas Hwy, Monterey (93940). Phone 831/647-1444. www.tarpys.com.* Tarpy's is located in a historic country stone house dating to 1917. The dining area is a former wine-tasting room, and the kitchen produces upscale country-style dishes. American menu. Closed July 4, Thanksgiving, Dec 25. Lunch, dinner, Sun brunch. Bar. Children's menu. Outdoor seating. **$$$**
[D]

San Luis Obispo North Coast Byway
ROUTE 1 ✹ CALIFORNIA
A continuation of the Big Sur Coast Highway.

Quick Facts

LENGTH: 57 miles.

TIME TO ALLOW: 2 hours or more.

BEST TIME TO DRIVE: Year-round.

SPECIAL CONSIDERATIONS: Temporary seasonal closures are expected each year north of San Luis Obispo County. These closures occur most often along the rugged Big Sur Coast during heavy rainfall months.

BICYCLE/PEDESTRIAN FACILITIES: The Byway corridor offers incredible opportunities for hiking and bicycling; many cyclists even ride the entire stretch of Route 1 between San Luis Obispo and Monterey. Bike lanes exist from the city of San Luis Obispo to Hearst Castle, but in many areas of the Byway, bike lanes and shoulders are absent. Trails along portions of the Byway allow you to stroll leisurely and enjoy the great scenery and sunset views the Byway offers.

Route 1 in north San Luis Obispo County winds past and through some of the finest views in the western United States. The Byway blends the rural beauty associated with much of Route 1 in the northern portion of the state with the convenience and amenities found in the more heavily populated southern sections of California.

Whether you're taking your first trip on the Byway or you're an adventuring local making one of many repeat visits, this stretch of Route 1 is sure to enrich your spirit and engage your imagination. Navigating along this coastal Byway will surely reconnect your soul to natural and historical treasures that lurk within sight and close proximity.

THE BYWAY STORY

The San Luis Obispo North Coast Byway tells historical, natural, recreational, and scenic stories that make it a unique and treasured Byway.

Historical

From historical points in the city of San Luis Obispo to Hearst Castle in San Simeon, the San Luis Obispo North Coast Byway is rich in history.

The city of San Luis Obispo has its beginnings in the 1772 founding of the Mission San Luis Obispo de Tolosa by Father Junípero Serra; it was named for the Franciscan saint known as Louis, Bishop of Toulouse (France). Built on a knoll beside a sparkling creek, the mission became the hub of a growing settlement, serving as the center of both the community and the county. Mission San Luis Obispo is considered by many to be the most beautiful of all California missions.

California

ROUTE 1 ✱ San Luis Obispo North Coast Byway

During the 1880s, the Southern Pacific Railroad built a railroad south from San Jose. After a five-year delay, the railroad came to San Luis Obispo in 1894. Construction of the railroad helped bring both industry and variety to the small community and changed the face of the city. Remnants of the historical railroad system remain at the Ramona Railroad Depot and the San Luis Obispo Railroad Museum. The museum collects, restores, displays, and operates historic railroad equipment.

Hearst Castle, a California State Historical Monument, is just off of the Byway, north of Cambria. The castle, a living monument to the area's early 20th-century history, was built by publisher William Randolph Hearst, who entertained the rich and famous here. He intended it to be an elaborate getaway, complete with fine art and architecture. This historic treasure now provides a look into the windows of the past; it one of the most heavily visited facilities in the California State Park System.

Natural

The San Luis Obispo North Coast Byway's prominent resource is the ocean, including its sea life and nationally recognized bays: Morro Bay, Morro Estuary, and Monterey Bay. The bays and ocean along the route often afford travelers views of otters, seals, sea lions, and whales. Morro Estuary serves a critical environmental function of the Pacific Coast by supporting many species of migratory birds protected by international treaties.

One of the most remarkable recent activities along this stretch of Route 1 is the establishment of breeding colonies of elephant seals near Piedras Blancas Point. As you drive, elephant seal colonies are easily viewable from the Byway. In addition, the California Department of Transportation, working closely with Hearst Ranch Corporation, has provided excellent vista points and informational kiosks about the seals, which are the largest of all pinnipeds and can exceed 2 tons in weight and 10 feet in length. Like many marine mammals, elephant seals were hunted to near extinction in the 19th century and, until recently, the huge seals lived in isolated areas far from humans. Then, in 1990, they started colonizing the unspoiled beaches and coves just south of Point Piedras Blancas.

The San Luis Obispo North Coast Byway also bisects lush valleys and rural farmland. The Byway skirts the Morros Peaks and the Santa Lucia coastal mountain range and goes through the state's southernmost native Monterey pine forest. Equally important is the fertile land of the area, a significant natural resource for farming, which is one of the important industries of central and northern California.

Recreational

The San Luis Obispo corridor is blessed with pristine opportunities for outdoor recreation. Visitors may hike, cycle, surf, ride horses, watch birds, wind surf, hang glide, kayak, and fly kites, among many other activities. The excellent climate of the area allows for year-round recreation.

The Byway's close proximity to countless cycling routes makes it a desirable destination for cyclists. The highway itself generally has generous shoulders and makes for a great bike ride, allowing you to move along at a pace that gives you more time to take in the beauty of the route.

Perhaps the best way to take in the immense scenic opportunities of the Byway is to hike or ride horses right along the coastline. Coastal access adjacent to the southern boundary of the Monterey Bay National Marine Sanctuary, for example, gives you the opportunity to experience the magnificence of the Pacific Ocean. The area also offers horse enthusiasts the opportunity to explore miles of coastline along the Byway. You can bring your own horses or utilize one of the local outfitters who rent horses for rides along the Byway.

The Harmony Coast contains unique opportunities to explore rocky coastal inlets by kayak. Just north of the California beach community of Cayucos on rural Route 1, rocky sections support some of the state's richest and most extensive tide pool habitat areas. Kayaking allows for in-depth exploration of these intriguing natural habitats.

Scenic

Many travelers have daydreamed of traveling along a peaceful coastal road, with the blue waters of the ocean washing the beach or crashing craggy rock walls on one side and serene hills, farmland, and mountain peaks on the other side. The San Luis Obispo North Coast Byway turns these daydreams into reality.

The Byway travels along a coastline containing rocky headlands, hundreds of coves, dozens of uncrowded beaches, and clean blue water stretching to the distant horizon. The air above the Byway is without pollution, and the horizon is free of giant oil tankers and freight ships that inhibit similar coastal drives. The Byway takes you past wide coastal terraces, sandy shores and dune areas, rocky inshore areas, and sheer granite cliffs and bluffs high above the sea.

The harbors and bays found along the Byway have undoubtedly served as inspiration for artistic seascape paintings. Morro Bay, a working fishing village and a protected harbor, is also home to the Morro Bay Estuary and Morro Rock. Morro Rock, abruptly rising over 500 feet above the bay, provides a dreamy backdrop for activities in the clean harbor. Other scenic bays along the route include Estero Bay, San Simeon Bay, and the southern portion of part of the Monterey Bay National Marine Sanctuary.

The spectacular shoreline of the San Luis Obispo North Coast Byway is backed by a series of coastal terraces that rise to the foothills and then to the high ridges of the Santa Lucia Range. The land is covered with open rangelands, including coastal prairie grasslands, oak savannas, pine forest meadows, and grassland-covered upland slopes. In spring, these areas are mantled in the lush green of new growth, followed by vibrant displays of orange California poppy, purple lupine, and other colorful native wildflowers. Later in the year, these same grasslands are toasted to a golden brown, providing rich contrast to the somber and dark evergreen forests around Cambria. Softly sculptured hills ring the city, with a series of steep, conical peaks, called morros. Morros are the remains of ancient volcanoes jutting up from the valley floor.

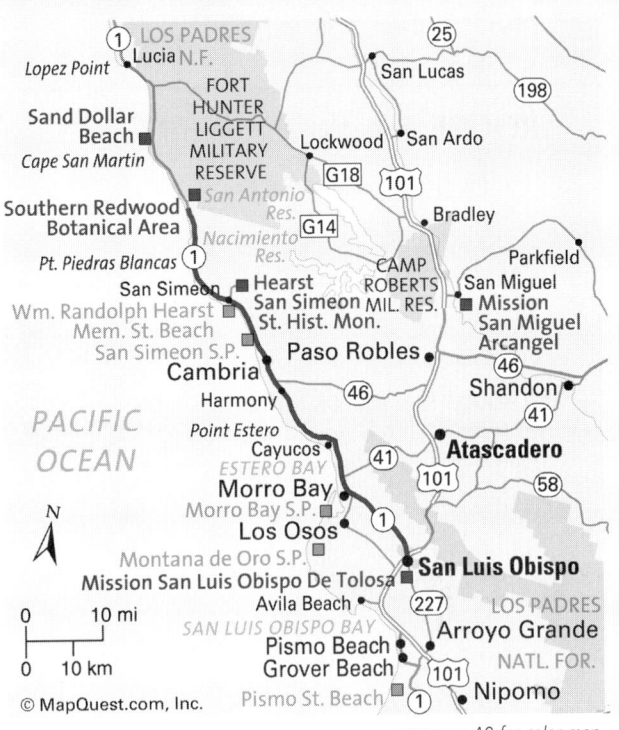

THINGS TO SEE AND DO

Driving along the San Luis Obispo North Coast Byway will certainly keep your senses engaged, but if you yearn to get out of the car and stretch your legs, or if you'd like to make a mini-vacation out of your trip, check out these attractions along the route.

AH LOUIS STORE. *800 Palm St, San Luis Obispo (93401). Phone 805/543-4332.* A leader of the Chinese community, Ah Louis was an extraordinary man who achieved prominence at a time when Asians were given few opportunities. The two-story building, dating to 1874, served as

California

ROUTE 1 ❊ San Luis Obispo North Coast Byway

the Chinese bank, post office, and general merchandise store and was the cornerstone of the Chinese community. Open Mon-Sat; closed holidays.

HEARST SAN SIMEON STATE HISTORICAL MONUMENT. *750 Hearst Castle Rd, San Simeon (93452). 805/927-2020. 800/444-4445. www.heartcastle.com.* In the Santa Lucia Mountains of California on a hilltop overlooking the Pacific Ocean, craftsmen labored nearly 28 years to create a magnificent estate of 165 rooms and 127 acres of gardens, terraces, pools, and walkways. Rooms were furnished with a magnificent collection of Spanish and Italian antiques and art. Called La Cuesta Encantada (the Enchanted Hill), it is better known as Hearst Castle, once the home of newspaper publisher, art collector, and builder William Randolph Hearst. Day tours take approximately one hour and 45 minutes; evening tours take approximately two hours and 15 minutes. The main house itself, La Casa Grande, is a grand setting for Hearst's collection of European antiques and art pieces. It was also a most fitting site for hosting the many influential guests who stayed at Hearst's 250,000-acre San Simeon ranch. Guests included President Calvin Coolidge, Winston Churchill, George Bernard Shaw, Charles Lindbergh, Charlie Chaplin, and a diverse array of luminaries from show business and the publishing industry. Open daily; closed Jan 1, Thanksgiving, and Dec 25. Five tours daily. **$$-$$$$**

MADONNARI ITALIAN STREET PAINTING FESTIVAL. *751 Palm St, San Luis Obispo (93401). Phone 805/781-2777. www.rain.org/~imadonna.* Local artists decorate the streets around the mission with chalk drawings. Also music, Italian cuisine, and an open-air market. Held at the Mission San Luis Obispo de Tolosa in September.

MISSION SAN LUIS OBISPO DE TOLOSA. *751 Palm St, San Luis Obispo (93401). Phone 805/543-6850. www.missionsanluisobispo.org.* Fifth of the California missions, founded in 1772, this mission still serves as the parish church. Eight-room museum contains extensive Chumash collection and artifacts from early settlers. First olive orchard in California was planted here; two original trees still stand. Open daily 9 am-4 pm; closed holidays. **FREE**

MONTANA DE ORO STATE PARK. *350 Pecho Valley Rd, Los Osos (93402). Phone 805/528-0513. www.parks.ca.gov.* Spectacular scenery along 7 miles of shoreline, with tide pools, beaches, and camping. Hiking trails up 1,350-foot Valencia Peak. Popular for whale-watching and viewing harbor seals and sea otters along the shore. **$$$**

MORRO BAY AQUARIUM. *595 Embarcadero, Morro Bay (93442). Phone 805/772-7647. www.morrobay.com/morrobayaquarium/index.html.* Displays 300 live marine specimens, including seals, sharks, and harbor seals. Open daily. **$**

MORRO BAY STATE PARK. *Morro Bay (93442). Phone 805/772-7434. www.parks.ca.gov.* Approximately 2,400 acres on Morro Bay. Fishing, boating; 18-hole golf course (fee), picnicking, hiking, tent and trailer camping (showers; water and electric hookups).

ALL-AMERICAN ROADS

MORRO ROCK. *Morro Bay, Morro Bay (93442). Phone 805/772-4467. www.morrobay.com/rock.htm.* A 576-foot-high volcanic boulder often called the Gibraltar of the Pacific is now a bird sanctuary. Drive to the base of the rock for optimal viewing. Open daily.

MOZART FESTIVAL. *1160 Marsh St, San Luis Obispo (93401). Phone 805/781-3008. www.mozartfestival.com.* Recitals, chamber music, orchestra concerts, and choral music. Held at various locations throughout the county, including Mission San Luis Obispo de Tolosa and Cal Poly State University campus. Held in late July-early Aug.

MUSEUM OF NATURAL HISTORY. *State Park Rd, Morro Bay (93442). Phone 805/772-2694. www.morrobaymuseum.org.* Films, slide shows, displays; nature walks. Open daily 10 am-5 pm; closed Jan 1, Thanksgiving, Dec 25. **$**

PERFORMING ARTS CENTER SAN LUIS OBISPO. *Grand Ave, San Luis Obispo (93407). Phone 805/756-2787. www.pacslo.org.* This 91,500-square-foot center offers professional dance, theater, music, and other performances all year. The 1,350-seat Harmon Concert Hall is JBL Professional's exclusive North American test and demonstration site. Ticket prices vary by event; call or check the Web site for the current performance schedule.

RENAISSANCE FESTIVAL. *1087 Santa Rosa St, San Luis Obispo (93408). Phone 707/864-5706; toll-free 800-688-1477. www.hisrev.org/slo.html.* Celebration of the Renaissance; period costumes, food booths, entertainment, arts and crafts. Held in July.

SAN LUIS OBISPO CHILDREN'S MUSEUM. *1010 Nipomo St, San Luis Obispo (93401). Phone 805/544-KIDS.* A hands-on museum for children in preschool through elementary school (must be accompanied by an adult); houses many interactive exhibits; themes change monthly. Open Tues-Sun; closed holidays. **$$**

SAN LUIS OBISPO COUNTY MUSEUM AND HISTORY CENTER. *696 Monterey St, San Luis Obispo (93401). Phone 805/543-0638. www.slochs.org.* Local history exhibits; decorative arts. Open Wed-Sun 10 am-4 pm; closed holidays. **FREE**

SHAKESPEARE PRESS MUSEUM. *Cal Poly's Graphic Communication Building, California Polytechnic State University, San Luis Obispo (93401). Phone 805/756-1108. www.grc.calpoly.edu/pages/shakes.html.* Collection of 19th-century printing presses, type, and related equipment; demonstrations for prearranged tours. Open Mon, Wed; closed holidays. **FREE**

SLO INTERNATIONAL FILM FESTIVAL. *817 Palm St, San Luis Obispo (93401). Phone 805/546-3456. www.slofilmfest.org.* Showcases the history and art of filmmaking. Screenings of new releases and classics are held over four days in November.

PLACES TO STAY

If you choose to include an overnight stay in your trip along this All-American Road, Mobil Travel Guide recommends the following lodgings.

Cambria

★★★ **BURTON DRIVE INN.** *4022 Burton Dr, Cambria (93428). Phone 805/927-5125; toll-free 800/572-7442. www.burtondriveinn.com.* A bright blue entrance welcomes you to this inn located in the center of town. All units are spacious at 600 square feet each. 10 rooms, 2 story. No A/C. Complimentary continental breakfast. Check-out 11 am, check-in 2 pm. TV; cable (premium). Totally nonsmoking. **$**

★ **CAMBRIA SHORES INN.** *6276 Moonstone Beach Dr, Cambria (93428). Phone 805/927-8644; toll-free 800/433-9179. www.cambriashores.com.* 24 rooms. No A/C. Pet accepted, some restrictions; fee. Complimentary continental breakfast. Check-out 11 am. TV. **$**

37

California

ROUTE 1 ❋ San Luis Obispo North Coast Byway

★★ **CASTLE INN BY THE SEA.** 6620 Moonstone Beach Dr, Cambria (93428). Phone 805/927-8605. www.cambria-online.com/CastleInnbytheSea. 31 rooms. Complimentary continental breakfast. Check-out 11 am. TV. Outdoor pool, whirlpool. $

★ **SAN SIMEON PINES RESORT.** 7200 Moonstone Beach Dr, Cambria (93428). Phone 805/927-4648; toll-free 866/927-4648. www.sspines.com. 60 rooms, 1-2 story. No A/C. Complimentary continental breakfast. Check-out 11 am. TV. Outdoor pool. Golf. Lawn games. Hiking. $

★★★ **SQUIBB HOUSE.** 4063 Burton Dr, Cambria (93428). Phone 805/927-9600; toll-free 866/927-9600. www.squibbhouse.com. This yellow Italianate structure has been painstakingly restored to its original 1877 splendor. You'll find the same handcrafted pine furniture in your room in the 100-year-old Shop Next Door. 5 rooms, 2 story. No A/C. No room phones. Complimentary continental breakfast. Check-out 11 am, check-in 3-6 pm. Antiques. Wine tasting. Totally nonsmoking. $$

Cayucos

★★★ **BEACHWALKER INN.** 501 S Ocean Ave, Cayucos (93430). Phone 805/995-2133; toll-free 800/750-2133. www.beachwalkerinn.com. The individually designed rooms of this inn are cozy, but don't miss this quaint town's beaches, magnificent gardens, and other attractions, including water sports, golf, whale- and seal-watching, and wineries. 24 rooms, 2 story. No A/C. Complimentary continental breakfast. Check-out 11 am, check-in 2 pm. TV; cable (premium), VCR available (movies). Opposite beach. Totally nonsmoking. $$

Morro Bay

★ **BAY VIEW LODGE.** 225 Harbor St, Morro Bay (93442). Phone 805/772-2771. 22 rooms, 2 story. No A/C. Check-out 11 am. TV; cable (premium), VCR (movies fee). Fireplaces. Laundry services. Bay 1 block. $

★★★ **INN AT MORRO BAY.** 60 State Park Rd, Morro Bay (93442). Phone 805/772-5651; toll-free 800/321-9566. www.innatmorrobay.com. Nestled in Morro State Park, this inn offers a wide variety of activities, including golf and the Blue Herron Rookery. 98 rooms, 2 story. No A/C. Check-out noon. TV; cable (premium). Restaurant, bar; entertainment. Health club privileges. Massage. Outdoor pool, poolside service. Guest bicycles. On Morro Bay. $

★★ **LA SERENA INN.** 990 Morro Ave, Morro Bay (93442). Phone 805/772-5665; toll-free 800/248-1511. www.laserenainn.com. 37 rooms, 3 story. Complimentary continental breakfast. Check-out 11 am. TV; cable (premium). In-room modem link. Sauna. $

San Luis Obispo

★★★ **APPLE FARM.** 2015 Monterey St, San Luis Obispo (93401). Phone 805/544-2040; toll-free 800/255-2040. www.applefarm.com. This delightful inn successfully combines country Victorian charm with modern conveniences. Guest rooms are charmingly furnished with fireplaces, canopy

ALL-AMERICAN ROADS

beds, and window seats. 69 rooms, 3 story. Check-out noon. TV. In-room modem link. Fireplaces. Restaurant. Pool, whirlpool. Free airport transportation. Bakery, millhouse. $

★★★ **GARDEN STREET INN.** *1212 Garden St, San Luis Obispo (93401). Phone 805/545-9802. www.gardenstreetinn.com.* Built in 1887 and beautifully restored in 1990, this Italianate/Queen Anne home is remarkable. Guest rooms are spacious and handsomely appointed with lovely wall coverings and antiques. 13 rooms, 2 story. Children over 16 years only. Complimentary breakfast. Check-out 11 am, check-in 3-7 pm. Free airport transportation. Totally nonsmoking. $$

★★ **MADONNA INN.** *100 Madonna Rd, San Luis Obispo (93405). Phone 805/543-3000; toll-free 800/543-9666. www.madonnainn.com.* 109 rooms, 1-4 story. Some A/C. No elevator. Check-out noon. TV; cable (premium). Restaurant, dining room, bar; entertainment. Free airport transportation. Individually decorated rooms, each in a motif of a different nation or period. On a hill with mountain views. Totally nonsmoking. $$

★★★ **SANDS SUITES & MOTEL.** *1930 Monterey St, San Luis Obispo (93401). Phone 805/554-0500; toll-free 800/441-4657. www.sandssuites.com.* 70 rooms, 1-2 story. Pet accepted; fee. Complimentary continental breakfast. Check-out 11 am. TV; VCR (free movies). In-room modem link. Laundry services. Outdoor pool, whirlpool. Free airport transportation. $

★ **VILLA.** *1670 Monterey St, San Luis Obispo (93401). Phone 805/543-8071. www.villamotelslo.com.* 14 rooms, 1-2 story. Complimentary continental breakfast. Check-out 11 am. TV; cable (premium). ¢

San Simeon

★★ **BEST WESTERN CAVALIER OCEANFRONT RESORT.** *9415 Hearst Dr, San Simeon (93452). Phone 805/927-4688; toll-free 800/826-8168. www.cavalierresort.com.* 90 rooms, 2 story. No A/C. Pet accepted. Check-out noon. TV; cable (premium), VCR available. In-room modem link. Fireplaces. Restaurant, bar. Room service. In-house fitness room. Outdoor pool, whirlpool. $

PLACES TO EAT

A long day of driving is sure to make you hungry. At the end of your journey, take a table at one of the following restaurants.

Cambria

★★ **ROBIN'S RESTAURANT.** *4095 Burton Dr, Cambria (93428). Phone 805/927-5007. www.robinsrestaurant.com.* Asian, vegetarian menu. Closed Thanksgiving, Dec 25. Lunch, dinner. Outdoor seating. Garden. Totally nonsmoking. $$

★★ **THE BRAMBLES DINNER HOUSE.** *4005 Burton Dr, Cambria (93428). Phone 805/927-4716. www.bramblesdinnerhouse.com.* Continental menu. Dinner, Sun brunch. Bar. Children's menu. Victorian décor; antiques. Outdoor seating. Totally nonsmoking. $$

Morro Bay

★★★ **GALLEY.** *899 Embarcadero, Morro Bay (93442). Phone 805/772-2806.* This dining spot features the freshest locally caught seafood in Morro Bay and is consistently chosen as a favorite of locals and visitors alike. Seafood menu. Closed late Nov-Dec 25. Lunch, dinner. Children's menu. Totally nonsmoking. $$$

39

California

ROUTE 1 ✻ San Luis Obispo North Coast Byway

★★ **ROSE'S LANDING.** *725 Embarcadero, Morro Bay (93442). Phone 805/772-4441.* Seafood, steak menu. Lunch, dinner. Bar. Entertainment. Children's menu. Outdoor seating. **$$**
[D]

San Luis Obispo

★ **APPLE FARM.** *2015 Monterey St, San Luis Obispo (93401). 805/554-6100; toll-free 800/255-2040. www.applefarm.com.* American menu. Breakfast, lunch, dinner. Outdoor seating. Totally nonsmoking. **$$**
[D]

★★ **CAFÉ ROMA.** *1020 Railroad Ave, San Luis Obispo (93401). 805/541-6800.* Italian menu. Closed Sun, major holidays. Lunch, dinner. Bar. Outdoor seating. Totally nonsmoking. **$$**
[D]

★ **IZZY ORTEGA'S.** *1850 Monterey St, San Luis Obispo (93401). 805/543-3333.* Mexican menu. Closed Jan 1, Thanksgiving, Dec 24-25. Lunch, dinner. Bar. Children's menu. Outdoor seating. Totally nonsmoking. **$**
[D]

Volcanic Legacy Scenic Byway

❈ CALIFORNIA

Part of a multistate Byway; see also OR.

Quick Facts

LENGTH: 360 miles.

TIME TO ALLOW: 1 day.

BEST TIME TO DRIVE: Summer and fall provide for the best travel conditions. The winter months offer beautiful snowscapes. High season is June to September.

BYWAY TRAVEL INFORMATION: Siskiyou County Visitor's Bureau: 888/66-BYWAY; Volcanic Legacy National Scenic Byway Information: 866/772-9929; Byway local Web site: www.volcaniclegacybyway.org.

RESTRICTIONS: The geometry of this Byway makes it the most restrictive of the routes with respect to large vehicles, including recreational vehicles (RVs) and tour buses. Tour buses are allowed on the Byway, subject to specific permitting by the park. All route segments of the Volcanic Legacy Scenic Byway are open to traffic year-round, with the exception of the roadway within Lassen Volcanic National Park. Portions of this road are subject to seasonal closures, typically from November through June. Other portions of the route may be subject to periodic temporary closures or restrictions due to inclement weather and maintenance. Small fees are collected at Lassen Volcanic National Park and Lava Beds National Monument.

BICYCLE/PEDESTRIAN FACILITIES: Bicyclists and pedestrians are permitted along the corridor route segments with the exception of I-5. Pedestrians are, however, discouraged from using some portions of the roadway, particularly in Lassen Volcanic National Park, due to the lack of sufficient shoulder area along the existing roadways. In several areas, particularly the National Park Service and Forest Service lands, trails leading off the Byway are used by bicyclists and pedestrians for recreation, as well as for travel to points of interest.

California's Volcanic Legacy Scenic Byway stretches from Mount Lassen in northern California to the California-Oregon border. From the border, the Byway continues north to Oregon's Crater Lake, making this Byway America's volcano-to-volcano highway. The volcanic activity of the past has created unique geological formations, such as wavy lava flows and lava tube caves. Surrounding this volcanic landscape is a wide diversity of scenery. The Byway travels through or near dense forests, broad wetlands and habitat areas, pastoral grasslands, farms and ranches, and well-managed timber resource lands.

The Volcanic Legacy Scenic Byway offers even more benefits than just the fascinating volcanic geology and scenery. Each season offers a different array of outdoor recreational opportunities. The beautiful green forests and mountains along the Byway are home to hiking trails, including the nationally recognized Pacific Crest Trail; ski slopes; and great fishing and kayaking in clear, cool mountain streams and lakes. Traveling the Byway, you can also enjoy viewing the hundreds of species of wildlife along the way.

THE BYWAY STORY

The Volcanic Legacy Scenic Byway tells historical, natural, recreational, and scenic stories that make it a unique and treasured Byway.

Historical

Although the name may not imply it, the Volcanic Legacy Scenic Byway contains not only natural and scenic qualities, but also rich historical qualities. Much of the historical significance of the Byway arises from its Native

California

✸ Volcanic Legacy Scenic Byway

American roots, and the Byway is dotted with historic mining and logging towns. Many features along the Byway are listed as historical landmarks.

Captain Jack's Stronghold, a national monument located in the Lava Beds National Monument, is historically significant because it was the site of the Modoc War. During the Modoc War of 1872-1873, the Modoc Tribe took advantage of the unique geography of their homelands. Under the leadership of Kintuashk, who came to be known as Captain Jack, the Modoc people took refuge in a natural lava fortress. The site of the fortress is now known as Captain Jack's Stronghold. From this secure base, Captain Jack and his group of 53 fighting men and their families held off US Army forces, which numbered up to ten times more than Kintuashk's tribe. However, the tribe was still able to hold off the Army forces for five months.

Mount Shasta is another site of historical significance along this Byway. The major history of the mountain lies in its geological greatness. It also has a spiritual history. Native Americans of the area believed Mount Shasta to be the abode of the Great Spirit. Out of respect, the natives never ascended past the timberline. A long history of mythology surrounds the mountain, including legends of Lemurians, Atlanteans, secret commonwealth citizens, dwarfs, fairies, Bigfoot, and space beings that materialize at will. Mount Shasta draws visitors from all over the world, some seeking spiritual insight, others the experience of the beauty and natural wonders that Mother Nature has to offer here in this unique alpine region. The upper elevation of Mount Shasta Wilderness was designated in 1976 as a National Natural Historic Landmark.

The Volcanic Legacy Scenic Byway is dotted with historic towns, many of which began as logging communities. McCloud is one example, being a company-built mill town, still revealing its colorful railroad and logging history. The Heritage Junction Museum in the city offers exhibits displaying 100 years worth of historical artifacts and photographs depicting the region. The still-functioning McCloud Railway is also evidence of the logging history of the town. Likewise, the town of Weed was a logging town, built in 1897. The Weed Historic Lumber Museum helps to reveal the part Weed played in the logging industry of the time. Other historical towns along the Byway include Westwood, one of the largest company towns in the West during the early to mid-1900s, and Mount Shasta City.

Unfortunately, not all of the history along the Byway is bright. The Tulelake Relocation Center was one of ten American concentration camps established during World War II to incarcerate 110,000 persons of Japanese ancestry. The majority of these people were American citizens. A large monument of basalt rock and concrete along the north side of State Highway 139 commemorates the relocation center. The monument, dedicated in 1979, incorporates multiple levels of rock walls, a concrete apron, and a state historical marker. The Tule Lake Relocation Center is located off the Byway about 10 miles from the town of Tule Lake. The new Tule Lake Museum in the town of Tule Lake has a restored camp building and watch tower on display, as well as information about the relocation center.

Natural

The Volcanic Legacy Scenic Byway includes some of the most spectacular natural wonders in the nation and takes you around magnificent Mount Shasta, a solitary peak rising to a height of 14,162 feet. The Byway allows you to experience the effects of the geological and volcanic history of the region. These geological and volcanic natural wonders are reason enough to travel the Byway, but the Byway also contains an abundance of natural wildlife and vegetative habitats.

This Byway traverses two major geological areas. Lassen Volcanic National Park is located in the southern portion of the Byway. The park contains Lassen Peak, one of the largest plug dome volcanoes in the world. Lassen Peak was a major source of the many geological formations of the area. Lava Beds National Monument, located along the northern part of the Byway, near California's border with Oregon, is the site of the largest concentration of lava tube caves in the world. To finish this exciting volcano-to-volcano journey, continue north on Highway 97 to Crater Lake National Park.

The Volcanic Legacy Scenic Byway stretches across the convergence of the Nevada Mountains with the Great Basin. This convergence provides a vast diversity of habitats. The diversity allows for a significantly higher number of plant and animal species than most other regions of the West, with habitat for more than 360 species of animals and more than 1,000 plant species. The many state parks, recreation areas, and wildlife reserves along the Byway provide the best opportunities to observe these natural living resources. At the refuges, such as the Lower Klamath National Wildlife Refuge, visitors can view the largest concentration of bald eagles in the lower 48 states during the winter, and the largest annual concentration of waterfowl in North America.

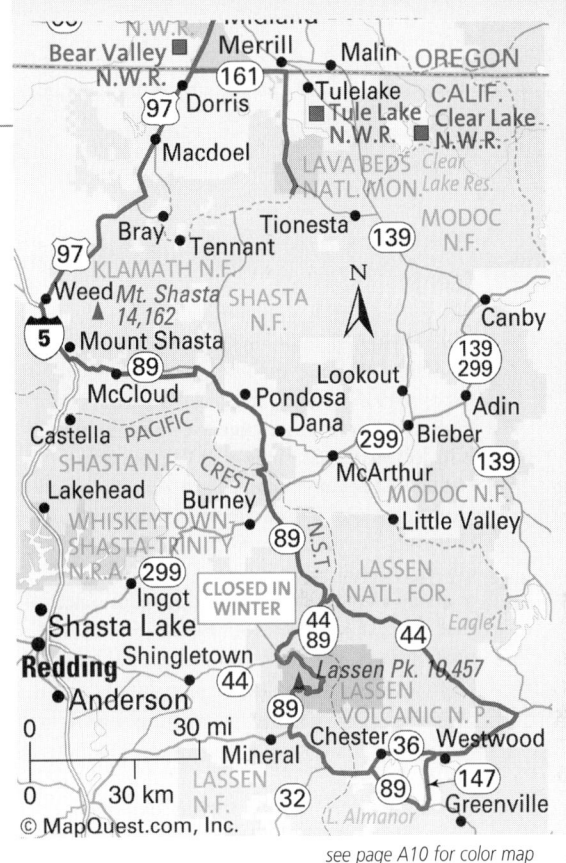

see page A10 for color map

Recreational

The Volcanic Legacy Scenic Byway's length and vast diversity of landscapes provide a wide variety of year-round recreational opportunities. You can tour a lighted lava tube or spelunk on your own at Lava Beds National Monument, see bubbling mud pots and steam vents at Lassen Volcanic National Park, or drive to an elevation of 7,900 feet on Mount Shasta to view the surrounding landscape. The Byway offers hikes through national forest lands that cover much of the area along the Byway. Crisp lakes, streams, and rivers offer great fishing, boating, swimming, or quiet contemplation. Also available are cross-country skiing, snowshoeing, and snowmobiling in the winter months. If that isn't enough, hang gliding and parasailing are popular in the Hat Creek area of Lassen National Forest.

California

❋ *Volcanic Legacy Scenic Byway*

Scenic

The volcanic landscape of the Volcanic Legacy Scenic Byway includes distinctive features of mountain lakes and streams, three volcanoes (all nationally recognized), lava flows, and lava tube caves. You can experience these volcanic features through attractions at Crater Lake National Park (in Oregon), Lava Beds National Monument, and Lassen Volcanic National Park. However, the volcanic landscape is visible throughout the entire Byway. The Byway offers extended views of majestic volcano peaks, an abundance of beautiful forest vistas, and up-close views of crisp mountain lakes and streams.

Perhaps the most captivating of the Volcanic Legacy Scenic Byway's scenic qualities are its vast volcano mountain peaks. Mount Shasta is the tallest of the peaks. Others include Lassen Peak and Mount Scott on the rim of Crater Lake. The immensity of the peaks allows them to be viewed from hundreds of miles away. The Byway circles around Mount Shasta, providing views from every angle. The majority of peaks along the Byway are above the timberline and provide views of broad snowfields and craggy rock outcroppings. At lower elevations, broad grassy meadows with extensive wildflowers offer outstanding foreground settings for views of the more distant peaks.

THINGS TO SEE AND DO

Driving along the Volcanic Legacy Scenic Byway will certainly keep your senses engaged, but if you yearn to get out of the car and stretch your legs, or if you'd like to make a mini-vacation out of your trip, check out these attractions along the route.

LAKE ALMANOR. *Chester (96020). Phone 530/258-2426.* Located about 20 miles southeast of Lassen Peak, Lake Almanor is a favorite vacation destination and summer-home spot for residents of north-central California. Tucked between Lassen and Plumas national forests, the lake and the surrounding area offer a mix of recreational opportunities from golf to fishing, as well as a number of resorts and quaint lakeside towns. In winter, the area attracts snowmobilers and cross-country skiers.

LAKE SISKIYOU. *4239 W A Barr Rd, Mount Shasta (96067). www.lakesis.com.* Box Canyon Dam impounds the Sacramento River, creating a 430-acre lake for fishing and swimming. Open Apr-Oct.

LASSEN VOLCANIC NATIONAL PARK. *44 miles E of Redding via CA 44; 51 miles E of Red Bluff via CA 36, 89. Phone 530/595-4444. www.nps.gov/lavo/.* This 165-square-mile park was created to preserve the area that includes the 10,457-foot Lassen Peak, a volcano last active in 1921. Lassen Park, in the southernmost part of the Cascade Range, contains glacial lakes, virgin forests, mountain meadows, and snow-fed streams. Hydrothermal features, the Devastated Area, and Chaos Jumbles can be seen from Lassen Park Road. Boiling mud pots and fumaroles (steam vents) can be seen a short distance off the road at Sulphur Works. At Butte Lake, colorful masses of lava and volcanic ash blend with the forests, meadows, and streams. The peak is named for Peter Lassen, a Danish pioneer who used it as a landmark in guiding immigrant trains into the northern Sacramento Valley.

After being denuded in 1915 by a mudflow and a hot blast, the Devastated Area is slowly being reclaimed by small trees and flowers. The

ALL-AMERICAN ROADS

Chaos Crags, a group of lava plugs, were formed some 1,100 years ago. Bumpass Hell, a colorful area of mud pots, boiling pools, and steam vents, is a 3-mile round-trip hike from Lassen Park Road. Clouds of steam and sulfurous gases pour from vents in the thermal areas. Nearby is Lake Helen, named for Helen Tanner Brodt, the first white woman to climb Lassen Peak, in 1864.

At the northwest entrance is a visitor center (late June-Labor Day, daily) where you can find information about the park's human, natural, and geological history. There are guided walks during the summer, self-guided nature trails, and evening talks at some campgrounds. Camping (fee) is available at eight campgrounds; there's a two-week limit except at Lost Creek and Summit Lake campgrounds, which impose a seven-day limit; check at a ranger station for regulations. Lassen Park Road is usually open mid-June-mid-Oct, weather permitting. The Sulphur Works entrance to the south and the Manzanita Lake entrance to the northwest are open during the winter months for winter sports. There are facilities for the disabled, including a visitor center, comfort station, and amphitheater at Manzanita Lake.

✴ **LAVA BEDS NATIONAL MONUMENT.** *30 miles SW of Tulelake, off CA 139. Phone 530/667-2282. www.nps.gov/labe/.* Seventy-two square miles of volcanic formations are preserved here in the extreme northeastern part of the state. Centuries ago, rivers of molten lava flowed here. In cooling, they formed a strange and fantastic region. Cinder cones dot the landscape, one rising 476 feet from its base. Winding trenches mark the collapsed roofs of lava tubes, an indicator of the 380 caves beneath the surface. Throughout the area are masses of lava hardened into weird shapes. Spatter cones may be seen where vents in the lava formed vertical tubelike channels, some only 3 feet in diameter but reaching downward 100 feet. Outstanding caves include Sentinel Cave, named for a lava formation in its passageway; Catacombs Cave, with passageways resembling Rome's catacombs; and Skull Cave, with a broad entry cavern reaching approximately 80 feet in diameter. (The name comes from the many skulls of mountain sheep that were found here.) The National Park Service provides ladders and trails in the 24 caves that are easily accessible to the public.

One of the most costly Native American campaigns in history took place in this rugged, otherworldly setting. The Modoc War of 1872-1873 saw a small band of Native Americans revolt against reservation life and fight a series of battles with US troops. Although they were obliged to care for their families and live off the country, the Modocs held off an army almost ten times their number for more than five months.

There is a campground at Indian Well (fee, water available mid-May-Labor Day), and there are picnic areas at Fleener Chimneys and Captain Jacks Stronghold (no water). Guided walks, audiovisual programs, cave trips, and campfire programs are held daily, mid-June-Labor Day. Park headquarters has a visitor center (daily). No gasoline is available in the park, so fill your gas tank before entering. Per vehicle **$**.

✴ **MOUNT SHASTA.** *E of I-5, in Shasta-Trinity National Forest, Mount Shasta (96067).* This perpetually snow-covered double peak volcano towers to 14,162 feet. Five glaciers persist on the slopes, feeding the McCloud and Sacramento rivers. A scenic drive on the Everitt Memorial Highway climbs from the city of Mount Shasta up the slope to 7,840 feet for a magnificent view. White pine, the famous Shasta lily, and majestic stands of red fir are found at various elevations.

SISSON MUSEUM. *1 N Old State Rd, Mount Shasta (96067). Phone 530/926-5508.* Features exhibits on area history, opportunities for mountain climbing, a fish hatchery, and exhibits of local Native American culture. Open daily; closed Easter, Dec 25; also Jan-Feb. **FREE**

California

❋ *Volcanic Legacy Scenic Byway*

SHASTA SUNSET DINNER TRAIN. *28 Main St, McCloud (96057). Phone 530/964-2142; toll-free 800/733-2141. www.shastasunset.com.* The Shasta Sunset Dinner Train takes the same route that the lumber-heavy McCloud Railway did in the late 19th century, departing from the historic station in McCloud, soaring over the southern foothills of 14,162-foot Mount Shasta, and then coming back again. The three-hour ride is filled with breathtaking views as the vintage gold-finished cars (which were originally built in 1916 for the Illinois Central Railroad and are now lavish inside and out) climb inclines and switchbacks and cross trestles and bridges. The dinner menu changes monthly, but it is best described as continental with a regional spin; the extensive wine list emphasizes California labels. There are also sightseeing excursions on open-air railcars and luncheon trips. $$$-$$$$

STATE FISH HATCHERY. *1 N Old Stage Rd, Mount Shasta (96067). Phone 530/926-2215.* The State Fish Hatchery raises trout and has been in continuous operation since 1888. You can take a self-guided tour of trout ponds. Open daily. **FREE**

PLACES TO STAY

If you choose to include an overnight stay in your trip along this All-American Road, Mobil Travel Guide recommends the following lodgings.

★★ **BIDWELL HOUSE BED AND BREAKFAST.** *1 Main St, Chester (96020). Phone 530/258-3338. www.bidwellhouse.com.* 14 rooms, 1 cottage, 2 story. No A/C. Room phones available. Holidays 2-day minimum. Complimentary full breakfast. Check-out 11 am, check-in 3-6 pm. TV available. Game room. Some fireplaces. Antiques. Built in 1901. Flower and vegetable gardens. Totally nonsmoking. ¢
D SC

★ **MCCLOUD HOTEL BED AND BREAKFAST.** *408 Main St, McCloud (96057). Phone 530/964-2823; toll-free 800/964-2823. www.mccloudhotel.com.* 16 rooms, 2 story. No room phones. Adults only. Complimentary full breakfast. Check-out 11 am, check-in 3-7 pm. TV in common room. Massage. Concierge service. Built in 1915. Totally nonsmoking. ¢

★ **BEST WESTERN TREE HOUSE MOTOR INN.** *111 Morgan Way, Mount Shasta (96067). Phone 530/926-3101; toll-free 800/528-1234. www.bestwestern.com.* 95 rooms, 2-3 story. Pet accepted. Complimentary full breakfast. Check-out noon. TV. In-room modem link. Restaurant, bar. Indoor pool, whirlpool. Downhill, cross-country ski 10 miles. Meeting rooms, business center. View of Mount Shasta. ¢

★ **FINLANDIA MOTEL.** *1612 S Mt Shasta Blvd, Mount Shasta (96067). Phone 530/926-5596.* 25 rooms, 3 kitchen units, 1-2 story. Pet accepted. Check-out 11 am. TV. Downhill ski 9 miles; cross-country ski 8 miles. ¢

★ **MOUNT SHASTA RESORT.** *1000 Siskiyou Lake Blvd, Mount Shasta (96067). Phone 530/926-3030; toll-free 800/958-3363. www.mountshastaresort.com.* 50 cottages, 2 story. Package plans; weekends, holidays 2-3 day minimum. Check-out 11 am, check-in 3 pm. TV. In-room modem link. Refrigerators, microwaves, fireplaces. Restaurant, bar. Spa. 18-hole golf, greens fee $42. Putting green, driving range. Lighted tennis, pro. Downhill, cross-country ski 10 miles. Tobogganing. Camping. Business services. Totally nonsmoking. $

ALL-AMERICAN ROADS

★ **STRAWBERRY VALLEY INN.** *1142 S Mt Shasta Blvd, Mount Shasta (96067). Phone 530/926-2052. www.strawberryvalleyinn.com.* 25 rooms, 7 suites. Some A/C. Complimentary continental breakfast. Check-out 11 am. TV. In-room modem link. Restaurant nearby. Downhill, cross-country ski 10 miles. Totally nonsmoking. ¢

★ **SWISS HOLIDAY LODGE.** *2400 S Mt Shasta Blvd, Mount Shasta (96067). Phone 530/926-3446.* 21 air-cooled rooms, 2 story. Pet accepted; $5. Complimentary continental breakfast. Check-out 11 am. TV; cable (premium). Outdoor pool; whirlpool. Downhill, cross-country ski 10 miles. Refrigerators available. Picnic tables, grills. View of Mount Shasta. Totally nonsmoking. ¢

PLACES TO EAT

A long day of driving is sure to make you hungry. Along the way, try the following restaurants.

★★★ **CAFÉ MADDALENA.** *5801 Sacramento Ave, Dunsmuir (96025). Phone 530/235-2725. www.cafemaddalena.com.* Mediterranean menu. Closed Mon. Dinner. Innovative menu featuring Spanish, Italian, and Provencal cuisine. $$

★★ **THE HIGHLAND HOUSE.** *1000 Siskiyou Lake Blvd, Mount Shasta (96067). Phone toll-free 800/958-3363. www.mountshastaresort.com.* American menu. Lunch, dinner. Upscale white-tablecloth dining room featuring modern American cuisine and outdoor seating with views of Mount Shasta. $$$

★★ **PIEMONT.** *1200 S Mt Shasta Blvd, Mount Shasta (96067). Phone 530/926-2402.* American, Italian menu. Closed Mon; Thanksgiving, Dec 24-25; also Tues in Jan and Feb. Dinner. Bar. Children's menu. Totally nonsmoking. $

★★ **SERGE'S RESTAURANT.** *531 Chestnut St, Mount Shasta (96067). Phone 530/926-1276.* French menu. Closed Mon-Tues. Dinner. Intimate country restaurant with outdoor seating available. $$

San Juan Skyway
❄ COLORADO

Quick Facts

LENGTH: 233 miles.

TIME TO ALLOW: 1 to 2 days.

BEST TIME TO DRIVE: June through October. The Byway can be enjoyed year-round, and each season has its own attractions. Fall is one of the most spectacular seasons along the Byway because of the many fall colors. High season is in July and August.

BYWAY TRAVEL INFORMATION: San Juan National Forest Visitors Center: 970/247-4874; Byway local Web site: www.coloradobyways.org.

SPECIAL CONSIDERATIONS: The country along the San Juan Skyway is exciting to explore, but safety should always be a major concern. Old, unstable mills, mines, and timber structures may be decaying and hazardous. Be prepared for changing weather both while driving and while hiking. If you are not accustomed to high altitudes, get plenty of rest and resist overdoing activities during your first two days at high altitude.

RESTRICTIONS: This Byway is maintained year-round. Mountain passes are sometimes closed for an hour or two (sometimes even a day or two) in the case of heavy snowstorms or slides during the winter. The two-lane road between Ouray and Silverton has incredibly beautiful views; it is also narrow and steep, has many hairpin switchbacks and a tunnel, includes tremendous drop-offs with no railings or shoulders, and offers few places to pass. Some curves are signed at 10 miles per hour.

BICYCLE/PEDESTRIAN FACILITIES: The San Juan Skyway is a popular and extremely challenging bicycle route. Shoulders are always adequate, but in some places they are tight. Be particularly alert on the Ouray to Silverton segment, where the road is narrow, high, steep, and curvy, and views ahead are limited.

Travel to the top of the world and back in time on the San Juan Skyway. This loop trip through the San Juan Mountains of southwest Colorado follows over 200 miles of state-maintained highways on a journey from towering mountains and alpine forests to the rolling vistas and ancient ruins of Native American country.

On this Byway, you drive through the heart of 5 million acres of the San Juan and Uncompahgre national forests. The skyway takes you over high mountain passes and through quaint historic towns. Crashing waterfalls can be seen in the spring as the snow melts in the higher mountains; wildflowers are in full bloom during the pleasant summer months; the golden colors of aspens delight visitors in the fall; and winter brings a quieting blanket of snow to the Byway.

You also find plenty of action along the route: four-wheeling, hiking, backpacking, bicycling, hunting, fishing, kayaking, dirt biking, and motorcycle touring.

You find rest and relaxation, too, by browsing town shops, soaking in historic hot springs, staying in a Victorian lodge, or sleeping under the stars in a forest campground. During the winter, skiing is one of the premier activities you can enjoy at quality resort areas like Telluride and Purgatory. The beauty of the surrounding mountains and the historic towns will remind you of the varied and complex history of the area. Ancestral Pueblos lived and worked the land long ago, and the cliff dwellings at Mesa Verde National Park exemplify the complexity of this culture. Spanish exploring parties made their way through the area, and the discovery of gold in the Rocky

Colorado

San Juan Skyway

Mountains forever changed the nature of the surrounding country. Mining towns sprung up in the mountains, and the railroad helped maintain this growth.

THE BYWAY STORY

The San Juan Skyway tells archeological, historical, natural, recreational, and scenic stories that make it a unique and treasured Byway.

Archaeological

Among this Byway's many archaeological sites, Mesa Verde (located in Mesa Verde National Park) is arguably the most outstanding site. Mesa Verde (Spanish for "green table") offers an unparalleled opportunity to see and experience a unique cultural and physical landscape. The culture represented at Mesa Verde reflects more than 700 years of history. From approximately AD 600 through AD 1,300, people lived and flourished in communities throughout the area. They eventually built elaborate stone villages, now called cliff dwellings, in the sheltered alcoves of the canyon walls. In the late 1200s and within only one or two generations, they left their homes and moved away.

The archaeological sites found in Mesa Verde National Park are some of the most notable and best preserved in the United States. Mesa Verde National Park offers visitors a spectacular look into the lives of the ancestral Pueblo. Scientists study the ancient dwellings of Mesa Verde in part by making comparisons between the ancestral Pueblo and their descendants who live in the Southwest today—24 Native American tribes in the Southwest have an ancestral affiliation with the sites at Mesa Verde.

Historical

The discovery of precious metals led to the exploration and settlement of areas along the San Juan Skyway during the late 19th century. Narrow-gauge railroads played an important role during the mining era and in the history of southwest Colorado as a whole.

With their rails set 3 feet apart as opposed to the standard gauge of nearly 5 feet, the narrow-gauge lines made it possible for trains to operate in mountainous country with tight turns and steep grades. Evidence of these defunct, narrow-gauge lines is manifested by the water tanks, bridges, trestles, and sections of railroad bed found along the Byway. One narrow-gauge railroad, the Durango & Silverton, continues to operate as a tourist line. It was constructed in 1881-1882 by the Denver & Rio Grande Railroad to haul ore and provisions, and in 1968 the line was designated a National Historic Civil Engineering Landmark. As it travels along the Animas River amidst majestic mountains, the Durango & Silverton Railroad offers you spectacular scenic vistas and the experience of riding an authentic coal-fired, steam-powered railroad. It is one of southwest Colorado's major attractions and carries over 200,000 passengers a year.

Natural

The already spectacular San Juan Skyway takes on especially vibrant beauty in the fall. The lush green of deciduous vegetation on the mountainsides is transformed into shades of gold, red, bronze, and purple, with evergreens adding their contrasting blues and greens.

The aspen trees are the first to turn shades of gold and rosy red. With their shimmering leaves, the aspen groves glow when the sun shines through them. The cottonwood trees, located along rivers and creeks, are next to turn gold, and a variety of shrubs complement the scene with their fall hues of red, purple, bronze, and orange.

Autumn is a favorite time for locals and tourists alike to enjoy the warm days, cool and crisp nights, and breathtakingly beautiful scenery of the San Juan Skyway.

Recreational

Summer activities include hiking, mountain biking, kayaking, four-wheeling, hunting, and fishing. Winter activities include snowshoeing, ice climbing, snowmobiling, and cross-country and downhill skiing.

Durango Mountain Resort at Purgatory offers downhill skiing and a Nordic center with a groomed track. In summer, the lift takes visitors up the mountain for sightseeing and wildflower viewing. The lift is also a way to get to the top of the mountain biking trail system and to the top of the toboggan-like Alpine Slide.

Scenic

The brawny and pine-furrowed Rockies lounge around this Byway, and their uneven ridges yield to tree-packed forests, flashing streams, and slate-blue lakes. The scene extends into stretches of breezy grasslands divided occasionally by hand-hewn weathered fences. This Byway is known as the Million Dollar Highway not only for its connection to gold and silver mining, but also for its first-class scenery.

HIGHLIGHTS

The following tour begins in Mesa Verde National Park and ends in the town of Ouray. If you are beginning the tour from Ouray, simply begin at the bottom of the list and work your way up.

- **Mesa Verde:** At this national park, explore cliff dwellings made by the Anasazi Indians. These dwellings were mysteriously abandoned by the Anasazi approximately 200 years before Columbus discovered America.
- **Durango:** This authentic Old West town, founded in 1880, still retains its Victorian charm. Restored historic landmarks line downtown streets, while nearby ski resorts beckon to adventurous winter travelers.
- **Silverton:** This remote mining community can be reached either by taking the historic Durango & Silverton narrow-gauge railroad or by driving over the 10,910-foot Molas Divide pass. Many of the beautiful Victorian buildings in Silverton are registered as National Historical Sites.
- **Ghost towns:** The ghost towns of Howardsville, Eureka, and Animas Forks are all located within 14 miles of Silverton. At Animas Forks, you can walk through the remnants of a 19th-century mining town or wander through beautiful meadows of wildflowers.
- **Million Dollar Highway:** The section of highway from Silverton to Ouray has been named the Million Dollar Highway because of the immense amounts of silver and gold that were carted through these passes. This road is quite possibly the most beautiful section of Byway anywhere in the country and is not to be missed.

THINGS TO SEE AND DO

Driving along the San Juan Skyway will certainly keep your senses engaged, but if you yearn to get out of the car and stretch your legs, or if you'd like to make a mini-vacation out of your trip, check out these attractions along the route.

BACHELOR-SYRACUSE MINE TOUR. *1222 County Rd 14, Ouray (81427). Phone 970/325-0220.* This mine has been in continuous operation since 1884. You can take a guided tour aboard a mine train, advancing 3,350 feet horizontally into Gold Hill. Within the mine,

Colorado

✹ *San Juan Skyway*

you'll see mining equipment, visit work areas, and find out how explosives are used. Gold panning is available, as is an outdoor café. Open late May-Sept, daily; closed July 4. $$$$

BEAR CREEK FALLS AND TRAIL. *1230 Main, Box 145, Ouray (81427). Phone 970/325-4746.* This area offers a 2-mile canyon walk with views of a tiered waterfall. Open May-Oct.

BOX CAÑON FALLS PARK. *1/2 mile S on US 550, Ouray (81427). Phone 970/325-4464.* Canyon Creek has cut a natural canyon 20 feet wide, 400 feet deep—a view of thundering falls from the floor of the canyon is reached by stairs and a suspended bridge. Picnic tables are available in beautiful settings. Children must be accompanied by an adult. Open daily.

BRIDAL VEIL FALLS. *2 1/2 miles E on CO 145, Telluride (81435).* Bridal Veil Falls is the highest waterfall in Colorado. The structure at top of the falls was once a hydroelectric power plant that served the Smuggler-Union Mine operations. It has been renovated and now provides auxiliary electric power to Telluride.

DIAMOND CIRCLE THEATRE. *7th and Main, Durango (81302). Phone 907/247-3400. www.diamondcirclemelodrama.com.* Professional turn-of-the-century melodrama and vaudeville performances, located in the Strater Hotel. Advance reservations are advised. Performances June-Sept, nightly (except Sun). $$$$

✪ **DURANGO & SILVERTON NARROW GAUGE RAILROAD.** *479 Main Ave, Durango (81301). Phone 970/247-2733. www.durangotrain.com.* This historic narrow gauge railroad, in operation since 1881, links Durango in southwest Colorado with the Victorian-era mining town of Silverton, 45 miles away. A journey on this coal-fired, steam-powered locomotive up the Animas River and through the mountainous wilderness of the San Juan National Forest gives you the chance to relive history while taking in some of the most breathtaking scenery Colorado has to offer. Round-trip travel takes approximately nine hours. Same-day travelers may opt to return by bus; others can stay overnight in historic Silverton with a return train ride the next day. During the winter season, the train makes a shorter round-trip journey to and from Cascade Canyon. Wheelchair-accessible cars are available; reservations for all riders are highly recommended. Open May-Oct, with shorter routes during the winter months. $$$$

DURANGO & SILVERTON NARROW GAUGE RAILROAD MUSEUM. *479 Main Ave, Durango (81301). Phone 970/247-2733.* This museum, operated in conjunction with Durango & Silverton Narrow Gauge Railroad, contains exhibits on steam trains, historic photos, railroad art, and restored railroad cars. You can even enter a locomotive. $$

HOT SPRINGS POOL. *1200 Main, Box 468, Ouray (81427). Phone 970/325-4638.* This outdoor, million-gallon pool is fed by natural mineral hot springs and is sulphur-free. Bathhouse; spa. Open daily. $$

✪ **MESA VERDE NATIONAL PARK.** *Cortez (81321). Phone 970/529-4465. www.nps.gov/meve/.* In the far southwest corner of Colorado exists the largest—and arguably the most fascinating—archaeological preserve in the nation. Mesa Verde National Park, with 52,000 acres encompassing 4,000 known archaeological sites, is a treasure trove of ancestral Pueblo cultural artifacts, including the magnificent, mysterious Anasazi cliff dwellings. Constructed in the 13th century, these huge, elaborate stone villages built into the canyon walls are spellbinding. To fully appreciate their significance, first take a walk through the park's **Chapin Mesa Museum** for a historical overview. A visit to the actual sites can be physically challenging but is well worth the effort. Several of the sites can be explored year-round, free of charge; others require tickets for ranger-guided tours in summer months only. Tour tickets can be purchased at the park's Far View Visitors Center. Open daily. $$

OLD HUNDRED GOLD MINE TOUR. *721 County Rd 4A, Silverton (81433). Phone 970/387-5444.* This guided one-hour tour of an underground mine offers a view of mining equipment, crystal pockets, and veins. Find out more about methods of hard-rock mining. Open Memorial Day-Sept, daily. **$$$$**

OURAY COUNTY HISTORICAL MUSEUM. *420 6th Ave, Ouray (81427). Phone 970/325-4576. www.ouraycountyhistoricalsociety.org.* This former hospital constructed in 1887 now houses artifacts from mining and ranching and exhibits Ute relics. Open daily. **$$**

RED MOUNTAIN PASS. *1315 Snowden, Silverton (81433). Phone 970/387-5838.* Traveling through the towering San Juan Mountains, the 23-mile stretch of US 550 between Ouray and Silverton passes through some of Colorado's wildest country. Traversing numerous gorges, past cascading falls and tunnels, the road rises to 11,075 feet to cross the Red Mountain Pass, a favorite spot for hikers, rock climbers, mountain bikers, and backcountry ski enthusiasts. Abandoned log cabins and mining equipment still visible from the roadside are evidence of the region's history. Open as weather permits.

SAN JUAN COUNTY HISTORICAL SOCIETY MUSEUM. *1315 Snowden, Silverton (81433). Phone 970/387-5838. www.silvertonhistoricalsociety.org.* Located in an old three-story jail, this museum exhibits mining and railroad artifacts from Silverton's early days. Open Memorial Day-mid-Oct, daily. **$$**

★ **SAN JUAN NATIONAL FOREST.** *15 Burnette Ct, Durango (81301). Phone 970/247-4874. www.fs.fed.us/r2/sanjuan/.* This forest of nearly 2 million acres includes the Weminuche Wilderness, Colorado's largest designated wilderness, with several peaks topping 14,000 feet. The forest also includes the South San Juan and Lizard Head wildernesses. The Colorado Trail begins in Durango and traverses the backcountry all the way to Denver. Recreation includes fishing in high mountain lakes and streams, boating, whitewater rafting, hiking, biking, camping, and four-wheel driving. Open daily.

TELLURIDE GONDOLA. Passengers are transported from downtown Telluride, over a ski mountain, and to Mount Village. You can find four gondola terminals: Station Telluride, Oak St; Station St. Sophia, on the ski mountain; and stations Mount Village and Village Parking in Mount Village. Open early June-early Oct and late Nov-mid-Apr, daily. **FREE**

TELLURIDE HISTORICAL MUSEUM. *317 N Fir St, Telluride (81435). Phone 970/728-3344. www.telluridemuseum.com.* Built in 1893 as a community hospital, this historic building houses artifacts, historic photos, and exhibits that show what Telluride was like in its Wild West days. Open Tues-Sun. **$**

Colorado

❋ *San Juan Skyway*

TELLURIDE SKI RESORT. *565 Mt Village Blvd, Telluride (81435). Phone toll-free 800/801-4832. www.telski.com.* The ski resort offers a three-stage gondola; four quad, two triple, and two double chairlifts; one surface lift; patrol, school, rentals; restaurants, nursery. Sixty-six runs; longest run 3 miles; vertical drop 3,522 feet. Cross-country skiing, heliskiing, ice skating, snowmobiling, sleigh rides. Shuttle bus service and two in-town chairlifts. Open Thanksgiving-early Apr, daily. $$$$

PLACES TO STAY

If you choose to include an overnight stay in your trip along this All-American Road, Mobil Travel Guide recommends the following lodgings.

Bayfield

★★★ **WIT'S END GUEST RANCH AND RESORT.** *254 County Rd 500, Bayfield (81122). Phone 970/884-4113; toll-free 800/236-9483. www.witsendranch.com.* 35 kitchen cabins, 1-2 story. No A/C. Check-out 10 am, check-in 4 pm. TV; VCR (free movies). In-room modem link. Stone fireplaces, knotty pine interiors. Laundry services. Dining room. Bar; entertainment. Room service. Free supervised children's activities (June-Labor Day), from 5 years. Heated pool; whirlpool. Tennis. Cross-country ski on site. Horse stables. Hay rides. Snowmobiles, sleighing. Mountain bikes. Social director. Fishing, hunting guides. Picnic tables, grills. Airport transportation. In a valley on 550 acres; all cabins are adjacent to a river or pond. Totally nonsmoking. $$$$

Dolores

★★ **RIO GRANDE SOUTHERN HOTEL AND BED & BREAKFAST.** *101 S 5th St, Dolores (81323). Phone toll-free 800/258-0434. www.riograndesouthernhotel.com.* 7 rooms, 2 story. Historic building constructed in 1892 with wood floors and an on-site restaurant. $

Durango

★★ **LELAND HOUSE BED & BREAKFAST SUITES.** *721 E 2nd Ave, Durango (81301). Phone 970/385-1920; toll-free 800/664-1920.* 10 air-cooled rooms, 2 story. Pet accepted. Complimentary full breakfast. Check-out 11 am, check-in 3 pm. TV; cable (premium), VCR available. In-room modem link. Fireplaces. Restored apartment building (1927); many antiques. Totally nonsmoking. $

★★★ **LIGHTNER CREEK INN.** *999 County Rd 207, Durango (81301). Phone 970/259-1226; toll-free 800/268-9804. www.lighnercreekinn.com.* A mountain getaway located only five minutes from downtown and fine dining. This inn resembles a French country manor and offers finely decorated rooms. 10 rooms, 2 story. No A/C. Children over 6 years only. Check-out 11 am, check-in 4 pm. Built in 1903; many antiques. Totally nonsmoking. $

★★★ **NEW ROCHESTER HOTEL.** *726 E 2nd Ave, Durango (81301). Phone 970/385-1920; toll-free 800/664-1920. www.rochesterhotel.com.* Built in 1892, this hotel offers guest rooms named after historic figures from the Old West. It is located close to all the area's historic attractions. 15 rooms, 2 story. Pet accepted, some restrictions. Complimentary continental breakfast. Check-out 11 am, check-in 3 pm. TV; cable (premium), VCR available. Totally nonsmoking. $

Mesa Verde

★★ **FAR VIEW LODGE.** *1 Navajo Hill, Mile 15, Mesa Verde National Park (81328). Phone 970/529-4421.* 150 rooms, 1-2 story. No A/C. No room phones. Pet accepted, some restrictions. Check-out 11 am. Restaurant, bar. Room service 24 hours. Hiking trails. Mesa Verde tours available. General store, take-out service, coin showers. Educational programs. Camping sites, trailer facilities. View of canyon. Totally nonsmoking. ¢

Ouray/Ridgway

★ **BOX CANYON LODGE & HOT SPRING.** *45 Third Ave, Ouray (81427). Phone 970/325-4981; toll-free 800/327-5080. www.boxcanyonouray.com.* 38 rooms, 2 story. No A/C. Check-out 11 am. TV; cable (premium). Fireplace in suites. At the mouth of the canyon; scenic view. Near the river. $

★ **CASCADE FALLS LODGE.** *120 6th Ave, Ouray (81427). Phone 970/325-4394; toll-free 888/466-8729.* 19 rooms, 1-2 story. No A/C. Closed mid-Oct-mid-Apr. Complimentary continental breakfast. Complimentary coffee in rooms. Check-out 10:30 am. TV; cable (premium). Balconies. Refrigerators, microwaves. Restaurant nearby. Playground. Whirlpool. Picnic tables. ¢

★★★ **DAMN YANKEE COUNTRY INN.** *100 6th Ave, Ouray (81427). Phone 970/325-4219; toll-free 800/845-7512.* This inn, complete with natural hot springs pool, is located in the San Juan Mountains. Rooms are furnished with ceiling fans, two-person whirlpools, and remote-controlled gas fireplaces. 10 air-cooled rooms, 3 suites, 3 story. Children over 16 years only. Complimentary full breakfast. Check-out 11 am, check-in 3 pm. TV; cable (premium), VCR available. Balconies. Restaurant nearby. Whirlpool in gazebo. Street parking. Totally nonsmoking. ¢

★★ **OURAY VICTORIAN INN & TOWNHOMES.** *50 3rd Ave, Ouray (81427). Phone 970/325-7222; toll-free 800/846-8729.* 38 rooms, 4 suites, 2 story. No A/C. Pet accepted. Complimentary continental breakfast (Oct-May). Check-out 11 am. TV; cable (premium). In-room modem link. Restaurant nearby. Playground. Two whirlpools. Picnic tables. Meeting rooms, business services. On the river. ¢

★★★ **ST. ELMO HOTEL.** *426 Main St, Ouray (81427). Phone 970/325-4951. www.stelmohotel.com.* The guest rooms at this inn are all individually decorated in Victorian style and feature period antiques. It is located in the town of Ouray, which is nestled in the majestic San Juan Mountains. Guests can enjoy a wine and cheese social hour every afternoon in the parlor. 9 rooms, 2 story. No room phones. Complimentary full breakfast. Check-out 11 am, check-in 1 pm. TV in sitting room; cable (premium). Restaurant, bar. Whirlpool. Sauna. Business services. Restored 1898 hotel. Totally nonsmoking. ¢

★★ **CHIPETA SUN LODGE BED & BREAKFAST.** *304 S Lena, Ridgway (81432). Phone toll-free 800/633-5868. www.chipeta.com.* 24 rooms, 3 story. An architectural masterpiece featured in national magazines with beautiful views, luxurious suites, and a spacious spa. $$

Silverton

★★ **ALMA HOUSE BED AND BREAKFAST.** *220 E 10th St, Silverton (81433). Phone 970/387-5336.* 10 air-cooled rooms, 6 with bath, 4 share bath, 2 1/2 story. No room phones. Pet accepted, some restrictions; $10. TV; cable (premium). Complimentary full breakfast. Check-out 11 am, check-in 2 pm. Business services available. Luggage handling. Built in 1898. Victorian furnishings. Some fireplaces. Totally nonsmoking. $

Colorado

❋ San Juan Skyway

★★★ **WYMAN HOTEL.** *1371 Greene St, Silverton (81433). Phone 970/387-5372; toll-free 800/609-7845. www.silverton.org/wymanhotel.* 18 air-cooled rooms, 2 story. Closed Nov, Dec, Mar, Apr. Pet accepted; $15. Complimentary full breakfast. Check-out 10:30 am, check-in after 3-8 pm. TV; cable (premium), VCR, free videos. In-room modem link. Some refrigerators. Restaurant nearby. Street parking. Business services. Built in 1902. Victorian furnishings. Totally nonsmoking. **$**

Telluride

★★★ **COLUMBIA HOTEL.** *300 W San Juan Ave, Telluride (81435). Phone 970/728-0660; toll-free 800/201-9505. www.columbiatelluride.com.* 21 rooms, 4 story. No A/C. Pet accepted, some restrictions; $25. Check-out 11 am. TV; cable (premium), VCR (movies). In-room modem link. Fireplaces. Laundry. Restaurant, bar. Room service. Exercise equipment. Downhill, cross-country ski, snowboard on site. **$$**

★ **MANITOU LODGE.** *333 S Fir St, Telluride (80751). Phone 970/728-4011.* 12 rooms, 2 story. No A/C. Complimentary continental breakfast. Check-out 10 am, check-in 4 pm. TV; cable (premium). Restaurant nearby. Downhill ski 1 block, cross-country ski on site. **$$**

★★★ **NEW SHERIDAN HOTEL.** *231 W Colorado Ave, Telluride (81435). Phone 970/728-4351; toll-free 800/200-1891. www.newsheridan.com.* Built in 1891, this hotel is located in the heart of Telluride. Many of the elegant guest rooms feature mountain views and separate sitting rooms. Warm up with a hearty gourmet breakfast and relax in the afternoon with a complimentary glass of Pine Ridge wine at the New Sheridan Bar. 26 rooms, 3 story. Closed mid-Apr-mid-May. Complimentary continental breakfast. Check-out 11 am, check-in 2 pm. TV; cable (premium). In-room modem link. Restaurant, bar. Babysitting services available. In-house fitness room. Game room. Whirlpool. Downhill, cross-country ski 2 blocks. Valet parking available. Concierge. Totally nonsmoking. **$$**

★ **THE VICTORIAN INN.** *401 W Pacific St, Telluride (81435). Phone 970/728-6601; toll-free 800/611-9893. www.tellurideinn.com.* 31 rooms, 2 story. No A/C. Complimentary continental breakfast. Check-out 10 am, check-in 4 pm. TV. Restaurant nearby. Sauna. Downhill, cross-country skiing. Totally nonsmoking. **$**

★★★ **WYNDHAM PEAKS RESORT.** *136 Country Club Dr, Telluride (81435). Phone 970/728-6800; toll-free 800/789-2220. www.thepeaksresort.com.* 174 rooms, 6 story. Closed mid-Apr-mid-May, mid-Oct-mid-Nov. Pet accepted; fee. Check-out noon, check-in 4 pm. TV; cable (premium), VCR. In-room modem link. Dining room, bar. Room service. Supervised children's activities. Babysitting services available. In-house fitness room, spa, massage, sauna. Indoor, outdoor pools; children's pool; whirlpool; poolside service. Golf; greens fee $160 (includes cart). Outdoor tennis, lighted courts. Downhill, cross-country ski on site; rentals. Hiking, sleighing, snowmobiles. Valet parking available. Free airport transportation. Business center. Concierge. **$$$**

PLACES TO EAT

A long day of driving is sure to make you hungry. At the end of your journey, take a table at one of the following restaurants.

Durango

★★ **ARIANO'S ITALIAN RESTAURANT.** *150 E College Dr, Durango (81301). Phone 970/247-8146.* Northern Italian menu. Closed

ALL-AMERICAN ROADS

Thanksgiving, Dec 25. Dinner. Bar. Children's menu. Turn-of-the-century building originally was a saloon and brothel. Casual attire. Totally nonsmoking. $$

★ **CARVER BREWING CO.** *1022 Main Ave, Durango (81301). Phone 970/259-2545.* American, Southwestern menu. Closed Jan 1, Thanksgiving, Dec 25. Breakfast, lunch, dinner. Bar, brewery. Children's menu. Casual attire. $
D

★★★ **CHEZ GRAND-MERE.** *3 Depot Pl, Durango (81301). Phone 970/247-7979. www.chezgrand-mere.com.* French menu. Lunch, dinner. Six-course prix fixe menu changes nightly. Largest wine list in the region. $$$

★★ **FRANCISCO'S.** *619 Main Ave, Durango (81301). Phone 970/247-4098.* Mexican, American menu. Mexican décor. Lunch, dinner. Bar. Children's menu. Casual attire. $
D SC

★ **LADY FALCONBURGH.** *640 Main St, Durango (81301). Phone 970/382-9664.* American menu. Lunch, dinner, late night. Bar. Children's menu. Casual attire. $

★ **PALACE.** *505 Main Ave, Durango (81301). Phone 970/247-2018. www.palacerestaurants.com.* American menu. Closed Sun Nov-May; Dec 25. Lunch, dinner. Bar. Casual attire. Reservations accepted. Outdoor seating. $$
D

★★ **RED SNAPPER.** *144 E 9th St, Durango (81301). Phone 970/259-3417.* Seafood, steak menu. Closed Thanksgiving, Dec 25. Dinner. Bar. Children's menu. Turn-of-the-century building (1904). Casual attire. Totally nonsmoking. $$
D

Ouray

★★ **BON TON.** *426 Main St, Ouray (81427). Phone 970/325-4951.* Italian menu. Closed Dec 25. Dinner, Sun brunch. Bar. Children's menu. Built in 1898. Outdoor seating. Totally nonsmoking. $$
D

★ **BUEN TIEMPO.** *515 Main St, Ouray (81427). Phone 970/325-4544.* Mexican, Southwestern menu. Closed Dec 25. No A/C. Dinner. Bar. Outdoor seating. Casual dining. In an 1891 building, originally a hotel. Totally nonsmoking. $$
D

★ **CECILIA'S.** *630 Main St, Ouray (81427). Phone 970/325-4223.* American menu. Closed mid-Oct-mid-May. Breakfast, lunch, dinner. Children's menu. Specializes in homemade soup, pastries. Entertainment. In a vintage movie theater. $$
D

Telluride

★★★ **ALLRED'S.** *2 Coonskin Ridge, Telluride (81435). Phone 970/728-7474.* American menu. Closed mid-Apr-mid-June, late Sept-mid-Dec. Dinner. Bar. Children's menu. Casual attire. Reservations required. $$$
D

★★★ **COSMOPOLITAN.** *300 W San Juan, Telluride (81435). Phone 970/728-1292.* Located just across from the gondola in the Hotel Columbia, this fine-dining restaurant features a weekly changing menu comprised of dishes from around the globe. French, American menu. Closed mid-Apr-mid-May, also the last week of Oct. Dinner. Bar. Entertainment. Children's menu. Casual attire. Reservations required. Totally nonsmoking. $$
D

★ **FLORADORA.** *103 W Colorado Ave, Telluride (81435). Phone 970/728-3888.* Southwestern, American menu. Lunch, dinner. Bar. Children's menu. Specializes in steak, fajitas. Stained-glass windows, Tiffany-style lamps. Totally nonsmoking. $$
D

Trail Ridge Road/ Beaver Meadow Road
❋ COLORADO

Quick Facts

LENGTH: 53 miles.

TIME TO ALLOW: 2 hours or more.

BEST TIME TO DRIVE: Open to through traffic Memorial Day to mid- or late October; closed by snow the rest of the year. High season includes June, July, and August, and the heaviest traffic is between 10 am and 4 pm.

BYWAY TRAVEL INFORMATION: Rocky Mountain National Park Information Center: 970/586-1206; Byway local Web site: www.coloradobyways.org.

SPECIAL CONSIDERATIONS: You can't get fuel inside Rocky Mountain National Park, so you'll have to fill up in Estes Park or Grand Lake. Beware of vapor lock, a common occurrence for vehicles from low altitudes. Speed limits are generally 35 mph.

RESTRICTIONS: Rocky Mountain National Park is closed during the winter from mid- to late October until the Friday of Memorial Day weekend. Park entrance fees are required: $10 per carload for seven days, $5 per pedestrian, bicyclist, or motorcyclist for seven days; commercial bus fees vary.

BICYCLE/PEDESTRIAN FACILITIES: The road is narrow and has no shoulder or guardrail. At different points along the route, the drop-off is up to 2,000 vertical feet. Take extreme caution if biking this scenic road.

Sitting in a national park encompassed by national forests, the Trail Ridge Road/Beaver Meadow Road is arguably one of the most beautiful Byways in Colorado. The overarching characteristic of the Byway is its many overlooks, all of which bestow stirring vistas of 415 square miles of the towering (14,000+ feet) southern Rockies.

The clear atmosphere of this alpine tundra makes seeing the night sky from one of the overlooks incomparable. Constellations, planets, meteor showers, and phases of the moon seem brighter than ever and just beyond arm's reach.

Because this is such a protected area, elk, deer, mountain sheep, coyotes, moose, beavers, ptarmigans, marmots, pikas, eagles, and peregrine falcons can be seen more often than in other (nonprotected) areas of Colorado and the nation. Also, the tender tundra wildflowers, which generally peak in July, are an exceptional treat.

THE BYWAY STORY

The Trail Ridge Road/Beaver Meadow Road tells historical, natural, recreational, and scenic stories that make it a unique and treasured Byway.

Historical

The first white men to see this area were French fur traders. In 1859, Joel Estes and his son, Milton, rode into the valley that now bears their name. A few others had settled in this rugged county by 1909 when Enos Mills, a naturalist, writer, and conservationist, began to campaign for preservation of the pristine area, part of which became the Rocky Mountain National Park in 1915.

Colorado

✳ *Trail Ridge Road/Beaver Meadow Road*

Natural

One-third of the park is above the tree line, and the harsh, fragile alpine tundra predominates. The uniqueness of this area is a major reason why it has been set aside as a national park. Just below that, at the upper edges of the tree line, the trees are twisted, grotesque, and hug the ground. Here, more than one-quarter of the plants are also found in the Arctic.

Just below that, forests of Englemann spruce and subalpine fir take over, in a subalpine ecosystem. Openings in these cool, dark forests expose wildflower gardens of rare beauty and luxuriance in which the blue Colorado columbine reigns. And in the foothills, open stands of ponderosa pine and juniper grow on the slopes facing the sun; on cooler north slopes grow Douglas fir.

Recreational

The recreational opportunities on this route are varied and excellent. For example, you can enjoy horseback riding, camping, fishing, rock climbing, and various winter activities.

Several campgrounds beckon, some of which are open year-round. The Rocky Mountain National Park maintains more than 260 miles of trails for private and commercial horse users. Hire horses and guides at two locations on the east side of the park or from a number of liveries outside the park boundaries during the summer season.

Four species of trout live in the mountain streams and lakes of Rocky Mountain National Park: German brown, rainbow, brook, and cutthroat trout. These cold waters may not produce large fish, but you do get to enjoy the superb mountain scenery as you fish. Rocky Mountain National Park also offers a variety of challenging ascents throughout the year for climbers. The Colorado Mountain School is the park's concessionaire, operating a climbing school and guide service.

Winter brings cross-country skiing in the lower valleys and winter mountaineering in the high country. Access roads from the east are kept open and provide you with a panorama of the high mountains.

Scenic

The highest continuous road in the United States, this route affords an almost-too-rapid sequence of scenic overlooks as it skips along the roofs of some of the tallest Rockies (over 12,000 feet). From these wind-scoured peaks, you can gaze out to the dark masses of other Rockies, posed like hands of cards in the distance. The land adjacent to the Byway is otherworldly; the tundra's twisted, ground-creeping trees, crusted snow, and hard-faced boulders seem like they belong to a colder, more distant world.

HIGHLIGHTS

While visiting the Trail Ridge Road/Beaver Meadow Road, you can take a self-guided tour of the Byway. If you enter the park from the east (either the Fall River or Beaver Meadows entrance), start at the beginning and move down the list. If you are entering from the west (Grand Lake Entrance), begin at the bottom of the list and work your way up.

- **Rainbow Curve Overlook:** At 10,829 feet, this overlook is more than 2 vertical miles above sea level. At this elevation, every exposed tree is blasted by wind, ice, and grit into distinctive flag shapes. Tree branches here survive only on the downwind side of tree trunks. Higher still, trees survive only where the severely pruned shrubs are covered and protected by winter snowdrifts.

- **Forest Canyon Overlook:** Here, the erosive force of glacial ice is unmistakable. Although the ice did not reach as high as the overlook, it still lay more than 1,500 feet thick in a V-shaped stream valley. With the grinding of a giant rasp, the ice scoured the valley into the distinctive U shape of today.

- **Rock Cut Overlook:** Here on the roof of the Rockies, the climate is rigorous. Severe weather can come at any time. Periods of drought may occur in both summer and winter, and winter blizzards are frequent. Temperatures remain below freezing all winter, and they frequently drop below freezing in summer. Wind speeds here can exceed 150 miles per hour in either summer or winter, and ultraviolet radiation is twice what it is at sea level. Sunlight is 50 percent more intense.

- **Fall River Pass and Alpine Visitor Center:** Besides the Visitor Center, there is a gift shop and a short trail to an overlook at 12,003 feet.

- **Milner Pass:** Here, Trail Ridge Road crosses the Continental Divide. At this point, waters enter either the Atlantic or Pacific drainages. The Rockies divide these two great watersheds, but the Continental Divide may be a mountaintop, a ridge, or a pass.

- From this point, a short trail leads past Poudre Lake, headwaters of the Cache La Poudre River, and up to Old Fall River Road. This road was the original road over the Continental Divide. The trail then connects with another trail leading to Mount Ida, at 1,288 feet. This is a 4 1/2-mile hike.

THINGS TO SEE AND DO

Driving along the Trail Ridge Road/Beaver Meadow Road will certainly keep your senses engaged, but if you yearn to get out of the car and stretch your legs, or if you'd like to make a mini-vacation out of your trip, check out these attractions along the route.

ENOS MILLS ORIGINAL CABIN. *6760 Hwy 7, Estes Park (80517). Phone 970/586-4706.* On this family-owned 200-acre nature preserve stands the cabin of Enos Mills, regarded as the "Father of Rocky Mountain National Park."

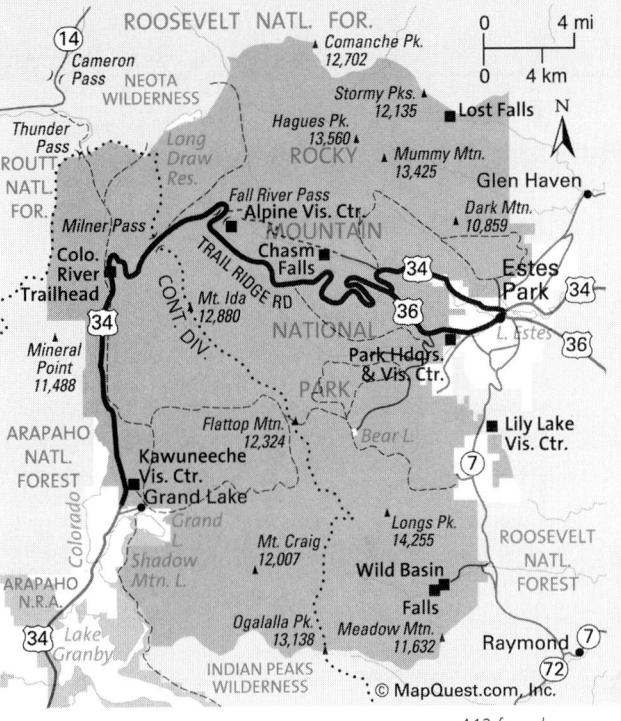

see page A12 for color map

In the shadow of Longs Peak, the cabin contains photos, notes, and documents of the famed naturalist. Nature guide (fee) and self-guided nature trails. Open May-Oct, daily; rest of year, by appointment. **FREE**

ESTES PARK AREA HISTORICAL MUSEUM.
200 Fourth St, Estes Park (80517). Phone 970/586-6256. www.estesnet.com/museum.
The museum includes three facilities, including a building that served as headquarters of Rocky Mountain National Park from 1915 to 1923. Exhibits on the history of the park, the town, and the surrounding area. Open Apr-Sept, daily; Oct-Mar, weekends only. **$$**

✪ ROCKY MOUNTAIN NATIONAL PARK.
Estes Park (80517). Phone 970/586-1206. www.nps.gov/romo/. More than 100 years ago, Joel Estes built a cabin on Fish Creek, one of the higher sections of north-central Colorado. Although the Estes family moved away, more settlers soon followed, and the area became known as Estes Park. Described by Albert Bierstadt (one of the great 19th-century landscape artists of the West) as America's finest composition for the painter, the land west of where Estes settled was set aside as Rocky Mountain National Park in 1915. Straddling

Colorado

❋ *Trail Ridge Road/Beaver Meadow Road*

the Continental Divide, with valleys 8,000 feet in elevation and 114 named peaks more than 10,000 feet high, the 415-square-mile park contains a staggering profusion of peaks, upland meadows, sheer canyons, glacial streams, and lakes. Dominating the scene is Longs Peak, with its east face towering 14,255 feet above sea level. The park's forests and meadows provide sanctuary for more than 750 varieties of wildflowers, more than 260 species of birds, and such indigenous mammals as deer, wapiti (American elk), bighorn sheep, beaver, and other animals. $$

ROOSEVELT NATIONAL FOREST. *240 W Prospect Rd, Estes Park (80517). Phone 970/498-1100. www.fs.fed.us/arnt/.* Forest lands include more than 780,000 acres of icy streams, mountains, and beautiful scenery. Trout fishing, hiking trails, winter sports area, picnicking, and camping. Of special interest are the Cache la Poudre River and five wilderness areas. **FREE**

PLACES TO STAY

If you choose to include an overnight stay in your trip along this All-American Road, Mobil Travel Guide recommends the following lodgings.

Estes Park

★ **ALPINE TRAIL RIDGE INN.** *927 Moraine Ave. Estes Park (80517). Phone 970/586-4585; toll-free 800/233-5023. www.alpinetrailridgeinn.com.* 48 rooms, 1 kitchen suite. No A/C. Closed mid-Oct-Apr. Check-out 10:30 am. TV. Heated pool. Restaurant, bar. Business services available. Airport transportation. Refrigerators; microwaves available. Some balconies. Mountain views. ¢

★★ **ASPEN LODGE RANCH.** *6120 Hwy 7, Estes Park (80517). Phone 970/586-8133; toll-free 800/332-6867.* 59 units, 36 rooms in lodge, 23 cottages. No A/C. Check-out 11 am, check-in 4 pm. TV in lobby. Dining room (public by reservation). Box lunches, barbecue, breakfast rides. Bar. Free supervised children's activities (June-Sept), ages 3-12. Playground. Exercise room, sauna. Sports director. Game room, recreation room. Pool, whirlpool. Tennis. Cross-country ski on site. Picnic tables, grills. Lawn games, handball. Paddle boats. Entertainment. Hayrides, overnight cookouts. Ice skating, snowshoeing. Mountain bike rentals. Airport transportation. Meeting rooms, business center. Concierge. Gift shop. Petting zoo (summer months). $$

★★★ **BOULDER BROOK ON FALL RIVER.** *1900 Fall River Rd, Estes Park (80517). Phone 970/586-0910; toll-free 800/238-0910. www.estes-park.com/boulderbrook.* Fall asleep listening to the Fall River gurgle outside your back door or watch it from the "Spa Room." Fishing is widely available in the lake, river, stream, or creek. 19 air-cooled kitchen suites, 1-2 story. May-Oct 3-day minimum. Check-out 10 am, check-in 2:30 pm. TV; cable (premium), VCR. In-room modem link. Some fireplaces. Cross-country ski 7 miles. Airport transportation. On the banks of the Fall River. Totally nonsmoking. $

★ **PONDEROSA LODGE.** *820 Fall River Rd, Estes Park (80517). Phone 970/586-4233; toll-free 800/628-0512. www.estes-park.com/ponderosa.* 23 rooms, 2 story. No A/C. No room phones. Summer 2-, 3-, 5-day minimum. Check-out 10 am. Check-in 2 pm. TV; cable (premium). Fireplaces. Restaurant nearby. $

★★★ **ROMANTIC RIVERSONG INN.** *1765 Lower Broadview Rd, Estes Park (80517). Phone 970/586-4666. www.romanticriversong.com.* A gurgling trout stream, gazebo, and pond all add to the charm of this bed-and-breakfast. Rooms are named after wildflowers. Located on 27 acres adjacent to Rocky Mountain National Park, the inn offers some breathtaking views. 16 rooms,

1-2 story. No A/C. No room phones. Children over 12 years only. Complimentary full breakfast. Check-out noon, check-in 4-7 pm. Fireplaces. Airport transportation. Built in 1928; decorated with a blend of antique and modern country furnishings. Dinner with advance reservation. Many ponds, trails. Totally nonsmoking. $$
D

★ **WIND RIVER RANCH.** *5770 S St. Vrain, Estes Park (80517). Phone 970/586-4212; toll-free 800/523-4212. www.windriverrance.com.* 15 units, 4 rooms in lodge, 13 (1-3 bedroom) cottages. June-Aug 3-day minimum. Closed rest of year. No room phones. Check-out 10 am, check-in 3 pm. Many private porches. Many fireplaces. Grocery, coin laundry, package store 7 miles. Dining room. Box lunches. Free supervised children's activities (June-Aug). Playground. Heated pool, whirlpool. Hiking, rafting. Airport transportation. Meeting rooms, business center. $$

Grand Lake

★ **BIGHORN LODGE.** *613 Grand Ave, Grand Lake (80447). Phone 970/627-8101; toll-free 888/315-2378.* 20 rooms, 2 story. TV. Whirlpool. Restaurant nearby. Check-out 10 am. Business services available. Some refrigerators, microwaves. ¢

★ **GRAND LAKE LODGE.** *15500 US 34, Grand Lake (80447). Phone 970/627-3967. www.grandlakelodge.com.* 56 kitchen units, 1-2 story. No room phones. Closed Oct-May. Check-out 10 am. Check-in 4 pm. Laundry services. Dining room. Bar; entertainment Wed-Sun. Game room. Heated pool, whirlpool. Lawn games. ¢

★★ **SPIRIT MOUNTAIN RANCH.** *3863 County Rd 41, Grand Lake (80447). Phone 970/887-3551.* 4 air-cooled rooms, 2 story. No room phones. Children over 10 years only. Complimentary full breakfast, afternoon refreshments. Check-out 11 am, check-in 4 pm. Whirlpool. Game room. Downhill ski 15 miles, cross-country ski on site. Picnic tables, grills. Lawn games. Bicycles. Business services. Luggage handling. Totally nonsmoking. $

★ **WESTERN RIVIERA.** *419 Garfield St, Grand Lake (80447). Phone 970/627-3580. www.westernriv.com.* 25 rooms, 2 story, 6 kitchen cabins. Check-out 10 am. TV. Fireplace in lobby. Cross-country ski 1 mile. On lakefront; scenic view. ¢

Colorado

❊ *Trail Ridge Road/Beaver Meadow Road*

PLACES TO EAT

A long day of driving is sure to make you hungry. At the end of your journey, take a table at one of the following restaurants.

Estes Park

★★★ **BLACK CANYON INN.** *800 MacGregor Ave, Estes Park (80517). Phone 970/586-9344.* Continental menu. Closed Mon. Reservations accepted. Lunch, dinner. Bar. Children's menu. Specializes in seafood, wild game. Built in 1927 of rough-cut logs. Two-story moss and rock fireplace. $$
D

★ **MAMA ROSE'S.** *338 E Elkhorn Ave, Estes Park (80517). Phone 970/586-3330.* Italian menu. Closed major holidays; Jan, Feb; also Mon-Wed (winter). Breakfast, dinner. Bar. Children's menu. Outdoor seating. Victorian décor; large fireplace. Totally nonsmoking. $$
D

★★ **NICKY'S.** *1350 Fall River Rd, Estes Park (80517). Phone 970/586-5376.* Continental menu. Breakfast, lunch, dinner. Bar. Children's menu. Outdoor seating. $$$
D

Grand Lake

★★★ **CAROLINE'S CUISINE.** *9921 US 34 #27, Grand Lake (80447). Phone 970/627-9404.* French, American menu. Closed two weeks in Apr, two weeks in Nov. Dinner. Bar. Children's menu. Entertainment: pianist (Sat). Outdoor seating. Three dining rooms; European décor. Art gallery upstairs. Large windows offer views of either the mountain or the hills. $$
D

★ **E. G.'S GARDEN GRILL.** *1000 Grand Ave, Grand Lake (80447). Phone 970/627-8404.* Closed Dec 25. Reservations accepted. No A/C. Lunch, dinner. Bar. Children's menu. Specialties: catfish, baby back ribs, enchiladas. Street parking. Outdoor seating. Totally nonsmoking. $$
D

★★ **GRAND LAKE LODGE RESTAURANT.** *15500 US 34, Grand Lake (80447). Phone 970/627-3967.* Steak menu. Closed mid-Sept-May. Breakfast, lunch, dinner. Bar. Children's menu. Casual attire. Outdoor seating. $$
D

The Historic National Road
✹ ILLINOIS
Part of a multistate Byway; see also IN, MD, OH, PA, WV.

Quick Facts

LENGTH: 165 miles.

TIME TO ALLOW: 12 hours.

BEST TIME TO DRIVE: All seasons have their unique attractions on this Byway. High season is during the fall.

BYWAY TRAVEL INFORMATION: Effingham Convention & Visitors Bureau: 800/772-0750; Collinsville Convention & Visitors Bureau: 618/345-4999; Cahokia Mounds State Historic Site: 618/346-5160; Byway local Web site: www.nationalroad.org.

RESTRICTIONS: Some delays may be experienced during severe weather, and seasonal storms may increase driving times.

BICYCLE/PEDESTRIAN FACILITIES: All counties, except for Madison (which is on the western end of the Byway), rate the route as suitable for bicycles. In Madison County, bicyclists are urged to be cautious; bicycling is not advisable due to high traffic.

The Historic National Road crosses the state of Illinois from near the Wabash River to the great Mississippi River. The rolling countryside, prairie fields, and small towns along the old trail whisper to you of an earlier time. Each of the seven counties of the old trail weaves its own story.

The Historic National Road is a road of history. Nineteenth-century river transportation and commerce, along with historic cemeteries, tell of the struggles of the early settlers on the western frontier. County fairs and main street storefronts speak of small towns where you can still find soda fountains, one-room schools, and old hotels where travelers stopped to rest.

Small and large museums, a National Register Historic District, and National Register Historic Sites are found all along the Byway. Prehistoric Native American life is evident here as well, along with giant earthwork mounds that took 300 years to build. This old trail still beckons as it did over a century and a half ago, with lakes, streams, wildlife refuges, nature preserves, and trails where white-tailed deer play. The atmosphere of old-fashioned travel is stored in the little shops and towns along the way. The western end of the Byway takes you to Eads Bridge and the gateway to the West.

THE BYWAY STORY

The Historic National Road tells archaeological, historical, natural, recreational, and scenic stories that make it a unique and treasured Byway.

Illinois

✽ The Historic National Road

Archaeological

The Cahokia Mounds State Historic Site, an archaeological site with worldwide recognition, bisects the Historic National Road. This remarkable World Heritage Archaeological Site consists of the largest mound buildings built by Native Americans on the North American continent. As you pass the site while driving the Byway, you see Monks Mound rising out of the ground on the north side of the Byway, covering 14 acres and rising 100 feet into the air. You may also notice a large circle of wooden posts, known as Woodhenge, next to the road. The visitor center is the pride of the Illinois Historic Preservation Agency and provides more information on the site and the people who created it.

Historical

In 1806, Congress appropriated funds to construct a National Road that ran westward from Cumberland, Maryland, to the Mississippi River. It was the first federally funded road system in this great new country. The Illinois section was surveyed in 1828 by Joseph Schriver, and construction was started in 1831 under the supervision of William C. Greenup. The section to Vandalia was completed in 1836. However, the western section was never funded due to high costs and waning interest in road building. With the coming of the Terre Haute-Vandalia-St. Louis Railroad that paralleled the road, the National Road fell into disrepair, only to be resurrected in the early 1920s when it was hard surfaced and designated US 40. Today, most of the original alignment of the 1828 surveyed National Road is still in place and is in public hands.

The route passes through many historic towns and villages that were established in the mid-1800s along this great road. On the eastern end of the Illinois section of the Byway is Marshall, a town that sports the oldest continuously operating hotel. Also on the eastern end is the village of Greenup, with its unique business section decorated with original overhanging porches. This village is designated as a Historic Business District on the National Register of Historic Places. In the central section is Vandalia, the second capital of Illinois, its original business district intact. The Capitol Building, in which Abraham Lincoln passed his test to practice law, is now a State Historic Site and sits on the Historic National Road.

Natural

The Historic National Road in Illinois is dominated at each end of the Byway by rivers. The Wabash River is on the east end, and the mighty Mississippi River lies on the west end. Rivers and lakes are interspersed throughout the middle area, with flat prairies and hilly landscapes combining to create many natural features along the Byway. Different species of wildlife make their homes all along the route, and fish are plentiful in the many lakes and rivers.

The topography along the Byway was created by glaciers that advanced and retreated over the land during the Pleistocene Period, leaving behind moraines and glacial deposits that created regions of undulating landscape in some areas and flat prairies in other areas. The landscape of the Byway is defined by three major areas: the Embarras River Basin on the east side, the Wabash River Basin in the central area, and the Sinkhole Plain on the west side (which is contained in the Mississippi River Basin).

The Mississippi River is the third largest river in the world, and as a result of its size, this river has played an important part in the lives of those who have called this area home. From flooding to fertile land, the river has shaped the lives of Native Americans, pioneers, settlers, and current residents of the many cities that dot the banks of the river. The river, through irrigation, has been the lifeblood of farmers, and also has been a recreational destination for many. In addition, over 400 species of wildlife—including ancient lineages of fish—live on and near the Mississippi River. In fact, 40 percent of North America's duck, goose, swan, and wading bird populations use the Mississippi as a migration corridor.

see page A13 for color map

Recreational

The Historic National Road in Illinois offers many recreational opportunities. You can bike or hike on the various trails that are accessible from the Byway. Numerous state parks allow you to enjoy the natural characteristics of the Byway; many of the towns have city parks and recreational facilities. From camping to bird-watching, there is something for everyone along this Byway.

At Lincoln Trail Lake State Park, you can travel the route that Abraham Lincoln took from Kentucky to Illinois. This park is on part of that route, and today it is a place where you can enjoy hiking, fishing, boating, or camping. Summer is not the only time to enjoy this area, however; wintertime sports include ice fishing, ice skating (when the lake allows it), and cross-country skiing.

Many lakes, rivers, and streams provide recreational opportunities. Carlyle Lake is a 26,000-acre multipurpose lake known for its great fishing and waterfowl hunting. You can catch bass, bluegill, crappie, catfish, walleye, and sauger fish. At Eldon Hazlet State Park, controlled pheasant hunting is available, and bird-watching is also a popular activity at the lakes. Carlyle Lake is well known among sailors, and you can rent a houseboat at the park. Camping and golf courses are available here as well.

Numerous small towns are spread across the Byway, providing a variety of activities. If more adventurous activities are what you are looking for, you can board the *Casino Queen,* a riverboat casino that is docked in East St. Louis. At Collinsville, the Gateway International Raceway hosts motor sports in a state-of-the-art facility.

Scenic

Diverse and changing, the landscape of the Historic National Road in Illinois offers many scenic views to the Byway traveler. The route is dotted with towns and rural communities, interspersed with rural lands and farms. The large metropolitan area of the western edge of the Byway, in Collinsville and East St. Louis, provides a different kind of scene. From historic buildings and bridges to gently rolling hills, this Byway exemplifies a scenic drive.

The natural layout of the land is one of variation. In the east, the rolling hills and interspersed forests provide a different view than the flat, unbroken views presented on the western edge of the Byway. In between, cultivated fields, distant barns, farmhouses, and grazing livestock all speak of the nature of the land. Small communities were developed around the agriculture of the area, and now these towns beckon visitors with historic buildings and one-of-a-kind features, such as Greenup's historic porches.

Many features of the Byway revolve around transportation because of the importance of the National Road. Bridges, such as the S-bridge, remain to provide visitors a chance to glimpse these engineering feats. Picturesque stone bridges, as well as covered bridges, may be seen on the Byway. In addition, the Eads Bridge stands in East St. Louis on the Mississippi, giving the metropolitan skyline a distinct look.

HIGHLIGHTS

The Illinois National Road Museum Tour takes you through some of the museums located on the National Road in Illinois. The tour begins in Martinsville and goes to Collinsville (east of St. Louis).

- **Lincoln School Museum:** This high-quality museum is located in Martinsville, about 18 miles west of the Indiana state line. The building itself was built in 1888, and the school is open to groups for an interpretation of early pioneer days.

- **My Garage Corvette Museum:** This museum, located in Effingham, about 30 miles west of Martinsville, is a must for automobile lovers. On display are vintage Corvettes from the 1950s and '60s—a perfect museum for the National Road.

67

Illinois

✸ The Historic National Road

- **Franciscan Monastery Museum:** Dating to 1858, this historic monastery has a wonderful museum that displays artifacts from early settlers as well as the Franciscan Fathers. Visitors can view pioneer items such as toys and kitchen utensils, and religious items such as Bibles and vestments. There are also antique legal documents on display, such as marriage licenses. The monastery is located about 5 miles east of Effingham.
- **Collinsville Historical Museum:** Located about 90 miles west of Effingham in Collinsville, this museum offers visitors a unique glance into the region's residents all the way back to John Cook, the first settler in 1810. Many interesting artifacts are on display, including a variety of Civil War objects and miners' tools. No museum tour would be complete without a visit to this high-quality museum.

THINGS TO SEE AND DO

Driving along the Historic National Road will certainly keep your senses engaged, but if you yearn to get out of the car and stretch your legs, or if you'd like to make a mini-vacation out of your trip, check out these attractions along the route.

LITTLE BRICK HOUSE MUSEUM. *621 St. Clair St, Vandalia (62471). Phone 618/283-0667.* In this museum, you'll find simple Italianate architecture with six restored rooms furnished primarily in the 1820-1839 period, including antique wallpapers, china, wooden utensils, dolls, doll carriages, pipes, parasols, powder horn, oil portraits, and engravings. The Berry-Hall Room contains memorabilia of James Berry, artist, and James Hall, writer. The museum pays tribute to members of the Tenth General Assembly of Illinois. Outbuildings and period garden with original brick pathways around the house. Open by appointment.

RAMSEY LAKE STATE PARK. *850 N and Intersection 700 E, Ramsey (62080). Phone 618/423-2215.* At approximately 1,960 acres, Ramsey Lake State Park offers a 47-acre lake stocked with bass, bluegill, and red ear sunfish. In addition to fishing, boating (ramp, rentals, electric motors only), hunting, hiking, horseback riding, picnicking (shelters), concession, and camping are available. **FREE**

RICHARD W. BOCK MUSEUM. *315 E College Ave, Greenville (62446). Phone 618/664-2800. www.greenville.edu/campus/bock/.* Inside the original Almira College house (1855) is a collection of works by sculptor Richard W. Bock (1865-1949), who, between 1895-1915, executed a number of works for Frank Lloyd Wright–designed buildings. Also on display are Wright-designed prototypes of leaded-glass windows and lamps for Wright's Dana House in Springfield. Open Wed, Fri, Sat; closed during the summer, call for an appointment. **FREE**

VANDALIA STATEHOUSE STATE HISTORIC SITE. *315 W Gallatin St, Vandalia (62471). Phone 618/283-1161. www.state.il.us/HPA/hs/vandalia.htm.* President Lincoln and Stephen Douglas served in the House of Representatives in this two-story, Classical Revival building built by townspeople in 1836 in an effort to keep the capital in Vandalia. Many antiques and period furnishings. Guide service. Open daily. **FREE**

PLACES TO STAY

If you choose to include an overnight stay in your trip along this All-American Road, Mobil Travel Guide recommends the following lodgings.

★★ **HOLIDAY INN.** *1000 Eastport Plaza Dr, Collinsville (62234). Phone 618/345-2800; toll-free 800/551-5133. www.holiday-inn.com.* 229 rooms, 5 story. Pet accepted, some restrictions. Complimentary full breakfast. Check-out noon. TV; cable (premium). In-room modem link. Restaurant, bar. Room service 24 hours. In-house fitness room, sauna. Health club privileges. Game room. Indoor pool, whirlpool. Free airport transportation. $

★ **MAGGIE'S BED & BREAKFAST.** *2102 N Keebler Rd, Collinsville (62234). Phone 618/344-8283. www.maggie's-b-n-b.* 5 rooms, 3 story. No room phones. Pet accepted, some restrictions. Complimentary full breakfast. Check-out noon, check-in 4-6 pm. TV; VCR (movies). Game room. Whirlpool. Built in 1900; former boarding house. Totally nonsmoking. Credit cards not accepted. $

★ **BEST INN.** *1209 N Keller Dr, Effingham (62401). Phone 217/347-5141; toll-free 888/237-8466. www.bestinn.com.* 83 rooms, 2 story. Pet accepted, some restrictions. Complimentary breakfast. Check-out 1 pm. TV. Pool. ¢

★★ **BEST WESTERN RAINTREE INN.** *1809 W Fayette Ave, Effingham (62401). Phone 217/342-4121; toll-free 800/780-7234. www.bestwestern.com.* 65 rooms, 2 story. Pet accepted, some restrictions. Complimentary continental breakfast. Check-out 11 am. TV; cable (premium). Restaurant, bar. Pool. ¢

★ **SUPER 8.** *1400 Thelma Keller Ave, Effingham (62401). Phone 217/342-6888; toll-free 800/800-8000. www.super8.com.* 49 rooms, 2 story. Pet accepted, some restrictions. Complimentary breakfast. Check-out 11 am. TV; cable (premium). ¢

★★ **THE DAISY INN BED & BREAKFAST.** *315 E Illinois St, Greenup (62428). Phone 217/923-3050; www.bbonline.com/il/daisy.* 5 rooms, 2 story. A restored Victorian inn with comfortable rooms and private baths. $

★ **BEST WESTERN COUNTRY VIEW INN.** *I-70 and IL 127. Greenville (62246). Phone 618/664-3030; toll-free 800/780-7234. www.bestwestern.com.* 83 rooms, 2 story. Pet accepted, some restrictions; fee. Complimentary continental breakfast. Check-out 11 am. TV. In-house fitness room. Pool. ¢

★ **THE RENCH HOUSE.** *316 W Main St, Greenville (62246). Phone 618/664-9698. www.greenville-chamber.com/renchhouse.* 3 rooms, 2 story. Built in 1852, this Victorian-style house is within walking distance of downtown Greenville. $

★★ **THE ARCHER HOUSE.** *717 Archer Ave, Marshall (62441). Phone 217/826-8023; www.thearcherhouse.com.* 8 rooms, 2 story. Built in 1841 as a stagecoach stop, the Archer House is the oldest operating hotel in Illinois. $$

Illinois

❋ The Historic National Road

★ **JAY'S INN.** 720 W Gochenour St, Vandalia (62471). Phone 618/283-1200. 21 rooms, 2 story. Pet accepted. Check-out noon. TV; cable (premium). Restaurant, bar. ¢

PLACES TO EAT

A long day of driving is sure to make you hungry. At the end of your journey, take a table at one of the following restaurants.

★ **RICHARD'S FARM RESTAURANT.** 607 NE 13th St, Casey (62420). Phone 217/932-5300. American menu. Lunch, dinner. Located in a converted barn. Home of the 1-pound pork chop. $

★ **EL RANCHERITO.** 1313 Keller Dr, Effingham (62401). Phone 217/342-4753. Mexican menu. Closed Thanksgiving. Lunch, dinner. Children's menu. $

★ **NIEMERG'S STEAK HOUSE.** 1410 W Fayette Ave, Effingham (62401). Phone 217/342-392. American menu. Closed Dec 25. Breakfast, lunch, dinner. Bar. Children's menu. Casual, family-style dining. $$$

★ **NUBY'S STEAKHOUSE.** 679 Hwy 40 W, Pocahontas (62275). Phone 618/669-2737. www.greenville-chamber.com/nubys. American menu. Closed Mon. Lunch, dinner. $

★ **DEPOT OF VANDALIA.** 107 S 6th St, Vandalia (62471). Phone 618/283-1918. French, Cajun menu. Lunch, dinner. Restaurant and lounge located in a turn-of-the-century train depot. $

The Historic National Road
✻ INDIANA
Part of a multistate Byway; see also IL, MD, OH, PA, WV.

Quick Facts

LENGTH: 156 miles.

TIME TO ALLOW: 3 hours to 1 day.

BEST TIME TO DRIVE: High seasons are spring and fall. In the spring, flowers like poppies, irises, and wildflowers are spread along the roadside. Black locusts and redbuds are also in bloom. During September and October, community festivals are occurring all along the Byway.

BYWAY TRAVEL INFORMATION: Indiana National Road Association: 765/478-3172.

RESTRICTIONS: As a primary east/west route through Indiana, the road experiences no seasonal accessibility limitations.

BICYCLE/PEDESTRIAN FACILITIES: In rural portions of the Historic National Road, you will not find sidewalks for pedestrians or shoulders specifically designated for bicycles. However, in rural portions of the Byway where traffic is often not heavy, bicyclists and pedestrians can travel many stretches of the route in relative safety and comfort.

One of America's earliest roads, the National Road was built between 1828 and 1834 and established a settlement pattern and infrastructure that is still visible today. Nine National Register Districts are found along the route, as are 32 individually designated National Register Sites offering education and entertainment. As you travel Indiana's Historic National Road, you find a landscape that has changed little since the route's heyday in the 1940s.

Historic villages with traditional main streets and leafy residential districts still give way to the productive fields and tranquil pastures that brought Indiana prosperity. From the Federal-style architecture of an early pike town (a town that offered traveling accommodations and little else) to the drive-ins and stainless-steel diners of the 1940s, you can literally track the westward migration of the nation in the buildings and landscapes that previous generations have left behind.

Along the way, you will find many of the same buildings and towns that were here during the earliest days of westward expansion. A visit to Antique Alley gives you a chance to do some antique shopping and exploring along this historic road. The Indiana Historic National Road is a unique way to experience the preserved pike towns along the route, such as Centerville and Knightstown.

THE BYWAY STORY

The Historic National Road tells archaeological, cultural, historical, natural, recreational, and scenic stories that make it a unique and treasured Byway.

Indiana

✹ *The Historic National Road*

Archaeological

Eastern Indiana was the home of two groups of Native Americans identified by scholars as the Eastern Woodland Societies, who made their homes in the area following the retreat of the glaciers. One group occupied the area around 7000 to 1000 BC, the other from approximately 1000 to 700 BC. Many of their campsites have been found in the area of the Whitewater River Gorge. The Whitewater River Gorge was an important area after glacier movement and activity had stopped in the area. The area was excellent for hunting and fishing, with flowing streams and an abundance of resources.

Cultural

The National Road brought the nation to Indiana. The lure of limitless opportunities and the romance of the West drew tens of thousands of pioneers through Indiana between 1834 and 1848. Many stayed and settled in the Hoosier State, thus creating a new culture—the foundation for our national culture. This is because religious and economic groups left the distinctive colonial societies of the eastern seaboard and merged in the Midwest. Settlers to Indiana brought with them their own particular mix of customs, languages, building styles, religions, and farming practices. Quakers, European immigrants, and African Americans looking for new opportunities all traveled the National Road. Evidence of this mix of cultural influences can be seen along the corridor today in the buildings and landscapes. It can also be learned at the Indiana State Museum's National Road exhibit, and it can be experienced on a Conestoga Wagon at Conner Prairie or at a Civil War encampment along the route.

As the region matured, the culture continued to evolve under the influence of the nation's primary east-west route. Richmond was home of the Starr Piano Company, and later the Starr-Gennet recording studios, where jazz greats like Hoagy Carmichael and Louis Armstrong made recordings in an early jazz center. The Overbeck sisters, noted for their Arts and Crafts pottery, lived and worked in Cambridge City. The poet James Whitcomb Riley, author of "Little Orphant Annie" and "Raggedy Man," lived in Greenfield. Indianapolis, the largest city on the entire Historic National Road, became an early center for automobile manufacturing. Today, visitors experience such attractions as the Children's Museum of Indianapolis (the largest in the world) and the Eiteljorg Museum of American Indian and Western Art, as well as a variety of other museums and cultural institutions.

The Historic National Road in Indiana represents one segment of the historic National Road corridor from Maryland to Illinois. The cultural resources within Indiana are intimately tied to traditions and customs from the eastern terminus of the road in Cumberland, Maryland, and are built on goals and expectations of a nation looking west.

Historical

The National Road was the first federally funded highway in the United States. Authorized by Thomas Jefferson in 1803, the road ran from Cumberland, Maryland, west to Vandalia, Illinois. Designed to connect with the terminus of the C&O Canal in Cumberland, the National Road gave agricultural goods and raw materials from the interior direct access to the eastern seaboard. It also encouraged Americans to settle in the fertile plains west of the Appalachians. For the first time in the United States, a coordinated interstate effort was organized and financed to survey and construct a road for both transportation purposes and economic development.

Built in Indiana between 1828 and 1834, the National Road established a settlement pattern and infrastructure that is still visible today. The historic structures along the National Road illustrate the transference of ideas and culture from the east as the road brought settlement and commerce to Indiana. The National Road still passes through well-preserved, Federal-style pike towns and Victorian streetcar neighborhoods, and it is lined with early automobile-era structures, such as gas stations, diners, and motels.

see page A13 for color map

Natural

The topography of Indiana was created by glaciers that advanced and retreated over the land during the Pleistocene Period. Leaving behind moraines and an undulating landscape, the glaciers also helped to create the Whitewater River Gorge, where fragments of limestone, clay, and shale bedrock can be seen. The gorge and surrounding region is known internationally among geologists for its high concentration of Ordovician Period fossils.

Recreational

You can find many opportunities for recreation along the Historic National Road in Indiana, as well as in nearby cities. Golf is a popular sport along the highway, as evidenced by the many golf courses, such as the Glen Miller Public Golf Course, the Hartley Hills Country Club, the Highland Lake Public Golf Course, and the Winding Branch Public Golf Course. Biking and hiking are other extremely popular sports along the Byway. Local park and recreation facilities are often directly accessible from the Byway or can be found nearby.

Professional sports can be enjoyed along the Byway as well. White River State Park in Indianapolis offers you an opportunity to enjoy a Triple-A baseball game at Victory Field (or to visit the Indianapolis Zoo). Just off the Historic National Road in downtown Indianapolis are the RCA Dome, home of the Indianapolis Colts, and Conseco Fieldhouse, home of the Indiana Pacers.

Scenic

The Historic National Road is a combination of scenes from rural communities, small towns, and a metropolitan city. This combination makes the Byway a scenic tour along one of the most historically important roads in America. Small-town antique shops and old-fashioned gas pumps dot the Byway, making the Historic National Road a relaxing and peaceful journey. Broad views of cultivated fields, distant barns and farmhouses, and grazing livestock dominate the landscape. In other areas, courthouse towers, church steeples, and water towers signal approaching communities that draw you from the open areas into historic settlements. The topography of the land affords vistas down the corridor and glimpses into natural areas that sit mostly hidden in the rural landscape. This repeating pattern of towns and rural landscapes is broken only by metropolitan Indianapolis.

HIGHLIGHTS

The following are just some of the points of interest available to you when traveling west across the Indiana portion of this Byway from the western border of Ohio. If you're traveling east, read this list from the bottom up.

- **Historic Richmond:** As one of Indiana's oldest historic towns (founded in 1806), Richmond has one of the Hoosier State's largest intact collections of 19th-century architecture. You can visit four National Register Historic Districts, **Hayes Regional Arboretum,** a bustling historic downtown full of unique shops and restaurants, and a fascinating collection of local museums, including the **Wayne County Museum,** the **Richmond Art Museum,** the **Gaar Mansion,** the **Indiana Football Hall of Fame,** the **Joseph Moore Museum** at Earlham College, and the **Rose Gardens** located along the road on the city's east side.

- **Centerville:** One of the historic highway's most intact and quaint National Road–era pike towns is listed in the National Register of Historic Places for its fine collection of architecture. Centerville also has a noteworthy collection of small antique and specialty shops and is home to the world's largest antique mall, just several blocks north of the National Road.

- **Pike towns and Antique Alley (Richmond to Knightstown):** You can meander along the National Road and enjoy the tranquil

Indiana

❋ The Historic National Road

agricultural landscape interspersed with pike towns that recall the early years when travelers needed a place to rest every 5 miles or so. This route is also heralded as Antique Alley, with over 900 antique dealers plying their trade in and between every community along the route.

- **Huddleston Farmhouse Inn Museum, Cambridge:** A restored National Road–era inn and farm tells the story of the historic highway and the people who formed communities along its length. The museum is owned and operated by the Historic Landmarks Foundation of Indiana and is the home office of the Indiana National Road Association, the National Scenic Byway management nonprofit group. The museum displays the way of life of an early Hoosier farm family and the experience of westward travelers who stopped for food and shelter. Cambridge City is also listed in the National Register of Historic Places and has unique historic buildings that are home to diverse shops and local eateries.

- **Knightstown:** Knightstown grew because of its location on the National Road between Richmond and Indianapolis. The town has retained its significant collection of 19th- and 20th-century architecture; a large section of the town is listed in the National Register of Historic Places. Today, you can visit four antique malls, watch a nationally known coppersmith, and stay in one of two bed-and-breakfasts. Also available is the **Big Four Railroad Scenic Tour.**

- **Greenfield: James Whitcomb Riley's Old Home and Museum** on the National Road in Greenfield tells the story of the Hoosier poet and allows you to experience his life and community with guided tours. The town also is rich in small-town local flavor, with many shops and restaurants to satisfy you.

- **Historic Irvington:** A classic 1870s Indianapolis suburb was developed as a getaway on the city's east side. Irvington has since been swallowed by the city but retains its stately architecture and peaceful winding cul-de-sacs. Listed in the National Register of Historic Places, Irvington recalls turn-of-the-century progressive design principles and allows the modern visitor a glimpse into the city's 19th-century development.

- **Downtown Indianapolis:** The center of Indiana's National Road is also its state capital. Downtown Indianapolis offers a growing array of activities and amenities, from the state's best shopping at **Circle Centre Mall,** an unprecedented historic preservation development that incorporates building facades from the city's past into a state-of-the-art mall experience, to gourmet dining and an active nightlife and sports scene. Along Washington Street just east of downtown, you can visit the **Indiana Statehouse, the Indianapolis Zoo, the Eiteljorg Museum of American and Indian Art,** and **White River State Park.** The **Indianapolis**

- **Colts** play at the RCA Dome, and the **Indiana Pacers** continue the ritual of Hoosier Hysteria at Conseco Fieldhouse downtown.
- **Plainfield:** Twentieth-century automobile culture dominates this area. Motels and gas stations remain from the early days and are interspersed with the sprawl and development of the modern city. **The Diner,** on the east side of Plainfield, is a remnant from the early days of travel, a stainless-steel café with an atmosphere reminiscent of the 1940s, an atmosphere that is quickly disappearing. From Plainfield to Brazil, look for roadside farmers' markets.
- **Brazil:** The western extension of the National Road was surveyed through what is now Brazil in 1825; today, its National Register–listed Meridian Street remains an classic example of how the historic highway promoted the growth of communities along its length. The village is also full of curios and collectibles.
- **Terre Haute:** The western edge of Indiana's National Road is anchored by Terre Haute, a community offering historic points of interest and cultural experiences of various kinds. The **Rose-Hulman Institute of Technology** on the city's east side was founded in 1874 and is an exceptionally beautiful college campus; just west of the city on State Road 150, the **St. Mary-of-the-Woods College** campus offers a touch of European elegance in the Indiana forest. Its campus is in a beautiful wooded setting and has several buildings dating to its 1841 founding. You can choose National Road restaurants along the city's **Wabash Avenue,** located in historic buildings. **Dobbs Park,** 1/2 mile south of the highway at the intersection of Highways 46 and 42, is home to a nature center and **Native American Museum. The Sheldon Swope Art Museum** at 25 S 7th Street features 19th- and 20th-century artworks in a 1901 Renaissance Revival-style building with an Art Deco interior. The **Children's Science and Technology Museum** at 523 Wabash Avenue houses rooms full of hands-on learning displays and special exhibits. Larry Bird fans can see memorabilia at **Larry Bird's Boston Connection** (55 S 3rd Street) and view a museum of his career keepsakes, including his Olympic medal, MVP trophies, photographs, and other mementos. Continue on Indiana's Old National Road onto the Illinois portion of the road.

THINGS TO SEE AND DO

Driving along the Historic National Road will certainly keep your senses engaged, but if you yearn to get out of the car and stretch your legs, or if you'd like to make a mini-vacation out of your trip, check out these attractions along the route.

ANTIQUE ALLEY. *5701 National Rd E, Richmond (47374). Phone 765/935-8687. www.antiquealley.us.* More than 900 dealers display their treasures within a 33-mile loop. Hours vary. **FREE**

CARDINAL GREENWAY RAIL TRAIL. *Richmond (47374). Phone 765/287-0399.* This asphalt trail connects Richmond to Muncie. When completed, the trail will be 60 miles long and run all the way to Marion. It's open to walkers, joggers, skaters, and horseback riders. Open daily.

★ **THE CHILDREN'S MUSEUM OF INDIANAPOLIS.** *3000 N Meridian St, Indianapolis (46208). Phone 317/334-3322. www.childrensmuseum.org.* The largest museum of its kind in the nation, with ten major galleries. Exhibits cover science, social cultures, space, history, and exploration and include the Welcome Center, SpaceQuest Planetarium (fee), 30-foot-high Water Clock, Playscape gallery for preschoolers, Computer Discovery Center, hands-on science exhibits, simulated limestone cave, carousel rides (fee), and a performing arts theater. The largest gallery, the Center for Exploration, is designed for ages 12 and up. Open Mar-Labor Day, daily; rest of year, Tues-Sun; closed Easter, Thanksgiving, Dec 25. **$$**

Indiana

✻ *The Historic National Road*

CIRCLE CENTRE MALL. *49 W Maryland St, Indianapolis (46204). Phone 317/681-8000. www.simon.com.* Indianapolis' newest mall in the heart of downtown offers more than 100 shopping, dining, and entertainment options. Anchor stores Nordstrom and Parisian are flanked by national chains such as Gymboree, Banana Republic, and Williams-Sonoma in this four-story structure that spans two city blocks. Open Mon-Sat 10 am-9 pm, Sun noon-6 pm; closed Thanksgiving, Dec 25. **FREE**

CITY MARKET. *222 E Market St, Indianapolis (46204). Phone 317/634-9266.* This renovated marketplace was constructed in 1886 and includes this building and two adjacent areas. The market features smoked meats, dairy, specialty bakery and fruit stands, and ethnic foods. Open Mon-Sat; closed holidays. **FREE**

✪ **CONNER PRAIRIE.** *13400 Allisonville Rd, Indianapolis (46038). Phone 317/776-6000; toll-free 800/966-1836. www.connerprairie.org.* This 250-acre nationally acclaimed living history museum offers costumed interpreters who depict the life and times of early settlement in this 1836 village. The area contains 39 buildings, including a Federal-style brick mansion (1823) built by fur trader William Conner (self-guided tours). Working blacksmith, weaving, and pottery shops; woodworkers complex. Visitor center with changing exhibits. Hands-on activities at Pioneer Adventure Area; games, toys. Picnic area, restaurant, gift shop. Special events throughout year. Open Tues-Sun; closed holidays. **$$$**

CRISPUS ATTUCKS MUSEUM. *1140 Dr. Martin Luther King Jr. St, Indianapolis (46202) Phone 317/226-4613.* Four galleries have been established to recognize, honor, and celebrate the contributions made by African Americans. Open Mon-Fri; closed holidays. **FREE**

CROWN HILL CEMETERY. *700 W 38th St, Indianapolis (46208). Phone 317/925-8231.* This is the third largest cemetery in the nation. President Benjamin Harrison, poet James Whitcomb Riley, novelist Booth Tarkington, and gangster John Dillinger are among the notables buried here.

EAGLE CREEK PARK. *7840 W 56th St, Indianapolis (46254). Phone 317/327-7110. www.indygov.org/indyparks/.* Approximately 3,800 acres of wooded terrain with a 1,300-acre reservoir make up the nation's second largest city park. Fishing, boat ramps, rentals, swimming beach (open Memorial Day-Labor Day), bathhouse, water sports center; shelters, golf course, cross-country skiing, hiking trails, playgrounds, picnicking. Open daily; some facilities closed in winter. **$**

✪ **EITELJORG MUSEUM OF AMERICAN INDIAN AND WESTERN ART.** *500 W Washington St, Indianapolis (46204). Phone 317/636-9378. www.eiteljorg.org.* The museum features collections of Native American and American Western art, considered one of the finest collections of its kind. Open Memorial Day-Labor Day, Mon-Sat, also Sun afternoons; rest of year, Tues-Sat, also Sun afternoons; closed Easter, Thanksgiving, Dec 25. **$$**

FOWLER PARK PIONEER VILLAGE. *3000 E Oregon Church Rd, Terre Haute (47802). Phone 812/462-3391.* An 1840s pioneer village with 12 log cabins, a general store, schoolhouse, and gristmill. Open summer weekends; also by appointment. **FREE**

THE GERMAN FRIENDSHIP GARDEN. *2500 National Rd E, Richmond (47374).* Features 200 German hybridized roses sent by the German city of Zweibrücken from its own rose garden. In bloom May-Oct. **FREE**

GLEN MILLER PARK. *2514 E Main St, Richmond (47374). Phone 765/983-7285.* A 194-acre park; E. G. Hill Memorial Rose Garden, 9-hole golf (fee), natural springs, picnic shelters, concessions, fishing, paddleboats, playground, tennis courts, and outdoor amphitheater (summer concerts). **FREE**

ALL-AMERICAN ROADS

HAYES REGIONAL ARBORETUM. *801 Elks Rd, Richmond (47374). Phone 765/962-3745. www.hayesarboretum.org.* A 355-acre site with trees, shrubs, and vines native to this region; 40-acre beech-maple forest; auto tour (3 1/2 miles) of the site. Fern garden; spring house. Hiking trails; bird sanctuary; nature center with exhibits; gift shop. Open Tues-Sun; closed holidays. **FREE**

HISTORIC LOCKERBIE SQUARE. *528 Lockerbie St, Indianapolis (46202). Phone 317/631-5885.* Late 19th-century private houses have been restored in this 6-block area. Cobblestone streets, brick sidewalks, and fine architecture make this an interesting area for sightseeing.

HOLCOMB OBSERVATORY & PLANETARIUM. *4600 Sunset Ave, Indianapolis (46208). Phone 317/940-9333. www.butler.edu/holcomb/.* Features the largest telescope in Indiana, a 38-inch Cassegrain reflector. Planetarium shows (call for schedule). **$$**

HUDDLESTON FARMHOUSE INN MUSEUM. *838 National Rd, Cambridge City (47327). Phone 765/478-3172.* Restored 1840s farmhouse/inn complex with outbuildings once served National Road travelers. Open May-Aug, Tues-Sat, also Sun afternoons; rest of year, Tues-Sat only; closed holidays and the month of Jan. **$**

INDIANA STATE MUSEUM. *202 N Alabama St, Indianapolis (46204). Phone 317/232-1637. www.in.gov/ism/.* Depicts Indiana's history, art, science, and popular culture with five floors of displays. Exhibits include the Indiana Museum of Sports, Indiana radio, forests of 200 years ago, a small-town community at the turn of the century, and paintings by Indiana artists. Changing exhibits. Open daily; closed holidays. **$$**

★ **INDIANAPOLIS MOTOR SPEEDWAY AND HALL OF FAME MUSEUM.** *4790 W 16th St, Indianapolis (46222). Phone 317/484-6747. www.brickyard.com.* Site of the famous 500-mile automobile classic held each year the Sunday before Memorial Day. Many innovations in modern cars have been tested at races here. The oval track is 2 1/2 miles long, lined by grandstands, paddocks, and bleachers. Hall of Fame Museum (fee) has exhibits of antique and classic passenger cars, many built in Indiana; more than 30 Indianapolis-winning race cars. Open daily; closed Dec 25. **$$**

INDIANAPOLIS ZOO. *1200 W Washington St, Indianapolis (46222). Phone 317/630-2010. www.indyzoo.com.* This 64-acre facility includes the state's largest aquarium, an enclosed whale and dolphin pavilion, and more than 3,000 animals from around the world. Sea lions, penguins, sharks, polar bears; daily whale and dolphin shows; camels and reptiles of the deserts; lions, giraffes, and elephants in the plains; tigers, bears, and snow monkeys in the forests. Encounters features domesticated animals from around the world, and a 600-seat outside arena offers daily programs and demonstrations. Living Deserts of the World is a conservatory covered by an 80-foot-diameter transparent dome. New **White River Gardens** is a conservatory and gardens. Commons Plaza includes a restaurant and snack bar; additional animal exhibits; and an amphitheater for shows and concerts. Horse-drawn streetcar, elephant, camel, carousel, and miniature train rides. Open daily. **$$$**

JAMES WHITCOMB RILEY HOME. *250 W Main St, Greenfield (46140). Phone 317/462-8539.* Boyhood home of the poet from 1850-1869. Riley wrote "When the Frost is on the Punkin" and many other verses in Hoosier dialect. Tours. Museum adjacent. Open Apr-late Dec, Mon-Sat, also Sun afternoons. **$**

77

Indiana

✳ *The Historic National Road*

JOSEPH MOORE MUSEUM OF NATURAL SCIENCE. *801 National Rd W, Richmond (47374). Phone 765/983-1303.* On the Earlham College campus. Birds and mammals in natural settings, fossils, mastodon and allosaurus skeletons. Open during the academic year, Mon, Wed, Fri, Sun; rest of year, Sun only. **FREE**

LEVI COFFIN HOUSE STATE HISTORIC SITE. *113 US 27N, Fountain City (47341). Phone 765/847-2432.* Federal-style brick home of the Quaker abolitionist who helped 2,000 fugitive slaves escape to Canada; period furnishings. Tours. Open Tues-Sat, afternoons; closed July 4. **$**

LIEBER STATE RECREATION AREA. *1317 W Lieber Rd, Greencastle (46120). Phone 765/795-4576.* This area contains approximately 775 acres on Cataract Lake (1,500 acres). Swimming, lifeguard, bathhouse, water-skiing, fishing, boating (dock, rentals); picnicking, concession, camping. Activity center. Adjacent are 342 acres of state forest and 7,300 acres of federal land, part of the Cagles Mill Flood Control Reservoir Project. Open Memorial Day-Labor Day. **$**

MADAME WALKER THEATRE CENTER. *617 Indiana Ave, Indianapolis (46202). Phone 317/236-2099. www.walkertheatre.org.* The Walker Theatre, erected and embellished in an African and Egyptian motif, was built in 1927 as a tribute to Madame C. J. Walker, America's first self-made female millionaire. The renovated theater now features theatrical productions, concerts, and other cultural events. The center serves as an educational and cultural center for the city's African-American community. Tours. Open Mon-Fri. **$**

MADONNA OF THE TRAILS. *22nd and E Main sts, Richmond (47374). Phone 765/983-7200.* One of 12 monuments erected along the National Road (US 40) in honor of pioneer women. **FREE**

MIDDLEFORK RESERVOIR. *IN 27 and Sylvan Nook Dr, Richmond (47374). Phone 765/983-7293.* A 405-acre park with a 175-acre stream and a spring-fed lake. Fishing, boating (dock rental), bait and tackle supplies; hiking trails, picnicking, playground. **FREE**

NATIVE AMERICAN MUSEUM. *5170 E Poplar St, Terre Haute (47803). Phone 812/877-6007.* Exhibits include dwellings, clothing, weapons, and music of Eastern Woodland Native American cultures. Hands-on activities. **FREE**

OLD LOG JAIL AND CHAPEL-IN-THE-PARK MUSEUMS. *28 N Apple, Greenfield (46140). Phone 317/462-7780.* Historical displays include arrowheads, clothing, china, and local memorabilia. Open Apr-Nov, Sat and Sun. **$**

PRESIDENT BENJAMIN HARRISON HOME. *1230 N Delaware St, Indianapolis (46202). Phone 317/631-1898. www.presidentbenjaminharrison.org.* This residence of 23rd president of the United States includes 16 rooms with original furniture, paintings, and the family's personal effects. Herb garden. Guided tours (every 30 minutes). Open daily; closed holidays and 500 Race day. **$$**

SHAKAMAK STATE PARK. *6265 W State Rd 48, Jasonville (47438). Phone 812/665-2158.* More than 1,766 acres with three artificial lakes stocked with game fish. Swimming pool, lifeguard, bathhouse; boating (rentals, no gasoline motors). Picnicking, playground, hiking, camping, trailer facilities; cabins. Naturalist service. nature center. Open May-Aug.

SHELDON SWOPE ART MUSEUM. *25 S 7th St, Terre Haute (47807). Phone 812/238-1676. www.swope.org.* The museum's permanent collections include 19th- and 20th-century American art. Special exhibits, films, lectures, classes, and performing arts events. Open daily; closed holidays. **FREE**

ALL-AMERICAN ROADS

VIGO COUNTY HISTORICAL MUSEUM. *S 6th St, at Washington Ave, Terre Haute (47802) Phone 812/235-9717.* Local exhibits in 12 rooms of an 1868 house; one-room school, country store, military room, and dressmaker's shop. Open Tues-Sun; closed holidays.

WAYNE COUNTY HISTORICAL MUSEUM. *1150 N A St, Richmond (47374). Phone 765/962-5756.* Pioneer rooms include a general store; bakery, cobbler, print, bicycle, blacksmith, and apothecary shops; log cabin (1823); loom house; agricultural hall; decorative arts gallery; antique cars and old carriages; Egyptian mummy; and collections of the Mediterranean world. Open Feb-Dec, Tues-Sun; closed holidays. $$

PLACES TO STAY

If you choose to include an overnight stay in your trip along this All-American Road, Mobil Travel Guide recommends the following lodgings.

★ **MCKINLEY HOUSE.** *3273 E US Hwy 40, Brazil (47834). Phone 812/442-5308; toll-free, 866/442-5308.* 2 rooms, 2 story. This nicely restored inn was built in 1872 by Green McKinley, one of the original contractors of Highway 40, and is constructed of red brick made from clay dug at nearby Croy Creek. It has been operated as an inn continuously since it was built. $

★ **LANTZ HOUSE INN B&B.** *214 W Main St, Centerville (47330). Phone 765/855-2936; toll-free 800/495-2689.* 5 rooms, 2 story. This inn is located in a historical commercial building in the heart of old Centerville, within walking distance of shops and restaurants. All rooms have private baths. $

★★★ **THE WALDEN INN.** *2 W Seminary St, Greencastle (46135). Phone 765/653-2761; toll-free 800/225-8655. www.waldeninn.com.* This country inn on the campus of DePauw University has warmth and charm. Guests can stroll through town and check out the area's covered bridges. 55 rooms, 2 story. Check-out 1 pm, check-in 4 pm. TV. Restaurant. Amish furniture. $

★ **LEES INN.** *2270 N State St, Greenfield (46140). Phone 317/462-7112; toll-free 800/733-5337. www.leesinn.com.* 100 rooms, 2 story. Pet accepted. Complimentary continental breakfast. Check-out noon. TV. ¢

★★★ **CANTERBURY HOTEL.** *123 S Illinois St, Indianapolis (46225). Phone 317/634-3000; toll-free 800/538-8186. www.canterburyhotel.com.* The Canterbury Hotel transplants the charm and elegance of England to downtown Indianapolis. Since the 1850s, it has enjoyed a proud history as the city's leading hotel. This intimate hotel provides visitors with a convenient city location and private access to the adjacent shopping mall, filled with upscale stores and restaurants. Mahogany furniture and traditional artwork complete the classic décor in the guest rooms. Spacious and inviting, the accommodations are well suited for modern travelers. The lovely restaurant dishes up American and continental favorites for breakfast, lunch, and dinner, while the traditional afternoon tea is a local institution. 99 rooms, 12 story. Complimentary continental breakfast. Check-out noon. TV; VCR available. In-room modem link. Restaurant. Concierge. Formal décor; four-poster beds, Chippendale-style furniture. Historic landmark. $$

79

Indiana

✱ *The Historic National Road*

★★★ **EMBASSY SUITES INDIANAPOLIS-DOWNTOWN.** *110 W Washington St, Indianapolis (46204). Phone 317/236-1800. www.embassysuites.com.* Within walking distance of the business district, shopping, and local attractions, this hotel is conveniently located. Guest suites are large, comfortable, and affordable. 360 rooms, 18 story. Complimentary full breakfast. Check-out noon. TV; VCR available. In-room modem link. Restaurant, bar. In-house fitness room. Indoor pool, whirlpool. $$

★ **HAMPTON INN.** *105 S Meridian St, Indianapolis (46225). Phone 317/261-1200; toll-free 800/426-7866. www.hamptoninn.com.* 180 rooms, 9 story. Complimentary continental breakfast. Check-out noon. TV; cable (premium). In-room modem link. Restaurant, bar. Room service. In-house fitness room. Valet parking available. $

★ **COMFORT INN.** *912 Mendelson Dr, Richmond (47374). Phone 765/935-4766; toll-free 800/228-5150. www.choicehotels.com.* 52 rooms, 2 story. Pet accepted. Check-out 11 am. Game room. Indoor pool, whirlpool. ¢

★★ **THE FARRINGTON BED & BREAKFAST.** *931 S 7th St, Terre Haute (47807). Phone 812/238-0524.* 5 rooms, 3 story. Located in the historical district of Terre Haute and built in 1898. $

★★ **HOLIDAY INN.** *3300 US 41 S, Terre Haute (47802). Phone 812/232-6081; toll-free 800/465-4329. www.holiday-inn.com.* 230 rooms, 2-5 story. Pet accepted. Check-out noon. TV; cable (premium). In-room modem link. Guest laundry. Restaurant, bar. Room service. In-house fitness room. Indoor pool, whirlpool. $

PLACES TO EAT

A long day of driving is sure to make you hungry. At the end of your journey, take a table at one of the following restaurants.

★★ **PALAIS ROYAL CAFÉ.** *822 E Main St, Centerville (47330). Phone 765/939-1199. www.palaisroyalcafe.com.* American menu. Closed Sun-Wed. Dinner. Elegant dining in a turn-of-the-century farmhouse. $$

★★★ **A DIFFERENT DRUMMER.** *2 W Seminary St, Greencastle (46135). Phone 765/653-2761.* Inside the Walden Inn, diners will find conservative fare such as chicken cordon bleu, roasted eggplant with spinach, lamb chops, and veal medallions. Closed Dec 25. Breakfast, lunch, dinner. Bar. $$

★ **CARNEGIE'S.** *100 W North St, Greenfield (46140). Phone 317/462-8480.* American menu. Closed Sun, Mon. Lunch, dinner. This chef-owned restaurant features regional cuisine and is located in the town's first library. $

★★ **THE MAJESTIC.** *47 S Pennsylvania, Indianapolis (46204). Phone 317/636-5418. www.majesticrestaurant.com.* Continental menu. Closed Sun; some major holidays. Lunch, dinner. Bar. Children's menu. $$$

★★★ **RESTAURANT AT THE CANTERBURY.** *123 S Illinois, Indianapolis (46225). Phone 317/634-3000. www.canterburyhotel.com.* Decorated more like an English club than a restaurant, this elegant, tranquil hotel dining room serves American continental cuisine, focusing on game dishes. Lunch prices can be very reasonable. Don't miss the afternoon tea service with live piano music. Continental menu. Breakfast, lunch, dinner, Sun brunch. Bar. Jacket required. Valet parking. $$$

★★ **ST. ELMO STEAK HOUSE.** *127 S Illinois, Indianapolis (46225). Phone 317/637-1811. www.stelmos.com.* Turn-of-the-century décor and old photographs lend a historic feel to this longstanding and popular spot. Steak menu. Closed major holidays. Dinner. Bar. **$$$**
[D]

★ **PLAINFIELD DINER.** *3122 E Main St, Plainfield (46168). Phone 317/839-9464.* Diner menu. Breakfast, lunch, dinner. One of the oldest historic roadside diners in Indiana. **$**

★★ **OLDE RICHMOND INN.** *138 S 5th St, Richmond (47374). Phone 765/962-2247.* Continental menu. Closed Jan 1, Labor Day, Dec 25. Lunch, dinner. Bar. Children's menu. Restored mansion built in 1892. Outdoor seating. **$$$**
[D]

★ **TASTE OF THE TOWN.** *1616 E Main St, Richmond (47374). Phone 765/935-5464.* Italian, American menu. Closed Mon; some major holidays. Lunch, dinner. Bar. Children's menu. Casual attire. **$$**
[D]

★★ **FROG'S BISTRO AND WINE SHOPPE.** *810 Wabash Ave, Terre Haute (47802). Phone 812/478-9663.* American menu. Lunch, dinner. This New Orleans-style bistro has an emphasis on wine and jazz. **$$**

Creole Nature Trail
✹ LOUISIANA

Quick Facts

LENGTH: 180 miles.

TIME TO ALLOW: 4 to 8 hours.

BEST TIME TO DRIVE: Great year-round, although the best months for alligator watching are April through October. Summer is the high season.

BYWAY TRAVEL INFORMATION: Southwest Louisiana/Lake Charles Convention and Visitors Bureau: toll-free 800/456-SWLA.

SPECIAL CONSIDERATIONS: Bring insect repellent and watch out for dangerous wildlife in the refuges by keeping your distance. Do not try to feed, tease, or prod an alligator into moving by throwing rocks or other things at him; he is perfectly capable of defending himself.

RESTRICTIONS: Wildlife refuges are closed on federal holidays. Some hunting and fishing grounds require permits. Also, it is advised not to take dogs along at Marsh Trail because alligators may consume them.

BICYCLE/PEDESTRIAN FACILITIES: The Creole Nature Trail National Scenic Byway has always been a popular route for bike touring, even though it is primarily a two-lane facility with limited or no shoulders. Pedestrians have the opportunity to explore aspects of the trail at the Wetland Walkway, a mile-and-a-half walking trail on the Sabine National Wildlife Refuge; on the boardwalk at the Cameron Prairie National Wildlife Refuge; and at the Cameron jetties fishing pier and RV park. The beaches are public and fully accessible, and a public ferry that crosses the Calcasieu Ship Channel accommodates bicyclists as well.

Join in an authentic Louisiana Festival or capture alligators with your camera. Offering an up-close and personal view of Louisiana's unique environment, the Creole Nature Trail travels through thousands of acres of untouched wetlands that reflect a peace blessed with some of the most beautiful scenery imaginable. Besides pine trees, you'll see fields of rice and soybeans, cattle, and country homesteads during the summer. In the spring, the water lilies and blossoming water hyacinth growing in the marsh are like paradise to photographers.

If you like to photograph or hunt wildlife, the trail takes you to four different wildlife refuges and a bird sanctuary. Alligators, birds, wildflowers, gulf beaches, and all kinds of southwest Louisiana wildlife can be found in this area. If you're not a duck hunter, you may want to try your hand at a little Louisiana fishing. The combination of fresh and saltwater areas provides a unique habitat for many of the plants and creatures that live along the Byway.

For surf fishing, crabbing, and shrimping, the Louisiana coastline can be a lot of fun. In the Calcasieu and Cameron parishes, you have access to boat launches, campgrounds, hunting services, recreational facilities, swimming areas, bird-watching, and cabins. At Lake Charles, you can swim or sunbathe on the beach, launch a boat at a nearby facility, or take a cruise on one of the gambling boats.

Traveling the edge of the Gulf of Mexico, you will be enchanted by the entwining ecosystems of the coastland and the marshland.

Louisiana

✽ *Creole Nature Trail*

THE BYWAY STORY

The Creole Nature Trail tells archaeological, cultural, historical, natural, recreational, and scenic stories that make it a unique and treasured Byway.

Archaeological

Comparatively large concentrations of Native American archaeological finds, such as pots, shards, and arrowheads, have been unearthed throughout Cameron Parish, and burial mounds were found on Little Chenier, indicating that the earlier Native American populations must have been large and widespread.

Cultural

The culture along the Creole Nature Trail is one that has been mixing and evolving for hundreds of years. Spanish, French, and African influences have all collided here in this coastal outback where alligators roam and hurricanes are known to swallow entire villages. The people of southwest Louisiana understand the place they live and revel in it. Festivals celebrate living on the Creole Nature Trail throughout the year. Along the Byway, you may learn how to skin an alligator or enjoy some real Cajun cooking. Historic buildings, nature trails, and even wildlife refuges provide a few more details about the way people live and enjoy life on the Byway.

To account for Louisiana's cultural mix and regional differences, this state has sometimes been called "the Creole State." This is appropriate for Louisiana because the term "creole" (from the Portuguese *crioulo,* meaning "native to a region") has many hues of meaning. Initially, in Louisiana, the West Indies, and Latin America, "Creole" referred to the colonial French/Spanish population. The word later came to refer to the *gens libres de couleur* (free people of color) in Louisiana who were of mixed Afro-European descent. The word "creole" was then used to describe the Afro-French language called Creole, as well as a variety of foodways, music styles, architecture, and attitudes that reflect the mingling of cultures in Louisiana. Many people now recognize "creole" or "creolization" to be a combination of cultures that make a new culture.

Whatever you decide about the meaning of "creole," you are sure to find Byway culture delightful. When you aren't exploring a wildlife refuge or enjoying a community festival, you may get a chance to see how the Byway residents live today. Although the local economy uses the discovery of petroleum as a resource, it once relied entirely on the ocean and the marshes. Shrimp boats and ships in the Cameron Ship Channel reflect the importance of the ocean in the area. Shrimp, crabs, oysters, and a host of fresh and saltwater fish are harvested daily, and when you sample cooking on the Creole Nature Trail, you'll find a new appreciation for seafood.

More than 75 festivals and events occur in the area throughout the year, from the Alligator Harvest Festival to Mardi Gras. Wherever you go along the Byway, be sure to dip in to the local culture and enjoy the flavor.

Historical

As a coastal Byway on the Gulf of Mexico, the Creole Nature Trail has a history of tropical storms and maritime incidents. Many places along the way reflect pieces of local and national history. The Byway is the *Creole Nature Trail*—mixing different cultures and histories. The French and the Spanish both had an influence here, as did many other settlers from different regions and the native culture of the Attakapas tribe. The Creole Nature Trail began as an even more rugged country than it is today, full of alligators, deer, waterfowl, and even panthers. For a time, dangerous scoundrels and pirates inhabited the area, too, leaving legends of treasure behind. Later, the Civil War and two World Wars changed the face of southwest Louisiana.

An infamous history prevails throughout much of the early 1800s on the Byway. The pirate Jean Lafitte made a huge profit from capturing Spanish slave ships and selling the slaves to

Louisiana cotton and sugar cane planters. His exploits involved everything from the African slave trade to liaisons with French spies. Some even say the treasure of Napoleon might be buried somewhere in Calcasieu Parish. The illicit slave trade continued near Lake Sabine and Lake Calcasieu, and Lafitte is rumored to have buried riches and treasure chests along the Calcasieu River. Long after Lafitte disappeared from the shores of southwest Louisiana, many of the ex-pirates who sailed with him remained in the area traveled by the Byway until the end of their days.

When the Civil War came to Louisiana, battles that occurred along the Byway often centered around a particular landmark. Battles were fought over Sabine Pass and Calcasieu Pass, where the Confederates were successful. After the battle over Calcasieu Pass, the dead from both sides were buried in unmarked graves on Monkey Island, and they are commemorated with a monument at Cameron Parish Courthouse. Standing today as a stalwart landmark, the Sabine Pass Lighthouse was built in 1854, and it also became a point of conflict during the Civil War. The light was extinguished to deter a possible Union attack on Fort Griffin. After the Civil War, the lighthouse continued to stand through hurricanes, tidal waves, and storms and continues to stand today.

As the Byway entered the 20th century, an effort began to preserve the elements that make the Byway unique. This effort included beautiful wetlands that became National Wildlife Refuges and the historic courthouses and lighthouses that already existed.

Natural

The marshlands of coastal Louisiana are teeming with wildlife: they are a bird-watcher's paradise and a photographer's dream. The marshes are alive with the rhythms of nature, the coming of new life, and the passing of old. They also witness the ebbing and flowing of water, the greening and browning of plant life, and the coming and going of ducks and geese by the hundreds of thousands as the seasons change.

These marshes are filled with the music of life, including the songs of the cardinal and blackbird, the quacking and honking of ducks and geese, the chatter of squirrels, the croaking of frogs, and the bellowing of alligators. If you listen closely, you can hear the hooting of the owl, the screeching of the hawk, the hissing and barking of the nutria, or the constant knocking and tapping of the woodpecker. Millions of birds stop and stay on the 300,000 acres of refuges and marsh along the Byway, and birds are not the only creatures thriving here. Once an endangered species, alligators are now a common sight in places all along the route.

In southwestern Louisiana, marshes and other wetlands can be viewed in the Sabine National Wildlife Refuge, the Rockefeller National Wildlife Refuge, Lacassine National Wildlife Refuge, and the Cameron Prairie National Wildlife Refuge. Parts of these refuges and game preserves are readily accessible, and the public is invited to take a closer look. The

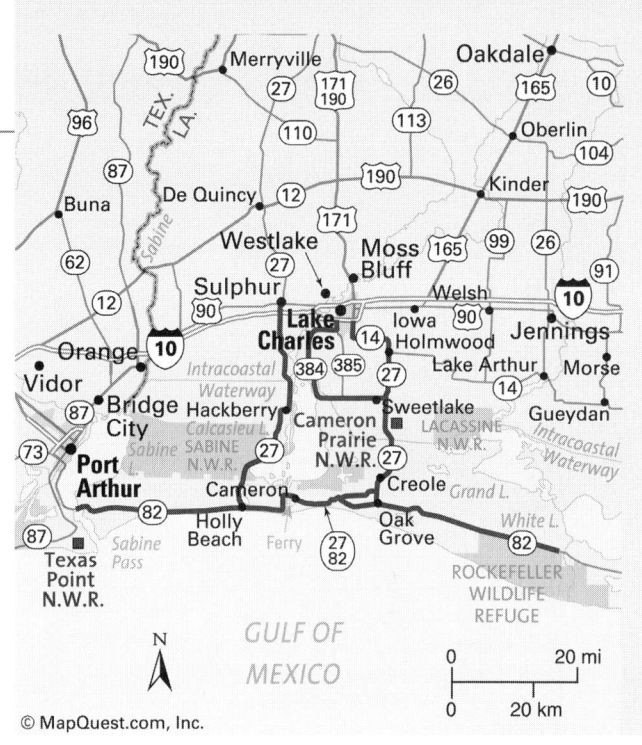

see page A14 for color map

Louisiana

✹ Creole Nature Trail

Marsh Trail allows visitors to get a good look at plant and animal life in the Sabine Refuge as they stroll along a 1 1/2-mile raised circular walkway that traverses through a marsh and is filled with alligators, rabbits, and waterfowl. The Rockefeller Refuge is open nine months each year for sightseeing and fishing. Travel here is mostly by boat, because there are few roads on this 84,000-acre refuge.

At Peveto Bird and Butterfly Sanctuary, you will find creatures living amid the cheniers. Beautiful butterflies find this habitat to be the perfect place to spend the winter. Characterized as coastal oak woods, cheniers are ancient beach ridges formed by the forces of the ocean and the Mississippi River. Found primarily on the Louisiana coast, these natural landforms are a build-up of sandy beach that became high enough above sea level to support hardwood trees like oak. These beautiful features can be seen all along the Byway.

As a coastal prairie, much of the land along the Byway displays beautiful wildflowers throughout the warmer months. Many of the flowers have memorable names, like the maypop passionflower and the duck potato. Unique plants can be found growing everywhere along the Byway. Cordgrass grows where nothing else will, and a plant called alligatorweed is a food source for deer, herons, and egrets. Alligatorweed grows in freshwater in large dense clusters. Sometimes, it is so dense that alligators can be seen basking in the sun on top of a mat of alligatorweed.

Recreational

Between bird-watching and alligator hunting, adventure peeks around every corner. But the Byway offers more than just a marsh. Be sure to explore all the celebrations and events that occur in Byway communities year-round, including opportunities to learn about the Civil War events that took place in this area and the cultures that were involved. Of course, looking for wildlife will likely lead to a nature hike through one of the four wildlife refuges on the Byway. And getting out of the car is half the fun of driving!

One of the most popular activities for locals and visitors alike is the excellent fishing on Louisiana's coastline, where freshwater, saltwater, and brackish fishing are all available to you. Here, visitors catch more than just fish—crab, shrimp, and oyster are also popular items to pull from the sea. Every so often, an alligator may want to try the bait, but they aren't the most desirable catch.

Swimming, boating, and beachcombing are also available to visitors who want to explore a place where the ocean meets the marsh. Hike through the marshes and take a boat along the coastline.

Visitors love to stop in places like Lake Charles and the towns of Cameron County to take a look at the historic sites that make each town memorable. In Lake Charles, explore the historic Calcasieu Courthouse or take a walking tour through the Charpentier Historic District. Classic architectural styles of the South are preserved here, building an atmosphere for the Byway. So whether you explore the fantastic natural coastline or the communities along the way, you'll find something to satisfy your urge for exploration. And you'll want to come back for more.

Scenic

The Creole Nature Trail provides scenery just as it should be in an outback wilderness—untamed and

ALL-AMERICAN ROADS

intriguing. These characteristics are preserved in the way wetland birds roam freely across the countryside and in the way that the ocean waves curl into the salt marshes. The Creole Nature Trail provides scenery of extraordinary natural quality formed from the interactions of the Gulf of Mexico and the lowlands of Louisiana, and the Byway travels past lakes and streams that create the waterways of the Creole Nature Trail. Tidal canals line the Byway in some places, changing with the sea. They carry waters from the Gulf of Mexico into the low-lying flats where freshwater gathers from runoff. The result is the thriving sight of an estuary.

As you drive along the Byway, keep the windows rolled down for an offshore breeze of salty air. As you drive through the marshes, search the reeds and grass for a glimpse of a heron or an alligator. (On a sunny day, the gators may be so bold as to bask on the boardwalks.) Tufts of salt-meadow cordgrass reflect off the blue waters below them. Past the beach and on the ocean, fleets of boats gather for shrimping.

Mineral soils and higher ground form cheniers; the most significant of these ridges is Blue Buck Ridge. The chenier ridges are where the live oaks grow, offering a habitat for songbirds and a beautiful photo opportunity. The trees are said to be sculpted by sea spray and ocean winds that give them a peculiar appearance. The silhouette of the trees at sunset is especially appealing.

HIGHLIGHTS

This tour of the Creole Nature Trail begins in Sulphur, Louisiana (or, if you prefer, start at the other end of the Byway and read this list from the bottom up).

- At Sulphur, the area is characterized by rolling pasture land that gradually turns to wetland. Small ponds and bayous begin to appear as well.
- After crossing Ellender Bridge, you enter **Cameron Parish,** the largest parish in the state. The vegetation in the area is mostly of the salt marsh variety. Additionally, the landscape is dotted with oil wells and oilfield pumping stations.
- Next, you approach **Hackberry.** In this vicinity, you find an abundance of shrimp and crab houses along Kelso Bayou. Here, seafood is cheap and plentiful. The area is important to the commercial fishing industry because of the abundance of natural resources.
- A bit farther down the Byway, you come upon the **Sabine National Wildlife Refuge.** Here, you get views of birds and other marsh animals. The refuge includes the 1.5-mile self-guided Marsh Trail with interpretation stations, an observation tower, and panoramic view of miles of marsh terrain.
- Following the Creole Nature Trail south, you reach the Gulf Coast at **Holly Beach.** This area is know as the Cajun Riviera. The beach provides 25 miles of year-round beaches, campsites, accommodations, and a variety of outdoor recreation. From this point, the Byway moves west along the Gulf Coast.
- Approximately 30 miles down the Byway, following the Gulf Coast, you come upon the **Rockefeller Wildlife Refuge.** This area is home to a variety of wintering waterfowl and resident mammals. The refuge is also an important area for research studies on a number of marsh-management strategies. While you can enjoy recreational fishing in this area, hunting is prohibited. Be cautious of the alligators that inhabit the area.
- From this area, you may choose to turn back west toward Cameron Prairie National Wildlife Reserve or continue east toward the western terminus of the Byway.

THINGS TO SEE AND DO

Driving along the Creole Nature Trail will certainly keep your senses engaged, but if you yearn to get out of the car and stretch your legs, or if you'd like to make a mini-vacation out of your trip, check out these attractions along the route.

Louisiana

❈ *Creole Nature Trail*

BRIMSTONE HISTORICAL SOCIETY MUSEUM. *800 Picard Rd, Lake Charles (70601). Phone 337/527-7142.* This museum commemorates the turn-of-the-century birth of the local sulphur industry, with exhibits explaining the development of the Frasch mining process. Other exhibits deal with southwest Louisiana. Open Mon-Fri; closed holidays. **FREE**

✪ **HISTORIC CHARPENTIER.** *Lake Charles (70601). Phone 318/436-9588; toll-free 800/456-SWLA.* The historic district includes 20 square blocks of downtown area; architectural styles range from Queen Anne, Eastlake, and Carpenter's Gothic (known locally as Lake Charles style) to Western stick-style bungalows. Tours (fee) and brochures describing self-guided tours may be obtained at the Convention & Visitors Bureau. **FREE**

IMPERIAL CALCASIEU MUSEUM. *204 W Sallier St, Lake Charles (70601). Phone 337/439-3797.* Exhibits include items of local historical interest. Complete rooms and shops, toy collection, rare Audubon prints. The Gibson-Barham Gallery houses art exhibits. On the premises is the 300-year-old Sallier Oak tree. Open Tues-Sat; closed holidays. **$**

PORT OF LAKE CHARLES. *150 Marine St, Lake Charles (70601).* The port consists of docks and a turning basin. Ships pass down the Calcasieu ship channel and through Lake Calcasieu.

SAM HOUSTON JONES STATE PARK. *107 Sutherland Rd, Lake Charles (70611). Phone 337/855-2665; toll-free 888/677-7264.* The approximately 1,000 acres include lagoons in a densely wooded area at the confluence of the west fork of the Caslcasieu and Houston rivers and Indian Bayou. Fishing, boating (rentals, launch); nature trails, hiking, picnicking, tent and trailer sites (hookups, dump station), cabins. Open daily. **$**

PLACES TO STAY

If you choose to include an overnight stay in your trip along this All-American Road, Mobil Travel Guide recommends the following lodgings.

★★ **AUNT RUBY'S BED & BREAKFAST.** *504 Pujo St, Lake Charles (70601). Phone 318/430-0603. www.auntrubys.com.* 6 rooms, 2 story. Constructed in 1911, this bed-and-breakfast has six guest rooms with private baths and offers a gourmet breakfast in the morning. **$**

★ **BEST WESTERN RICHMOND SUITES HOTEL.** *2600 Moeling St, Lake Charles (70615). Phone 337/433-5213; toll-free 800/528-1234. www.bestwestern.com.* 140 rooms, 30 kitchen suites, 2 story. Complimentary full breakfast. Check-out noon. TV; cable (premium). In-room modem link. Laundry services. Exercise equipment. Pool, whirlpool. Airport transportation. **$**

★★ **C. A.'S HOUSE BED & BREAKFAST.** *624 Ford St, Lake Charles (70601). Phone 337/439-6672. www.waltersattic.com.* 5 rooms, 3 story. A three-story colonial house built in the early 1900s. It is located in the Charpentier Historic District and was once owned by the president of the Huber Motor Oil Company and Quality Oil Company and then later owned by C. A. King II. **$$**

★★ **PLAYERS ISLAND RIVERBOAT HOTEL & CASINO.** *505 N Lakeshore Dr, Lake Charles (70602). Phone 318/437-1500; toll-free 800/977-7529.* 269 rooms, 4 story. Check-out noon. TV; cable (premium). Pool; poolside service. Restaurant, bar. Room service. Convention facilities. Business services available. In-room modem link. Bellhops. Valet service. Some refrigerators, wet bars. On lake. **¢**

ALL-AMERICAN ROADS

★★ **WALTER'S ATTIC BED & BREAKFAST.** 618 Ford St, Lake Charles (70601). Phone 337/439-6672; toll-free 866/439-6672. www.waltersattic.com. 5 rooms, 2 story. This inn is located in the Charpentier Historic District and caters to honeymoon and anniversary couples. It features a heated pool and fireplaces. $$

★★ **A RIVERS EDGE BED & BREAKFAST.** 2035 Gus St, Westlake (70669). Phone 337/497-1525. www.lakecharlesbedbreakfast.com. 3 rooms, 1 story. Set between a winding bayou and its own private island. Guests are greeted with smoothies, homemade cookies, cold cuts, cheese, and crackers. Pool. $

PLACES TO EAT

A long day of driving is sure to make you hungry. At the end of your journey, take a table at one of the following restaurants.

★★★ **CAFE MARGAUX.** 765 Bayou Pines E, Lake Charles (70601). Phone 337/433-2902. Continental, French menu. (Mon-Fri) Closed Sun; Dec 25. Lunch, dinner. Bar. Reservations accepted. $$
[D]

★★ **HARLEQUIN STEAKS & SEAFOOD.** 1717 Hwy 14. Lake Charles (70601). Phone 337/439-2780. Steak, seafood menu. Closed Sun, major holidays. Dinner reservations accepted. Bar. Children's menu. Several dining rooms provide an intimate atmosphere; attractive landscaping. Family-owned. $$

★ **JEAN LAFITTE INN.** 501 W College St, Lake Charles (70605). Phone 318/474-2730. Cajun/Creole menu. Closed major holidays. Lunch, dinner. Bar. Children's menu. $$
[D]

★ **PAT'S OF HENDERSON.** 1500 Siebarth Dr, Lake Charles (70615). Phone 337/439-6618. American, Cajun/Creole menu. Closed Thanksgiving, Dec 25. Lunch, dinner. Bar. Children's menu. Reservations accepted. $$
[D]

★ **PEKING GARDEN.** 2433 E Broad St, Lake Charles (70601). Phone 337/436-3597. Chinese menu. Closed Thanksgiving, Dec 25. Lunch, dinner. Bar. Children's menu. Specializes in Hunan cuisine. Chinese artifacts in dining room. $$
[D]

★★ **PUJO STREET CAFE.** 901 Ryan St, Lake Charles (70601). Phone 337/439-2054. www.pujostreet.com. Cajun/Creole menu. Closed Sun evening. Lunch, dinner. Updated Creole cuisine in downtown Lake Charles. $

★ **STEAMBOAT BILL'S.** 732 Martin Luther King Hwy, Lake Charles (70601). Phone 337/494-1700. Creole menu. Lunch, dinner. Famous for catfish and po' boys. $

★ **TONY'S PIZZA.** 335 E Prien Lake Rd, Lake Charles (70601). Phone 337/477-1611. Specializes in pizza, deli sandwiches, and salads. Closed Thanksgiving, Dec 25. Italian menu. Lunch, dinner, late night. Friendly, family-oriented atmosphere. Family-owned. $
[D] [SC]

★ **CAJUN CHARLIE'S SEAFOOD RESTAURANT.** 202 Henning Dr, Sulphur (70663). Phone 337/527-9044. www.cajuncharlies.com. Creole menu. Lunch, dinner. Known for authentic Creole seafood recipes and being a very local attraction. $

Acadia Byway
✵ MAINE

Quick Facts

LENGTH: 40 miles.

TIME TO ALLOW: 3 hours.

BEST TIME TO DRIVE: This Byway is excellent year-round, with beautiful foliage in autumn; hiking and cross-country skiing in winter; and bird-watching, hiking, and bicycling in spring. High season runs from late June though September; tourism is especially heavy on July 4 and Labor Day weekends.

BYWAY TRAVEL INFORMATION: Bar Harbor Chamber of Commerce: 207/288-5103; Acadia National Park Service: 207/288-3888.

SPECIAL CONSIDERATIONS: Mount Desert Island now has a free seasonal bus service that visitors are encouraged to use; the central terminal is in downtown Bar Harbor. The buses stop at many of the hotels and campgrounds along the way. They also stop anywhere that offers adequate space to pull over. You can easily flag them down.

RESTRICTIONS: The Park Loop Road is closed from late November to mid-April. Other roads can be closed during extreme weather conditions. You must pay a car toll to get on Park Loop Road at the national park. This pass is good for three days.

BICYCLE/PEDESTRIAN FACILITIES: The Park Loop Road was designed around biking and walking recreational activities. It is a one-way road, and the right lane is specifically designated for both bikers and walkers. There are also plenty of other places to walk and bike along this Byway. For example, Acadia National Park alone boasts 120 miles of hiking trails and 45 miles of carriage roads.

Fog is a common sight along this Byway, muting the landscape with its romantic gray mists. In the midday sun, the sea's bright blue surface is studded with colorful lobster buoys. Seen at sundown from Cadillac Mountain, the sea glows in soft pinks, mauves, and golds.

As the name suggests, the Acadia area was French before it was American. French explorer Samuel Champlain sailed into Frenchman Bay in 1604, naming the area Mount Desert Island because of its landmark bare top. Today, the National Park Service owns approximately half of the island that makes up Acadia National Park. The island boasts lush forests, tranquil ponds, and granite-capped mountains, where exploring is made easy by an extensive system of carriage roads and hiking trails. This alternate transportation network provides access to all areas of the park for walkers, equestrians, bicyclists, and cross-country skiers.

Villages on Mount Desert present a variety of lifestyles on the island today. Bar Harbor offers many accommodations and amusements. Northeast Harbor shelters sailboats, both large and small, and a summer colony. Bass Harbor and Southwest Harbor retain more of a traditional flavor of Maine's coastal villages.

THE BYWAY STORY

The Acadia Byway tells archaeological, cultural, historical, natural, recreational, and scenic stories that make it a unique and treasured Byway.

Archaeological

Many aspects indicate Native American encampments, but prehistoric records are scant.

Maine

❋ Acadia Byway

For example, deep shell heaps suggest Native American encampments dating back 6,000 years in Acadia National Park. The first written descriptions of Maine coast Native Americans were recorded 100 years after European trade contacts began. In these records, Native Americans were described as people who lived off the land by hunting, fishing, collecting shellfish, and gathering plants and berries.

The Wabanaki Indians called Mount Desert Island Pemetic, or "the sloping land." They built bark-covered conical shelters and traveled in delicately designed birch bark canoes. Archaeological evidence suggests that the Wabanaki wintered on the coast and summered inland in order to take advantage of salmon runs upstream in the winter and avoid harsh inland weather.

Cultural

While Maine is rich in culture, perhaps the best-known sights along the coast are the lobster traps and colorful buoys. Catching lobster has been a profitable activity in Maine since the 1840s. In fact, lobster was so plentiful during the age of elegant "cottages" in Acadia that the wealthy commonly fed their servants lobster because it was so inexpensive. Today, the sight of a lobsterman reeling in his trap is common.

Lobstermen use buoys to mark their trap sites, and every lobsterman has a different combination of colors to differentiate his buoys from someone else's. Often, one buoy is atop the wheelhouse of the lobster boat to display his colors. While the lobster boats are not the same wooden dories originally used, they are still a unique sight along the waters. They generally have a round bottom and a double wedge hull, ranging from 20 to 40 feet. The actual lobster traps come in various designs. Two of the best known are the parlor trap and the double-header trap, and they're set anywhere from 50 feet to miles apart. During the summer, lobster can be found in shallow waters (60 to 100 feet), but during the winter, lobster descend to depths of over 200 feet. You'll see lobstermen out hauling in their catch anytime weather permits and often when it does not.

Historical

Acadia's long history of settlement and colonization began with Samuel Champlain, who led the expedition that landed on Mount Desert on September 5, 1604. He wrote in his journal, "The mountain summits are all bare and rocky . . . I name it Isles des Monts Desert." Because Champlain, who made the first important contribution to the historical record of Mount Desert Island, visited 16 years before the Pilgrims landed at Plymouth Rock, this land was known as New France before it became New England.

The land was in dispute between the French to the north and the English to the south for about 150 years. No one wanted to settle in the contested land until Antoine Laumet immigrated to New France in 1688 and bestowed upon himself the title Sieur de la Mothe Cadillac. He asked for, and received, 100,000 acres of land along the Maine Coast, including Mount Desert. He and his bride resided there for a time, but soon abandoned their enterprise of establishing a feudal estate in the new world.

After a century and a half of conflict, British troops triumphed at Quebec, ending French dominion in Acadia. Hence, lands along the Maine coast opened for English settlement. Soon, an increasing number of settlers homesteaded on Mount Desert Island. By 1820, farming and lumbering vied with fishing and shipbuilding as major occupations. Outsiders—artists and journalists—revealed and popularized the island to the world in the mid-1800s. Painters, called rusticators, inspired patrons and friends to flock to the island. Soon, tourism became a major industry.

For a handful of Americans, the 1880s and Gay Nineties meant affluence on a scale without precedent. Mount Desert, still remote from the cities of the east, became a retreat for prominent people of the times. The Rockefellers, Morgans, Fords, Vanderbilts, Carnegies, and Astors chose to spend their summers on the island. The families transformed the area with elegant estates, euphemistically called "cottages." For over 40 years, the wealthy held sway at Mount Desert until the Great Depression, World War II, and the fire of 1947 marked the end of such extravagance.

Although the wealthy came to the island to play, they also helped to preserve the landscape. George B. Dorr, in particular, was a tireless spokesman for conservation. He devoted 43 years of his life, energy, and family fortune to preserving Acadia. Dorr and others established the Hancock County Trustees of Public Reservations. This corporation's sole purpose was to preserve land for the perpetual use of the public, and it acquired some 6,000 acres by 1913. In 1916, the land became the Sieur de Monts National Monument, and in 1919 it became the first national park east of the Mississippi, with Dorr as the first park superintendent. In 1929, the park name changed to Acadia, and today the park encompasses 35,000 acres of land.

Natural

Acadia Byway runs right along Acadia National Park, where the sights are outstanding. Catching sight of an animal in its native environment will charm the casual visitor into an enthusiast, yet Acadia is home to a menagerie of wildlife that captivates the most experienced nature watcher. Whether you yearn to catch a glimpse of whales and seals or native and migratory birds, Acadia offers it all.

A variety of whales can be seen in the Gulf of Maine with antics that bring a smile, along with a sense of awe. Although finback, minke, and right whales can be seen, humpbacks are

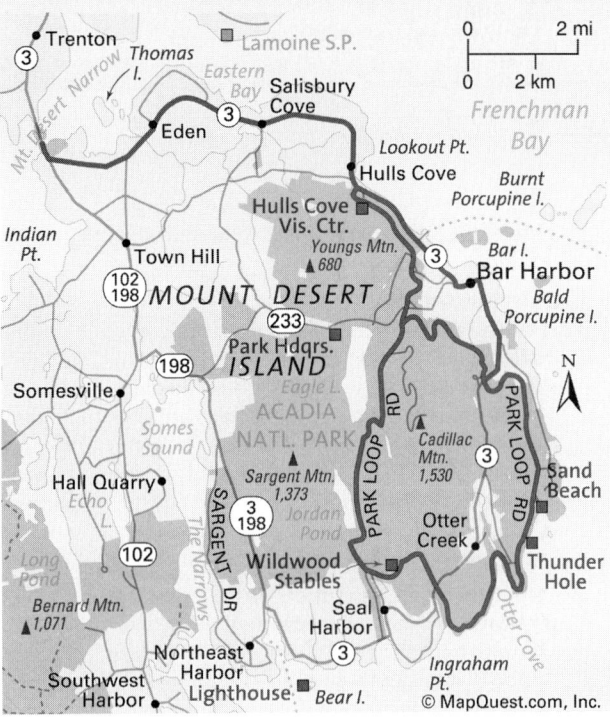

see page A15 for color map

among the most playful of the whales. They are known for spy hopping (sticking their heads out of the water to look around), lobe tailing (throwing the lower half of their bodies out of the water), and tail slapping. To witness a humpback whale breaching (jumping completely out of the water) is a particularly amazing sight. Pay careful attention to the humpback's tail during its aerobatics—each whale's tail is unique.

After watching mammoth mammals in the water for a time, take a look above you. Acadia is an especially fertile area for bird sightings. In fact, 213 species—some migratory and some native—frequent the area. The peregrine falcon, once nearly extinct, can be seen winging overhead. They seem to circle lazily, but these raptors can attack prey at speeds of more than 100 miles per hour. They are most active at dawn and dusk in open areas. Puffins, also once nearly extinct, are making a comeback on islands along the Maine coast. Visitors may see this clown of the sea during offshore excursions.

Recreational

For outdoor recreation and fun, Acadia Byway is a dream come true. Relatively small at only 13 miles wide and 16 miles long, Acadia

Maine

✻ *Acadia Byway*

National Park offers a multitude of activities. Acadia maintains 45 miles of carriage roads for walking, riding, biking, and skiing and over 100 miles of trails just for hiking. Situated right along the coast, the area is perfect for boating, sailing, and kayaking. You can find an activity that best allows you to experience the tree-fringed lakes and streams, flower-filled meadows, or revitalizing sea breeze.

Hiking is one of the best ways to see all that Acadia has to offer. Trails that encourage meditation on the magnificence of nature crisscross the entire island. Take time to steal softly through a still forest, skip along the thundering coast, or meander through a swaying meadow. Up Cadillac Mountain is a particularly inspiring hike; its summit is the highest point on the Atlantic coast north of Rio de Janeiro. If you reach it before dawn and stand at the summit, you will be the first person in the continental United States to see the sun begin its journey across the sky and witness the beginning of a brand new day.

Want to see as much of the park as possible? Try cycling. Bicyclists experience the same closeness to nature as hikers but see more of the countryside and cover more ground. If you prefer paved roads, you'll find Acadia's smooth rides beckoning, while mountain bikers are in for a pleasant surprise: 45 miles of carriage roads wind around rippling lakes, through tunnels of leafy branches, over hills, and under a number of stone bridges. One ride that begins at Jordan Pond is a rolling 23 miles. This ride takes cyclists around the western portion of the eastern half of Mount Desert Island, between Somes Sound and Jordan Pond. If you enjoy flowering paths, two exquisite gardens along this ride bid you to stop and explore the sweet-smelling paths with a stunning view of the harbor.

For water enthusiasts, Acadia offers a number of alternatives. Ocean canoeing and kayaking are drawing new converts every day. The thrill of gliding on the surface of the rolling sea is an experience never to be forgotten. You can immerse yourself more fully in the ocean experience by swimming at one of the beaches, although water temperatures rarely exceed 55 degrees. Echo Lake Beach, a freshwater lake, is somewhat warmer. Take a trip on one of the schooners for a glimpse into sailing experiences of the late 1800s. Relax in the gentle breeze, try your hand at deep-sea fishing, or help the crew with the lines.

Scenic

Acadia National Park preserves the natural beauty of Maine's coasts, mountains, and offshore islands. Acadia Byway takes you through a diverse area of scenery, from the seashore to the green vegetation inland. Park Loop Road, constructed specifically to take visitors through the variety of sights that Acadia has to offer, leads you along a path of breathtaking delight. Acadia's mountains are the highest rocky headlands on the Atlantic shore of the United States, and the views from these mountaintops encompass shadowy forests, gleaming lakes, hushed marshes, bold rocky shores, and coastal islands. The ocean, which surrounds Acadia on all sides, strongly influences the atmosphere of the park.

Travel along the Byway and stop to enjoy the tidepools along the beaches. Pockets in the rocky shore trap pools of water as the tide recedes, and remarkable plants and creatures grow and live in them, surviving the inhospitable world between tides. A little farther along, step into part of the woodlands where sunlight filters through the branches of spruce-fir, birch, aspen, and oak, leaving patches of light on your face and the sweet-smelling pine that crunches underfoot. Around another curve, a clear, shimmering freshwater lake appears. Filling a glacially carved valley, the solitude and peace the still water offers make the lakes in the interior of Acadia a place for reflection. At yet another place along the Byway, climb through the mountains and enjoy the stark beauty of the cliff faces and numerous plant species.

HIGHLIGHTS

While traveling this Byway, take your time. Because this route is on the coast and in a national park, you'll find no end to the brilliant views. Although the Byway runs just 40 miles, you can spend several days here.

Before you start out, pick up some hiking guides and other brochures and pamphlets at the visitor center, which is at the beginning of the Byway. If you're planning to hike, you'll want to know how difficult each of the hikes is so that you can plan according to your level of expertise. You'll also want to find out the cost of ferries if you plan to go out to the Cranberry Islands or go whale-watching.

- **Day 1:** Spend a day in the city of Bar Harbor, soaking in the relaxed atmosphere, eating at a fine or local-flavor charming restaurant, and exploring a few of the hundreds of specialty shops. Some of the items the shops offer are so unique and distinctive that you'll never see their like again. You can seek out plenty of nightlife: bars, clubs, concerts, and specialty movie theaters (one is Art Deco; one has couches and pizza). You may even be able to catch one of the two annual music festivals, part of the annual film festival, or an opening night at an art gallery.
- **Day 2:** Spend the day hiking around Dorr and Champlain Mountains and the Tarn. Explore off-road Acadia National Park on a mountain bike; take the 50+ miles of carriage roads that are safe, serene, gorgeous, and well maintained. You could even spend an overnighter in the park. There are plenty of places in Bar Harbor to pick up food and supplies if you need them.
- **Day 3:** Make sure to hit Thunder Hole (and its associated historical ranger station). Otter Cliffs and the adjoining Otter Point are simply remarkable. You may want to don a jacket as you sit on the rocks and have a picnic lunch. Hop a ferry out to the Cranberry Islands to explore or take a ferry to whale-watch. You can see many other kinds of wildlife while whale-watching: bald eagles, puffins, and peregrine falcons (endangered). While out near the water, you can ocean kayak or canoe, deep-sea fish, or take a windjammer cruise. All of this equipment may be rented, and plenty of guides are available.

THINGS TO SEE AND DO

Driving along the Acadia Byway will certainly keep your senses engaged, but if you yearn to get out of the car and stretch your legs, or if you'd like to make a mini-vacation out of your trip, check out these attractions along the route.

THE ABBE MUSEUM. *PO Box 286, Bar Harbor (04609). Phone 207/288-3519. www.abbemuseum.org.* Large collection of Native American artifacts. Open May-Oct. **$**

Maine

✣ *Acadia Byway*

◩ **ACADIA NATIONAL PARK.** *Bar Harbor (04609). Phone 207/288-3338. www.nps.gov/acad/.* At 40,000 acres, Acadia is small compared to other national parks; however, it is one of the most visited national parks in the United States and the only national park in the northeastern United States. A 27-mile-loop road connects the park's eastern sights on Mount Desert Island, and ferry services take travelers to some of the smaller islands. Visitors can explore 1,530-foot Cadillac Mountain, the highest point on the Atlantic Coast of the United States; watch waves crash against Thunder Hole, creating a thunderous boom; or swim in the ocean at various coastal beaches. A road to the summit of Cadillac provides views of Frenchman, Blue Hill, and Penobscot bays. Like all national parks, Acadia is a wildlife sanctuary. Fir, pine, spruce, many hardwoods, and hundreds of varieties of wildflowers thrive. Nature lovers will be delighted with the more than 120 miles of trails; 45 miles of carriage roads offer bicyclists scenic rides through Acadia. There is saltwater swimming at Sand Beach and freshwater swimming at Echo Lake. Snowmobiles are allowed in some areas, and cross-country skiing is available. Most facilities are open Memorial Day-Sept; however, portions of the park are open year-round, and the picnic grounds are open May-Oct; closed Jan 1, Thanksgiving, Dec 24-25. The park entrance fee (subject to change) is $2-$5; per vehicle $5-$10.

BAR HARBOR HISTORICAL SOCIETY MUSEUM. *4 Mount Desert St, Bar Harbor (04609). Phone 207/288-0000. www.barharborhistorical.org.* Collection of early photographs of hotels, summer cottages, and Green Mountain cog railroad; hotel registers from the early to late 1800s; maps, scrapbook of the 1947 fire. Open mid-June-Oct, Mon-Sat; closed holidays. **FREE**

BAR HARBOR WHALE WATCH COMPANY. *39 Cottage St, Bar Harbor (04609). Phone 207/288-2386; toll-free 800/WHALES-4. www.whalesrus.com.* This company offers variety of cruises aboard catamarans *Friendship V* or *Helen H* to view whales, seals, puffins, ospreys, and more. Also nature cruises and lobster and seal watching. Cruises vary in length and destination and depart from Bluenose Ferry Terminal. Open May-Oct, daily.

FERRY SERVICE TO YARMOUTH, NOVA SCOTIA. *121 Edens St, Bar Harbor (04609). Phone toll-free 888/249-7245.* Passenger and car carrier *Cat Ferry* makes three-hour trips. **$$$$**

LOBSTER HATCHERY. *1 West St, Bar Harbor (04609). Phone 207/288-2334.* Young lobsters hatched from eggs are allowed to grow to 1/2 inch in length and then are returned to the ocean to supplement the supply; guides narrate the process. Open mid-May-mid-Oct, Mon-Sat.

NATURAL HISTORY MUSEUM. *109 Eden St, Bar Harbor (04609). Phone 207/288-5015. www.coamuseum.org.* More than 50 exhibits depict animals in their natural settings; the most spectacular may be the 22-foot Minke whale skeleton. Interpretive programs; evening lectures in summer (Wed). Open June-Labor Day, Mon-Sat; rest of year, Fri-Sun; closed Thanksgiving-mid-Jan, last two weeks in Mar. **$**

OCEANARIUM-BAR HARBOR. *Rte 3, Bar Harbor (04609). Phone 207/288-5005. www.theoceanarium.com.* Features include a lobster hatchery, salt-marsh walks, and a viewing tower; also a lobster museum with hands-on exhibits. Open mid-May-mid-Oct, Mon-Sat. $$

PLACES TO STAY

If you choose to include an overnight stay in your trip along this All-American Road, Mobil Travel Guide recommends the following lodgings.

★ **ACADIA INN.** *98 Eden St, Bar Harbor (04609). Phone 207/288-3500; toll-free 800/638-3636. www.acadiainn.com.* 95 rooms, 3 story. Closed mid-Nov.-Mar. Complimentary continental breakfast. Check-out 11 am. TV; cable (premium). In-room modem link. Refrigerators available. Coin laundry. Restaurant nearby. Playground. Heated pool, whirlpool. Picnic tables. Meeting rooms, business services available. Gift shop. $$

★★ **CANTERBURY COTTAGE.** *12 Roberts Ave, Bar Harbor (04609). Phone 207/288-2112. www.canterburycottage.com.* 4 rooms, 2 story. No A/C. No room phones. Children over 10 years only. Complimentary breakfast. Check-out 11 am, check-in 2 pm. TV; VCR available. Built in 1900. Totally nonsmoking. $

★ **CROMWELL HARBOR MOTEL.** *359 Main St, Bar Harbor (04609). Phone 207/288-3201; toll-free 800/544-3201. www.cromwellharbor.com.* 25 rooms. Check-out 11 am. TV; cable (premium). $$

★★★ **HOLIDAY INN SUNSPREE RESORT.** *123 Eden St, Bar Harbor (04609). Phone 207/288-9723; toll-free 800/465-4329. www.holiday-inn.com.* This inn is located close to the Hancock County Airport and is 50 miles from Bangor International Airport. The restaurant specializes in serving local seafood with a view, and the Edenfield lounge serves cocktails until late evening. 221 rooms, 4 story. Closed Nov-Apr. Check-out noon. TV. Balconies. Refrigerators. Restaurant, bar. Room service. Supervised children's activities (July-Aug). Exercise equipment, sauna. Heated pool, poolside service. Putting green. Lighted tennis courts. Lawn games. On ocean; marina, dockage. Business services available. Gift shop. Whale-watching tours. $$

★★★ **MIRA MONTE INN & SUITES.** *69 Mt Desert St, Bar Harbor (04609). Phone 207/288-4263; toll-free 800/553-5109. www.miramonte.com.* This Victorian inn is located in the center of Bar Harbor. It has nicely appointed rooms and luxury suites. 16 rooms in 2 buildings, 2 suites, 2 story. Closed mid-Oct-Apr. Complimentary breakfast. Check-out 11 am, check-in 3 pm. TV. Fireplaces. Lawn games. Restored Victorian home (1864) on 2 1/2 acres; wrap-around porch, period furnishings. Totally nonsmoking. $$

★ **PARK ENTRANCE OCEANFRONT MOTEL.** *15 Ocean Dr, Bar Harbor (04609). Phone 207/288-9703.* 58 rooms, 6 kitchen units, 24 with A/C, 2 story. Closed Nov-Apr. Check-out 11 am. TV; cable (premium). Whirlpool. Lawn games. Mooring, dock; fishing pier. $

Maine

✻ *Acadia Byway*

PLACES TO EAT

A long day of driving is sure to make you hungry. At the end of your journey, take a table at one of the following restaurants.

★★ **124 COTTAGE STREET.** *124 Cottage St, Bar Harbor (04609). Phone 207/288-4383.* Continental menu. Specializes in fresh fish. Closed Nov-May. Reservations accepted. Dinner. Bar. Children's menu. Outdoor seating. In a restored turn-of-the-century cottage. $$

★ **FISHERMAN'S LANDING.** *35 West St, Bar Harbor (04609). Phone 207/288-4632.* Blackboard menu. Closed Oct-May. Lunch, dinner. Bar. Built over the water. Outdoor deck seating. Lobster tanks; diners select their own lobster. $
D

★★★ **GEORGE'S.** *7 Stephens Ln, Bar Harbor (04609). Phone 207/288-4505.* This restaurant has perfected its Mediterranean-inspired menu. Creative tastes and unique flavors appear throughout the dishes, and adventurous guests do not leave disappointed. Mediterranean menu. Closed Nov-late May. Dinner. Bar. Children's menu. In a restored mid-1800s home; near the ocean. Outdoor seating. Totally nonsmoking. $

★★ **MAGGIE'S CLASSIC SCALES.** *6 Summer St, Bar Harbor (04609). Phone 207/288-9007.* Specializes in fresh local seafood. Own desserts. Closed mid-Oct-late June. Dinner. Bar. Reservations accepted. Totally nonsmoking. $$

★ **MIGUEL'S MEXICAN.** *51 Rodick St, Bar Harbor (04609). Phone 207/288-5117.* Mexican menu. Mexican artifacts, tiled floors. Closed mid-Nov-Mar. Dinner. Bar. Children's menu. Outdoor seating. $$
D

★★★ **READING ROOM.** *Newport Dr, Bar Harbor (04609). Phone 207/288-3351.* Specializes in fresh local seafood. Own baking. Closed mid-Nov-Easter. Reservations accepted. Breakfast, dinner, Sun brunch. Bar. Children's menu. Pianist or harpist. Valet parking available. Panoramic view of harbor and docks. $$
D

The Historic National Road

✱ MARYLAND

Part of a multistate Byway; see also IL, IN, OH, PA, WV.

Quick Facts

LENGTH: 170 miles.

TIME TO ALLOW: 4.5 hours.

BEST TIME TO DRIVE: April through October. Many migratory birds return in the spring, and autumn paints the area in vibrant reds and oranges. The busiest season is from June to August, while November to March is considered Maryland's off-season. Despite the bare trees and chill in the air, you will still enjoy traveling the Byway during the less-crowded times.

BYWAY TRAVEL INFORMATION: Byway local Web site: www.marylandroads.com/exploremd/scenicbyways/scenicbyways.asp; Byway travel and tourism Web site: www.mdisfun.org.

SPECIAL CONSIDERATIONS: You may want to plan stops for gas and food, because this is a long Byway. You'll also find numerous historic sites and museums to visit, so you may wish to plan additional time to drive the Byway.

BICYCLE/PEDESTRIAN FACILITIES: The roadways on this Byway vary in width and traffic. However, a majority of the Byway roads have paved shoulders that allow plenty of room for bikers.

As the first federally funded road, the Historic National Road provided a gateway to the West for thousands of settlers who followed it from Baltimore through the Appalachians to Vandalia, Illinois. The road's history traces the evolution of transportation and commemorates the movement that ultimately stretched the nation's boundaries from the Atlantic to the Pacific.

It all began in 1806, when Congress authorized a road running west from Cumberland, Maryland. The proposed Historic National Road was the impetus for Maryland's General Assembly to create a turnpike, run by private interests, connecting Baltimore and Cumberland. Maryland's Baltimore to Cumberland section of the road was designated the Historic National Pike.

Many layers of urbanization have modified this historic route, but the diligent traveler still may follow the old Historic National Pike through the streets of Baltimore westward into the historic Maryland countryside. Today, with the construction of new roads, many historic towns and sites originally connected to the Historic National Pike lure modern travelers with rugged charm, including a host of antique shops, specialty shops, and unique restaurants. These elements make the National Historic Road a treat for everyone.

THE BYWAY STORY

The Historic National Road tells cultural, historical, natural, recreational, and scenic stories that make it a unique and treasured Byway.

Maryland

✷ *The Historic National Road*

Cultural

The culture along the Historic National Road is one of pioneering spirit. As the first federally funded road, this Byway originally blazed a trail for the emerging nation to follow. Maryland's Baltimore to Cumberland section of the Historic National Road was designated the Historic National Pike. Soon, hardy travelers began seeking faster routes west, leading to a system of canals and railroads. Towns and cities along the pike began to spring up to provide comforts for weary travelers heading west. Even in modern times, travelers along the Historic National Pike can find a ready smile and a warm handshake.

Modern travelers of the Historic National Pike will find communities proud of their vibrant historical heritage. With Interstate 70 bypassing many of the original Historic National Pike cities, they have developed into artistic communities with a passion for diversity. Coffeehouses, small restaurants, antique shops, and cafés welcome modern travelers of the Historic National Pike to share in central Maryland's pioneering spirit.

Historical

In the late 18th century, as the population of the United States began to grow, President Thomas Jefferson convinced the US Congress to undertake a massive investment in new territory to the west. In 1803, the Louisiana Purchase more than doubled the size of the United States. Almost immediately, Jefferson dispatched Lewis and Clark on their mission to explore the new territory. At the same time, closer to home, Jefferson encouraged the development of a transportation infrastructure that would connect the eastern seaboard with points farther inland.

The construction of the National Road westward from Cumberland was the first such investment by the federal government. The construction of an "eastern connection" from Baltimore to Cumberland started before construction on the National Road had begun. This early start had a practical purpose: connecting the burgeoning population of Baltimore with new markets to the west. Without a road, the region's prosperity would not be assured. In the 1830s, the federal government gave the road back to the state of Maryland.

Natural

From the shores of the Chesapeake Bay to the majestic Negro Mountain, the Historic National Road offers many natural wonders. Many state parks along the Byway offer quiet breaks in the long drive. As the Byway continues into western Maryland, it passes through many mountain peaks, which constantly hindered early travel west. Before the Byway continues into Pennsylvania, it journeys through the city of Cumberland, which is nestled in a small mountain valley. Here, mountains tower 1,000 feet around the city.

The most magnificent feature to note in the Byway is the Narrows, located northwest of Cumberland. The Narrows is an unusual geologic formation near Cumberland that provides a pass through the Allegheny Mountains. Wills Creek runs north and south through the Narrows, creating the narrow gorge through Wills Mountain. The National Road was rerouted through the Narrows in 1834 because the original grade that traversed Wills Mountain was too steep. It was easier to take the water-level route up Mechanic Street through the Narrows and beyond. A good six-horse hitch could make this grade relatively easily with a few stops to let the team rest. Today, however, it accommodates automobiles quite well.

Recreational

Without question, the Historic National Road has a stellar array of recreational activities. Many people come here expecting to spend a day relaxing but change their plans to stay longer because of the large number of

see page A13 for color map

outstanding activities. This Byway is known not only for its historical highlights but also for its recreational qualities.

Perhaps the most popular destination in all of Maryland is Baltimore's Inner Harbor, where you'll find outdoor performances, numerous eateries, the Baltimore National Aquarium and Marine Mammal Pavilion, the Maryland Science Center and Davis Planetarium, the Pier 6 Concert Pavilion, historic ships, Harborplace shops, and much more.

If you love outdoor activity, this Byway features fantastic biking, boating, hiking, and rock climbing. If you're a sportsman, you won't get bored on the Historic National Road. You can find numerous places to fish as well as hunt deer, turkey, grouse, squirrel, rabbits, quail, and waterfowl. Furthermore, this area features one of the only special hunting spots in the nation dedicated to disabled persons. If you like to view animals but not necessarily hunt them, you can also find excellent bird-watching areas.

Scenic

From the picturesque shores of the Chesapeake Bay to the towering mountains surrounding Cumberland, the Historic National Road delivers breathtaking scenery every step of the way. You will see early stone bridges, Pennsylvania-German back barns with limestone-faced gable ends, and the last toll-booth left on the Maryland part of the Historic National Road.

The Blue Ridge is a mountain chain with two ridges in Maryland (South Mountain to the west and Catoctin Mountain to the east). Views are quite beautiful approaching South Mountain, from the top of the mountain (Washington Monument State Park), and around Middletown. Washington Monument State Park on South Mountain contains a spectacular overlook located approximately 1 mile from the Byway, from which the surrounding Middletown Valley can be admired. The Appalachian Trail crosses by this landmark.

Leaving South Mountain, the Byway passes through historic and scenic Turner's Gap on its way into Middletown. You can stop off at an overlook here to admire the view into town.

THINGS TO SEE AND DO

Driving along the Historic National Road will certainly keep your senses engaged, but if you yearn to get out of the car and stretch your legs, or if you'd like to make a mini-vacation out of your trip, check out these attractions along the route.

ANTIETAM NATIONAL BATTLEFIELD. *11 miles S on MD 65, Hagerstown (21740). www.nps.gov/anti/.* On September 17, 1862, the bloodiest day in Civil War annals, more than 23,000 men were killed or wounded as Union forces blocked the first Confederate invasion of the North. Clara Barton, who founded the Red Cross 19 years later, tended the wounded at a field hospital on the battlefield. Approximately 350 iron tablets, monuments, and battlefield maps, located on 8 miles of paved avenues, describe the events of the battle. The Visitor Center houses a museum and offers information, literature, and a 26-minute orientation movie (shown on the hour). Visitor Center (open daily; closed Jan 1, Thanksgiving, Dec 25); battlefield (open daily); ranger-conducted walks, talks, and demonstrations (open Memorial Day-Labor Day, daily). **$**

THE AVENUE IN HAMPDEN. *36th St, Baltimore (21211).* Although the four blocks that make up the Avenue total only 1/2 mile, visitors will be amazed at all there is to see in this eclectic North Baltimore neighborhood. Novelty shops, vintage clothing stores, casual restaurants, and art galleries line Hampden's main drag, and the treasures that guests can find in these shops range from kitschy to sublime. **FREE**

Maryland

✽ *The Historic National Road*

◼ **B & O RAILROAD MUSEUM.** *901 W Pratt St, Baltimore (21223). Phone 410/752-2490. www.borail.org.* This museum, affiliated with the Smithsonian, celebrates the birthplace of railroading in America and depicts the industry's economic and cultural influences. Encompassing 40 acres, the museum's collection of locomotives is the oldest and most comprehensive in the country. Its exhibits are divided among three main buildings. In the Roundhouse, visitors can board and explore more than a dozen of the "iron horses," which include a rail post office car and the Tom Thumb train. The second floor of the Annex building has an impressive display of working miniature-scale trains. The Mount Clair Station, exhibiting the story of the B & O Railroad, was built in 1851 to replace the 1829 original, which was the first rail depot in the country. Outside, the museum features more trains, such as the Chessie, the largest steam locomotive. On certain weekends, visitors can take a train ride. Open daily; closed major holidays. $$

BABE RUTH BIRTHPLACE AND MUSEUM. *16 Emory St, Baltimore (21230). Phone 410/727-1539. www.baberuthmuseum.com.* Although Babe Ruth played for the New York Yankees, Baltimore calls him one of its native sons. The house where this legend was born has been transformed into a museum that showcases his life and career. Visitors can see rare family photographs as well as a complete record of his home runs. The museum also features exhibits about the Baltimore Colts and Orioles. Every February 6, the museum commemorates Babe Ruth's birthday by offering free admission to all visitors. Open daily 10 am-5 pm, until 4 pm Nov-Mar; closed Jan 1, Thanksgiving, Dec 25. $$

BALTIMORE MARITIME MUSEUM. *802 S Caroline St, Baltimore (21231). Phone 410/396-3453. www.baltimoremaritimemuseum.org.* This museum's featured ships include the USS *Torsk*, a World War II submarine; the Coast Guard cutter *Taney*; and the lightship *Chesapeake*. All the ships have been designated National Historic Landmarks. Open spring, summer, and fall, Sun-Thurs 10 am-5:30 pm, Fri-Sat until 6:30 pm; winter, Fri-Sun 10:30 am-5 pm. $$

BALTIMORE MUSEUM OF ART. *10 Art Museum Dr, Baltimore (21218). Phone 410/396-7100. www.artbma.org.* Located near Johns Hopkins University, this museum opened in 1923 and was designed by John Russell Pope, the architect of the National Gallery in Washington, DC. The museum has eight permanent exhibits featuring works from the periods of Impressionism to modern art. It boasts the second largest collection of works by Andy Warhol. However, its jewel is the Cone collection, which includes more than 3,000 pieces by artists such as Picasso, Van Gogh, Renoir, Cezanne, and Matisse. The Matisse collection is the largest in the western hemisphere. Visitors will also want to see the 3-acre sculpture garden, which contains art by Alexander Calder and Henry Moore. Open Wed-Fri 11 am-5 pm, Sat-Sun 11 am-6 pm; free admission first Thurs of each month; closed Mon, Tues, major holidays. $$

BALTIMORE MUSEUM OF INDUSTRY. *1415 Key Hwy, Inner Harbor South, Baltimore (21230). Phone 410/727-4808. www.thebmi.org.* This museum educates visitors about the vital role that industry and manufacturing played in Baltimore's economic and cultural development. Located in a renovated oyster cannery on the west side of the Inner Harbor, the museum opened in 1977. Its exhibits showcase such trades as printing, garment making, canning, and metalworking. You can learn about the invention of Noxema, the disposable bottle cap, and even the first umbrella. Or you can explore the SS *Baltimore*, the only operating coal-fired tugboat on the East Coast that is now a National Historic Landmark, or the *Mini-Mariner*, a restored 1937 working prototype of the World War II boat bomber. The museum also has **Theatre on the Harbor,**

which presents touring and in-house productions. Past shows have included "Gizmo's Invention Show" and "Right Place, Right Time, Wright Brothers." Open Mon-Sat; closed Thanksgiving, Dec 24-25. $$$

BALTIMORE STREETCAR MUSEUM. *1901 Falls Rd, Baltimore (21201). Phone 410/547-0264. www.baltimoremd.com/streetcar/.* This museum features 11 electric streetcars and two horse cars used in the city between 1859 and 1963. 1 1/4-mile rides (fee). Open June-Oct, Sat and Sun afternoons; rest of year, Sun afternoons only; also open Memorial Day, July 4, Labor Day. $$

BALTIMORE ZOO. *1 Druid Hill Park Lake Dr, Baltimore (21217). Phone 410/366-5466. www.baltimorezoo.org.* Located in Druid Hill Park, this third oldest zoo in the United States covers 180 acres and features more than 2,250 animals. Children will be intrigued by the scaly inhabitants of the reptile house. They can travel to another continent by visiting the giraffes and elephants in the African Safari exhibit, and also ride the carousel or try out the climbing wall. The zoo also hosts special events during Halloween and the Christmas season. Open daily; closed Thanksgiving, Dec 25. $$$$

BARBARA FRITCHIE HOUSE AND MUSEUM. *154 W Patrick St, Frederick (21701). Phone 301/698-0630.* Exhibits include quilts, clothing made by Fritchie, her rocker and Bible, the bed in which she died, and other items; ten-minute film; also a garden. Open Apr-Sept, Mon, Thurs-Sun; Oct-Nov, Sat-Sun. $$

BASILICA OF THE NATIONAL SHRINE OF THE ASSUMPTION. *408 N Charles St, Baltimore (21201). Phone 410/727-3565.* Now a co-cathedral, this was the first Roman Catholic cathedral in the United States. Bishop John Carroll, head of the diocese of Baltimore from its establishment in 1789, blessed the cornerstone in 1806. The church was dedicated in 1821 and designed by architect B. H. Latrobe. Tours (by appointment). Open daily.

BRUNSWICK RAILROAD MUSEUM. *40 W Potomac St, Brunswick (21703). Phone 301/834-7100.* Furnishings and clothing interpret life in a turn-of-the-century railroad town; large model train exhibit; gift shop. Special events are held on selected weekends. Open June-Sept, Thurs-Sun; Apr-May and Oct-late Dec, Sat and Sun; limited hours. $$

CHESAPEAKE AND OHIO CANAL NATIONAL HISTORICAL PARK. *PO Box 4, Sharpsburg (21782). Phone 301/739-4200. www.nps.gov/choh/.* The unfortunate demise of the Chesapeake and Ohio Canal Company, which operated the rail lines in this area, is now a blessing for hikers, canoeists, and bikers, who can find access to the towpath along the banks of the waterway. Remaining as one of the least altered of old American canals, the Chesapeake and Ohio is flanked by ample foliage throughout most of its 20,239 acres. Many points of interest can be seen along the waterway. Exhibits are offered in Cumberland, Georgetown, Hancock, and Williamsport and at a museum stands near the Great Falls of the Potomac. At the Great Falls are interpretive programs, including self-guided trails, picnic facilities, and a working lock. Mule-drawn canal boat rides are offered Apr-Oct at Georgetown and Great Falls (fee). Camping for hikers and bikers is available throughout the park. $

CITY OF BALTIMORE CONSERVATORY. *2600 Madison Ave, Baltimore (21217). Phone 410/396-0180.* This graceful building (circa 1885) houses a large variety of tropical plants. Special shows during Easter, Nov, and the Christmas season. Open Thurs-Sun. **FREE**

CLYBURN ARBORETUM. *4915 Greenspring Ave, Baltimore (21209). Phone 410/396-0180.* Marked nature trails, nature museum, ornithological room, and horticultural library in a restored mansion. Outdoor shade and formal gardens, plus an All-American Selection Garden and the Garden of the Senses. Open daily. **FREE**

Maryland

✹ The Historic National Road

EDGAR ALLAN POE HOUSE AND MUSEUM. *03 N Amity St, Baltimore (21223). Phone 410/396-7932. www.nps.gov/edal/.* The famed author and father of the macabre lived in this house from 1832 to 1835. The faint of heart should beware, as several psychics have reported ghostly presences here. Haunted or not, the house and museum scare up many Poe artifacts, such as period furniture, a desk and telescope owned by Poe, and Gustave Dore's illustrations of "The Raven." Around January 19, the museum hosts a birthday celebration that includes readings and theatrical performances of Poe's work. Open Apr-Dec. $

FELLS POINT. *812 S Ann St, Baltimore (21231). www.fellspoint.us.* A shipbuilding and maritime center, this neighborhood dates back to 1730, with approximately 350 original residential structures. Working tugboats and tankers can be observed from the docks.

FORT CUMBERLAND TRAIL. *Cumberland (21502).* This walking trail covers several city blocks downtown around the site of Fort Cumberland and includes boundary markers and narrative plaques.

FORT FREDERICK STATE PARK. *11100 Fort Frederick Rd, Big Pool (21711). Phone 301/842-2155.* Erected in 1756 during the French and Indian War, the fort is considered a fine example of a pre-Revolutionary stone fort. It overlooks the Chesapeake and Ohio Canal National Historical Park. Barracks, interior, and wall of fort restored; military reenactments throughout the year. Fishing, boating (rentals); nature and hiking trails, picnicking (shelter), playground, unimproved camping. Museum, orientation film, historical programs. Winter hours may vary.

FORT McHENRY NATIONAL MONUMENT AND HISTORIC SHRINE. *End of E Fort Ave, Baltimore (21230). Phone 410/962-4299. www.nps.gov/fomc/.* Fort McHenry boasts a stunning view of the harbor, authentic re-created structures, and a wealth of living history that will fascinate both history buffs and casual visitors. In addition to being the site of the battle that inspired Francis Scott Key to pen "The Star-Spangled Banner" in 1814, the fort was a defensive position during the Revolutionary War, a POW camp for Confederate prisoners during the Civil War, and an army hospital during World War I. The fort's exhibits showcase these exciting events. Park rangers are knowledgeable and helpful, and they encourage visitors to participate in the twice-daily flag changes. Summer weekends feature precision drill and music performed by volunteers in Revolutionary War uniforms. Open daily; closed Jan 1, Dec 25. $

GAMBRILL STATE PARK. *8602 Gambrill Park Rd, Frederick (21702). Phone 301/791-4767.* The park has 1,136 acres with two developed areas. Fishing; nature and hiking trails, picnicking, tent and trailer sites (standard fees). Tea room. Two overlooks.

GORDON-ROBERTS HOUSE. *218 Washington St, Cumberland (21502). Phone 301/777-8678.* Restored 18-room Victorian house (circa 1867) with nine period rooms; costumes; research room. Open June-Oct, Tues-Sun; rest of year, Tues-Sat. **$$**

GREEN RIDGE STATE FOREST. *28700 Headquarters Dr NE, Cumberland (21502). Phone 301/478-3124.* These 44,000 acres of forest land stretch across the mountains of western Maryland and occupy portions of Town Hill, Polish Mountain, and Green Ridge Mountain. Abundant wildlife. Fishing, boat launch, canoeing; hiking trails, camping, winter sports. The C & O Canal runs through here into the 3,118-foot Paw-Paw Tunnel.

GUNPOWDER FALLS STATE PARK. *2813 Jerusalem Rd, Kingsville (21087). Phone 410/592-2897.* Approximately 16,000 acres, located in the Gunpowder River Valley. The Hammerman Area, E on US 40, right onto Ebenezer Rd, 5 miles to the park entrance in Chase, is a developed day-use area. The parks offers a swimming beach, windsurfing beach, boating, a marina (Dundee Creek), picnicking, and a playground. Other areas offer hiking/biking trails, canoeing, and trout fishing.

HAGERSTOWN ROUNDHOUSE MUSEUM. *300 S Burhans Blvd, Hagerstown (21740). Phone 301/739-4665.* The museum houses photographic exhibits of the seven railroads of Hagerstown; historic railroad memorabilia, tools, and equipment; archives of maps, books, papers, and related items. Open Fri-Sun afternoons. **$**

★ **HARBORPLACE.** *200 E Pratt St, Baltimore (21202). Phone 410/332-4191.* This shopping center is the most recognizable symbol of Baltimore's downtown and harbor renaissance. With its architecture of glass and exposed pipes and beams, Harborplace serves as a model for other cities' revitalization plans. Developed by James W. Rouse, the shopping mecca opened in 1980 and boasts more than 130 stores and restaurants. Visitors who want to take a break can go outside and walk on the brick-paved promenade that runs along the water's edge. Harborplace also has a small outdoor amphitheater, where, in good weather, guests are treated to free performances by jugglers, musicians, singers, and military and concert bands. Open daily. **FREE**

HISTORICAL SOCIETY OF FREDERICK COUNTY MUSEUM. *24 E Church St, Frederick (21701). Phone 301/663-1188. www.hsfc.org/.* This house, built in the early 1800s, shows both Georgian and Federal details and features leaded side and fanlights, Doric columns inside, double porches in rear, and boxwood gardens. Portraits of early Frederick residents hang on the walls. Genealogy library (Tues-Sat). Open Mon-Sat; also Sun afternoons. **$**

JONATHAN HAGER HOUSE AND MUSEUM. *110 Key St, Hagerstown (21740). Phone 301/739-8393.* This 1739 stone house sits in a park setting and features authentic 18th-century furnishings. Open Apr-Dec, Tues-Sun. **$$**

LEXINGTON MARKET. *400 W Lexington St, Baltimore (21201). Phone 410/685-6169. www.lexingtonmarket.com.* This under-roof market is more than two centuries old. Covering two blocks, it has more than 130 stalls offering fresh vegetables, seafood, meats, baked goods, and prepared foods that will whet any appetite. Vendors outside the market sell clothing, jewelry, T-shirts, and other miscellaneous items. Throughout the year, the market hosts several events, such as the Chocolate Festival in October, which boasts free samples and a chocolate-eating contest. But the most anticipated event at the market is Lunch with the Elephants. Every March, Ringling Brothers and Barnum & Bailey Circus elephants parade up Eutaw Street accompanied by fanfare, live music, and clowns. When they finally reach the market, they are served "lunch," which consists of 1,100 oranges, 1,000 apples, 500 heads of lettuce, 700 bananas, 400 pears, and 500 carrots. Open Mon-Sat; closed holidays. **FREE**

Maryland

✿ *The Historic National Road*

MARINE MAMMAL PAVILION. *Pier 4, 501 E Pratt St, Baltimore (21202).* This unique structure features a 1,300-seat amphitheater surrounding a 1.2-million-gallon pool, which houses Atlantic bottlenose dolphins; underwater viewing areas enable you to observe the mammals from below the surface. Special video programs about dolphins and whales; educational arcade with computerized video screens and other participatory exhibits around the pavilion's upper deck. Visitor service area located in the atrium. A life-size replica of a humpback whale spans two levels of the atrium. The Discovery Room houses a collection of marine artifacts. The Resource Center is an aquatic learning center for school visitors; the library boasts an extensive collection of marine science material. Open daily.

✪ **MARYLAND SCIENCE CENTER & DAVIS PLANETARIUM.** *601 Light St, Baltimore (21230). Phone 410/685-5225. www.mdsci.org.* This interactive center proves that science is anything but boring. Located in the Inner Harbor, the three-story building contains hundreds of exhibits guaranteed to spark young (and older) minds. In the Chesapeake Bay exhibit, you can learn about the delicate ecosystem that exists beneath the water. Or you can explore the mysteries of the human body in BodyLink. The Kids Room, for guests age 8 and younger, gives children the chance to operate a fish camera or dress up like turtles. Don't miss the Hubble Space Telescope National Visitor Center, a 4,000-square-foot interactive space gallery, which has more than 20 hands-on activities and 120 high-resolution images that allow guests to see space through the Hubble's eye. If you can't get enough of outer space, visit the Davis Planetarium and the Crosby-Ramsey Memorial Observatory, both on site. The center's IMAX theater will thrill you with its five-stories-tall movie screen and 3-D capability. Open daily. **$$$**

MILLER HOUSE. *135 W Washington St, Hagerstown (21740). Phone 301/797-8782.* Washington County Historical Society Headquarters. Federal town house (circa 1820); three-story spiral staircase; period furnishings; garden; clock, doll, and Bell pottery collections; Chesapeake & Ohio Canal and Civil War exhibits; 19th-century country store display. Open Apr-Dec, Wed-Sat; closed holidays and the first two weeks of Dec. **$$**

MONOCACY NATIONAL BATTLEFIELD. *4801 Urbana Pike, Frederick (21701). Phone 301/662-3515. www.nps.gov/mono/.* On July 9, 1864, Union General Lew Wallace with 5,000 men delayed General Jubal Early and his 23,000 Confederate soldiers for 24 hours, during which General Grant was able to reinforce—and save—Washington, DC. Monuments from New Jersey, Vermont, Pennsylvania, and the Confederacy mark the area. **FREE**

✪ **NATIONAL AQUARIUM.** *501 E Pratt St, Baltimore (21202). Phone 410/576-3800. www.aqua.org.* This aquarium's glass-and-steel pyramid shape is as unusual and stunning as the more than 15,000 sea creatures it houses. Located in the Inner Harbor, the National Aquarium introduces guests to stingrays, sharks, puffins, seals, and even a giant Pacific octopus. Explore the danger and mystery of a living South American tropical rain forest, complete with poisonous frogs, exotic birds, piranha, and swinging tamirin monkeys, or delight in the underwater beauty of the replicated Atlantic coral reef. The Children's Cove, a touch pool, provides an interactive experience for kids. In the Marine Mammal Pavilion, a high-tech dolphin show entertains and teaches guests about these intelligent creatures. Visitors particularly enjoy watching trainers feed the animals. Daily feeding schedules are posted in the lobby. Open daily 9 am-7 pm, Fri until 10 pm; closed Thanksgiving, Dec 25. **$$$$**

ORIOLE PARK AT CAMDEN YARDS. *333 W Camden St, Baltimore (21201). Phone 410/685-9800. orioles.mlb.com.* The crack of the bat and the roar of the crowd signal that the Orioles are home. Opened in 1992 and located just blocks from the Inner Harbor, Camden Yards is considered by many to be the best baseball stadium in the United States. With its steel trusses, arched brick façade, and natural turf, the stadium's design is reminiscent of the great ballparks built in the early 1900s. It holds 48,876 fans and memorializes local legends Brooks Robinson, Earl Weaver, and Cal Ripken, Jr. The old B & O Warehouse sits behind right field and has long been a target for batters aiming for a home run. Guests can sit anywhere in the stadium and enjoy an unobstructed view of the game. Tours of the stadium are also available and allow you to sit in the dugout, see the press box, and explore the clubhouse. Open during the season (Mar-Sept); tours held mid-Feb-late Dec, daily except on days of afternoon home games.

PORT DISCOVERY. *35 Market Pl, Baltimore (21202). Phone 410/727-8120. www.portdiscovery.org.* Port Discovery is three floors and 80,000 square feet of pure imagination. Ranked the fourth best children's museum in the country by *Child Magazine*, the museum opened in 1998 in collaboration with Walt Disney Imagineering. Its exhibits are interactive, innovative, and educational. Kids will have a blast exploring the three-story urban tree house. In MPT Studioworks, they can become producers of their own television broadcasts. Sensation Station will overload their senses of sight, sound, and touch. Kids can even travel back to ancient Egypt and uncover the mystery of the pyramids and Pharaoh's tomb. The museum also operates the HiFlyer, a giant helium balloon that's anchored 450 feet above the Inner Harbor. The enclosed gondola holds 20-25 passengers and offers a spectacular view of the city. Open Memorial Day-Labor Day, daily; rest of year, Tues-Sun; closed Thanksgiving, Dec 25. $$$$

ROCKY GAP STATE PARK. *12500 Pleasant Valley Rd NE, Cumberland (21502). Phone 301/777-2139.* Mountain scenery around a 243-acre lake with three swimming beaches. Swimming, fishing, boating (electric motors only; rentals); nature and hiking trails, picnicking, cafe, improved camping (reservations accepted one year in advance), winter activities. Resort; 18-hole golf course. $

ROGER BROOKE TANEY HOME. *121 S Bentz St, Frederick (21701). Phone 301/663-8687.* The Chief Justice of the United States from 1835 to 1864, Taney was chosen by Andrew Jackson to succeed John Marshall. He swore in seven presidents, including Abraham Lincoln, and issued the famous Dred Scott Decision. He is buried in the cemetery of St. John's Catholic Church at E 3rd and East sts. Open Apr-Oct, weekends. $$

STAR-SPANGLED BANNER FLAG HOUSE AND WAR OF 1812 MUSEUM. *844 E Pratt St, Baltimore (21202). Phone 410/837-1793.* Open to the public for over 75 years, this museum was the home of Mary Pickersgill, sewer of the flag that Francis Scott Key eternalized in America's national anthem. Although the flag now hangs in the Smithsonian's National Museum of American History, you can tour the house to learn about its origins and Pickersgill's life. The house has an adjoining **War of 1812 museum,** which exhibits military and domestic artifacts and presents an award-winning video. Open Tues-Sat. $

USS *CONSTELLATION*. *Pier 1, 301 E Pratt St, Baltimore (21202). Phone 410/539-1797. www.constellation.org.* This retired sloop has a proud naval history that spans from the Civil War to World War II. Anchored at Pier 1 in the Inner Harbor, you can board the ship for a self-guided audio tour. Kids can participate in the Powder Monkey program, in which they learn what it was like to serve in President Lincoln's navy. In 1999, a restoration project returned the ship to its original Civil War appearance. Open daily; closed Jan 1, Thanksgiving, Dec 25. $$

Maryland

❋ *The Historic National Road*

WALTERS ART MUSEUM. *600 N Charles St, Baltimore (21201). Phone 410/547-9000. www.thewalters.org.* This museum's collection is so comprehensive that it spans 55 centuries and traces the history of the world from ancient times to the present day. Father and son William and Henry Walters gifted the museum and its numerous holdings to Baltimore, although the New York Metropolitan Museum of Art also coveted it. Located in the historic neighborhood of Mount Vernon and containing more than 30,000 pieces of art, the collection, which is housed in three buildings, is renowned for its French paintings and Renaissance and Asian art. The museum also exhibits Faberge eggs, paintings by the Old Masters, such as Raphael and El Greco, and an impressive assortment of ivories and Art Deco jewelry. Check out the unique Roman sarcophagus. Open Tues-Sun; closed major holidays. **$$**

WASHINGTON COUNTY MUSEUM OF FINE ARTS. *91 Key St, Hagerstown (21740). Phone 301/739-5727. www.washcomuseum.org.* The museum offers paintings, sculpture, changing exhibits; concerts, lectures. Open Tues-Sun; closed holidays. **FREE**

WESTERN MARYLAND SCENIC RAILROAD. *13 Canal St, Cumberland (21502). Phone 301/759-4400; toll-free 800/TRAIN-50. www.wmsr.com.* This excursion train makes a scenic trip 17 miles to Frostburg and back. Open May-Oct, Tues-Sun; Nov-mid-Dec, weekends. **$$$$**

PLACES TO STAY

If you choose to include an overnight stay in your trip along this All-American Road, Mobil Travel Guide recommends the following lodgings.

★★ **QUALITY INN & SUITES.** *793 W Bel Air Ave, Aberdeen (24382). Phone 410/272-6000. www.qualityinn.com.* 124 rooms, 2 story. Complimentary continental breakfast. Check-out noon. TV; cable (premium). VCR available. Pool; wading pool. Restaurant adjacent. Coin laundry. Meeting rooms. Business services available. ¢

★★ **DAYS INN INNER HARBOR HOTEL.** *100 Hopkins Pl, Baltimore (21201). Phone 410/576-1000; toll-free 800/329-7465. www.daysinn.com.* 250 rooms, 9 story. Check-out 11 am. TV; cable (premium). In-room modem link. Some refrigerators; microwaves available. Valet service. Restaurant, bar. Room service. Health club privileges. Pool, poolside service, lifeguard. Meeting rooms, business center. Concierge. **$**

★★★ **RENAISSANCE HARBORPLACE HOTEL.** *202 E Pratt St, Baltimore (21202). Phone 410/547-1200; toll-free 800/535-1201. www.renaissance.com.* Located on the waterfront at Baltimore's scenic Inner Harbor and amidst all of downtown's delights, this hotel offers guests scenic views, friendly service, and elegantly appointed guest rooms. Nearby attractions include the Gallery, Convention Center, and World Trade Center. 657 rooms, 12 story. Check-out noon. Check-in. TV; cable (premium), VCR available. In-room modem link. Restaurant, bar; entertainment. Room service 24 hours. Health club privileges. Exercise equipment, sauna. Whirlpool, poolside service. Garage, valet parking available. Business center. Concierge. Luxury level. **$$**

★★ **BEST WESTERN BRADDOCK MOTOR INN.** *1268 National Hwy, Cumberland (21502). Phone 301/729-3300; toll-free 800/296-6006. www.bestwestern.com.* 107 rooms, 3 story. Check-out 11 am, check-in 2 pm. TV; cable (premium), VCR available (movies). In-room modem link. Restaurant, bar; closed Sun. Room service. Exercise equipment, sauna. Game room. Indoor pool, whirlpool, poolside service. Airport transportation. **$**

ALL-AMERICAN ROADS

★★★ **INN AT WALNUT BOTTOM.** *120 Greene St, Cumberland (21502). Phone 301/777-0003; toll-free 800/286-9718. www.iwbinfo.com.* At this elegant retreat, guests are offered their choice of two equally charming accommodations. The Georgian-style architecture of the Cowden House welcomes guests with a formal doorway and chimneys at each end, while the Queen Anne-style Dent House delights guests with a distinctly round turret on the corner. Either place is guaranteed to enchant guests with the history behind it, the charmingly appointed guest rooms, and wonderful antiques. 14 rooms, 4 share bath, 2 suites, 2-3 story. Complimentary full breakfast. Check-out 11 am, check-in 3 pm. TV; cable (premium). Restaurant. Health club privileges. Two buildings (1820, 1890). Totally nonsmoking. ¢

★ **SUPER 8.** *1301 National Hwy, Cumberland (21502). Phone 301/729-6265; toll-free 800/800-8000. www.super8.com.* 63 rooms, 3 story. Complimentary continental breakfast. Check-out 11 am. TV. ¢

★★ **ROCKY GAP LODGE & GOLF RESORT.** *16701 Lakeview Rd NE, Flintstone (21530). Phone 301/784-8400; toll-free 800/724-0828.* 220 rooms, 6 story. Check-out 11 am, check-in 3 pm. TV; cable (premium). Restaurant, bar. Room service. Children's activity center. In-house fitness room. Indoor pool, whirlpool, poolside service. Outdoor tennis. Boats, fishing, hiking. Business center. $$

★★★ **TURNING POINT INN.** *3406 Urbana Pike, Frederick (21704). Phone 301/831-8232. www.turningpointinn.com.* An elegant Edwardian estate built in 1910 and lovingly renovated with modern amenities. 5 rooms, 2 with shower only, 2 kitchen cottages, 3 story. Complimentary full breakfast; afternoon refreshments. Check-out 11 am, check-in 3 pm. TV; cable (premium). Dining room. Business services. View of Sugarloaf Mountain and adjacent farmland. ¢

★★ **PLAZA HOTEL.** *1718 Underpass Way, Hagerstown (21740). Phone 301/797-2500; toll-free 800/826-4534.* 163 units, 6 story. Check-out noon. TV; cable (premium), VCR available. In-room modem link. Restaurant, bar. Room service. Exercise equipment, sauna. Indoor pool, whirlpool. Free airport transportation. ¢

★★ **VENICE INN.** *431 Dual Hwy, Hagerstown (21740). Phone 301/733-0830.* 220 rooms, 2-5 story. Pet accepted, some restrictions. Check-out noon. TV; cable (premium), VCR (movies). Refrigerators, microwaves available. Valet services. Restaurant, bar; entertainment Tues-Sat. Room service. Exercise equipment. Game room. Pool. Golf adjacent. Beauty shop. Airport transportation. Meeting rooms. ¢

PLACES TO EAT

A long day of driving is sure to make you hungry. At the end of your journey, take a table at one of the following restaurants.

★★★ **ATLANTIC.** *2400 Boston St, Baltimore (21224). Phone 410/675-4565. www.atlanticrestaurant.com.* Seafood menu. Closed major holidays. Lunch, dinner, Sun brunch. Entertainment. Children's menu. An adventurous mix of Asian and American seafood in a modern room. $$

★ **BERTHA'S.** *734 S Broadway, Baltimore (21231). Phone 410/327-5795.* Specializes in mussels, seafood. Closed major holidays. Reservations required for Scottish afternoon tea (Mon-Sat). Lunch, dinner, Sun brunch. Bar; entertainment. Eclectic décor. Historic 19th-century building. $$$

Maryland

❋ *The Historic National Road*

★★★ **BLACK OLIVE.** *814 S Bond St, Baltimore (21231). Phone 410/276-7141.* Greek, Middle Eastern menu. Closed major holidays. Dinner. Entertainment. Casual attire. $$$
[D]

★★★★ **CHARLESTON.** *1000 Lancaster St, Baltimore (21202). Phone 410/332-7373. www.charlestonrestaurant.com.* Chef-owner Cindy Wolf's stunning regional American restaurant offers one of the most exciting and luxurious dining experiences to be had in Baltimore. This upscale bistro-style room is warmed by an amber glow, and the food is even better. Sautéed heads-on gulf shrimp with andouille sausage and Tasso ham with creamy stone-milled grits, a signature dish, is a perfect example of the robust, home-style low-country cooking served here. American menu. Menu changes daily. Closed Sun, holidays. Dinner. Bar. Entertainment. Outdoor seating. $$$

★★ **VELLEGGIA'S.** *829 E Pratt St, Baltimore (21202). Phone 410/685-2620.* Italian menu. Closed Dec 24-25. Lunch, dinner. Bar. Children's menu. Casual attire. $$
[D]

★★ **BROWN PELICAN.** *5 E Church St, Frederick (21701). Phone 301/695-5833.* American menu. Closed Jan 1, Super Bowl Sun, Thanksgiving, Dec 25. Lunch (Mon-Fri), dinner. Bar. Reservations required Fri, Sat. Unique décor and home-style food in historic downtown Frederick, in the basement of an antebellum bank. $
[D]

★★ **TAURASO'S.** *6 East St, Frederick (21701). Phone 301/663-6600.* Italian, American menu. Closed Dec 25. Reservations accepted. Lunch, dinner. Bar. Specializes in fresh fish, veal, steak. Outdoor seating. In a restored factory building (late 1800s). $$
[D]

★ **JUNCTION 808.** *808 Noland Dr, Hagerstown (21740). Phone 301/791-3639.* American menu. Closed Sun. Breakfast, lunch, dinner. Children's menu. Railroad-themed diner with model trains circling the ceiling. Totally nonsmoking. $
[SC]

★★ **RED HORSE STEAK HOUSE.** *1800 Dual Hwy, Hagerstown (21740). Phone 301/733-3788.* Seafood, steak menu. Closed major holidays. Dinner. Bar. Children's menu. $
[D]

★★ **RICHARDSON'S.** *710 Dual Hwy, Hagerstown (21740). 301/733-3660.* Seafood menu. Closed Dec 24 evening, Dec 25. Buffet; breakfast, lunch, dinner. Bar. Children's menu. $
[D]

North Shore Scenic Drive
❋ MINNESOTA

Quick Facts

LENGTH: 154 miles.

TIME TO ALLOW: 1 day.

BEST TIME TO DRIVE: Late spring through late fall.

BYWAY TRAVEL INFORMATION: Minnesota Office of Tourism: 612/296-5027; Grand Portage Traveler Information Center: 218/475-2592; Byway local Web site: www.superiorbyways.org; Byway travel and tourism Web sites: www.northshorescenicdrive.com, www.lakecnty.com.

SPECIAL CONSIDERATIONS: The weather along the shore can be quite cool at times, so a jacket is recommended even in summer. Each town along the Byway offers plenty of visitor services, including gasoline and lodging.

RESTRICTIONS: The North Shore Scenic Drive can be traveled year-round. At times in winter, snowfall is heavy. However, because homes and businesses exist along the route, the plowing of this road is a priority.

BICYCLE/PEDESTRIAN FACILITIES: The North Shore Scenic Drive has sidewalks and 6- or 8-foot shoulders in places along the route that provide safe biking and pedestrian opportunities. Most pedestrian traffic concentrates around the various state parks. Trails and pedestrian warning signs and crossings are in place. Be aware that this route is a major transport route to and from the Canadian border, so large semi trucks and other similar vehicles are frequently seen along the Byway.

The North Shore of Lake Superior, the world's largest freshwater lake, is 154 miles of scenic beauty and natural wonders. It has what no other place in the Midwest can offer—an inland sea, a mountain backdrop, an unspoiled wilderness, and a unique feeling all its own.

The North Shore Scenic Drive runs from Duluth to the Canadian border. The drive along the lakeshore is rich with the history of Native Americans, French and British explorers, lumbering, and iron-ore mining. On one side of the highway, Superior National Forest, one of the great wilderness areas of the United States, carpets the hills of the Sawtooth Mountains with balsams, birch, and pine. On the other side, Lake Superior offers spectacular views from the rocky shore. The region offers unlimited opportunities to get out and enjoy the outdoors. Each of the eight state parks has beautiful trails, and the 200-mile Superior Hiking Trail provides the chance to experience this magnificent landscape firsthand. For those who want to get out on the lake, there are charter fishing, sailing, kayaking, and excursion boats.

The North Shore also has a rich history deeply rooted in its plentiful natural resources. The Grand Portage National Monument features a reconstructed North West Company fur-trading post. Grand Marais is a quaint harbor town that is the entrance to the Gunflint Trail, a paved trail leading inland to the Boundary Waters Canoe Area Wilderness. Giant ore boats pull up to the docks at Two Harbors, and the much smaller, 100-year-old tugboat the *Edna G.* is displayed here. Small museums in Two Harbors and Tofte, as well as interpretive programs at the state parks, tell the story of this area.

Minnesota

❋ *North Shore Scenic Drive*

Whether you are looking for a wilderness expedition or the comforts of a modern lodge, the lofty pines of the Superior National Forest and crashing waves of Lake Superior seem to have a magic that whispers, "Come back."

THE BYWAY STORY

The North Shore Scenic Drive tells historical, natural, recreational, and scenic stories that make it a unique and treasured Byway.

Historical

The North Shore includes the rich and colorful heritage of settlers who were attracted to the area's bounty of natural resources. Many examples of this heritage can be found along the route, from the Voyageur era at Grand Portage National Monument to more recent times at the Split Rock Lighthouse State Historic Monument or the *Edna G.* Steam Tug Boat National Monument in Two Harbors. A host of interpretive resources and festivals keep this heritage alive, allowing you to experience the story of the North Shore.

It is believed that the first people to settle the North Shore region arrived about 10,000 years ago. These Native Americans entered the region during the final retreat of the Wisconsin glaciation. Many waves of Native American peoples inhabited the North Shore prior to European contact.

The first Europeans, French explorers, and fur traders reached Lake Superior country around AD 1620. By 1780, the Europeans had established fur-trading posts at the mouth of the St. Louis River and at Grand Portage. During the fur trading days, Grand Portage became an important gateway into the interior of North America for exploration, trade, and commerce. The trading post came alive for a short time each summer during a celebration called the Rendezvous, when voyageurs and traders from the western trading posts met their counterparts from Montreal to exchange furs and trade goods. Grand Portage is now a national monument and an Indian reservation. At this national monument, some of the original structures of the fur-trading days have been reconstructed.

In 1854, the Ojibwe signed the Treaty of La Pointe, which opened up northeastern Minnesota for mineral exploration and settlement. The late 1800s saw a rise in commercial fishing along the North Shore. Some of the small towns along the North Shore, such as Grand Marais and Little Marais, were first settled during this period. Many of the small towns still have fish smokehouses, thus keeping the fishing heritage alive. The North Shore Commercial Fishing Museum in Tofte interprets this period.

Lumber barons moved into the region between 1890 and 1910, and millions of feet of red and white pine were cut from the hills along the North Shore. Temporary railroads transported the logs to the shore, where they were shipped to sawmills in Duluth, Minnesota, and Superior, Bayfield, and Ashland, Wisconsin. Today, many of those old railroad grades are still visible, and some of the trails still follow these grades.

Miners digging for high-grade ore from the Iron Ranges in northeastern Minnesota established shipping ports like Two Harbors in 1884. With the rise of taconite in the 1950s, they developed shipping ports at Silver Bay and Taconite Harbors along Superior's Shores. These harbors are still in use, and visitors driving the route may see large 1,000-foot-long ore carriers being loaded or resting close to shore. The shipping history and Lake Superior's unpredictable storms have left the lake bottom dotted with shipwrecks, which now provide popular scuba diving destinations.

With the completion of the North Shore highway in 1924, tourism became an important industry along the shore. However, even earlier (in the 1910s), Historic Split Rock Lighthouse attracted tourists who arrived by sailboat. Split Rock Lighthouse is still the best-known North Shore landmark. Visitors who explore

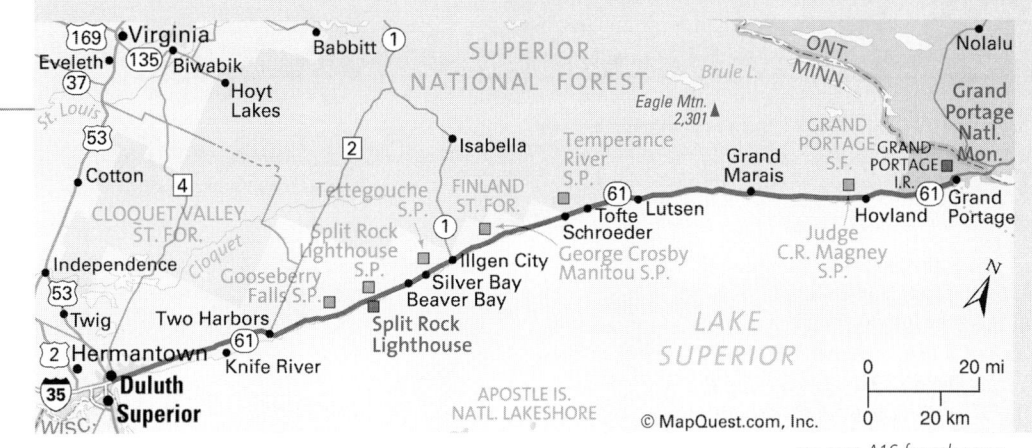

see page A16 for color map

the North Shore today will come to know not only this landmark, but many others that point to past times in this area of Minnesota.

Natural

The North Shore Scenic Drive allows you to experience a number of unique natural and geological features. The Byway follows the shoreline of the world's largest freshwater lake, Lake Superior, which contains 10 percent of the world's fresh-water supply. This Byway is a marvelous road to travel, never running too far from the lakeside and at times opening out onto splendid views down the bluffs and over the blue water. This gives visitors a chance to experience a landscape that has seen little alteration from its original state. During the winter, the many parks and hundreds of miles of groomed trails draw outdoor enthusiasts for cross-country skiing, snowshoeing, and snowmobiling. Lutsen Mountain is the largest and highest downhill ski area in the Midwest. During the fall color season, the shore displays bright red sugar maples and warm gold birches and aspens. The vibrant colors attract many travelers to the area to tour the shore and some of the back roads.

The North Shore's spectacular topography originated a billion years ago, when molten basalt erupted from the mid-continental rift. The Sawtooth Mountains, which frame the North Shore, are remnants of ancient volcanoes. The glaciers that descended from Canada 25,000 years ago scoured the volcanic rock into its current configuration. Cascading rivers coming down from the highlands into Lake Superior continue to reshape the landscape today. Northeastern Minnesota is the only part of the US where the expansive northern boreal forests dip into the lower 48 states. The Lake Superior Highlands have been identified to be of great importance for biodiversity protection by the Minnesota Natural Heritage Program and the Nature Conservancy. This landscape contains significant tracts of old-growth northern hardwood and upland northern white cedar forest.

The natural environment along the corridor supports a number of wildlife species. Wildlife that may be observed from the road or at the state parks adjacent to the road include beavers, otters, timberwolves, white-tailed deer, coyotes, red foxes, black bears, and moose. Federally listed threatened species of bald eagle, gray wolf, and peregrine falcon also have populations here. Northeastern Minnesota is recognized as one of the better areas in the nation for viewing rare birds. Diversity of habitat, geography, and proximity to Lake Superior combine to attract a variety of bird life that draws bird-watchers from across the nation and around the world. In the fall, hawks migrating along the shore of Lake Superior number in the tens of thousands. Winter is an excellent time to see northern owls, woodpeckers, finches, and unusual water birds.

Besides the state parks, a number of scientific and natural areas have been set aside along the route. These sites were selected because they contain excellent examples of the area's geologic history or harbor unique plant communities. Due to the unique geography of the landscape and climate changes during the ice ages, remnant species of arctic plants can be found along the shore. Examples of rare alpine plants that can be found include butterwort, northern eyebright, alpine bistort, small false asphodel, and moonwort.

113

Minnesota

❋ *North Shore Scenic Drive*

Recreational

Imagine yourself nestled next to a fireplace in a lodge after a long day of skiing or drying out next to a campfire from an afternoon of kayaking on a Minnesota river. The North Shore is one of the primary destinations for recreational activities in the Midwest, as well as for recreational driving, with well-developed facilities for outdoor activities that include camping, hiking, biking, skiing, snowmobiling, fishing, and canoeing.

The North Shore Scenic Drive is home to one of the greatest trail systems in the nation. The Superior Hiking Trail stretches 200 miles from Two Harbors to the Canadian border, connecting the eight state parks and giving travelers the opportunity to enjoy the natural beauty and vistas from the highlands and the cliffs. The trail system is well signed and offers everything from day hikes to multiple-week treks through a rugged wilderness setting. The trail is designated as a National Recreation Trail by the US Forest Service. A shuttle service offers transportation between trail heads. The Lake Superior Water Trail enables visitors to travel the coastline of Lake Superior by kayak. The trail uses public land for designated rest areas and will eventually be part of the Lake Superior Water Trail encircling all of Lake Superior. The Gitchi-Gami Trail is planned to accommodate bicyclists, pedestrians, and inline skaters following the right of way of the North Shore Scenic Drive.

When you're ready for a break from outdoor excitement, try touring some of the classic historical sites in the area. The Minnesota Historical Society takes care of the Split Rock Lighthouse site and provides interpretive programs. The Lake County Historical Museum, which is housed in the old Duluth & Iron Range Railway Depot, contains excellent exhibits on the region's history. In Two Harbors, you can tour an operating lighthouse and the *Edna G.*, which was the last steam tug to work the Great Lakes. So pack up your sled or your river raft and try them out in northeastern Minnesota. Be sure to bring your camera, too, because there are memorable sights to see!

Scenic

One of the main draws of the North Shore is its reputation as one of the most scenic drives in the US. The route offers splendid vistas of Lake Superior and its rugged shoreline, as well as views of the expansive North Woods. The road crosses gorges carved out by cascading rivers, offering views of waterfalls and adding diversity to the landscape. The attraction of the falls at Gooseberry State Park make this the most visited state park in Minnesota.

Different seasons and changes in weather continually alter the landscape's appearance, keeping the route fresh and interesting. During the fall, the corridor displays bright-red sugar maples and warm gold birches and aspens. The vibrant colors attract many day and weekend travelers to the North Shore. After the leaves have fallen and the ground is snow covered, new views of the lake open up, with opportunities to spy wildlife like deer, moose, and wolves that use the frozen lakeshore as a way to travel. Spring ice break-up offers another fascinating scene as glimmering mountains of ice are driven up the shore. In summer, the lake, with an average water temperature of 40 degrees, offers a welcome breeze to cool down the summer heat.

ALL-AMERICAN ROADS

A few charming towns dot the shoreline. Most started out as small fishing and harbor towns, shipping ore and timber. These towns still have a distinct sense of connection with the lake. For many travelers, the quaint town of Grand Marais is as far as they will go; however, the scenery becomes even more spectacular as you continue driving north toward the Canadian border. For long stretches, there is nothing alongside the road but trees, cliffs, beaches, and the whitecap-crested lake. The Byway ends at Grand Portage. Here, a national monument marks the beginning of a historic 9-mile portage trod by Indians and Voyageurs. A few miles farther at Grand Portage State Park, you can view the High Falls. At 120 feet, these are the highest waterfalls in Minnesota. The falls' magnificence is a fitting end to a trip up the North Shore.

HIGHLIGHTS

The North Shore Scenic Drive is comprised of the northern 154 miles of Minnesota Trunk Highway 61, from Duluth to Two Harbors all the way up to Grand Portage near the US/Canadian border.

- Begin your experience on the North Shore Scenic Drive in **Canal Park** in Duluth. Follow Canal Park Drive over Interstate 35 to Superior Street.
- Take a right on Superior Street and follow this road through a portion of historic **downtown Duluth** and past the refurbished **Fitger's Brewery Complex,** with its many fine shops and restaurants.
- To continue along the Byway, take a right onto London Road. This intersection is at 10th Avenue East and Superior Street. Follow London Road for the next 5.4 miles, driving past **Leif Erikson Park,** which contains the **Rose Garden,** a popular attraction for visitors.
- To continue on the route, follow the signs for the North Shore Scenic Drive. The route proceeds along the lake, passing through small settlements and stunning lake vistas. There are no fewer than six rivers that cross under the Byway during this 19-mile segment to Two Harbors.
- Connect with the Byway loop in downtown **Two Harbors** by turning right onto Highway 61 just west of town. Follow Highway 61 to 6th Street (Waterfront Drive), where you take a right and pick up the Byway once again.
- Follow 6th Street to South Avenue, where you take a left. Prior to taking a left, be sure to stop at the **3M Museum.** As you drive down South Avenue, you begin to see the massive ore docks that extend from the waterfront.
- Continue on the route by taking a left onto First Street (Park Road) and following it to Highway 61. First Street takes you past hiking trails that line the shoreline and the peaceful setting of **Burlington Bay,** the second of the two harbors that give the community its name.
- Taking a right on Highway 61 and continuing on that route will lead you along the remainder of the North Shore Scenic Drive, which ends approximately 122 miles later at the Canadian border.

THINGS TO SEE AND DO

Driving along the North Shore Scenic Drive will certainly keep your senses engaged, but if you yearn to get out of the car and stretch your legs, or if you'd like to make a mini-vacation out of your trip, check out these attractions along the route.

AERIAL LIFT BRIDGE. *525 Lake Ave S, Duluth (55802). Phone 218/722-3119.* 138 feet high, 336 feet long, 900 tons in weight. The bridge connects the mainland with Minnesota Point, rising 138 feet in less than a minute to let ships through. **FREE**

DEPOT MUSEUM. *520 South Ave, Two Harbors. Phone 218/834-4898.* Historic depot (1907) highlights the geological history and the discovery and mining of iron ore. A mallet locomotive (1941) and the world's most powerful steam engine

Minnesota

❋ North Shore Scenic Drive

are on display. Open May, weekends; Memorial Day-Oct, daily.

DEPOT SQUARE. *Duluth.* Reproduction of a 1910 Duluth street scene with an ice cream parlor, storefronts, gift shops, and trolley rides.

DULUTH LAKEWALK. *Duluth. Phone toll-free 800/4-DULUTH.* The Duluth Lakewalk stretches for 4.2 miles along Lake Superior. An entrance point is just feet from the beginning of the North Shore Scenic Drive. The Lakewalk features a boardwalk and an adjacent trail for bikers, runners, and in-line skaters. Never more than a few feet from Lake Superior, the Lakewalk offers excellent views of the harbor. **FREE**

THE *EDNA G.* *Waterfront Dr, Two Harbors. Phone 218/834-4898.* The *Edna G.* served Two Harbors from 1896 to 1981. It was designated a National Historic Site in 1974, as the only steam-powered tug still operating on the Great Lakes. Now retired, the *Edna G.* features seasonal tours where visitors can see her beautiful interior décor of wood paneling and brass fittings. Visitors get a look at the captain's quarters, the engine room, the crew's quarters, the galley, and the pilot house.

FITGER'S BREWERY COMPLEX. *600 E Superior St, Duluth. Phone 218/722-8826; toll-free 888/FITGERS. www.fitgers.com.* Historic renovated brewery transformed into more than 25 specialty shops and restaurants on the shore of Lake Superior. Summer courtyard activities. Open daily; closed holidays. **FREE**

GLENSHEEN. *3300 London Rd, Duluth. Phone 218/726-8910.* Circa 1905-1908. A historic 22-acre Great Lake estate on the western shore of Lake Superior; owned by the University of Minnesota. Tours. Grounds open daily. Mansion open May-Oct, daily; rest of year, weekends; closed holidays. **$$**

GOOSEBERRY FALLS STATE PARK. *3206 Hwy 61, Two Harbors (55616). Phone 218/834-3855.* Known as the gateway to the North Shore Scenic Drive, Gooseberry Falls State Park entices visitors to stop and enjoy the area before continuing on the rest of the drive. The Gooseberry River plummets down a wall of rock, creating the scenic falls that make the area so popular. Learn more about the park's history and nature at the Joseph N. Alexander Visitor Center or explore it yourself on some of the hiking trails that are provided. 1,662 acres. Fishing, hiking, cross-country skiing, snowmobiling, picnicking, camping (dump station). State park vehicle permit required.

GRAND PORTAGE NATIONAL MONUMENT. *315 S Broadway, Grand Portage (55604). Phone 218/387-2788. www.nps.gov/grpo/.* Located on the magnificent shore and boreal forest of Lake Superior, Grand Portage National Monument preserves a vital headquarters of 18th-, 19th-, and 20th-century fur trade activity and Ojibwe heritage. The monument is enclosed within Grand Portage Indian Reservation, for centuries home to Ojibwe Indian families. Within a reconstructed palisade wall, the great hall and kitchen complex have been rebuilt. Nearby, a canoe warehouse houses the vessels, crafted from birch, cedar, and spruce raw materials, essential for travel along east-west fur trade routes. The 8 1/2-mile "Great Carrying Place," or Grand Portage, connects the summer headquarters compound of the North West Company to an unrestored Fort Charlotte located across the Pigeon River from Canada. This centuries-old Grand Portage became a major gateway into the interior of North America for exploration, trade, and commerce, linking Lake Superior with a westward system of lakes and rivers. During the late 18th century, Grand Portage served as the inland headquarters for the North West Fur Company and was the location for a summer rendezvous involving Indian families, voyageurs, clerks, wintering partners, and agents. Primitive camping at Fort Charlotte (accessible only by hiking the Grand Portage or by canoe). Buildings and grounds open mid-May-mid-Oct, daily. Trail open all year. $$

GUNFLINT TRAIL. *Grand Marais. Phone toll-free 800/338-6932. www.gunflint-trail.com.* Penetrates into an area of hundreds of lakes where camping, picnicking, fishing, and canoeing are available. Starting at the northwest edge of town, the road goes north and west 58 miles to Saganaga Lake on the Canadian border.

★ ISLE ROYALE NATIONAL PARK. *Grand Portage. Contact the Superintendent, 800 E Lakeshore Dr, Houghton, MI (49931). Phone 906/482-0984. www.nps.gov/isro/.* This unique wilderness area, covering 571,790 acres, is the largest island in Lake Superior, 15 miles from Canada (the nearest mainland), 18 miles from Minnesota, and 45 miles from Michigan. There are no roads, and no automobiles are allowed. The main island, 45 miles long and 8 1/2 miles across at its widest point, is surrounded by more than 400 smaller islands. Moose, wolves, foxes, and beavers are the dominant mammals. More than 200 species of birds have been observed, including loons, bald eagles, and ospreys. More than 165 miles of foot trails lead to beautiful inland lakes, more than 20 of which have game fish, including pike, perch, walleye, and, in a few, whitefish cisco. There are trout in many streams and lakes. Fishing is under National Park Service and Michigan regulations. Isle Royale can be reached by boat from Grand Portage in Minnesota. The park is open approximately May-Oct.

LAKE SUPERIOR MARITIME VISITORS CENTER. *600 Lake Ave S, Duluth (55802). Phone 218/727-2497.* Located at the beginning of the North Shore Scenic Drive. Ship models, relics of shipwrecks, reconstructed ship cabins; exhibits related to maritime history of Lake Superior and Duluth Harbor and the Corps of Engineers. Vessel schedules and close-up views of passing ship traffic. Open Apr-mid-Dec, daily; rest of year, Fri-Sun; closed Jan 1, Thanksgiving, Dec 25. **FREE**

LIGHTHOUSE POINT AND HARBOR MUSEUM. *520 South Ave, Two Harbors. Phone 218/834-4898.* Displays tell the story of iron-ore shipping and the development of the first iron-ore port in the state. A renovated pilot house from an ore boat is located on the site. Shipwreck display. Tours of operating lighthouse. Open May-Nov 1, daily. $$

LUTSEN MOUNTAINS SKI AREA. *467 Ski Hole Rd, Lutsen. Phone 218/663-7281. www.lutsen.com.* Seven double chairlifts, surface lift; school, rentals; snowmaking; lodge, cafeteria, bar. Longest run 2 miles; vertical drop 1,088 feet. Gondola. Cross-country trails. Open mid-Nov-mid-Apr, daily. $$$$

SPLIT ROCK LIGHTHOUSE STATE PARK. *3755 Split Rock Lighthouse, Two Harbors (55616). Phone 218/226-6377.* 1,987 acres. As one of the best known landmarks along the North Shore Scenic Drive, Split Rock Lighthouse is a beacon in more ways than one. Built in 1909 as a result of so many shipwrecks resulting from storms, the lighthouse now operates a historical site where visitors can tour the structure and learn more about life in a lighthouse. This historic complex (fee) includes a fog-signal building, keeper's dwellings, several outbuildings, and the ruins of a tramway (open mid-May-mid-Oct, daily). Waterfalls. Cart-in camping (fee) on Lake Superior; access to the Superior Hiking Trail. State park vehicle permit required. $

Minnesota

❋ North Shore Scenic Drive

SUPERIOR NATIONAL FOREST. *Contact the Forest Supervisor, 8901 Grand Avenue Pl, Duluth (55808). Phone 218/626-4300. www.superiornationalforest.org.* With more than 2,000 beautiful clear lakes, rugged shorelines, picturesque islands, and deep woods, this is a magnificent portion of Minnesota's famous northern area. The Boundary Waters Canoe Area Wilderness, part of the forest, is perhaps the finest canoe country in the United States (travel permits required for each party, $9 for advance reservations, phone 800/745-3399). Scenic water routes through wilderness near the international border offer opportunities for adventure. Adjacent Quetico Provincial Park is similar. Boating, swimming, water sports; fishing and hunting under Minnesota game and fish regulations; winter sports; camping (fee), picnicking, and scenic drives along Honeymoon, Gunflint, Echo, and Sawbill trails.

WILLIAM A. IRVIN. *301 Harbor Dr, Duluth. Phone 218/722-5573. www.williamairvin.com.* Guided tours of the former flagship of United States Steel's Great Lakes fleet that journeyed inland waters from 1938-1978. Explore decks and compartments of the restored 610-foot ore carrier, including the engine room, elaborate guest staterooms, galley, pilothouse, observation lounge, and elegant dining room. May-mid-Oct. $$

PLACES TO STAY

If you choose to include an overnight stay in your trip along this All-American Road, Mobil Travel Guide recommends the following lodgings.

★★ **BEST WESTERN EDGEWATER.** *2400 London Rd, Duluth (55812). Phone 218/728-3601; toll-free 800/780-7234. www.bestwestern.com.* 282 rooms, 5 story. Pet accepted, some restrictions. Complimentary continental breakfast. Check-out noon. TV; cable (premium). Many rooms with balconies, view of Lake Superior. Restaurant adjacent. Playground. In-house fitness room, sauna. Game room. Indoor pool, whirlpool. Downhill ski 7 miles, cross-country ski 1 mile. Lawn games. Miniature golf. Business center. ¢

★ **COMFORT SUITES.** *408 Canal Park Dr, Duluth (55802). Phone 218/727-1378; toll-free 800/228-5151. www.choicehotels.com.* 82 rooms, 3 story. Complimentary continental breakfast. Check-out 11 am. TV; cable (premium). In-room modem link. Laundry services. Indoor pool, whirlpools. Restaurant adjacent. Downhill, cross-country ski 5 miles. $

★★★ **FITGERS INN.** *600 E Superior St, Duluth (55802). Phone 218/722-8826; toll-free 888/348-4377. www.fitgers.com.* Housed in what was once a thriving brewery, this historic hotel has European style with modern facilities. Well-designed guest suites, luxurious amenities, a dinner theater, restaurants, and shopping make this a popular choice in Duluth. Most rooms overlook Lake Superior. 62 rooms, 20 story. Pet accepted, some restrictions. Check-out noon. TV; cable (premium), VCR available. In-room modem link. Some fireplaces, in-room whirlpools. Bar; entertainment weekends. In-house fitness room. Health club privileges. ¢

★★ **HOLIDAY INN HOTEL & SUITES.** *200 W First St, Duluth (55802). Phone 218/722-1202; toll-free 800/477-7089. www.holiday-inn.com.* 353 rooms, 16 story. Check-out noon. TV. In-room modem link. Restaurant, bar. Health club privileges. Indoor pools, whirlpool. Downhill, cross-country ski 7 miles. Free garage parking. Adjacent to a large shopping complex. ¢

★★ **RADISSON HOTEL.** *505 W Superior St, Duluth (55802). Phone 218/727-8981; toll-free 800/333-3333. www.radisson.com.* Located downtown and connected to the indoor skyway system. 268 rooms, 16 story. Pet accepted. Check-out noon. TV; VCR available. Restaurant, bar. Health club privileges. Sauna. Indoor pool, whirlpool, poolside service. Downhill, cross-country ski 10 miles. ¢

★ **SUPER 8.** *4100 W Superior St, Duluth (55807). Phone 218/628-2241; toll-free 800/800-8000. www.super8.com.* 59 rooms, 2 story. Complimentary continental breakfast. Check-out 11 am. TV; cable (premium). Coin laundry. Restaurant opposite open 24 hours. Sauna. Whirlpool. Downhill, cross-country ski 5 miles. ¢

★★ **BEARSKIN LODGE.** *124 E Bearskin Rd, Grand Marais (55604). Phone 218/388-2292; toll-free 800/338-4170. www.bearskin.com.* 4 rooms, 11 cabins. No A/C. Check-out 10 am, check-in 4 pm. Fireplaces. Coin laundry. Dining room (reservations required). Free supervised children's activities (June-Aug), ages 3-13. Playground. Whirlpool. Sauna. Private swimming beach. Cross-country ski on site. Boats, motors, canoes. Private docks. Hiking trails, mountain bikes. Nature program. $

★ **DREAM CATCHER BED & BREAKFAST.** *2614 County Rd 7, Grand Marais (55604). Phone 218/387-2876; toll-free 800/682-3119. www.dreamcatcherbb.com.* 3 rooms, 2 story. Situated in the woods of northeastern Minnesota, high above Lake Superior's rugged North Shore, this bed-and-breakfast offers unique rooms and a full breakfast each morning. $

★★ **EAST BAY HOTEL AND DINING ROOM.** *Wisconsin St, Grand Marais (55604). Phone 218/387-2800; toll-free 800/414-2807. www.eastbayhotel.com.* 36 rooms, 2-3 story. No A/C. Pet accepted. Check-out 11 am. TV. Fireplaces. Restaurant, bar. Entertainment. Room service. Massage. Whirlpool. Cross-country ski 5 miles. On lake. ¢

★★ **NANIBOUJOU LODGE.** *20 Naniboujou Trail, Grand Marais (55604). Phone 218/387-2688. www.naniboujou.com.* 24 rooms, 2 story. No A/C. No room phones. Check-out 10:30 am. Some fireplaces. Restaurant. On lake/river. Cross-country ski on site. Totally nonsmoking. ¢

★★ **STONE HEARTH INN.** *5698 Lakeside Estates Rd, Little Marais (55614). Phone 218/226-3020; toll-free 888/206-3020.* 8 rooms, 2 story. Romantic 1920s inn on Lake Superior. Old-fashioned porch, large stone fireplace in living room. Guest rooms are furnished with antiques; some have whirlpools, gas fireplaces, and kitchens. All rooms have private baths. $

★★ **LIGHTHOUSE BED & BREAKFAST.** *1 Lighthouse Point, Two Harbors (55616). Phone 218/834-4898; toll-free 888/532-5606. www.lighthousebb.org.* 3 rooms, 2 story. Built in 1892, the Two Harbors Lighthouse is listed on the National Register of Historic Places and is a working lighthouse. Guests become assistant lighthouse keepers and become registered keepers of the light during their stay. $

PLACES TO EAT

A long day of driving is sure to make you hungry. At the end of your journey, take a table at one of the following restaurants.

★★★ **BELLISIO'S.** *405 Lake Ave S, Duluth (55802). Phone 218/727-4921.* This restaurant features wine racks from floor to ceiling and white tablecloths with full table settings to help guests enjoy a true Italian experience. Italian menu. Lunch, dinner. Bar. Wine cellar. $$

★★ **BENNETT'S ON THE LAKE.** *600 E Superior St, Duluth (55802). Phone 218/722-2829. www.bennettsonthelake.com.* American menu. Breakfast, lunch, dinner. Situated in a turn-of-the-century factory building, with views of Lake Superior and displays of local artwork. $$

Minnesota

❋ *North Shore Scenic Drive*

★ **FITGER'S BREWHOUSE.** 600 E Superior St, Duluth (55802). Phone 218/726-1392. www.brewhouse.net. Bar food. Lunch, dinner. Duluth's oldest operating brewery and pub, established in 1857. $
D SC

★ **GRANDMA'S CANAL PARK.** 522 Lake Ave S, Duluth (55802). Phone 218/727-4192. www.grandmasrestaurants.com. Under the Aerial Lift Bridge at the entrance to the harbor. Closed some major holidays. Lunch, dinner. Bar. Children's menu. $
D SC

★★ **PICKWICK.** 508 E Superior St, Duluth (55802). Phone 218/727-8901. The wood-paneled dining area and antique-filled rooms of this historic family-owned bar and restaurant offer incredible views of Lake Superior. The continental menu is an eclectic mix of regional and internationally influenced dishes, from smoked whitefish to Grecian lamb chops. Closed Sun; major holidays. Lunch, dinner. Bar. Children's menu. $$
D

★ **SCENIC CAFÉ.** 5461 North Shore Dr, Duluth (55804). Phone 218/525-2286. www.scenic-cafe.com. International menu. Lunch, dinner. Creative, worldly cuisine with excellent desserts and an extensive beer and wine selection. $

★ **TOP OF THE HARBOR.** 505 W Superior St, Duluth (55802). Phone 218/727-8981. www.radisson.com/duluthmn. This 16th-floor revolving restaurant offers panoramic views of the city, Duluth Harbor, and Lake Superior. American menu. Breakfast, lunch, dinner. Children's menu. $$
SC

★ **BIRCH TERRACE.** W 6th Ave, Grand Marais (55604). Phone 218/387-2215. This Northwoods mansion was built in 1898. Two fireplaces warm the interior dining room during the winter, and a deck overlooking the marina provides pleasant summertime views. American menu. Dinner. Bar. Children's menu. $$
D

Natchez Trace Parkway

✸ MISSISSIPPI

Part of a multistate Byway; see also AL, TN.

Quick Facts

LENGTH: 310 miles.

TIME TO ALLOW: 2 days.

BEST TIME TO DRIVE: Summer is best to see the lush vegetation along the way, late March-April for spring flowers, and September-October for fall colors. High season is March-April.

BYWAY TRAVEL INFORMATION: Natchez Trace Parkway: toll-free 800/305-7417; Byway local Web site: www.nps.gov.natr.

SPECIAL CONSIDERATIONS: Be alert for animals on the parkway, as well as copperheads, cottonmouths, and rattlesnakes. Fire ants can inflict painful bites, so do not disturb their mounds. Poison ivy grows throughout the area. You'll find one service station on the parkway (located at milepost 193.1), but gas, food, and lodging are available in the communities near the parkway.

RESTRICTIONS: The speed limit along this Byway is 50 mph. Tent and trailer camping is allowed at designated campgrounds only.

BICYCLE/PEDESTRIAN FACILITIES: The Natchez Trace Parkway is popular among bicyclists—both for distance touring and for local riders out for a day of fresh air. Pedestrian facilities along the parkway consist of separate hiking/nature/horse trails. Bicyclists are encouraged to avoid the following two areas during heavy traffic periods: Ridgeland, Mississippi, I-55 North to milepost 103, from 7-9 am and from 4-6 pm; and Tupelo, Mississippi, milepost 258 to 268, from 7-8:30 am and from 3-5 pm on weekdays.

The Natchez Trace Parkway tells the story of people on the move, the story of the age-old need to get from one place to another. It is a story of Natchez, Chickasaw, and Choctaw Indians following traditional ways of life; of French and Spanish people venturing into a new world; and of people building a new nation.

At first, the Trace was probably a series of hunters' paths that slowly came together to form a trail that led from the Mississippi River over the low hills into the Tennessee Valley. By 1785, Ohio River Valley farmers searching for markets had begun floating their crops and products down the rivers to Natchez or New Orleans. Because they sold their flatboats for lumber, returning home meant either riding or walking. The trail from Natchez offered the most direct route for them to follow.

The parklands along the Trace preserve important examples of our nation's natural and cultural heritage. Since the late 1930s, the National Park Service has been constructing a modern parkway that closely follows the course of the original Trace. Today, the parkway gives travelers an unhurried route from Natchez, Mississippi, to Nashville, Tennessee. It is a subtle driving experience. Motorists and bicyclists alike enjoy the scenery, from the rock-studded hills of Tennessee, past the cotton fields of Alabama, to the flat and meandering southern extremes shaded by trees and Spanish moss. The Natchez Trace Parkway winds along 445 scenic miles through three states, including Alabama, Mississippi, and Tennessee.

Mississippi

❋ *Natchez Trace Parkway*

THE BYWAY STORY
The Natchez Trace Parkway tells archaeological, cultural, historical, natural, recreational, and scenic stories that make it a unique and treasured Byway.

Archaeological
Archaeological sites on the Natchez Trace date from the Paleo-Indian period (12,000 BC-8,000 BC) through historic Natchez, Choctaw, and Chickasaw settlements (AD 1540-1837). Campsites, village sites, stone quarry sites, rock shelters, shell heaps, and burial sites are among the archaeological treasures along the Trace. The most visually obvious are burial and ceremonial earthen mounds associated with the Woodland and Mississippian periods. The Mississippians were highly skilled farmers and artists who may have traded with people from as far away as Mexico and Central America. They established elaborate political systems and lived in large permanent towns that were often fortified with stockades.

Of the seven mound locations found within the boundaries of the Natchez Trace Parkway (all of which are located in Mississippi), five are burial mound sites and two are ceremonial mound sites. Burial mounds are generally conical or rounded in shape, while ceremonial mounds are generally flat-topped and are built to accommodate a religious structure or an official's house. On the parkway, six of the seven mound sites are identified and interpreted.

Cultural
The cultural aspects of the Natchez Trace can be seen in its heritage. From rough frontier towns on the edge of Indian Territory to the rise of Southern comforts, the people who live along the Trace embody its rich culture. Southern traditions and hospitality are apparent as you meander through the heart of Dixie. From Natchez to Memphis, you'll enjoy the people you meet along the Natchez Trace.

Because the Natchez Trace is a long Byway, take an extra day or two to fully appreciate Southern living. On your extended stay, take in one of the many opportunities for cultural entertainment. These range from concerts by community bands to performances by small-stage theater troupes. Spend a night at the opera or attend some of the special events on the Byway, such as the Belhaven Singing Christmas Tree in Jackson, Mississippi. Just be sure to keep your camera handy for some good ol' Southern memories.

Historical
The Natchez Trace Parkway was established to commemorate the historical significance of the Old Natchez Trace as a primitive trail that stretched some 500 miles through the wilderness from Natchez, Mississippi, to Nashville, Tennessee. Although generally thought of as one trail, the Old Natchez Trace was actually a number of closely parallel routes. The Trace probably evolved from the repeated use of meandering game trails by the earliest human inhabitants. Over time, these paths were gradually linked and used for transportation, communication, and trade, first by Native Americans and later by European explorers, American traders, and others.

History has witnessed several phases in the development of the Natchez Trace, each with a distinct origin and purpose. The first phase was an Indian trail, actually known as the Chickasaw Trace by residents of Fort Nashborough (present-day Nashville, Tennessee). Heading southwest from Nashville, the Chickasaw Trace led to the Chickasaw Nation, near present-day Tupelo, Mississippi. From there, other trails led southwest through country controlled by the Choctaw Nation and onward to Natchez. The southern portion of this trail appeared on 18th-century British maps as the "Path to the Choctaw Nation."

Word spread among the early white settlers that it was possible to travel by foot between Nashville and Natchez through the Indian nations. Traffic increased along this "Boatman's Trail," with men returning home to the north after selling cargo and flatboats at Natchez or New Orleans. Added usage caused discontent to grow due to the harsh conditions of this new route. In 1806, Thomas Jefferson directed the Postmaster General to oversee a route improvement project. Unfortunately, funds for maintenance weren't included in the appropriation. Complaints concerning conditions on the rugged wilderness trail flooded in as river trade boomed along with the increasing population.

However, before improvements were ever made, the need for them diminished. After his victory at the Battle of New Orleans in 1815, Andrew Jackson marched his troops home along the Trace—an event that signaled not only the war's end, but also the decline of the Natchez Trace's importance as a transportation corridor. By 1820, steamboats were common on the Mississippi River, making upriver travel easy. Boatmen chose to return home by water rather than by the overland route.

Not until the years following 1820, when much of the route fell into disuse, was it referred to as the Natchez Trace. Speculation is that those who had experienced hardships and adventure on the Natchez Road spoke of it more glamorously as the Natchez Trace when reminiscing about it. By the 1830s, this term had replaced Natchez Road.

Natural

The Natchez Trace Parkway encompasses a diversity of natural resources. The motor road cuts through six major forest types and eight major watersheds. The parkway ranges from 70 to 1,100 feet in elevation and covers a distance of 445 miles, resulting in a variety of habitats.

Along the parkway, approximately 800 species of plants help to support 57 species of mammals, 216 species of birds, 57 species of reptiles, 36 species of amphibians, and a variety of other vertebrates and invertebrates. Three of these species are classified as endangered—the southern bald eagle, the red-cockaded woodpecker, and the gray bat; three more are classified as threatened—the Bayou darter, the slackwater darter, and the ringed sawback turtle.

Natchez, the southern terminus of the Natchez Trace Parkway, is located on a bluff 100 feet above the Mississippi River. From here, the parkway winds northeastward through a forest of beech and oak trees, some of which are draped with Spanish moss. This forest is located in the Loess Bluffs province. The road then enters the Southern Pine Hills near Raymond, Mississippi, and passes through the Jackson Prairie, which is now occupied by the Jackson metropolitan area and the Ross Barnett Reservoir. From the northeastern tip of the reservoir, the parkway crosses pine and dry oak forests in Mississippi's North Central Hills,

see page A5 for color map

Mississippi

❋ *Natchez Trace Parkway*

Flatwoods, and Pontotoc Ridge provinces. Many of these woodlands were leased by European settlers for the purpose of planting cotton in the red-clay soil, which in turn gave rise to the region's antebellum plantation society. The plantations have long since vanished, but agriculture remains important in this part of the state. The alluvial agricultural soils around Tupelo are part of the Black Belt Prairie and were an important resource of the Chickasaw and prehistoric Indians.

The more fertile farm lands along the parkway are devoted to the production of milo, soybeans, corn, wheat, and cotton, while the marginal agricultural lands are used primarily for the grazing of cattle and horses. Some of the more common wildlife along the entire length of the parkway include whitetailed deer, turkeys, bobcats, raccoons, opossums, foxes, coyotes, and field- and forest-dwelling songbirds.

Recreational

You can find numerous opportunities for recreation along the Natchez Trace Parkway. By far, the most popular is simply enjoying the historic and natural beauty, which abounds all along the parkway. Take in one of the many museums located throughout the Byway or take a walk among the dogwoods. The Byway has many historic battlefields, allowing you the chance to stretch your legs and reminisce about the past. Pack a picnic and see the many Southern mansions along the route or hunt for souvenirs in one of the many quaint shops along the way.

At least ten months of fine weather each year and a combination of natural resources, including lakes, woodlands, and wildlife, make outdoor recreation along the Trace favorable. Hunting is excellent, as are golfing, bicycling, jogging, swimming, tennis, baseball, football, soccer, and other sports. If you're a fisherman, take advantage of the many rivers located throughout the Byway and wet your line.

Scenic

As the interstate highway of its time, the Natchez Trace entertained travelers along its well-trod path with its picturesque views of the surrounding countryside. You can enjoy these same wonders today. From blossoming flowers and trees to historical Native American earthen mounds, the Natchez Trace offers scenic vistas at every turn. By winding through six major forest types and eight major watersheds, you are afforded the opportunity to see a variety of habitats and wildlife; the changing seasons enhance the scenic qualities of the Natchez Trace.

HIGHLIGHTS

The Mississippi section of the Natchez Trace Parkway includes these points of interest between mile 310 and mile 0. If you're traveling in the other direction, simply read this list from the bottom up.

- **Mile 308.8—Bear Creek Mound:** This ceremonial structure was built between AD 1200 and AD 1400.

- **Mile 302.8—Tishomingo State Park:** The park was named for a famous Chickasaw chief. Camping, picnicking, swimming, canoeing, and fishing are available here.

- **Mile 293.2—Tennessee-Tombigbee Waterway and Jamie L. Whitten Bridge:** The waterway provides 459 miles of navigable water between the Gulf of Mexico and the Tennessee River. The waterway and the nearby visitor center are administered by the US Army Corps of Engineers.

- **Mile 286.7—Pharr Mounds:** This 90-acre complex of eight burial mounds was built from about AD 1 to AD 200.

- **Mile 278.4—Twentymile Bottom Overlook:** The low area along the stream is typical of the landscape through which the old Trace passed.

- **Mile 275.2—Dogwood Valley:** A nature trail goes through a large stand of dogwood trees. The walk takes about 15 minutes.
- **Mile 269.4—Confederate gravesites:** A short walk on the old Trace goes to the graves of 13 unknown Confederate soldiers.
- **Mile 266.0—Tupelo Visitor Center (park headquarters):** A nature trail leads through an area of forest regrowth; the walk takes 20 minutes. Rest rooms, exhibits, information, and an orientation program are available.
- **Mile 261.8—Chickasaw Village:** The Chickasaws' daily life and early history are described in exhibits at the site of one of their villages. A nature trail features plants they used.
- **Mile 259.7—Tupelo National Battlefield:** The 1864 battle took place 1 mile east on Mississippi 6.
- **Mile 251.1—Chickasaw Council House:** This is the site of Pontatok, the capital of the Chickasaw Nation during the 1820s.
- **Mile 243.3—Hernando DeSoto site:** The Spanish explorer and the first European to travel the Mississippi spent the winter of 1540-1541 near here.
- **Mile 243.1—Davis Lake:** This is the access point to the US Forest Service picnicking and summer camping area.
- **Mile 232.4—Bynum Mounds:** Exhibits describe the life of the prehistoric peoples who built these mounds between 100 BC and AD 200.
- **Mile 203.5—Pigeon Roost:** Folsom's stand and trading post, operated by Nathaniel and David Folsom, once stood near here. Millions of passenger pigeons, now extinct, once roosted here.
- **Mile 180.7—French Camp:** Louis LeFleur established a stand here in 1812. It became a school in 1822 and has remained one to this day. Sorghum is made here in the fall.
- **Mile 160.0—Information Center:** Travel information is provided for the parkway and the Kosciusko area by local chamber of commerce volunteers.
- **Mile 122.0—Cypress Swamp:** The nature trail takes you through a water tupelo/bald cypress swamp. The walk takes about 20 minutes.
- **Mile 106.9—Boyd Mounds:** These earthen burial mounds were built from AD 800 to AD 1100.
- **Mile 104.5—Brashear's Stand:** This inn was advertised as "a house of entertainment in the wilderness" to travelers in 1806. A portion of the original Trace is nearby.
- **Mile 102.4—Mississippi Crafts Center:** Sales and demonstrations of Mississippi crafts are featured. Exhibits, information, and rest rooms.
- **Mile 78.3—Battle of Raymond:** This Civil War battle, a part of the Vicksburg campaign in 1863, was fought nearby.
- **Mile 54.8—Rocky Springs:** The old townsite can be reached by a short trail from the upper parking area. You'll find camping, picnicking, ranger station, rest rooms, and a section of the old Trace.
- **Mile 45.7—Grindstone Ford/Mangum site:** Artifacts found here have revealed much about the prehistoric people who once lived in this area. Early-day travelers heading north considered themselves in wild country after they crossed the ford on Bayou Pierre.
- **Mile 18.4—Bullen Creek:** A nature trail leads through a mixed hardwood-pine forest. The walk takes 15 minutes.
- **Mile 15.5—Mount Locust:** This restored historic house, which was one of the first stands in Mississippi, has interpretive programs from February through November, plus rest rooms, exhibits, and a ranger station.

Mississippi

✱ Natchez Trace Parkway

- **Mile 10.3—Emerald Mound:** Ancestors of the Natchez built this ceremonial mound about AD 1400. The second largest of its type in the nation, the mound covers nearly 8 acres. A trail leads to the top.

THINGS TO SEE AND DO

Driving along the Natchez Trace Parkway will certainly keep your senses engaged, but if you yearn to get out of the car and stretch your legs, or if you'd like to make a mini-vacation out of your trip, check out these attractions along the route.

◪ ANTEBELLUM HOUSES. *1601 Church St, Port Gibson (39150). Phone 601/437-4351.* Open year-round by appointment; special schedule during Spring Pilgrimage.

BRICES CROSS ROADS NATIONAL BATTLEFIELD SITE. *2680 Natchez Trace Pkwy, Tupelo (38801). Phone 601/680-4025. www.nps.gov/brcr/.* Once the site of a crucial and hard-fought battle of the Civil War, Brices Cross Roads is dedicated to the memory of those who lost their lives here. Located on Hwy 370 west of Baldwyn, this 1-acre battlefield site commemorates the battle that had one objective—to make it impossible for Confederate General Nathan Bedford Forrest to interfere with General William T. Sherman's railroad supply line from Nashville to Chattanooga during the Atlanta campaign. Forrest scored a decisive victory over General S. D. Sturgis' Union forces when they met at Brices Cross Roads on June 10, 1864. The Union lost five men to every Southern casualty, and General Forrest's troops managed to capture desperately needed supplies, including guns, ammunition, cannons, and wagons. The battle was considered a major tactical victory for the Confederacy but did not diminish the effectiveness of Sherman's campaign, as supplies continued to flow. **FREE**

◪ CANAL STREET DEPOT. *Canal and State sts, Natchez (39120). Phone toll-free 800/647-6724.* The depot houses the official Natchez Pilgrimage Tour and Tourist Headquarters, which provides information on historic Natchez and the surrounding area. Offers tours (fee) of 15 antebellum mansions and tickets for spring, fall, and Christmas pilgrimages. Open daily 9 am-5:30 pm.

ELVIS PRESLEY PARK AND MUSEUM. *306 Elvis Presley Dr, Tupelo (38801). Phone 662/841-1245. www.elvispresleybirthplace.com.* In the park is a small, white frame house, where Presley lived for the first three years of his life. The museum houses a collection of Elvis memorabilia. Chapel (free). Open daily; buildings closed Thanksgiving, Dec 25. **$$$**

EMERALD MOUND. *2680 Natchez Trace Pkwy, Natchez (39120). Phone 601/442-2658.* This 8-acre Mississippian mound, the second largest in the United States, dates roughly from 1250-1600. Unlike earlier peoples, who constructed mounds to cover tombs and burials, the Mississippians (ancestors of the Natchez, Creek, and Choctaw tribes) built mounds to support temples and ceremonial buildings. When DeSoto passed through this area in the 1540s, the flat-topped temple mounds were still in use. Open daily. **FREE**

GRAND GULF MILITARY PARK. *Grand Gulf Rd, Port Gibson (39150). Phone 601/437-5911. www.grandgulfpark.state.ms.us.* This site marks the former town of Grand Gulf, which lost 55 of 75 city blocks to Mississippi floods between 1855 and 1860. The Confederacy chose to fortify the banks when the population was only 160 and the town was dying. In the spring of 1862, Admiral David G. Farragut sent his powerful naval squadron upriver; Baton Rouge and Natchez fell, but Vicksburg refused to surrender. Confederate artillery and supporting troops were sent to Grand Gulf, where intermittent fighting between Union warships and Confederate shore batteries continued until a

Union column landed at Bayou Pierre, marched on Grand Gulf, and burned what remained of the town. War returned to Grand Gulf when Admiral D. D. Porter's ironclads opened fire on forts Cobun and Wade on the morning of April 29, 1863. After more than five hours, two ironclads were disabled and the guns of Fort Wade were silenced. The park today includes fortifications, an observation tower, a cemetery, a sawmill, a dog-trot house, a memorial chapel, a water wheel and grist mill, a carriage house with vehicles used by the Confederates, a four-room cottage reconstructed from the early days of Grand Gulf, and several other pre-Civil War buildings. A museum in the visitor center displays Civil War, Native American, and prehistoric artifacts (open daily; closed Jan 1, Thanksgiving, Dec 25). Park (open daily). Picnic facilities, 42 camper pads (hookups). **$**

HOMOCHITTO NATIONAL FOREST. *NE and SE via US 84, 98, MS 33, Natchez (39120). Phone 601/965-4391.* This 189,000-acre forest is located near the picturesquely eroded loess country. You can view the regular timber management activities. Swimming (Clear Springs Recreation Area), fishing, hunting, picnicking, and camping (Clear Springs Recreation Area). Fees may be charged at recreation sites.

MISSISSIPPI PETRIFIED FOREST. *124 Forest Park Rd, Flora (39071). Phone 601/879-8189. www.mspetrifiedforest.com.* Surface erosion exposed giant (up to 6 feet in diameter) petrified logs that were deposited in the Mississippi area as driftwood by a prehistoric river. Self-guided nature trail. Museum at visitor center has dioramas; wood, gem, mineral, and fossil displays; and an ultraviolet (black light) room. Picnicking. Camping. Open daily; closed Dec 25. **$$**

MOUNT LOCUST. *2680 Natchez Trace Pkwy, Natchez (39120). Phone 601/445-4211.* One of the earliest inns on the Trace; restored to its 1810s appearance. Interpretive program. Open Feb-Nov, daily; grounds only, Dec-Jan. **FREE**

MUSEUM OF NATURAL SCIENCE. *2148 Riverside Dr, Jackson (39202). Phone 601/354-7303. www.mdwfp.com/museum.* Collections, designed for research and education, cover Mississippi's vertebrates, invertebrates, plants, and fossils. Exhibits and aquariums depict the ecological story of the region; educational programs and workshops are offered for all ages. Professional library. Division of Mississippi Department of Wildlife Conservation. Open Mon-Sat; closed holidays. **$$**

MYNELLE GARDENS. *4736 Clinton Blvd, Jackson (39209). Phone 601/960-1894. www./nstar.com/mynelle/.* A 5-acre display garden with thousands of azaleas, camellias, daylilies, flowering trees, and perennials; reflecting pools and statuary; Oriental garden, miniature flower gardens, and an all-white garden. Turn-of-the-century Westbrook House is open for viewing. Changing art and photography exhibits. Picnicking. Open daily; closed some major holidays. **$**

Mississippi

❋ *Natchez Trace Parkway*

NATCHEZ STATE PARK. *230B Wickliff Rd, Natchez (39120). Phone 601/442-2658.* Park has horse trails that are believed to be abandoned plantation roads leading to Brandon Hall, house of the first native Mississippi governor, Gerard Brandon (1826-1831). Fishing lake; boating (ramp, rentals). Nature trail. Picnicking. Primitive and improved camping, cabins.

ROSS R. BARNETT RESERVOIR. *115 Madison Landing Cir, Ridgeland (39157). Phone 601/354-3448.* Reservoir (43 miles in length) created by damming the Pearl River. Swimming, water-skiing, fishing, boating. Picnicking. Camping. Open daily.

SMITH ROBERTSON MUSEUM. *528 Bloom St, Jackson (39202). Phone 601/960-1457.* History and culture of African-American Mississippians from Africa to the present; large collection of photos, books, documents, and arts and crafts. Open Mon-Fri, Sat mornings, Sun afternoons; closed major holidays. $

SPRINGFIELD PLANTATION. *20 miles NE via US 61, Natchez Trace Pkwy, then 12 miles N on MS 553, Fayette (39069). Phone 601/786-3802.* Believed to be the first mansion erected in Mississippi; remains nearly intact with little remodeling over the years; original hand-carved woodwork. Built for Thomas Marston Green, Jr., wealthy planter from Virginia; site of Andrew Jackson's wedding. Displays include Civil War equipment, railroad memorabilia, and a narrow-gauge locomotive. Open daily; closed Dec 25. $$

TOMBIGBEE NATIONAL FOREST. *20 miles S, off Natchez Trace Pkwy, Tupelo (38826). Phone 662/285-3264. www.fs.fed.us/r8/tombigbee/.* This section of the forest, along with a tract to the south on MS 15 near Louisville, totals 66,341 acres. Davis Lake provides swimming (fee), fishing, picnicking, and camping (electric hookups; fee; dump station). Recreation area (Mar-mid-Nov). $$

TRACE STATE PARK. *2139 Faulkner Rd, Tupelo (38826). Phone 662/489-2958.* This park sits on 2,500 acres with a 600-acre lake. Swimming beach; water-skiing; fishing for bass, catfish, bluegill, and crappie; boating (ramp, rentals). Hiking, horseback riding trail, golf, picnicking. Tent and trailer camping (electric and water hookups, dump station), cabins.

TUPELO NATIONAL BATTLEFIELD. *2680 Natchez Trace Pkwy, Tupelo (38801). Phone 601/680-4025. www.nps.gov/tupe/.* One-acre tract near the area where a Confederate line was formed to attack a Union position. Marker with texts and maps explains the battle. Open daily. **FREE**

✪ **VICKSBURG NATIONAL MILITARY PARK AND CEMETERY.** *3201 Clay St, Vicksburg (39183). Phone 601/636-0583.* This historic park, the site of Union siege lines and a brave Confederate defense, borders the eastern and northern sections of the city. A visitor center is at the park entrance, on Clay St at I-20. Museum; exhibits and audiovisual aids. Self-guided, 16-mile tour. Open daily; closed Dec 25. $$

PLACES TO STAY

If you choose to include an overnight stay in your trip along this All-American Road, Mobil Travel Guide recommends the following lodgings.

★ **LA QUINTA JACKSON NORTH.** *616 Briarwood Dr, Jackson (39211). Phone 601/373-6115; toll-free 800/687-6667. www.laquinta.com.* 101 rooms, 2-3 story. Pet accepted. Check-out noon. TV. In-room modem link. Valet services. Pool. Airport transportation. Business services. ¢

★★★ **MONMOUTH PLANTATION BED & BREAKFAST.** *36 Melrose Ave, Natchez (39120). Phone 601/442-5852; toll-free 800/828-4531. www.monmouthplantation.com.* This plantation offers a cluster of beautifully restored rooms. The

ALL-AMERICAN ROADS

dining experience is as exceptional as its décor, together creating a romance all its own. Enjoy the vast courtyards or a five-course dinner in the evening while taking advantage of the historic plantation tours and carriage rides during the day. 30 rooms, 2 story. Children over 14 years only. Complimentary full Southern breakfast. Check-out 11 am, check-in 3 pm. TV. Tennis. Fishing. Free tour of mansion. $$

★ **PRENTISS INN.** *45 Sergeant Prentiss Dr, Natchez (39120). Phone 601/442-1691; toll-free 800/541-1720.* 139 rooms, 1-2 story. Check-out noon. TV; VCR available. Pool. Meeting rooms. Business center. In-room modem link. ¢

★★ **OAK SQUARE COUNTRY INN.** *1207 Church St, Port Gibson (39150). Phone 601/437-4350; toll-free 800/729-0240.* 12 rooms, 2 story. Complimentary breakfast. Check-out 11 am. TV. Restored antebellum mansion (circa 1850) and guest house. Free tour of mansion, grounds. $

★ **COMFORT INN.** *1190 N Gloster St, Tupelo (38804). Phone 662/842-5100; toll-free 800/228-5150. www.comfortinn.com.* 83 rooms, 2 story. Complimentary continental breakfast. Check-out 11 am. TV; cable (premium). In-room modem link. Meeting rooms, business services. ¢

★★★ **EXECUTIVE INN.** *1011 N Gloster St, Tupelo (38801). Phone 662/841-2222; toll-free 800/533-3220.* Located on the north side of town, this inn has an airy atrium lobby. 115 rooms, 5 story. Check-out noon. TV; cable (premium). In-room modem link. Restaurant, bar. Room service. Sauna. Indoor pool, whirlpool. Meeting rooms, business services. ¢

★★ **MOCKINGBIRD INN BED & BREAKFAST.** *305 N Gloster St, Tupelo (38804). Phone 662/841-0286.* 7 rooms, 2 story. Children over 10 years only. Complimentary full breakfast. Check-out noon, check-in 3-8 pm. TV. Restaurant opposite. Built in 1925; porch. ¢

PLACES TO EAT

A long day of driving is sure to make you hungry. At the end of your journey, take a table at one of the following restaurants.

★★★ **NICK'S.** *1501 Lakeland Dr, Jackson (39216). Phone 601/981-8017.* Seafood menu. Closed Sun, major holidays. Lunch (Mon-Fri), dinner. Bar. Children's menu. Extensive wine list and seafood selections in an upscale environment. $$

★★ **CARRIAGE HOUSE.** *401 High St, Natchez (39120). Phone 601/445-5151.* American menu. Closed Jan 1, July 4. Lunch. Bar. $$

★ **COCK OF THE WALK.** *200 N Broadway, Natchez (39120). Phone 601/446-8920.* Specializes in catfish. Closed most major holidays. Limited menu. Dinner. Children's menu. Entertainment. Rustic décor; old train station on river. $$

★★ **TICO'S STEAK HOUSE.** *1536 E County Line Rd, Ridgeland (39157). Phone 601/956-1030.* Steak menu. Closed Sun; major holidays. Dinner. Bar. $$

Mississippi

✻ *Natchez Trace Parkway*

★ **JEFFERSON PLACE.** *823 Jefferson St, Tupelo (38801). Phone 662/844-8696.* Specializes in steak, chicken, shrimp. Closed Sun; Thanksgiving, Dec 25. Lunch, dinner, late night. Bar. $$

★ **MALONE'S FISH & STEAK HOUSE.** *1349 MS 41, Tupelo (38801). Phone 662/842-2747.* Specializes in steak, catfish. Closed Sun, Mon; Thanksgiving; also two weeks in late Dec. Dinner. Children's menu. $
[D]

★★ **PAPA VANELLI'S.** *1302 N Gloster, Tupelo (38801). Phone 662/844-4410.* Greek, Italian menu. Closed Dec 25. Lunch, dinner. Bar. Children's menu. $$
[D][SC]

Beartooth Highway

❋ MONTANA

Part of a multistate Byway; see also WY.

Quick Facts

LENGTH: 54 miles.

TIME TO ALLOW: 3 hours.

BEST TIME TO DRIVE: Driving from Red Lodge to Cooke City (east to west) in the morning and west to east in the afternoon reduces glare. High season extends throughout the summer.

BYWAY TRAVEL INFORMATION: Red Lodge Area Chamber of Commerce: 406/446-1718.

SPECIAL CONSIDERATIONS: The alpine climate is rigorous, and severe weather conditions can occur any month of the year. Summer temperatures range from the 70s on sunny days to below freezing during sudden snowstorms.

RESTRICTIONS: The entire length of the Byway is open from Memorial Day weekend through about mid-October. Snow conditions close sections. Check with the local ranger district office before planning a trip in May or September.

The Beartooth Highway is one of the most spectacular national forest routes on this continent. To many, it's known as "the most beautiful highway in America." From its beginning at the border of the Custer National Forest to its terminus near the northeast entrance to Yellowstone National Park, the Beartooth Highway (US 212) offers travelers the ultimate high country experience as it travels through the Custer, Shoshone, and Gallatin national forests.

Since its completion in 1936, the highway has provided millions of visitors a rare opportunity to see the transition from a lush forest ecosystem to alpine tundra in the space of a few miles. The Beartooths are one of the highest and most rugged areas in the lower 48 states, with 20 peaks over 12,000 feet in elevation. Glaciers are found on the north flank of nearly every mountain peak over 11,500 feet in these mountains.

Recreational opportunities are abundant in the area traversed by the Byway. You can cross-country ski in June and July, hike across the broad plateaus, view and photograph wildlife (Rocky Mountain goats, moose, black bears, grizzly bears, marmots, and mule deer), take a guided horseback trip, fish for trout in the streams and lakes adjacent to the Byway, and camp in the 12 national forest campgrounds in the area. Even when the highway is formally closed to automobiles, snowmobilers may travel the route and enjoy a spectacular winter wonderland.

Montana

✳ Beartooth Highway

THE BYWAY STORY

The Beartooth Highway tells archaeological, cultural, historical, natural, recreational, and scenic stories that make it a unique and treasured Byway.

Archaeological

Many of the ancient remains found here show a people who treasured their spirituality. We can best understand this by seeing the challenges they went through, from both severe climate and extreme environment, to come to this virulent area to practice religion. Archaeologists have found numerous small, limited-use camps that offer isolated finds and resource extraction sites. Because of the specimens found in the camps, the location of the camps, and even the frequency of the camps, archaeologists believe the area was used for spiritual purposes rather than primarily for food (which was previously thought).

Even though Native Americans dwelt in various places throughout present-day Montana, archaeological evidence from the Beartooth Mountains is somewhat limited. The high elevation most likely restricted living there on a permanent basis, largely because there is only a short time during the summer to hunt and gather plants specially adapted to high elevations before the cold returns. The rest of the year, deadly weather conditions contribute to making it a hostile environment. Coming here, rather than staying in the fertile plains in the low country, can mean only that the steep mountains held deep significance for them.

Despite the rugged climate, many people have found ancient obsidian arrowheads and spearheads from the people who lived hundreds of years ago, giving more evidence of archaeological activity. Some of these finds can be viewed in museums and visitor centers along the Byway. Whether these Native Americans came to hunt, worship, or a combination of the two, it is clear that they went through great physical strains to travel to the lofty Beartooth Mountains.

Cultural

The Beartooth Highway's most important cultural value is the chance to appreciate some of the activities that flourish in natural environments. By better understanding the people's occupations and interests in this part of Montana, you can more fully experience this Byway. Visitors often leave with a longing to return to the simple yet strenuous life found here. Furthermore, gaining this understanding gives a glimpse at the past, rugged life of Montana's homesteaders.

Some of the locals' occupations and hobbies include ranchers raising livestock that graze on the vast, open range; lumberjacks who spend their days in the dark timber lands managing wood in national forests; sportsmen hunting in steep, barren habitats; and anglers fishing in cold, wild streams. These and other similar activities thrive today along this Byway, continuing a long tradition of multiple uses on public lands.

Historical

The first recorded travel across the Beartooth Pass area occurred in 1882, when General Sheridan with a force of 129 soldiers and scouts, with 104 horses and 157 mules, pioneered and marked a route across the mountains from Cooke City to Billings. A year later, Van Dyke, a packer, modified the trail and located a route off the Beartooth Plateau into Rock Creek and Red Lodge. Van Dyke's trail was the only direct route between Red Lodge and Cooke City until the Beartooth Highway was constructed in 1934 and 1935. Remnants of Van Dyke's trail are visible from the Rock Creek Overlook parking lot, appearing as a Z on the mountain between the highway switchbacks about 1/2 mile south of the parking lot.

Doctor Siegfriet and other visionaries from the Bearcreek and Red Lodge communities foresaw, in the early 1900s, the value of a scenic route over the mountains to connect to Yellowstone Park. These men spent many years promoting

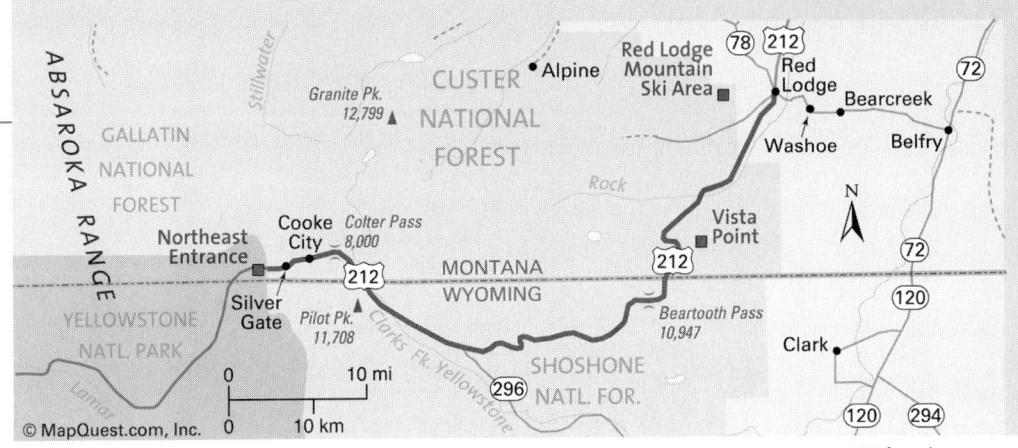

see page A17 for color map

the construction of a road over the mountains and even began the construction of a road with hand tools and horse-drawn implements.

Other routes were surveyed in the 1920 to 1925 period, and, in 1931, President Herbert Hoover signed the Park Approach Act, which was the forerunner to the funding of the road now known as the Beartooth Highway.

Natural

A variety of theories exist on the formation of the Beartooth Mountains, but geologists generally agree that the mountains resulted from an uplifting of an Archean block of metamorphic rocks that were eroded, flooded with volcanic lava on the southwest corner, and covered with glaciers. Seventy million years of formation went into making this section of the Rocky Mountains.

The Palisades that stretch along the Beartooth Front were first sedimentary rocks originally deposited as flat-lying beds in an ancient sea. Thrust skyward, they have become conspicuous spires. Pilot and Index peaks are the remainders of an extensive volcanic field that came into existence 50 million years ago.

Changes are continuing into the present. Yellowstone National Park has been an active volcanic center for more than 15 million years. Erosional forces are still at work. Glaciers have shaped the mountains into the range they comprise today. The glaciers edged their way down just 10,000 years ago. Younger rocks are the sources of coal exploited by the early settlers of Red Lodge.

The Stillwater Complex, a body of igneous magma formed along the northern edge of the mountain range 2.7 million years ago, is one of the rarest and least understood geologic occurrences in the world. It is the site of the only source of the platinum group metals in the western hemisphere, mined by Stillwater Mining Company of Nye, Montana.

Recreational

Recreational opportunities are abundant in the area traversed by the Beartooth Highway. You can cross-country ski on the snowfields in June and July; hike across the broad plateaus and on Forest Service trails (some of which are National Recreation Trails); camp; picnic; fish for trout in the streams and lakes adjacent to the highway; view wildflowers; view and photograph wildlife (moose, Rocky Mountain goats, mule deer, black bears, grizzly bears, marmots, pikas); visit a guest ranch; take a guided horseback trip from Cooke City; bicycle; downhill ski on the headwalls; and photograph nature at its finest. Even when the highway is formally closed to automobiles, snowmobilers may travel the route in a spectacular winter wonderland.

If you enjoy skiing, each summer in June and July, the Red Lodge International Ski Race Camp is conducted on the north side of the East Summit on the Twin Lakes Headwall. This camp is for aspiring Olympic-caliber skiers and provides a viewing opportunity for highway travelers. The ski area is not open to the public for skiing at this time.

Each summer, the Red Lodge Chamber of Commerce sponsors a one-day, unannounced "Top of the World Bar" in a snowbank at or near the West Summit and provides complimentary

Montana

✸ *Beartooth Highway*

nonalcoholic beverages, horse rides, complimentary photos at the Bar, and, on occasion, even a live pink elephant.

Scenic

The spire known as the Bears Tooth was carved in the shape of a large tooth by glacial ice gnawing inward and downward against a single high part of a rocky crest. Beartooth Butte is a remnant of sedimentary deposits that once covered the entire Beartooth Plateau. The red-stained rock outcrop near the top of Beartooth Butte was a stream channel some 375 million years ago, so fossils are found in abundance in the rocks of Beartooth Butte.

These treeless areas, near or above timberline, generally are areas that cannot grow trees. Vegetation is often small, low-growing, and compact—characteristics that are vital to the survival of the plants at this elevation. Wildflowers, often as tiny as a quarter-inch across, create a literal carpet of color during the 45-day or shorter growing season.

On the other hand, the common flowers found below timberline in wet meadows are Indian paintbrush, monkeyflower, senecio, and buttercups; in drier areas are lupine, beards-tongue, arrowleaf balsamroot, and forget-me-nots. The colors and the flowers change weekly as the growing season progresses, but mid-July is generally the optimum for wildflower displays.

Wildlife in Beartooth Country varies from the largest American land mammal, the moose, to the shrew, which is the smallest land mammal. Other animals commonly seen along the highway are mule deer, whitetail deer, elk, marmots (rock chucks), and pine squirrels. Bighorn sheep, Rocky Mountain goats, black bears, and grizzly bears are residents of the area, but none

is seen often. Birds include the golden eagle, raven, Clarks nutcracker, Stellars jay, robin, mountain bluebird, finch, hawk, and falcon. Watch for the water ouzel darting in and out of—and walking along the bottoms of—streams.

The snowbanks often remain until August near Beartooth Pass, and remnants of some drifts may remain all summer. A pink color often appears on the snow later in the summer, which is caused by the decay of a microscopic plant that grows on the surface of the snowbank. When the plant dies, it turns red and colors the snow pink.

THINGS TO SEE AND DO

Driving along the Beartooth Highway will certainly keep your senses engaged, but if you yearn to get out of the car and stretch your legs, or if you'd like to make a mini-vacation out of your trip, check out these attractions along the route.

GALLATIN NATIONAL FOREST. *10 E Babcock St, Bozeman (59715). Phone 406/587-6701. www.fs.fed.us.* Over 1.7 million acres, including mountain peaks, pine and fir forest, winter sports, pack trips, picnicking, camping, fishing, and hunting; 574,788-acre Absaroke-Beartooth Wilderness south of Livingston, 253,000-acre

Lee Metcalf Wilderness, and Gallatin Gateway to Yellowstone. Forest rangers provide interpretive programs in summer at the Madison River Canyon Earthquake Area.

GRASSHOPPER GLACIER. *14 miles NE on a mountain trail in the Absaroka-Beartooth Wilderness, Custer National Forest, Cooke City (59081).* One of the largest icefields in the United States; so named because of the millions of grasshoppers frozen in its 80-foot ice cliff. Accessible only by trail, the last 2 miles reached only by foot; be prepared for adverse weather. Grasshoppers are visible only during brief periods; glacial ice must be exposed by snow melt, which generally does not occur until mid-August, while new snow begins to accumulate in late August.

PLACES TO STAY

If you choose to include an overnight stay in your trip along this All-American Road, Mobil Travel Guide recommends the following lodgings.

★ **HOOSIER'S MOTEL & BAR.** *Corner Hwy 212 and Huston N, Cooke City (59020). Phone 406/838-2241.* 12 rooms, 1 story. No A/C. Check-out 10 am, check-in 12 pm. TV; cable (premium). Bar. Totally nonsmoking. $

★ **BEST WESTERN LUPINE INN.** *702 S Hauser Ave, Red Lodge (59068). Phone 406/446-1321; toll-free 888/567-1321. www.bestwestern.com.* 47 rooms, 2 story. Pet accepted, some restrictions. Complimentary continental breakfast. Check-out noon, check-in 3 pm. TV; cable (premium). In-room modem link. In-house fitness room, sauna. Game room. Indoor pool, whirlpool. Downhill, cross-country ski 6 miles. $

★ **COMFORT INN.** *612 N Broadway, Red Lodge (59068). Phone 406/446-4469; toll-free 888/733-4661. www.choicehotels.com.* 53 rooms, 2 story. Pet accepted; fee. Complimentary continental breakfast. Check-out 11 am, check-in 2 pm. TV; VCR available. In-room modem link. In-house fitness room. Indoor pool, whirlpool. Downhill, cross-country ski 6 miles. $

★★ **POLLARD HOTEL.** *2 N Broadway, Red Lodge (59068). Phone 406/446-0001; toll-free 800/765-5273. www.pollardhotel.com.* 38 rooms, 5 with shower only, 3 story. Complimentary full breakfast. Check-out noon, check-in 4 pm. TV; DVD available. In-room modem link. Restaurant. Room service. In-house fitness room, sauna. Whirlpool. Downhill, cross-country ski 6 miles. Racquetball courts. Restored hotel built in 1893. Totally nonsmoking. $

★★★ **ROCK CREEK RESORT.** *HC 49, Red Lodge (59068). Phone 406/446-1111; toll-free 800/667-1119. www.rockcreekresort.com.* Situated below Beartooth Pass and beside Rock Creek, this resort features such adventurous activities as snowmobiling, skiing, kayaking, and golfing. 85 rooms, 2-3 story. No A/C. Complimentary continental breakfast. Check-out 11 am, check-in 3 pm. TV; cable (premium), VCR available. In-room modem link. Restaurant, dining room. Room service. Children's activity center. In-house fitness room, sauna. Indoor pool, whirlpool. Outdoor tennis. Downhill ski 11 miles. Lawn games. Free airport transportation. $

★ **SUPER 8.** *1223 S Broadway Ave, Red Lodge (59068). Phone 406/446-2288; toll-free 800/813-8335. www.super8.com.* 50 rooms, 2 story. Pet accepted, some restrictions; fee. Complimentary continental breakfast. Check-out 11 am, check-in 2 pm. TV; cable (premium). Game room. Indoor pool; whirlpool. Downhill, cross-country ski 5 miles. ¢

Montana

❋ Beartooth Highway

PLACES TO EAT

A long day of driving is sure to make you hungry. At the end of your journey, take a table at one of the following restaurants.

★★★ **ARTHUR'S GRILL.** *2 N Broadway, Red Lodge (59068). Phone 406/446-0001.* American menu. Dinner, Sun brunch. Bar. Children's menu. Totally nonsmoking. $$
[D][SC]

★★ **OLD PINEY DELL.** *US 212, Red Lodge (59068). Phone 406/446-1196.* Dinner. Bar. Casual attire. Totally nonsmoking. $$
[D]

★ **LOG CABIN CAFÉ.** *US 212, Silver Gate (59081). Phone 406/838-2367.* Continental menu. Closed mid-Sept-mid-May. Dinner. Children's menu. Casual attire. Outdoor seating. Totally nonsmoking. $$

Las Vegas Strip
✷ NEVADA

Quick Facts

LENGTH: 4.5 miles.

TIME TO ALLOW: From half an hour to several hours.

BEST TIME TO DRIVE: Las Vegas is warm year-round. The Strip is usually fairly crowded and congested. Nighttime is usually busier than day, and holidays are especially busy.

BYWAY TRAVEL INFORMATION: Nevada Commission on Tourism: 775/687-4322.

SPECIAL CONSIDERATIONS: This is a pedestrian-rich environment, so be on the alert when driving. Consider driving the Byway once each direction. This way, you will be able to view all the sites that line both sides of the street and catch some that you may have missed.

BICYCLE/PEDESTRIAN FACILITIES: Sidewalks line the Strip and provide plenty of room for walking. Cyclists are welcome, but you must observe the same traffic laws as automobiles.

Often referred to as "the Jewel of the Desert," Las Vegas has long been recognized as the entertainment vacation capital of the country, and the Las Vegas Strip—at the heart of this playland—sparkles like no other place on Earth. More than 31 million visitors from all around the world are drawn to the lights of the Strip each year to experience its unique blend of exciting entertainment, scenic beauty, and lavishly landscaped resorts. An array of theme resorts can transport you to various exotic realms—from a medieval castle to a Parisian sidewalk café, a lakeside Italian village, or a pyramid in ancient Egypt.

The Las Vegas Strip hosts thousands of motorists a week; after you arrive on the Strip, however, you may be surprised to find that it's also a very enjoyable walking environment. The Las Vegas Strip is the only Byway more scenic at night than during the day. In fact, 365 days of the year, 24 hours a day, the "Neon Trail" offers a fascinating foray past spectacular resorts featuring a variety of visual delights. Whether it's pirates plundering, fiery volcanoes spouting, or tropical gardens luring the weary, the Las Vegas Strip offers a variety of fascinating visual experiences that enchant and mesmerize visitors of all ages. The many facets of this corridor make it truly a one-of-a-kind destination.

THE BYWAY STORY

The Las Vegas Strip tells cultural, historical, recreational, and scenic stories that make it a unique and treasured Byway.

Cultural

While Las Vegas is perhaps best known for its gaming culture—the popularity and influence

Nevada

✥ Las Vegas Strip

of which have spread to cities all over the world—the Las Vegas Strip possesses many other outstanding cultural amenities. The diversity and virtuosity of the architecture of the hotels and resorts along the Strip are certainly worth noting. Some of the world's most talented architects have created complex fantasylands all along the Strip. Just a few of the more recent projects include reproductions of the streets of New York, a bayside Tuscany village, the canals of Venice, and a replica of the Eiffel Tower and the *Arc de Triomphe*.

Many of the resorts on the Las Vegas Strip also feature world-class art galleries full of paintings by world-renowned artists, such as Renoir, Monet, and Van Gogh. Other resorts hold galleries of other unique items, like antique automobiles or wax figures. The Guinness World of Records Museum offers an interesting array of the unusual, and the World of Coca-Cola Las Vegas features an interactive storytelling theater.

Various hotels on the Las Vegas Strip feature a variety of top-caliber theatrical and dance shows. Several hotels and casinos host world-class sporting events and concerts featuring top-name entertainers. And no matter where you go on the Strip, you are bound to run into the dazzling light displays that permeate the area. The magical re-creations found along the Byway are the symbols of our society's most fantastic dreams of luxury.

Historical

The Las Vegas Strip, world-renowned for its neon glitter, possesses an equally colorful historical past. The unique history of Las Vegas is undeniably entwined with the culture of gaming. Gambling was legalized in Nevada in 1931, and the first casino opened downtown that same year. Competition was intense, and casino builders soon were looking to land outside the city limits just south of downtown along Highway 91 (the Old Los Angeles Highway), which is now known as the Las Vegas Strip.

Most of the Las Vegas Strip is not really located within the Las Vegas city limits, but along a corridor of South Las Vegas Boulevard located in unincorporated Clark County. The area was sparsely developed until 1938, when the first "resort property" was built 4 miles south of downtown Las Vegas at the corner of San Francisco Avenue (now Sahara) and Highway 91 (South Las Vegas Boulevard). Reportedly, city officials had denied licenses to certain businessmen with questionable connections who had applied to build a casino downtown. Undaunted, they decided to build outside the city limits, just south of the downtown district.

In 1941, construction began on the El Rancho Vegas resort at the corner of San Francisco Avenue and Highway 91. The original El Rancho Vegas introduced a new style of recreation and entertainment to the Nevada desert by combining lodging, gambling, restaurants, entertainment, shops, a travel agency, horseback riding, and swimming in one resort. The El Rancho Vegas was followed a year later by the Last Frontier Resort Hotel & Casino. The well-known Little Church of the West was originally constructed in the resort's Frontier Village. Listed on the National Register of Historic Places, the small chapel has survived four moves on the Strip.

One of the Strip's more colorful (and infamous) characters, Ben "Bugsy" Siegel (reputed hitman for New York mobster Lucky Luciano), oversaw the construction of the fabulous Flamingo Hotel, the third major (and most extravagant) resort to be built on the Strip. Although Siegel met his unfortunate demise soon after the resort's 1946 opening, his prophecies for the future of Las Vegas came true. This new popular playground of Hollywood stars prospered, with the Flamingo setting the stage for the many luxurious resorts yet to be imagined.

As the 1950s began, only four major resorts stood along the Strip, but three more major players were about to hit the scene. The Desert Inn, the Sahara, and the Sands all arrived on the Strip in the early 1950s, further enhancing the Strip's image as a self-contained playground by featuring elaborate tennis courts, an 18-hole golf course, larger casinos, and fabulous showrooms with Broadway's and Hollywood's brightest stars. Las Vegas has continued to build on this legacy, developing newer and more elaborate resorts every year to make certain that Las Vegas retains the image of the most fabulous playground on Earth.

Recreational

The simplest and easiest recreation on the Strip is strolling and sightseeing along the Boulevard. Intriguing arrays of fantasylands in lush surroundings welcome you to the Strip. But the excitement only begins with sightseeing. From comfortable and plush hotels to exciting displays of lights and fountains, Las Vegas creates a dreamlike lifestyle with color, sound, and light all combined to make the experience on the Las Vegas Strip memorable.

For the more adventuresome, roller coasters featured at several hotels provide a ride that twists, loops, and turns to your delight. Other resorts provide 3-D ride films appealing to the senses of sight, sound, and motion. Many of these rides feature the latest technologies for extra thrills. Most of the resorts along the Strip offer displays of grandeur for every visitor to enjoy. Anyone driving the Byway can stop to see erupting volcanoes, dueling ships, dancing fountains, circus acts, and lush tropical gardens.

In addition to a variety of theatrical and dance shows, the resorts offer varied spectator sports, such as boxing matches. There isn't a resort on the Strip that doesn't offer every visitor amenity imaginable. World-class spas, pools, and exercise rooms are as enticing as the casinos. When you aren't searching for slot machines, you may choose to browse through the many stores and boutiques each resort has to offer. You will find everything from designer fashion to specialty candies to Las Vegas souvenirs. Whatever you choose to do, Las Vegas is known as a playground for a reason.

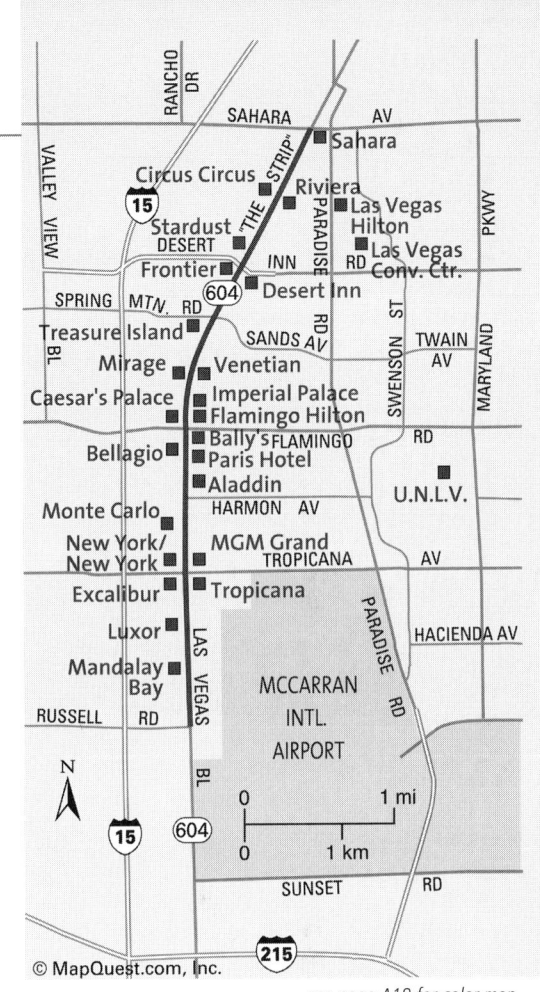

see page A18 for color map

Scenic

As one of the most geographically isolated major cities in the continental United States, Las Vegas provides you with an extraordinary visual experience. The matchless Las Vegas Strip serves as the gateway to a host of memorable experiences that are distinctly Las Vegas. The Strip's incredible array of resorts are constructed around themes that transport visitors to different exotic realms, including a medieval castle, the Parisian Eiffel Tower, a lakeside Italian village, and a pyramid in ancient Egypt. Day or night, the "Neon Trail" provides a fascinating foray past spectacular resorts that offer a variety of visual delights to pedestrians and motorists alike.

HIGHLIGHTS

The Southern Las Vegas Strip Walking Tour begins at South Las Vegas Boulevard and

Nevada

❋ Las Vegas Strip

Russell Road, although you can go the opposite way by reading this list from the bottom up.

- The famous "Welcome to Fabulous Las Vegas" sign announces that you're on the right track. On the east side of the Strip, you see **The Little Church of the West,** the site of many celebrity weddings and a favorite place today to have the perfect wedding.

- Park the car at the free parking garage at **Mandalay Bay** (most of the large hotels offer plenty of covered free parking). Explore the tropical themed hotel, including a fun sand and surf beach. Mandalay Bay is one of the newest hotels on the Strip (built in 1999), and that makes it a popular attraction.

- From Mandalay Bay, you can walk north to **Luxor,** the great black glass pyramid. (If you prefer, hop on the free tram that takes you right to the front doors of Luxor—you may want to save your energy for later in the trip.) While at Luxor, don't miss the **King Tut Tomb exhibit**—an exact replica of the ancient Egyptian pharaoh's tomb. A rotating **IMAX** film experience is also a popular attraction here. This unique hotel is amazing and has one of the largest atriums in the world.

- After spending time at Luxor, hop on the tram that takes you over to **Excalibur.** This is the place for an exciting dinner and show. The majestic castle offers adventure at its **Fantasy Faire Midway**—an arena of games appropriate for everyone in the family.

- After spending time at the medieval castle, cross the over street walkway into '30s- and '40s-inspired New York-New York. Billed as "the Greatest City in Las Vegas," **New York-New York** has attractions that are all themed to the New York life. Park Avenue shopping, a fast-paced Manhattan roller coaster, and Greenwich Village eateries help keep the theme intact.

- It's not time to stop yet. **The Monte Carlo,** just north of New York-New York, is just as classy, but with a purely European twist.

- After a jaunt to Monte Carlo, walk farther north, getting close to the halfway point. The big lake and fantastic fountains are part of **Bellagio,** a hotel that strives for utter perfection. Check out the art gallery here—it houses some fantastic pieces. The gallery has original paintings by Van Gogh, Monet, Renoir, Cezanne, and other masters.

- Now, at Flamingo Boulevard, cross the street to the east—over to **Paris.** This is the midpoint of the tour, and this area is full of areas to sit and rest or to grab a bite to eat. While at Paris, tour the **Eiffel Tower.** This is an exact replica, in half scale, of the original in France. The plans for the original were lent to the developers of the hotel so they could be as accurate as possible. There's also a two-thirds-scale replica of *L'Arc de Triomphe* near the hotel entrance—complete with Napoleon's victories inscribed on it.

- The next stop on this is the **MGM Grand.** This very large hotel strives to make visitors feel like stars. Elegance abounds at this hotel. Don't miss the **Lion Habitat** here: a walk-through tour that showcases some beautiful lions, some of which are descendants of Metro, the MGM marquee lion. The only thing separating you and the lions is a glass wall on both sides—an exciting experience.

- Just south of the MGM Grand is the famous **Tropicana,** home to the longest-running show on the Strip.

- After the Tropicana, cross the street again and take the tram from Excalibur to Mandalay Bay. At Mandalay Bay, get back in your car and cross the street to see the **Glass Pool Inn.** This motel was originally called The Mirage but sold the rights to its name to the much larger entity many years ago. The motel features an unusual above-ground pool with portal windows that has been featured in many movies.

- Finish off the tour of the southern Las Vegas Strip by driving north back past the Tropicana and MGM Grand and beyond. The drive provides amazing views that you may have missed along the walk.

THINGS TO SEE AND DO

Driving along the Las Vegas Strip will certainly keep your senses engaged, but if you yearn to get out of the car and stretch your legs, or if you'd like to make a mini-vacation out of your trip, check out these attractions along the route.

◆ BELLAGIO GALLERY OF FINE ART.
3600 Las Vegas Blvd S, Las Vegas (89109). Phone 702/693-7111. A refined retreat amid the Sin City madness, the Bellagio Gallery of Fine Art mounts rotating exhibitions organized by a New York gallery on subjects ranging from Faberge eggs to Calder mobiles. The gallery's fine shop stocks arty souvenirs. Open daily 9 am-9 pm. $$$

DESERT PASSAGE. *3663 Las Vegas Blvd S, Las Vegas (89109). Phone 702/866-0710.* Among the largest shopping centers on the Strip, Aladdin's Desert Passage models a North African bazaar with Moroccan archways, mosaic tiles, fountain courtyards, and stucco walls. The circular center tallies over 130 shops and 14 restaurants, most more affordable than those at Caesars Palace's designer-driven Forum Shops. Key tenants include cookware specialist Sur La Table, beauty supplier Sephora, trendsetter North Beach Leather, and outdoor outfitter Eddie Bauer. Direct from New Orleans, Commander's Palace restores the shop-weary lunch set. Open Sun-Thurs 10 am-11 pm, Fri-Sat 10 am-midnight.

EIFFEL TOWER EXPERIENCE. *3655 Las Vegas Blvd S, Las Vegas (89109). Phone 702/946-7000.* The City of Light immigrates to Las Vegas in the form of a 50-story half-scale replica of the Eiffel Tower. A glass elevator whisks you to 460 feet for panoramic views of the mountain-ringed valley by day and the neon canyon by night. The 11th-floor restaurant Eiffel Tower serves the fine French food of native Frenchman (and longtime Chicago chef) Jean Joho. Open daily 10 am-1 am. $$

◆ THE FORUM SHOPS AT CAESARS.
3500 Las Vegas Blvd S, Las Vegas (89109). Phone 702/893-4800. With piazzas, fountains, and an ever-changing (painted) sky overhead, the Forum Shops evoke an ancient Roman street in keeping with landlord Caesars Palace. Time your visit to catch one of the hourly shows at the Festival Fountain, where the statues of Bacchus, Venus, Apollo, and Mars come to life in an animatronic bacchanal (there's also a similar show at the other end of the mall involving Atlas). Stores scale toward luxury retailers like Bulgari, Escada, Gucci, and Fendi, but also include crowd-pleasers like Gap, FAO Schwarz, and Niketown. Several good restaurants, including Spago and Chinois, both from Wolfgang Puck, warrant a visit even for the shopping shy. Open Sun-Thurs 10 am-11 pm, Fri-Sat 10 am-midnight.

◆ FOUNTAINS OF BELLAGIO.
3600 Las Vegas Blvd S, Las Vegas (89109). Phone 702/693-7111. A Busby Berkeley chorus line with water cannons subbing for gams, the Fountains of the Bellagio perform daily to a roster of tunes ranging from campy to operatic. The razzle-dazzle really roils after dark, when 4,500 lights dramatize the 1,000-nozzle, 27 million-gallon performances. Crowds tend to stake out spots along the wall ringing the hotel-fronting lake several minutes before every evening show. But if you're a hotel guest, you can catch it on the TV's Bellagio channel. Open Mon-Fri 3 pm-midnight; Sat-Sun noon-midnight.

FREMONT STREET EXPERIENCE. *425 Fremont St, Las Vegas (89101). Phone 702/678-5600.* Old downtown Las Vegas aimed to compete with Strip neon via the Fremont Street Experience, a light and sound show broadcast on a 90-foot-high canopy over a four-block stretch of Fremont Street installed in 1995. And the $70 million gamble paid off. Embedded with 2.1 million lights and 218 speakers, the overhead show synchronizes music and colored-light-derived images in each six-minute show. Only the hottest hands in the

Nevada

❋ Las Vegas Strip

ten casinos that border the thoroughfare (also sponsors of the Experience) can resist filing outside for the on-the-hour shows. Each computerized performance per night is different, keying off various musical styles from calypso to disco to country western. Hourly shows dusk-midnight. **FREE**

GAMBLERS GENERAL STORE. *800 Main St, Las Vegas (89101). Phone 702/382-9903.* Take the casino action home with you courtesy of Gamblers General Store, an emporium for the wagering addicted. Wares range from portable poker chip sets and playing cards to roulette wheels, slot machines, and raffle drums—all shippable. Did the tables teach you an expensive lesson? Bone up for a return visit through the store's library of gaming books and videos. Open daily 9 am-5 pm; closed holidays.

GRAND CANAL SHOPPES AT THE VENETIAN. *3355 Las Vegas Blvd S, Las Vegas (89109). Phone 702/414-1000.* A 1,200-foot-long replica of the Grand Canal bisects the Grand Canal Shoppes, making this one of the Strip's more elegant retail emporiums. Venetian bridges, arches, and arcades dress up the mall. International luxury purveyors like Burberry, Jimmy Choo, and Wolford make a strong showing here. Try Il Prato or Ripa de Monte for Venetian paper goods, carnival masks, and Murano glass. When you're ready to drop, there's a food court and a number of full-service restaurants, many with patio seating. Open Sun-Fri 10 am-11 pm, Sat 10 am-midnight.

✪ GUGGENHEIM HERMITAGE MUSEUM. *3355 Las Vegas Blvd S, Las Vegas (89109). Phone 702/414-2440.* A venue for rotating exhibitions, the Guggenheim Hermitage is actually managed by a trio of museums, including the New York Guggenheim, Russia's Hermitage, and the Kunsthistorisches Museum in Vienna. Its open-ended, long-running show "Art Through the Ages" features 40 paintings that take a sweeping look at art history, from the 15th century's Jan Van Eyck, through the popular French Impressionist period, to the Expressionism of Jackson Pollack. Hot Dutch architect Rem Koohaas designed the showcase, breaking ground here by using textured industrial metal walls in place of the velvet used at the Hermitage and providing a modern counterpoint to the baroque trimmings of the Venetian that houses it. Open daily 9:30 am-8:30 pm. **$$$**

LION HABITAT. *3799 Las Vegas Blvd S, Las Vegas (89109). Phone 702/891-1111.* MGM's mascot lions lounge by day near the casino floor in a skylit habitat surrounded by waterfalls, acacia trees, and a pond. For close encounters, pass through it via a see-through tunnel as the lions pad above and below. Feline expert Keith Evans trucks up to six big cats daily to the Strip from his ranch 12 miles away. Open daily 11 am-11 pm. **FREE**

NEON MUSEUM. *3rd and Fremont sts, Las Vegas (89101). Phone 702/387-6366.* In an effort to preserve the outrageous neon signs for which the city is famed, Las Vegas' Neon Museum currently consists of ten vintage ads, refurbished and remounted in two outdoor "galleries," on 3rd and Fremont streets downtown. Neon touting Dot's Flowers (from 1949), the Nevada Motel (1950), Anderson Dairy's delivery boy (1956), and the Red Barn bar's martini glass (1960) seem almost quaint beside today's more elaborately evolved wattage. Guided tours $. Open 24 hours. **FREE**

RED ROCK CANYON NATIONAL CONSERVATION AREA. *From Las Vegas Blvd (the Strip), go W on Charleston Blvd for 17 miles to Red Rock Scenic Dr. Phone 702/515-5340. www.redrockcanyon.blm.gov.* Although only 10 miles from town limits, Red Rock Canyon couldn't be more dissimilar from the Neon Gulch. The 13-mile drive through the conservation area on a one-way road takes you to its most entertaining features, including several trailhead stops for day hikes and an almost certain photo op with the assertive wild burros that thrive here. Thirty miles of Mojave Desert trails take hikers deep into the petrified sand dunes, past ancient pictographs and mysterious waterfalls. Difficulty varies, but there's something here for everyone, from the Sunday stroller to the intermediate scrambler and advanced climber. Bureau of Land Management rangers often lead interpretive walks; call for details. Open winter 6 am-5 pm, spring and fall to 7 pm, summer to 8 pm; visitors center, winter 8 am-4:30 pm, summer to 5:30 pm.

RUMJUNGLE. *3950 Las Vegas Blvd S, Las Vegas (89119). Phone 702/632-7408.* One of the hottest scenes in Las Vegas, rumjungle pours on the eye candy, from platform-top dancing girls to gushing waterfalls. Until 9 pm weekdays and 11 pm on weekends, the nightspot opens as an eatery, dishing up global island fare with loads of sharable, martini-friendly finger foods. After hours, the place turns full-on nightclub with a blend of house and Latin music. When House of Blues shows nearby let out, rumjungle packs them in. Open Sun-Wed 5 pm-2 am, Thurs-Sat 5 pm-4 am.

SPORTS BOOK AT THE MIRAGE HOTEL AND CASINO. *3400 Las Vegas Blvd S, Las Vegas (89109). Phone 702/791-7111.* Most casinos have one, but sports books are shrinking in newer hotels. The Mirage boasts a 10,000-square-foot sports betting palace. If there's a sport that can be bet on, it's on the busy tote boards and televisions here, easily accounting for the visual confusion of neophytes. If you don't understand the odds, ask the window clerks. Sports bookies have dreamed up myriad ways to bet: not just who wins, who loses, and the point spread, but who wins the coin toss, what the halftime score will be, and who will score more points today, an individual NBA star or the Green Bay Packers. Big events, including the Super Bowl, the Kentucky Derby, and the NBA Finals, are predictably jammed. But niche sports like NCAA basketball and World Cup soccer draw sizable contingents to the book as well, making seats scarce. Open 24 hours.

WET 'N WILD LAS VEGAS. *2601 Las Vegas Blvd S, Las Vegas (89109). Phone 702/765-9700. www.wetnwildlv.com.* Primed to cool the kids in the desert dog days, the conveniently located Wet 'n Wild pumps nearly 2 million gallons of water through chutes, flumes, slides, a lazy river, and a wave pool. Some features, including seven-story plummets, are restricted to teens and adults. For the littlest, there's a pirate ship-cum-playground over the shallowest of pools. Rafts, tubes, and lockers are available for rent. Open May-Sept, daily at 10 am; closed Oct-mid-Apr. $$$$

PLACES TO STAY

If you choose to include an overnight stay in your trip along this All-American Road, Mobil Travel Guide recommends the following lodgings.

★★★★ **BELLAGIO.** *3600 Las Vegas Blvd S, Las Vegas (89109). Phone 702/693-7111; toll-free 888/987-6667. www.bellagiolasvegas.com.* The Bellagio Las Vegas is a visual masterpiece. From its bold designs and world-class artwork to its acclaimed entertainment and award-winning cuisine, Bellagio delights the senses. The lobby draws attention with its dazzling bursts of color from the 2,000 hand-blown glass flowers by renowned artist Dale Chihuly. The rooms delightfully combine European élan with American comfort. A fantastic casino is only the beginning at this all-encompassing resort, which hosts an impressive swimming pool and fountain area, an arcade of fine shopping, and a Conservatory and Botanical Gardens under its roof. Discriminating diners will applaud the culinary works of art created in the resort's many fine dining establishments. Figuring largely in the Bellagio experience is its 8-acre lake, where mesmerizing fountains perform to a symphony of sounds and lights every half-hour or so. Bellagio is also home to Cirque du Soleil's *O*, a heart-stopping aquatic performance that is simply not to be missed. 3,005 rooms, 36 story. Adults only. TV; cable

Nevada

❋ *Las Vegas Strip*

(premium). Restaurants. Exercise room. Spa. Massage. Heated pool; whirlpool, poolside service. Entertainment. **$$**

[D][SC][≈][🚶]

★★★ **CAESARS PALACE.** *3570 Las Vegas Blvd S, Las Vegas (89109). Phone 702/731-7110; toll-free 800/634-6661. www.caesars.com.* The Roman-themed Caesars was the Strip's first mega-resort when it opened in 1966. And though little lasts long in Vegas, Caesars still reigns, constantly growing and challenging competitors to keep up. To its Italian facade, Caesars recently added a replica of Rome's Coliseum in which singer Celine Dion entertains. The hotel's swimming deck, modeled on Pompeii, trims three pools in marble statues. The confusing layout of the casino floor is an open play to keep you in house. But there's plenty to recommend it, including 808 and Bradley Ogden restaurants as well as the high-end Forum Shops. Standard guest quarters include a couch as well as a marble bathroom. 2,500 rooms, 14-32 story. Check-out noon, check-in 3 pm. TV; cable (premium), VCR available (movies). In-room modem link. Restaurant, bar; entertainment. Exercise room, massage, sauna, steam room. Game room. Three pools, whirlpool. Handball. Racquetball. Free parking. Business center. Concierge. Casino. **$$**

[🚶][D][≈]

★★★★ **FOUR SEASONS HOTEL LAS VEGAS.** *3960 Las Vegas Blvd S, Las Vegas (89119). Phone 702/632-5000.* The Four Seasons Hotel is a palatial refuge in glittering Las Vegas. Located on the southern tip of the famous strip, the Four Seasons remains close to the attractions of this dynamic city while providing a welcome respite from the hustle and bustle. This non-gaming hotel occupies the 35th through 39th floors of the Mandalay Bay Resort tower, yet it is distinctively Four Seasons with its sumptuous décor and inimitable service. Guests surrender to the plush furnishings in the stylish rooms, and floor-to-ceiling windows showcase exhilarating views of the strip's neon lights or the stark beauty of the Nevada desert. Steak lovers rejoice at Charlie Palmer Steak, while the sun-filled Verandah offers a casual dining alternative. The glorious pool is a lush oasis with its swaying palm trees and attentive poolside service. Lucky visitors retreat to the sublime spa, where JAMU Asian techniques soothe the weary. 424 rooms, 5 story. Pet accepted, some restrictions. Check-out noon, check-in 3 pm. TV; cable (premium). Room service 24 hours. Restaurant, bar. Spa. Outdoor pool, children's pool. Concierge. **$$**

[D][➔][SC][≈]

★★★ **HARRAH'S HOTEL AND CASINO.** *3475 Las Vegas Blvd S, Las Vegas (89109). Phone 702/369-5000.* The gaming powerhouse Harrah's runs this Strip hotel, where the emphasis, as you might expect, is on the casino. Bolstering the hotel and casino's carnival theme décor, an outdoor plaza showcases entertainers, trinket vendors, and snack booths. Spacious but rather bland rooms are lodged in a 35-story tower behind the gaming floor, although guests spend most of their time at the many tables, Olympic-size swimming pool, boutique spa, or eight eateries. Popular entertainer Clint Holmes rules the showroom here with song and dance. 2,673 rooms, 35 story. Check-out noon, check-in 4 pm. TV. Laundry services. Restaurant, bar; entertainment. In-house fitness room, spa, massage, sauna. Game room. Outdoor pool. Valet parking available. Casino, wedding chapel. **$**

[D][SC][≈][🚶]

★★★ **LUXOR HOTEL AND CASINO.** *3900 Las Vegas Blvd S, Las Vegas (89119). Phone 702/262-4000.* A 30-story glass pyramid in the desert, the thoroughly thematic Luxor emulates ancient Egypt from its sphinx figurehead outdoors to gold-costumed employees within. Elevators travel the pyramid's incline to deposit guests at room hallways that overlook the world's largest atrium. Five pools, a fitness center, and a spa provide recreation, while an IMAX theater, two-story game room for the kids, and museum devoted to King Tut entertain. The inventive performance artists Blue Man Group headline Luxor's stage options. 4,400 rooms, 30 story. Check-out 11 am, check-in 3 pm. TV; cable (premium), VCR available. Restaurant, bar; entertainment. In-house fitness room, spa, massage, sauna. Outdoor pool, children's pool. Business center. Concierge. Casino. $

★★★ MANDALAY BAY RESORT AND CASINO.
3950 Las Vegas Blvd S, Las Vegas (89119). Phone 702/632-7777. Even in over-the-top Las Vegas, Mandalay Bay exceeds expectations. This all-encompassing resort captures the spirit of the tropics with its 11-acre sandy beach and three pools with lazy river ride. The stylish accommodations flaunt a tropical flavor, and the casino is a paradise of lush foliage and flowing water, yet this resort is perhaps best known for its mystifying Shark Reef. This facility goes far beyond the ordinary aquarium and takes the entire family on an unforgettable adventure. In true Vegas style, this resort has it all, including a 30,000-square-foot spa and terrific shopping. Thirteen restaurants offer a taste of the world, while an astounding variety of entertainment options include everything from live music to Broadway-style shows. 3,215 rooms, 403 suites, 36 story. Check-out 11 am, check-in 3 pm. TV; cable (premium). In-room modem link. Room service 24 hours. Restaurants, bar; entertainment. In-house fitness room, spa, massage. Beach. Outdoor pool, children's pool, whirlpool. $

★★★ MGM GRAND HOTEL AND CASINO.
3799 Las Vegas Blvd S, Las Vegas (89109). Phone 702/891-7777. The largest hotel on the Strip, the MGM Grand virtually pulses with Las Vegas energy. If you've come for nonstop thrills, check in here, where the attractions work well to keep you out of your comfortable room. In the casino, a glassed-in lion habitat with waterfalls showcases a wild pride. The outdoor pool includes a current-fed lazy river, and the spa specializes in cutting-edge treatments. MGM eateries Coyote Café, NobHill, and Craftsteak are thought to be some of the best in the city. The party crowd crows for the dance club Studio 54 and the lounge Tabu. 5,005 rooms, 29 story. Check-out 11 am. Check-in 3 pm. TV; cable (premium). Internet access. Restaurants, bar; entertainment. Supervised children's activities, ages 3-12. Exercise room, spa, steam room. Game room. Pool, whirlpool, poolside service. Free parking. Airport transportation. Business center. Concierge. ¢

★★★ THE MIRAGE HOTEL AND CASINO.
3400 Las Vegas Blvd S, Las Vegas (89177). Phone 702/791-7111. The Strip-side volcano—which erupts every 15 minutes at night—marks the Mirage and its exotic theme. Tropical fish tanks back the registration desks, the route to room elevators passes through a cascade of jungle foliage, and a lavish pool deck is ringed by towering palms. Among Mirage's many eateries, Renoir is one of town's tops for fine dining, while the Brazilian-style Samba makes a celebration of meat-eating. Two of Vegas' most popular shows—impersonator Danny Gans and lion-taming illusionists Siegfried & Roy—play the Mirage. Rooms, recently and smartly renovated, include spacious, marble-trimmed baths. 3,044 rooms, 30 story. Check-out noon, check-in 2 pm. TV; VCR available. In-room modem link. Restaurants, bar; entertainment. Exercise room, massage. Pool, whirlpool. Valet parking available. Business center. Concierge. Casino. $$

★★★ PARIS LAS VEGAS.
3645 Las Vegas Blvd, Las Vegas (89109). Phone 702/946-7000. A half-scale model of the Eiffel Tower landmarks Paris Las Vegas, an ode to French savoir faire complete with a copy of the Arc de Triomphe and costumed landscape painters fronting the Strip-side pavilion. Its charms continue inside, where three legs of the Eiffel Tower rest in the casino and a cobblestone street wends its way

Nevada

❋ *Las Vegas Strip*

through the shopping arcade. Rooms underscore the theme with French fabrics and custom furniture. Request a Strip view to see the dancing Bellagio fountains across the street. Most of the restaurants here are French, including the charming Mon Ami Gabi, which offers outdoor seating on a Las Vegas Boulevard terrace that offers prime people-watching. 2,916 rooms, 30 story. Pet accepted. Check-out 11 am, check-in 3 pm. TV. In-room modem link. Restaurants, bar; entertainment. In-house fitness room, massage, sauna. Outdoor pool, children's pool. Business center. Casino. $

★★ **RIVIERA HOTEL AND CASINO.** *2901 Las Vegas Blvd S, Las Vegas (89109). Phone 702/734-5110.* 2,072 rooms, 170 suites, 24 story. Check-out 11 am, check-in 3 pm. TV; cable (premium). In-room modem link. Restaurant, bar; entertainment. In-house fitness room, sauna, steam room. Outdoor pool, children's pool. Outdoor tennis, lighted courts. Business center. Casino. ¢

★★ **TROPICANA HOTEL & CASINO.** *3801 Las Vegas Blvd S, Las Vegas (89193). Phone 702/739-2222.* Over 1,800 spacious guest rooms including two towers of suites overlook 5 acres of gardens and pools at this popular resort. Guests can enjoy the *Folies Bergère*, said to be Las Vegas' longest running show. 1,878 rooms, 22 story. Check-out 11 am, check-in 3 pm. TV; cable (premium). In-room modem link. Restaurant, bar; entertainment. Sauna. Outdoor pool. Business center. Casino. $

★★★★ **THE VENETIAN RESORT HOTEL & CASINO.** *3355 Las Vegas Blvd S, Las Vegas (89109). Phone 702/414-1000.* From the masterfully re-created Venetian landmark buildings to the frescoed ceilings and gilded details, the Venetian Resort Hotel & Casino faithfully re-creates the splendor that is Venice in the heart of the Las Vegas Strip. Guests amble down the winding alleys and glide past ornate architecture in gondolas in this perfect reproduction of the golden island that has inspired countless artists for centuries. Inside, the Venetian is glamorous and refined. This all-suite property ensures the comfort of its guests in its spacious and luxurious accommodations. After winning a hand in the casino, head for the upscale boutiques displaying world-famous brands alongside signature Murano glass and Carnival masks. Some of the biggest names in American cuisine operate award-winning restaurants here, while the Venetian's Guggenheim and Madame Tussaud's Wax Museum always delight. Guests soak away their sins at the Canyon Ranch Spa Club, the only outpost of the famous destination spa. 3,036 rooms, 35 story. Check-out noon, check-in 3 pm. TV; cable (premium). In-room modem link. Restaurants, bar; entertainment. In-house fitness room, sauna, spa. Outdoor pool, children's pool. Valet parking available. Business center. Casino. $$

PLACES TO EAT

A long day of driving is sure to make you hungry. At the end of your journey, take a table at one of the following restaurants.

★★★★ **AQUA.** *3600 Las Vegas Blvd S, Las Vegas (89109). Phone 702/693-7223.* After strolling through the Bellagio Conservatory & Botanical Gardens on the way to dinner, guests find a luxurious, contemporary dining room bathed in blond wood, creamy neutral tones, and golden light. The menu here is in the care of a talented group of chef-creators trained and transported from the original Aqua in San Francisco. The kitchen is passionate about the sea; delicious dishes tend to concentrate on the creatures of the deep blue ocean jazzed up with California ingredients. Aqua serves the kind of food that begs to be licked off the plate. You won't be able to contain yourself. The menu

is extensive and offers à la carte selections in addition to a pair of five-course tasting menus, one vegetarian and one seasonal. The wine list focuses on American producers and contains some gems from small vineyards as well; you'll find lots of fish-friendly options. Contemporary American menu. Dinner. Jacket required. Reservations required. Valet parking available. $$$$
D

★★★★ **AUREOLE.** *3950 Las Vegas Blvd S (in the Mandalay Bay Resort and Casino), Las Vegas (89119). Phone 702/632-7401. www.aureolelv.com.* A branch of chef Charlie Palmer's New York original, Aureole wows patrons with its centerpiece four-story wine tower. Be sure to order a bottle just to see the catsuit-clad climber, suspended by ropes, locate your vintage. Its 12,000 bottles complement Palmer's seasonal contemporary American cuisine typified by dishes like Peking duck with foie gras ravioli and roast pheasant with sweet potato gnocchi. The modern but romantic room with encircling booths sets the stage for event dining at Mandalay Bay. Progressive American menu. Dinner. Bar. Jacket required. $$$$
D

★★★ **CHINOIS.** *3500 Las Vegas Blvd S, Las Vegas (89109). Phone 702/737-9700.* A spin-off of chef Wolfgang Puck's acclaimed Chinois on Main in Santa Monica, California, Las Vegas' Chinois features similar Asian fusion fare in the Forum Shops at Caesars Palace. The spare, artifact-decorated shop-level café, specializing in pan-Asian fare often lightened California style to please western palettes, is a well-located lunch spot. The broad-ranging menu includes sushi and sashimi, dim sum, wok-fried meat and vegetable recipes such as kung pao chicken, and Asian noodle dishes like pad Thai. Asian menu. Lunch, dinner. Bar. Children's menu. Reservations required. Valet parking available. $$$
D

★★ **CAMELOT.** *3850 Las Vegas Blvd S, in the Excalibur Hotel and Casino, Las Vegas (89109). Phone 702/597-7449.* Camelot serves gourmet dishes in a romantic setting. A cigar room, a wine cellar, a fireplace, and an open kitchen are some of the classic elements found here. Steak menu. Closed Mon, Tues. Dinner. Bar. Casual attire. Reservations accepted. Valet parking available. Large fireplace. $$$
D

★★ **IL FORNAIO.** *3790 Las Vegas Blvd S, Las Vegas (89109). Phone 702/650-6500. www.ilfornaio.com.* Italian menu. Dinner. Contemporary Italian cuisine and on-site bakery. $$$

★★★ **LE CIRQUE.** *3600 Las Vegas Blvd S, Las Vegas (89109). Phone 702/693-8100.* The hallowed temple of cuisine for New York's financial elite has made it to Las Vegas. Restaurateur and charmer Sirio Maccioni, the face and creative force behind the Gotham power scene, brought a branch to the Bellagio. Like its New York City sibling, this Le Cirque is a shining jewel of a restaurant, awash in bold colors and warm fabrics, with a bright, silk-tented ceiling that brings a festive big-top feel to the intimate dining room. The three-course prix fixe menu features rustic French fare that includes something for everyone: snails, fish, lamb, beef, and game, as well as salads and pasta. In signature Maccioni style, each dish is prepared with precision and delivered with care. Caviar service is available for those seeking extreme luxury, and the wine list boasts several stellar choices. French menu. Dinner. Jacket required. Reservations required. Valet parking available. $$$$
D

★★★★ **PICASSO.** *3600 Las Vegas Blvd S, Las Vegas (89109). Phone 702/693-7223.* The Bellagio is home to some of the finest restaurants in Las Vegas, and Picasso stands out among them. It offers exquisite food in a serene space, and it's one of those two-for-one

Nevada

✷ *Las Vegas Strip*

experiences. If you're trying to decide between visiting a museum and having an elegant and inspired meal, you can do both at Picasso. The master painter's original works don the walls of this beautiful, cozy, country-style room with soaring wood-beamed ceilings, sage-toned upholstery, and a stunning view of the lake. The menu is also artwork. The kitchen uses French technique as a canvas for layering Spanish and Mediterranean flavor. (You can opt for a four-course tasting menu or a chef's degustation option as well.) To match the museum-worthy food, you'll be offered a rare and magnificent selection of international wines. If the weather is warm, you can also dine al fresco by the lake—nature's art. French cuisine with Spanish flair. Closed Wed. Dinner. Jacket required. Reservations required. Valet parking available. $$$$
[D]

★★★ **PRIME.** *3600 Las Vegas Blvd S, Las Vegas (89109). Phone 702/693-7223.* Famed New York fusion chef Jean-Georges Vongerichten opened his first and only steakhouse with the stylish Prime. Located in the Bellagio with waterside views of the dancing fountains, Prime serves superior cuts of beef, veal, and lamb with a range of sauces, from standard béarnaise to very Vongerichten tamarind. Ample fish and chicken selections and creative appetizers entice lighter appetites. Elegant and romantic surrounds, including Baccarat crystal chandeliers and velvet draperies, distract from the expense-account prices. American menu. Dinner. Reservations required. $$$$
[D]

★ **STAGE DELI.** *3500 Las Vegas Blvd S, Las Vegas (89109). Phone 702/893-4045.* American, deli menu. Breakfast, lunch, dinner. Bar. Children's menu. Casual attire. Valet parking available. $
[D]

★★ **THE STEAK HOUSE.** *2880 Las Vegas Blvd, Las Vegas (89114). Phone 702/734-0410.* Dinner, Sun brunch. Bar. Reservations accepted. Valet parking available. $$$
[D]

★★★ **TOP OF THE WORLD.** *2000 S Las Vegas Blvd, Las Vegas (89104). Phone 702/380-7711.* In a town of few casino windows and even fewer restaurant views, Top of the World atop the Stratosphere Hotel Tower stands out. The circular room revolves once every 90 minutes, offering 360-degree nighttime views of Vegas by neon. Few scenery-centric restaurants push the culinary envelope, and Top of the World is no exception, although it does a nice job with steaks and continental classics like lobster bisque. A mini Stratosphere in chocolate is a must for dessert, serving two. American menu. Lunch, dinner. Bar. Entertainment. Reservations required. Valet parking available. $$$
[D]

★ **WOLFGANG PUCK CAFÉ.** *3799 Las Vegas Blvd S (in the MGM Grand Hotel and Casino), Las Vegas (89109). Phone 702/895-9653. www.wolfgangpuck.com.* International menu. Breakfast, lunch, dinner. $$

Lakes to Locks Passage – The Great Northeast Journey
❈ NEW YORK

Quick Facts

LENGTH: 234 miles.

TIME TO ALLOW: 2 to 7 days.

BEST TIME TO DRIVE: The springtime is ushered in with sugar season—watch the woods along the Byway, because nearly every sugarbush is tapped for sap collection. In the winter, Lake Champlain's bays become shanty villages for ice fishing. People gather along the passage for ice skating, cross-country skiing, and other winter activities.

BYWAY TRAVEL INFORMATION: Adirondack Regional Tourism Council: toll-free 800/487-6867.

SPECIAL CONSIDERATIONS: Many of the ferries crossing from New York to Vermont are closed in the winter.

BICYCLE/PEDESTRIAN FACILITIES: Most of the Byway route for the Lakes to Locks Passage is designated as NYS Bikeroute 9 and can accommodate bicycle and pedestrian travel. The terrain and outstanding landscape features of the Lakes to Locks Passage make it an outstanding destination for biking and walking as recreation, as well as the mode of transportation along the Byway. The Byway also allows for water-based travel: The interconnected lake and rivers allow access by water from anywhere in the world.

Past Lake Champlain and beneath the Adirondack Mountains, you find the Lakes to Locks Passage. Driving through the villages and hamlets of the Byway, travelers are swept into a place of old history and new adventures. State parks and preserves offer hiking trails, lakeside beaches, and wildlife-spotting opportunities. Paralleling Lake Champlain and the Champlain Canal, the Byway promises scenic views with plenty of history mixed in.

Pre-colonial history is woven throughout the names of places and historic sites. The French explorer Samuel de Champlain named Lake Champlain in 1609. The struggle between nations and people occurred here between the Huron, Algonquin, and Iroquois. During the French and Indian War, the French and British built settlements and fortifications all along the passage. Since then, many changes have moved through the Lakes to Locks Passage, but the natural beauty remains as a constant appeal to new explorers and visitors.

Explorers along the Lakes to Locks Passage travel the road by car, but those who know a little bit about the area bring a bicycle along, too. The Champlain Trail Bikeways are known as some of the best cycling trails in the country. But whether you travel by bicycle, on foot, or in the car, all the routes along the Byway offer access to unique points of interest.

THE BYWAY STORY

The Lakes to Locks Passage tells cultural, historical, natural, recreational, and scenic stories that make it a unique and treasured Byway.

New York

Lakes to Locks Passage–The Great Northeast Journey

Cultural

Residents along the Lakes to Locks Passage look at their part of the country as a working land; the seasons harmonize with the agricultural activities that take place along the Byway. From sugar in the winter to strawberries in the summer, the land along the passage is continually productive. This productivity began long ago with the Iroquois and Abenaki, who were able to develop strategies of survival there. The culture along the Byway today is one that cherishes resources both agricultural and natural.

With bountiful harvests of fresh-cut hay and ripening tomatoes and gardens, life along the Byway is bright and thriving. The people who live and work here enjoy the lakes, rivers, and forests as much as travelers do. During the Industrial Revolution, the rich iron deposits and the forests of the Adirondacks fueled the country. Later, another resource was discovered. Remember that yellow pencil you chewed on in grade school? Ticonderoga was the name written on the side of the pencil, and it was made from the rich graphite deposits found along the shores of Lake Champlain and Lake George. In fact, the region is known as the paper and pencil capital of America.

So as you travel the Lakes to Locks Passage, check out a few of the places where you'll get a glimpse of the local culture. The Waterford Historical Museum and Cultural Center offers a closer look at the oldest incorporated village in the United States. Many of the exhibits offer insight into colonial farming, and the museum overlooks the Mohawk River. Rogers Island Visitors' Center provides a look at the early cultures that lived in the area, and the Ticonderoga Heritage Museum exhibits the history of industry at Ticonderoga. Many other museums and centers offer a piece of Byway culture that allows you to understand the way of life along the Lakes to Locks Passage. You'll find that Byway culture enhances your ride and may even give you an inside look at the best things to do along the way.

Historical

Lakes to Locks is a passage of early American history. From the first Native Americans to the European explorers to the colonists, the geography and history of the land has played an important part in creating a passageway along the corridor that is now a Byway. Expeditions and battles have been carried out on its soil. The growth and development of a new nation has also occurred along the Byway, making it the well-known passage that it is today. The many historical sites along the Byway are evidence that it has always been a land much sought after.

When Samuel de Champlain arrived in the area in 1609, he found people there who loved the land and who struggled for it. The Iroquois were battling with the Algonquins and Hurons, who were joined by the French. As Champlain explored the area with the Algonquins and Hurons, they reached a beautiful lake with four islands and mountains in the distance. The lake was beautiful and, being the traditional explorer that he was, Champlain called it "Lake Champlain." Meanwhile, an English sea captain named Henry Hudson anchored his ship in what is now Albany on his journey to find the legendary Northwest Passage to China. His naming of the upper Hudson River through Lake George and Lake Champlain later influenced trade routes and Dutch settlements in the New World. By 1709, the British had settled the southern end of the passage, while the French had settled the northern end. Eventually, this separation determined the boundary of New York and Canada, but the arrangement would also play a part in the French and Indian War as several different nations fought for control of the land.

The French and Indian War continued for seven years until 1763, when Canada surrendered to Great Britain. For 15 years, the passageway that is now the Lakes to Locks Passage was under the control of Great Britain, but another war was about to take place. In 1776, American colonists began the Revolutionary War that changed the country forever. The American Navy gathered at the south end of Lake Champlain to delay British invasion. Meanwhile, victory at Saratoga won French support and further control of the area. The battles at Saratoga are now considered the turning point of the Revolutionary War as the colonists gained control and a new country was formed.

A new country meant new growth, and settlements were founded all along the Hudson and Champlain valleys. But the peace and prosperity was interrupted once again by war. This time, the War of 1812 set the British against the Americans once again. At the end of the war, the border between the United States and Canada was finally drawn, and peace and growth returned to the area. As the nation expanded, road and canal building became important endeavors. The Champlain Canal allowed movement of mineral and timber resources from the Adirondacks to throughout New York. As the land was developed and society grew, New York became the influential place that it is today. Drivers can see the history of a nation in the communities, forts, and battlefields all along the Lakes to Locks Passage.

Natural

The natural lakes and rivers of the Byway flow through a landscape dotted with mountains. Chasms and forests create scenic places for hiking and adventure. The natural qualities of the Lakes to Locks Passage are closely tied to the scenery and the recreational opportunities that abound on the Byway. Lake Champlain or one of its connecting waterways borders the Byway on its east side, while the Adirondack Mountains border the Byway on its west side. This arrangement creates scenic views and inviting places to stop along the way.

Glaciers from an ice age created the landscape along the Byway. The lakes, rivers, and mountains were all affected by the presence of these great blankets of ice. The mountains were

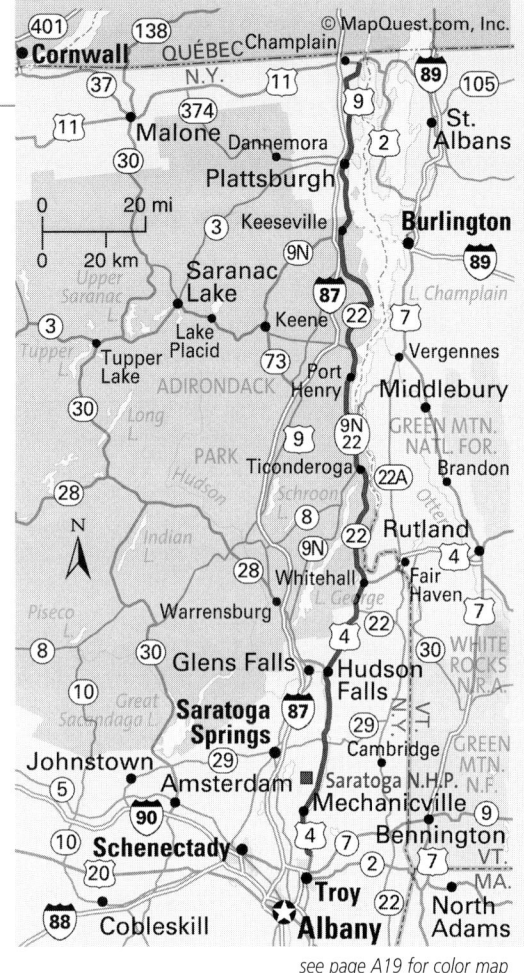

see page A19 for color map

eroded and rounded, the lakes were filled to the brim, and the rivers ran away with the surplus water. The discovery of a whale skeleton on the shores of modern Lake Champlain are an indication of the vastness of the ancient glacial lake. The gorge now known as the Ausable Chasm is sandstone sculpted by the fast-moving Ausable River.

Today, Lake Champlain is one of the largest freshwater lakes in the world, full of many varieties of trout, bass, perch, pike, and other fish. And fish aren't the only kind of wildlife along the Byway. The Lakes to Locks Passage is a host to a natural North American flyway. The Champlain Birding Trail allows you to watch for birds of all kinds as they migrate through the area. From Canadian geese to red-winged blackbirds, creatures with feathers are well represented on the Byway.

New York

✳ Lakes to Locks Passage—The Great Northeast Journey

Recreational

The land that surrounds the Lakes to Locks Passage has been a vacation destination since the early 1800s, when it was part of the "American Grand Tour." Artists, writers, and the elite of the time would enjoy the scenery on a train ride or from a canal boat. Today, gazing out the car window is only the beginning. The Lakes to Locks Passage is a place for boating, bird-watching, biking, and diving beneath the surface of Lake Champlain. The waterways are the center of recreation here, but even if you don't like the water, you'll find plenty to do.

Waterways connect Lake Champlain to an assortment of rivers and canals. Boaters will find access to this beautiful lake by the Champlain Canal, the Hudson River, or the Richelieu River. Lake Champlain being the sixth largest freshwater lake in the world, the boating and fishing opportunities are superb. Boaters, kayakers, and windsurfers can all find communities with marinas, supplies, and places to relax. And if you don't have a boat, boat rentals and tours are available all along the lakeshore. Trout, bass, pike, or perch may be the reason you decide to take a boat onto Lake Champlain—fishing Lake Champlain is such a dynamic experience that experts participate in fishing tournaments held there. With 585 miles of shoreline, professional and amateur anglers can fish and enjoy a picnic on the shore of the lake.

The sights beneath the surface of Lake Champlain also interest visitors to the Byway. America's best collection of freshwater shipwrecks can be found at the bottom of Lake Champlain, and diving is the best way to see them. You can find diving services as well as information on which sites are accessible. The Lake Champlain Underwater Historic Preserve and the Submerged Heritage Preserve are the places to start when searching for an exciting dive. Your dive may even include Champ, the legendary Lake Champlain Monster.

A name like Ausable Chasm just calls for adventure, and that is exactly what kayakers and rafters find as they travel down a 2-mile stretch of the Ausable River. If you prefer exploring on foot, steel bridges afford a bird's-eye view of the chasm. You can cross from one end of the gorge to the other to observe massive rock formations or walk along the cliffs through a forest. On the edge of the Adirondack Park, this part of the Byway is the perfect place for camping, hiking, or cycling. Lake Champlain Bikeways is one of the best cycling spots in the country. The route is nearly 360 miles long and goes through many parts of the Byway and into Quebec. The walkways and bikeways allow you to see the Byway and its recreational opportunities from several different perspectives.

Scenic

Part of the fun of driving the Lakes to Locks Passage is the variety of landscapes and terrains you pass along the way. Lakesides and forests are accented by historic buildings and quaint towns of America's early days. In the setting of lakes and agricultural countryside, the occasional colonial building or fort can be spotted. Meanwhile, the open valleys and rolling landscape of the passage provide a scenic route for cyclists and visitors who are interested in a

ALL-AMERICAN ROADS

scenic walk. The road gently curves past rivers and through bits of New England forest to bring you to destinations like Lake Champlain, the Ausable Chasm, and Adirondack Park.

The passage begins in a place where canals and rivers converge, and then it follows the path of the Champlain Canal where visitors and residents are boating and canoeing. You will definitely want to stop at Mount Defiance, where Lake Champlain, Fort Ticonderoga, and Mount Independence in Vermont are visible. At the north end of Lake Champlain, you can catch glimpses of Valcour Island and drive to Plattsburgh for a historic tour and scenic views of the lake. At Point Au Roche State Park, enjoy the Lake Shore Road that guides you through scenic farmland and views of the northern lake islands in Vermont. To make the journey through the Lakes to Locks Passage even more interesting, information and signs are placed all along the route to provide an extra story or two about the history of the land and the development of the lake, the canal, and its locks.

THINGS TO SEE AND DO

Driving along the Lakes to Locks Passage will certainly keep your senses engaged, but if you yearn to get out of the car and stretch your legs, or if you'd like to make a mini-vacation out of your trip, check out these attractions along the route.

CROWN POINT STATE HISTORIC SITE. *Bridge Rd, Crown Point (12928). Phone 518/597-3666.* Preserved ruins of fortifications occupied by French, British, and American forces during the French and Indian and Revolutionary wars: Fort St. Frederic (1734) and Fort Crown Point (1759). Site museum with exhibits and an audiovisual presentation on the history of the area. Self-guided tours; events. Grounds open May-Oct, daily; museum open Mon, Wed-Sun. **FREE**

PENFIELD HOMESTEAD MUSEUM. *Ironville Rd, Crown Point (12928). Phone 518/597-3804.* Site of the first industrial use of electricity in the US. A walk into history and the birthplace of the Electrical Age, this homestead museum will expose you to life in the 19th century. Museum of local history, Adirondack iron industry; self-guided tour through ironworks ruins. Open mid-May-mid-Oct, Wed-Sun. **$**

ALICE T. MINER COLONIAL COLLECTION. *9618 Main St, Chazy (12921). Phone 518/846-7336.* This 15-room colonial home includes furniture, painting, and decorative arts. Antiques, colonial household items, and appliances in 1824 house; sandwich glass collection; gardens. Open Tues-Sat; closed Jan, Dec 25. **$$**

AUSABLE CHASM. *Plattsburgh (12901) Phone 518/834-7454; toll-free 800/537-1211. www.ausablechasm.com.* This scenic gorge, accessible from US 9, was opened to the public in 1870. It is one of the oldest tourist attractions in the United States. Ausable (Aw-SAY-bl) Chasm leads eastward toward Lake Champlain for about a mile and a half. This spectacular gorge is 20 to 50 feet wide and from 100 to 200 feet deep. The Ausable River plunges in falls and rapids past curious rock formations, each with its own name: Pulpit Rock, Elephant's Head, Devil's Oven, Jacob's Well, the Cathedral. Paths and bridges crisscross the chasm. Camping is available on the grounds.

★ FORT TICONDEROGA. *Ticonderoga (12883). Phone 518/585-2821.* The fort was built in 1755 by the Quebecois, who called it Carillon, and was successfully defended by the Marquis de Montcalm against a more numerous British force in 1758. It was captured by the British in 1759 and by Ethan Allen and the Green Mountain Boys in 1775 (known as the first victory of the Revolutionary War). The stone fort was restored in 1909; the largest collection of cannons in North America is assembled on the grounds. The museum houses collections of weapons, paintings, and articles of daily life of

153

New York

❉ *Lakes to Locks Passage—The Great Northeast Journey*

the soldiers garrisoned here during the Seven Year and Revolutionary wars. Costumed guides give tours; cannon firings daily; fife and drum corps parade (July and Aug); special events. Museum shop; restaurant; picnic area. Scenic drive to the summit of Mount Defiance for a 30-mile view. Open early May-mid-Oct, daily.

HERITAGE MUSEUM. *Montcalm St and Tower Ave, Ticonderoga (12883). Phone 518/585-2696.* Displays of civilian and industrial history of Ticonderoga. Children's workshop. Open late June-Labor Day, daily; Labor Day-mid-Oct, weekends. **FREE**

KENT-DELORD HOUSE MUSEUM. *17 Cumberland Ave, Plattsburgh (12901). Phone 518/561-1035.* (1797) Historic house; British officers' quarters during the Battle of Plattsburgh (War of 1812); period furnishings. Tours. Open Mar-Dec, Tues-Sat afternoons; rest of year, by appointment only; closed Jan 1, Thanksgiving, Dec 25. **$$**

REPLICA OF HANCOCK HOUSE. *3 Wicker St, Ticonderoga (12883). Phone 518/585-7868.* The home of the Ticonderoga Historical Society is a replica of the house built for John Hancock on Beacon Street in Boston. It is maintained as a museum and research library. The rooms display various period furnishings as well as exhibits presenting social and civil history from the 1700s through the present. **FREE**

SARATOGA NATIONAL HISTORICAL PARK. *Saratoga Springs (12866). Phone 518/664-9821.* In two engagements, September 19 and October 7, 1777, American forces under General Horatio Gates defeated the army of General John Burgoyne in the Battles of Saratoga. This brought France into the war on the side of the colonies. The battle is regarded as the turning point of the Revolutionary War. The scene of this historic event is the rolling hill country between US 4 and NY 32, 5 miles north of Stillwater. Park folders with auto tour information are available at the Visitor Center. Open daily; closed Jan 1, Thanksgiving, Dec 25. **$$**

PLACES TO STAY

If you choose to include an overnight stay in your trip along this All-American Road, Mobil Travel Guide recommends the following lodgings.

★★ **MELODY MANOR RESORT.** *610 Lakeshore Dr, Bolton Landing (12814). Phone 518/644-9750.* 40 rooms, 1-3 story. Closed Nov-Apr. Check-out 11 am. TV. Heated pool. Restaurant, bar. Tennis. Recreation room. Lawn games. Rowboat, paddleboat. Some balconies. Picnic tables, grills. On 9 acres, 300-foot lakefront; private sand beach. **$**

★★★ **THE SAGAMORE.** *110 Sagamore Rd, Bolton Landing (12814). Phone 518/644-9400.* This stately, historic resort sits on an island on Lake George amidst the Adirondacks. 100 rooms in main hotel building, 3 story; 130 suites in lodge, 2 story. MAP available; package plans. Service charge $5 per person. Check-out noon, check-in 4 pm. TV; cable (premium). Indoor pool; whirlpool. Playground. Supervised children's activities (July-Aug; rest of year weekends only), ages 3-12. Dining room (public by reservation). Box lunches. Bar. Room service 24 hours (summer). Package store nearby. Convention facilities. Business center. In-room modem link. Bellhops. Concierge. Beauty shop. Valet parking available. Airport, train station transportation; horse-drawn carriages. Lighted and indoor tennis, pro. 18-hole golf privileges, pro, putting green. Private beach. Boats, motors; sightseeing boats, dinner cruises available; dockage. Cross-country ski on site. Ski store, rentals; ice skating. Nature trail. Bicycles. Social director; entertainment. Game room. Racquetball court. Exercise room; sauna, steam room. Spa. Many refrigerators, wet bars, fireplaces; microwaves available. Some private patios, balconies. **$$**

★ **VICTORIAN VILLAGE RESORT MOTEL.** *34818 Lake Shore Dr, Bolton Landing (12814). Phone 518/644-9401.* 3 rooms. No A/C. Late June-Labor Day 3-day minimum. Closed Dec-mid-Apr. Check-out 11 am. TV. Tennis. Lawn games. ¢

★★ **CROWN POINT BED & BREAKFAST.** *2695 Main St (Rte 9 N), Crown Point (12928). Phone 518/597-3651.* 6 rooms, 1 with shower only, 1 suite, 2 story. No A/C. No room phones. Closed Thanksgiving, Dec 25. Complimentary continental breakfast. Check-out 11 am, check-in 3 pm. TV in parlor. Victorian house built in 1886 for a banker; many antiques. Totally nonsmoking. $

★★★ **CANOE ISLAND LODGE.** *Lakeshore Dr, Diamond Point (12824). Phone 518/668-5592.* Guests return to the family vacations of their youth at this 50-year-old, knotty-pine-filled resort on Lake George in the Adirondack Mountains. The namesake island is actually 1 mile offshore; a perfect escape for enjoying the Thursday night barbeque dinners during summer season. 30 rooms in cottages, 18 rooms in 2-story lodges, 6 mini-chalets. MAP. Closed Nov-Apr. Check-out 11 am, check-in 1-4 pm. TV. Playground. Supervised children's activities (July-Aug), ages 3 and up. Dining room. Box lunches. Bar. Business services available. Tennis. Beach; water-skiing, boats, sailboats, rides; dockage. Lawn games. Recreation room. Entertainment; dancing. Barbecues on island. Some fireplaces in cottages. Some balconies. Rustic atmosphere. $

★ **JULIANA MOTEL.** *3842 Lakeshore Dr, Diamond Point (12824). Phone 518/668-5191.* 26 rooms, 9 kitchen units, 1-2 story, 7 kitchen cottages. Closed Labor Day-mid-May. Check-out 10 am. TV; cable (premium). Restaurant nearby. Playground. Recreation room. Pool. Picnic tables, grills. Private beach; rowboat. Sun deck. ¢

★ **TREASURE COVE RESORT MOTEL.** *3940 Lake Shore Dr, Diamond Point (12824). Phone 518/668-5334.* 50 rooms, 14 kitchen cottages, A/C in some cottages. Closed mid-Oct-mid-Apr. Check-out 10 am. TV. Pools. Playground. Restaurant nearby. Game room. Lawn games. Boat rentals; fishing charters. Refrigerators; some fireplaces. Picnic tables, grills. Private beach. $

★★ **BEST WESTERN THE INN AT SMITHFIELD.** *446 Cornelia St, Plattsburgh (12901). Phone 518/561-7750. www.bestwestern.com.* 120 rooms, 2 story. Pet accepted. Check-out noon. TV; cable (premium), VCR available. In-room modem link. Laundry services. Restaurant, bar. Exercise equipment. Indoor pool, poolside service. $

★ **CIRCLE COURT.** *440 Montcalm St W, Ticonderoga (12883). Phone 518/585-7660.* 14 rooms. Pet accepted. Check-out 11 am. TV. Refrigerators in rooms. Restaurant nearby. ¢

PLACES TO EAT

A long day of driving is sure to make you hungry. At the end of your journey, take a table at one of the following restaurants.

★ **FREDERICKS'S RESTAURANT.** *Rte 9 N, Lakeshore Dr, Bolton Landing (12814). Phone 518/644-3484. www.fredericksrestaurant.com.* Seafood menu. Lunch, dinner. Known for authentic local specialties and an extensive raw bar. $$

★★★ **TRILLIUM.** *110 Sagamore Rd, Bolton Landing (12814). Phone 518/644-9400.* In the Sagamore, a sprawling, gorgeously decorated inn on Lake George, diners will find chef David Britton creating a new feast every day. A typical entrée is roasted Maine lobster with vanilla fava bean risotto or "just cooked" salmon.

New York

❋ *Lakes to Locks Passage–The Great Northeast Journey*

Gourmet cuisine; own baking, ice cream. Reservations required. Dinner. Bar. Service charge 17%. Valet parking available. Elegant Greek Revival décor. Two-level dining area; view of lake. Jacket required. $$$
D

★ **ONE ONE ONE.** *111 Main St, Greenwich (12834). Phone 518/692-8016. www.111restaurant.com.* American. Closed Mon. Dinner. Unique regional cuisine in an art-gallery setting. $

★★ **THE VIEW RESTAURANT AT INDIAN KETTLES.** *9580 Lake Shore Dr, Rte 9 N, Hague (12836). Phone 518/543-8038. www.indian-kettles.com.* American menu. Built in 1946 and continuously operated as a restaurant on the banks of Lake George. Known for authentic local specialties. $

★★ **ANTHONY'S.** *538 Rte 3, Plattsburgh (12901). Phone 518/561-6420.* Continental menu. Closed some major holidays. Lunch, dinner. Bar. Children's menu. $$

★ **CARILLON RESTAURANT.** *61 Hague Rd, Ticonderoga (12883). Phone 518/585-7657. www.carillonrestaurant.com.* American menu. Closed Wed. Dinner. Chef-owned restaurant in the historic district of Ticonderoga. $

★ **FORT TICONDEROGA'S LOG HOUSE RESTAURANT.** *Rte 74, Ticonderoga (12883). Phone 518/585-2851. www.fort-ticonderoga.com.* American menu. Closed mid-Oct-mid-May. Breakfast, lunch. Regional cuisine in a historic setting. $

★ **GOLDEN ROOSTER.** *191 Montcalm St, Ticonderoga (12883). Phone 518/585-2673.* Hungarian menu. Closed Mon. Lunch, dinner. Owned and operated by a Hungarian couple who serve authentic Hungarian specialties. $

★ **HOT BISCUIT DINER.** *428 Montcalm St, Ticonderoga (12883). Phone 518/585-3483.* Closed some major holidays. Breakfast, lunch, dinner. Children's menu. $$
D

★ **FINCH & CHUBB RESTAURANT & INN.** *82 N Williams St, Whitehall (12887). Phone 518/499-2049. www.whitehall.com.* American menu. Lunch, dinner. Chef-owned establishment with regional cuisine and views of Whitehall Harbor. $

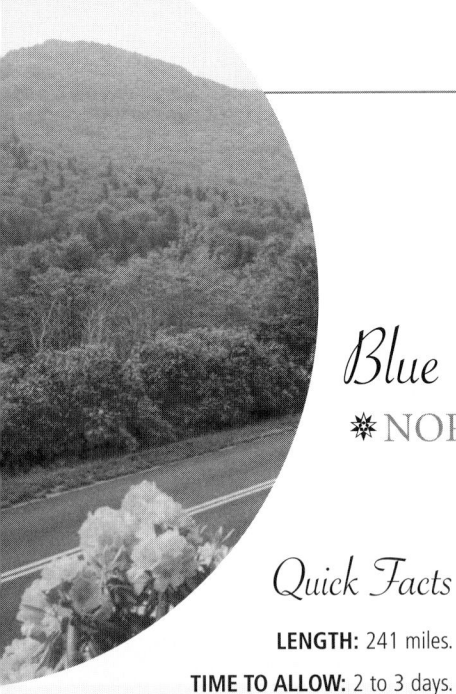

Blue Ridge Parkway
❈ NORTH CAROLINA

Quick Facts

LENGTH: 241 miles.

TIME TO ALLOW: 2 to 3 days.

BEST TIME TO DRIVE: June through October. Visitor Centers and recreational facilities are open from May through October. High season includes July 4 and Labor Day weekends and the month of October (fall foliage).

BYWAY TRAVEL INFORMATION: Byway local Web site: www.nps.gov/blri.

SPECIAL CONSIDERATIONS: Avoid traveling the parkway during periods of fog, snow, and ice. Bring a lightweight jacket for cool nights from spring through fall. Service stations are limited, but access points along the parkway allow for refueling in nearby communities. Also, watch for deer-crossing signs.

RESTRICTIONS: The parkway is open year-round, unless weather conditions (snow, ice, and windstorms) cause portions of the roadway to be closed. Speed is limited to 45 mph on the parkway. Swimming is not allowed in parkway lakes and ponds.

BICYCLE/PEDESTRIAN FACILITIES: The parkway was designed as a scenic leisure road for motorists; when bicycling, be prepared for significant distances between developed areas and services that vary by season.

The Blue Ridge Parkway is a scenic drive that crests the southern Appalachian Mountains and takes you through a myriad of natural, cultural, and recreational places. Many people drive the Blue Ridge Parkway for its natural botanical qualities. The shrubs and flowers that blossom throughout the spring and summer are a defining feature of the parkway, and in the fall, leaves burst into colors of red, yellow, and orange. And where there is lush vegetation, there is also abundant wildlife.

The diverse history and culture of the southern Appalachians are described at many overlooks and facilities along the parkway.

THE BYWAY STORY

The Blue Ridge Parkway tells archeological, cultural, historical, natural, recreational, and scenic stories that make it a unique and treasured Byway.

Archaeological

The story of the Blue Ridge Parkway is told partially through remnants of early Native Americans, mountain men, miners, and road builders of the Great Depression. Man and the area surrounding the Blue Ridge Parkway have been closely intertwined, and the artifacts and old buildings they leave behind provide information on the inhabitants that have lived in this area.

You find many signs of Native American culture and influence along the Blue Ridge Parkway, including those of the Cherokee. They have left behind artifacts and changes in the landscape as evidence of their lives here. Many of the fields still visible at the base of the mountains date back centuries to ancient

N. Carolina

✽ Blue Ridge Parkway

Native American agricultural methods of burning and deadening the trees and underbrush to provide needed grazing and crop land. Mountain and river names along the parkway also reflect the Native American influence. In North Carolina, the parkway enters the Qualla Reservation at milepost 457.7 and features an informational display on the reservation at the Lickstone Parking Overlook (milepost 458.9). Evidence of European settlements and homesteads are also found all along the parkway.

Cultural

Along the Blue Ridge Parkway, evidence of the local cultures are found in communities, museums, and shops. The cultures of the past are in abandoned cabins and structures left behind. Old family cemeteries, springhouses, and other indications of Appalachian habitation are scattered up and down the motor road, just waiting to be discovered. Mountain handicrafts are one of the most popular attractions along the Byway, and traditional crafts and music still thrive in the Blue Ridge Mountains along with more contemporary styles. Along the parkway in North Carolina are several places to view and purchase locally made items. The Folk Art Center in Asheville offers the most impressive collection of crafts on the Byway.

Historical

The parkway was conceived as a link between the Shenandoah National Park in Virginia and the Great Smoky Mountains National Park in North Carolina and Tennessee, and that vision came to fruition in 1935. The idea to build the parkway resulted from a combination of many factors, the primary one being the need to create jobs for trained engineers, architects, and landscape designers who had been left unemployed by the Great Depression, and for the thousands of mountain families already verging on poverty. In addition, recent openings of two popular eastern parks, the Great Smoky Mountains National Park and the Shenandoah National Park, were already attracting tourists to the naturally beautiful but financially poor area. The increasing availability of the automobile brought about a new generation of motoring vacations.

World War II halted construction, but road-building resumed soon after the war ended. By 1968, the only task left was the completion of a 7-mile stretch around North Carolina's Grandfather Mountain. In order to preserve the fragile environment on the steep slopes of the mountain, the Linn Cove Viaduct, a 1,200-foot suspended section of the parkway, was designed and built. Considered an engineering marvel, it represents one of the most successful fusions of road and landscape on the parkway. The Blue Ridge Parkway was officially dedicated on September 11, 1987, 52 years after the ground-breaking.

Natural

The creation of the Blue Ridge Mountains, perhaps hundreds of millions of years in the geologic past, was both violent and dramatic. Today, you can witness the flip-side to the mountain-building story—the mountain's gradual destruction. The slow, steady forces of wind, water, and chemical decomposition have reduced the Blue Ridge from Sierra-like proportions to the low profile of the world's oldest mountain range.

Diversity is the key word when understanding the ecology of the Appalachian Mountains. Park biologists have identified 1,250 kinds of vascular plants, 25 of which are rare or endangered. Four rare or endangered animals have also been identified on parkway lands. The reasons for this wide diversity are numerous. Elevation is a key factor, with parkway lands as low as 650 feet above sea level and as high as 6,047 feet above sea level. The parkway is also oriented on a north-south axis, with its two ends far apart. Combining these two factors, the parkway contains habitat as diverse as one may find when traveling from Georgia to Newfoundland, Canada.

Beginning at the parkway's lowest elevations and climbing up to its highest, you notice numerous transitions among a variety of forest types. Interspersed among these various forest types are small, unique habitats, like mountain bogs and heath balds. Many species of animals find their niche in these small pockets of habitat. Bog turtles and Gray's lily thrive in mountain bogs. Sheltered, wet coves are excellent for finding a variety of salamanders, some of which are unique to the southern Appalachians. A hemlock cove is an excellent place to find populations of red squirrel. Black-capped chickadees replace the Carolina chickadees as you climb up toward the spruce-fir forest. And of course, the Blue Ridge Mountains are also home to mountain lions, eagles, and even bears. For birding enthusiasts, the parkway offers a never-ending supply of beautiful birds, from the American bittern to the whippoorwill.

Recreational

The very nature of the Blue Ridge Parkway allows for outstanding recreational opportunities. You may choose to camp along the parkway in order to prolong your stay and make the most of all the area has to offer. Trails around the parkway let you hike into the inner regions of the Appalachian Mountains. If you're a bicyclist, you can enjoy the mountainous terrain and scenery. Anglers find a haven in the many streams and rivers that flow near the Byway. Nearby state parks and national forests have developed swimming areas perfect for a refreshing dip amid the forest-covered mountains. Rushing rivers create a playground for rafters and kayakers.

Festivals and events are often occurring in local towns and communities, from sports to outdoor adventure to drama to folk art.

Scenic

The parkway combines awesome natural beauty with the pioneer history of gristmills, weathered cabins, and split-rail fences to create the country's most popular national park. It encompasses a world of mountain forests, wildlife, and wildflowers thousands of feet above a patchwork of villages, fields, and farms.

Share the Blue Ridge magic by stopping at overlooks and campgrounds, picnic spots and mountain trails. Leave yourself time to explore the historic, hospitable towns along the way, where you'll find food and lodging, fuel and supplies, and lots of fun and good times. From the first explosion of colorful wildflowers in the spring to the refreshing coolness of summer to the fall extravaganza in red and gold to the stark beauty of snow-covered peaks in winter, each season provides you with a completely different Blue Ridge Parkway.

Wildlife is also a delight to see along the parkway. When the sun is high, groundhogs

see page A20 for color map

N. Carolina

✺ Blue Ridge Parkway

sit erect and chipmunks and squirrels chitter and chatter. At night, skunks, bobcats, foxes, opossums, and raccoons may be seen along the roadsides. Whitetail deer and black bears are present but seldom seen. Look for them in the early morning or evening. More than 100 bird species can be seen during the spring migration season as well. Because of the seasonal changes for both wildlife and vegetation, the Blue Ridge Parkway offers new sights year-round.

HIGHLIGHTS

The North Carolina section of the Blue Ridge Parkway begins at the state line at milepost 216.9 near Cumberland Knob. The following points of interest are the primary sights along the Byway. A few sites located just off the Byway, which are highly popular, are listed as well. Most services are available from May through October.

- **Milepost 217.5—Cumberland Knob,** at 2,885 feet, is a delightful spot to walk through fields and woodlands.
- **Milepost 238.5—Brinegar Cabin** was built by Martin Brinegar about 1880 and lived in until the 1930s. The original cabin is still standing.
- **Milepost 258.6—Northwest Trading Post** is sponsored by the Northwest Development Association to keep alive the old crafts within North Carolina's 11 northwestern counties.
- **Milepost 272—E. B. Jeffress Park** has a self-guiding trail to the Cascades and another trail to the old cabin and church.
- **Milepost 292 to 295—Moses H. Cone Memorial Park** has 25 miles of carriage roads, ideal for hiking and horseback riding. Flat Top Manor houses the Parkway Craft Center.
- **Milepost 304.4—Linn Cove Viaduct,** a highlight of the parkway and a design and engineering marvel, skirts the side of Grandfather Mountain.
- **Milepost 316.3—Linville Falls** roars through a dramatic, rugged gorge. Take trails to overlooks.
- **Milepost 331—Museum of North Carolina Minerals** has an interpretive display of the state's mineral wealth.
- **Milepost 355.4—Mount Mitchell State Park,** reached via NC 128, has a picnic area, a lookout tower, and the highest point east of the Mississippi River.
- **Milepost 382—Folk Art Center** offers sales and exhibits of traditional and contemporary crafts of the Appalachian Region. Interpretive programs, gallery, and library.
- **Biltmore Estate** is located 4 miles from the Highway 25-North exit near Asheville. George Vanderbilt's impressive 250-room mansion and grounds landscaped by the celebrated landscape architect Frederick Law Olmstead, designer of Central Park.
- **Milepost 408.6—Mount Pisgah** was once part of the Biltmore Estate. The estate became home of the first US forestry school and is the nucleus of the Pisgah National Forest.
- **Milepost 422.4—Devil's Courthouse** is a rugged exposed mountaintop rich in Cherokee legends. A walk to the bare rock summit yields a spectacular view of the Pisgah National Forest.
- **Milepost 431—Richland Balsam's** self-guiding trail takes you through a remnant spruce-fire forest. It's the highest point on the parkway at 6,047 feet.
- **Milepost 451.2—Waterrock Knob** provides a panorama of the Great Smokies, as well as a trail, exhibits, and comfort station.

THINGS TO SEE AND DO

Driving along the Blue Ridge Parkway will certainly keep your senses engaged, but if you yearn to get out of the car and stretch your legs, or if you'd like to make a mini-vacation out of your trip, check out these attractions along the route.

APPALACHIAN CULTURAL MUSEUM. *175 Mystery Hill Ln, Blowing Rock (28605). Phone 828/262-3117. www.museum.appstate.edu.* Regional museum presents an overview of the Blue Ridge area. Exhibits include Native American artifacts, Daniel Boone lore, mountain music, and the environment. Open Tues-Sat, also Sun afternoons. **$$**

APPALACHIAN SKI MOUNTAIN. *940 Ski Mt Rd, Blowing Rock (28605). Phone 828/295-7828. www.appskimtn.com.* Two quad, double chairlift; rope tow, handle-pull tow; patrol; French-Swiss Ski College; Ski-Wee children's program; equipment rentals; snowmaking; restaurant. Eight runs; longest run 2,700 feet; vertical drop 400 feet. Open Dec-mid-Mar; closed Dec 24 eve-Dec 25. Night skiing (all slopes lighted); half-day and twilight rates. **$$$$**

★ **BILTMORE ESTATE.** *One North Pack Square, Asheville (28801). Phone 828/255-1700; toll-free 800/624-1575. www.biltmore.com.* The 8,000-acre country estate includes 75 acres of formal gardens, numerous varieties of azaleas and roses, and the 250-room chateau (85 rooms are open for viewing), which is the largest house ever built in the United States. George W. Vanderbilt commissioned Richard Morris Hunt to design the house, which was begun in 1890 and finished in 1895. Materials and furnishings were brought from many parts of Europe and Asia; a private railroad was built to transport them to the site. Vanderbilt employed Gifford Pinchot, later governor of Pennsylvania and famous for forestry and conservation achievements, to manage his forests. Biltmore was the site of the first US forestry school. Much of the original estate in now part of the Pisgah National Forest. Tours of the estate include gardens, conservatory, and winery facilities (including tastings). Four restaurants on the grounds. Open daily; closed Thanksgiving, Dec 25. Guidebook (fee) is recommended. **$$$$**

BOTANICAL GARDENS OF ASHEVILLE. *151 WT Weaver Blvd, Asheville (28804). Phone 828/252-5190. www.ashevillebotanicalgardens.com.* A 10-acre tract with thousands of flowers, trees, and shrubs native to southern Appalachia; 125-year-old "dog trot" log cabin. Open daily. **FREE**

CHIMNEY ROCK PARK. *Hwy 64/74a Asheville (28720). Phone 828/625-9611; toll-free 800/277-9611. www.chimneyrockpark.com.* Towering granite monolith Chimney Rock affords a 75-mile view; four hiking trails lead to 404-foot Hickory Nut Falls, Moonshiner's Cave, Devil's Head balancing rock, and Nature's Showerbath. Trails, stairs, and catwalks. Picnic areas, playground; nature center; observation lounge with snack bar, gift shop. Twenty-six-story elevator shaft through granite. Open daily, weather permitting; closed Jan 1, Thanksgiving, Dec 25. **$$$$**

COLBURN GEM AND MINERAL MUSEUM. *2 S Pack Sq, Asheville (28801). Phone 828/254-7162.* Displays of 1,000 minerals from around the world; includes information on mineral locations in the state. **$$**

CROATAN NATIONAL FOREST. *160 Zillicoa St, Asheville (28801). Phone 252/638-5628.* A unique coastal forest (157,724 acres), with many estuaries and waterways; northernmost habitat of the alligator. Pocosins (Native American for "swamp on a hill") have many unusual dwarf and insect-eating plants. Swimming, boating, and fishing in Neuse River; hunting for deer, bear, turkey, quail, and migratory waterfowl; picnicking; camping (fee).

EMERALD VILLAGE. *McKinney Mine Rd and Blue Ridge Pkwy, Little Switzerland (28749). Phone 828/765-6463.* Historical area includes mines; North Carolina Mining Museum; Main Street 1920s Mining Community Museum;

N. Carolina

❋ Blue Ridge Parkway

Gemstone Mine, where visitors can prospect for gems under shaded flumes (fee; equipment furnished); Mechanical Music Maker Museum; waterfall and scenic overlook; shops and deli. Open daily; closed holidays. $$

FOLK ART CENTER. *382 Blue Ridge Vis, Asheville (28805). Phone 828/298-7928.* Home of the Southern Highland Craft Guild. Stone and timber structure; home of Blue Ridge Parkway information center; craft exhibits, demonstrations, workshops, related programs. Open daily; closed Jan 1, Thanksgiving, Dec 25. **FREE**

MOSES H. CONE MEMORIAL PARK. *Linville Rd, Blowing Rock (28605). Phone 828/295-7591.* Like Thoreau, Moses H. Cone wished to live deliberately. This park and stately home is a memorial to a remarkable textile magnate, nature lover, and perfectionist. Bridle paths, two lakes; 25 miles of hiking and cross-country skiing trails. Open May-Oct, daily. **FREE**

MOUNT MITCHELL STATE PARK. *Little Switzerland (28749). Phone 828/675-4611.* Adjacent to Pisgah National Forest, Mount Mitchell is a natural national landmark. A road leads to the summit (6,684 feet; the highest point east of the Mississippi River) for incomparable views. Trails, picnicking, restaurant, refreshment stands. Small tent camping area. Observation tower, museum.

MUSEUM OF NORTH CAROLINA MINERALS. *79 Parkway Maintenance Rd, Little Switzerland (28749). Phone 828/765-2761.* Mineral exhibits of the state. Open May-Nov, daily; rest of year, Wed-Sun; closed Jan 1, Thanksgiving, Dec 24-26. **FREE**

MUSEUM OF THE CHEROKEE INDIAN. *589 Psali Blvd, Cherokee (28719). Phone 828/497-3481.* Arts and crafts, audiovisual displays, portraits, prehistoric artifacts. Open daily; closed Jan 1, Thanksgiving, Dec 25. $$$

OCONALUFTEE INDIAN VILLAGE. *Hwy 441 N, Cherokee (28719). Phone 828/497-2111.* Replica of a Native American village of more than 250 years ago. Includes seven-sided council house; lectures; herb garden; craft demonstrations. Guided tours (mid-May-late Oct, daily). $$$

PARKWAY CRAFT CENTER. *667 Service Rd, Blowing Rock (28605). Phone 828/295-7938.* Demonstrations of weaving, wood carving, pottery, jewelry making, and other crafts. Open May-Oct, daily. Handcrafted items for sale. **FREE**

PISGAH NATIONAL FOREST. *160 Zillicoa St, Asheville (28801). Phone 828/257-4200.* This is a 499,816-acre, four-district forest. The Cradle of Forestry Visitor Center (summer, daily; fee) is the site of first forestry school in the United States. The forest surrounds Mount Mitchell State Park. Linville Gorge Wilderness is 10,975 acres of precipitous cliffs and cascading falls (permit required May-Oct for overnight camping). Wiseman's View looks into Linville Gorge. Shining Rock Wilderness contains 18,500 acres of rugged alpine scenery. The forest shares with Cherokee National Forest in Tennessee the 6,286-foot Roan Mountain, with its purple rhododendron and stands of spruce and fir. Offers swimming; good fishing for trout, bass, and perch; hunting for deer, bear, and small game; miles of hiking and riding trails; picnic sites; campgrounds (fee).

RIVER RAFTING AT THE NANTAHALA OUTDOOR CENTER. *13077 Hwy 19 W, Bryson City (28713). Phone toll-free 800/232-7238. www.noc.com.* Offers various trips on the Nantahala, French Broad, Ocee, Pigeon, Nolichucky, and Chattooga rivers ranging from 1 1/2 to 6 hours. $$$$

TWEETSIE RAILROAD. *296 Tweetsie Railroad, Blowing Rock (28605). Phone 828/264-9061. www.tweetsie.com.* A 3-mile excursion, with a mock holdup and raid on an old narrow-gauge railroad; Western Town with variety show at Tweetsie Palace; country fair; petting zoo; craft village; chairlift to Mouse Mountain Picnic Area. Open May-Oct, limited hours. $$$$

WOLF LAUREL SKI RESORT. *Valley View Cir, Mars Hill (28754). Phone 828/689-4111. www.skiwolflaurel.com.* Quad, double chairlifts; tow rope; patrol, school, rentals; snow making; restaurant, lodge. Longest run 3/4 mile; vertical drop 700 feet. Open mid-Dec-mid-Mar, daily. $$$$

PLACES TO STAY

If you choose to include an overnight stay in your trip along this All-American Road, Mobil Travel Guide recommends the following lodgings.

★★ BEST WESTERN ASHEVILLE BILTMORE. *22 Woodfin St, Asheville (28801). Phone 828/253-1851. www.bestwestern.com.* 154 rooms, 5 story. Complimentary continental breakfast. Check-out noon, check-in 3 pm. TV; cable (premium). In-room modem link. Restaurant. In-house fitness room, health club privileges. Outdoor pool. $

★ BLOWING ROCK INN. *788 N Main St, Blowing Rock (28605). Phone 828/295-7921.* 24 rooms. Closed Dec-Mar. Check-out 11 am. TV. Heated pool. ¢

★★★ CHETOLA RESORT AT BLOWING ROCK. *N Main St, Blowing Rock (28605). Phone 828/295-5500.* This Blue Ridge Mountain retreat, bordered on one side by a national forest, leaves guests wanting for nothing. The Highlands Sports and Recreation Center, conference center, professional tennis courts, and other amenities are all located within the resort's 78-acre property. 104 rooms, 62 condos, 1-3 story. Check-out 11 am, check-in 3 pm. TV; cable (premium), VCR available. Indoor pool; whirlpool. Playground. Supervised children's activities (June-Aug), ages 5-12. Dining room (public by reservation). Coin laundry. Meeting rooms. Business services available. Grocery, package store 1/2 mile. Sports director. Lighted tennis courts. Golf privileges. Boating, fishing. Downhill, cross-country ski 3 miles. Exercise equipment; sauna. Massage. Hiking. Bicycles. Social director. Entertainment. Racquetball court. Game room. Refrigerators. Some private balconies. Picnic tables, grills. Seven-acre lake. Adjacent to Moses Cone National Park. $

★ HOMESTEAD INN. *153 Morris St, Blowing Rock (28605). Phone 828/295-9559; fax 828/295-9551.* 15 rooms. Check-out 11 am. TV. Playground. Restaurant nearby. Downhill ski 4 miles. Refrigerators, microwaves available. Picnic tables, grills. ¢

★★ MAPLE LODGE. *152 Sunset Dr, Blowing Rock (28605). Phone 828/295-3331.* 11 rooms, some with A/C, 2 story. No room phones. No elevator. Weekends 2-day minimum. Closed Jan, Feb. Children over 12 years only. Complimentary full breakfast; afternoon refreshments. Check-out 11 am, check-in 3-9 pm. Some TVs. Luggage handling. Downhill ski 5 miles, cross-country ski 2 miles. Some refrigerators. Antiques. Totally nonsmoking. $$

N. Carolina

✳ *Blue Ridge Parkway*

★★★ **MEADOWBROOK INN.** *711 Main St, Blowing Rock (28605). Phone 828/295-4300.* This romantic, year-round inn is favored by summertime hikers and wintertime skiers alike. The rooms are furnished traditionally; one suite even has its own indoor pool. 61 rooms, 2-3 story. Complimentary continental breakfast. Check-out 11 am, check-in 3 pm. TV; VCR available. Dining room, bar. Exercise equipment. Indoor pool. Downhill ski 3 miles. $

★ **GREYSTONE LODGE.** *2419 NC 105, Boone (28607). Phone 828/264-4133.* 101 rooms, 4 story. Complimentary continental breakfast. Check-out 11 am. TV; cable (premium). Indoor pool. Restaurant nearby. Business services available. Downhill, cross-country ski 8 miles. Game room. ¢

★★★ **LOVILL HOUSE INN.** *404 Old Bristol Rd, Boone (28607). Phone 828/264-4204.* Captain E. F. Lovill, a Civil War hero and state senator, built this traditional farmhouse in 1875. The 11-acre, wooded property offers a charming wraparound porch with plenty of rocking chairs. 6 rooms, 2 story. No A/C. Closed Mar, two weeks in Sept. Children over 12 years only. Complimentary breakfast. Check-out 11 am, check-in 3 pm. TV. Downhill, cross-country ski 8 miles. Concierge. Restored country farmhouse built in 1875; grounds include gardens, stream with waterfall. Totally nonsmoking. $

★★ **QUALITY INN APPALACHIAN CONFERENCE CENTER.** *949 Blowing Rock Rd, Boone (28607). Phone 828/262-0020. www.qualityinn.com.* 132 rooms, 7 story. Check-out 11 am. TV; cable (premium). Indoor pool. Restaurant, bar. Guest laundry. Business services available. Golf privileges. Downhill ski 8 miles, cross-country ski 9 miles. Exercise equipment. Health club privileges. Refrigerators in suites. $

★ **COOL WATERS MOTEL.** *US 19 N, Cherokee (28719). Phone 828/497-3855.* 50 rooms. Check-out 11 am. TV. Pool; wading pool. Restaurant opposite. Tennis. Some patios. Picnic tables, grills. On stream; trout pond. ¢

PLACES TO EAT

A long day of driving is sure to make you hungry. At the end of your journey, take a table at one of the following restaurants.

★★★ **GABRIELLE'S.** *87 Richmond Hill Dr, Asheville (28806). Phone 828/252-7313.* American menu. Closed Tues. Dinner. Contemporary regional cuisine with formal service. Jacket required. $$$

★★ **GREENERY.** *148 Tunnel Rd, Asheville (28803). Phone 828/253-2809.* Closed Jan 1. Dinner. Bar. Reservations accepted. $$

★★ **THE MARKET PLACE RESTAURANT & WINE BAR.** *20 Wall St, Asheville (28801). Phone 828/252-4162.* Specializes in seafood, veal, lamb. Closed Sun, some major holidays. Dinner. Bar. Children's menu. Outdoor seating. Reservations accepted. Three formal dining areas. Totally nonsmoking. $$

★ **MCGUFFEY'S GRILL & BAR.** *1853 Hendersonville Rd, Asheville (28803). Phone 828/277-0440.* Specializes in beef, seafood, chicken. Closed Thanksgiving, Dec 25. Dinner. Bar. $$

★★★ **CRIPPEN'S.** *239 Sunset Dr, Blowing Rock (28607). Phone 828/295-3487.* This spacious, cozy dining room is located in Crippen's Country Inn. Continental menu. Closed Mon, most major holidays; also Super Bowl Sun. Dinner. Bar. Children's menu. Reservations accepted. Totally nonsmoking. $$$

★★ **RIVERWOOD.** *7179 Valley Blvd, Blowing Rock (28605). Phone 828/295-4162.* Closed Sun. Dinner. Bar. Specialties: stuffed rainbow trout, marinated beef tenderloin. Own desserts. Reservations accepted. Totally nonsmoking. **$$**
D

★★ **TWIG'S.** *Hwy 321 Bypass, Blowing Rock (28605). Phone 828/295-5050.* Regional American menu. Specializes in crab cakes, lamb, fresh seafood. Closed Mon; Dec 24-25. Dinner. Bar. Reservations accepted. Porch dining (summer). **$$**
D

★ **DAN'L BOONE INN.** *130 Hardin St, Boone (28607). Phone 828/264-8657.* Closed Dec 24-25. Breakfast (Sat-Sun), lunch (May-Nov), dinner. In one of the oldest buildings in Boone; country atmosphere. **$$**
D

★★ **MAKOTO.** *2124 Blowing Rock Rd, Boone (28607). Phone 828/264-7976.* Japanese menu. Closed Thanksgiving, Dec 25. Lunch, dinner. Service charge 15%. Children's menu. Sushi bar Fri-Sat. Tableside preparation. **$$**
D

The Historic National Road

❋ OHIO

Part of a multistate Byway; see also IL, IN, MD, PA, WV.

Quick Facts

LENGTH: 228 miles.

TIME TO ALLOW: 4 days.

BEST TIME TO DRIVE: Summer and fall, depending on which end (east or west) you will be spending most of your time. Summer is high season for festivals in Ohio. On the western section of the Byway, you find more agriculture, so summer and late summer have the most picturesque fields. The eastern section of the Byway offers hills and fall color.

BYWAY TRAVEL INFORMATION: Ohio Historic Preservation Office: 614/298-2000.

SPECIAL CONSIDERATIONS: Heavy snow or rain falls occasionally in this part of the country. It may impair drivability but does not result in lengthy road closures.

BICYCLE/PEDESTRIAN FACILITIES: In rural areas, on-road bicycling is feasible because of relatively low traffic volumes and generally wide shoulders. Similarly, small towns accommodate both pedestrians and bicyclists because of low traffic volumes, slow traffic speeds, and sidewalks. The large urban areas along the Byway all provide pedestrian sidewalks, and some have dedicated bicycle lanes.

The story of the Ohio Historic National Road is the story of our nation's aspirations and desires. The National Road literally paved the way west through the newly formed states of Ohio, Indiana, and Illinois and provided a direct connection to the mercantile and political centers of the East Coast, helping to secure the influence and viability of these new settlements. As much as the road's boom times during the early and mid-19th century signified its importance to national commerce and expansion, its decline during the late 19th and early 20th centuries revealed the meteoric rise of the railroad as the primary means of transport and trade across the nation. Likewise, the renaissance of the National Road in the mid-20th century reflected the growing popularity of the automobile.

Today, the Byway is a scenic journey across Ohio. The steep, wooded hills and valleys of the eastern edge of the Byway give way to the gently rolling farmland of the western part of the Byway. Picturesque farms, hiking trails, craft industries, and historic sites and museums await you along this portion of the Historic National Road.

THE BYWAY STORY

The Historic National Road tells archaeological, cultural, historical, natural, recreational, and scenic stories that make it a unique and treasured Byway.

Archaeological

Prehistoric civilizations once dominated the land surrounding what is now known as the Historic National Road in Ohio, and today, remnants of these early people can be found just off of the Byway. One important aspect for

Ohio

The Historic National Road

these early cultures was making tools and weapons. They found flint for these tools at what is known today as Flint Ridge State Memorial. The Hopewell culture frequented Flint Ridge because of the quality and beauty of the flint found there. This flint would have been a very important resource to that culture, the way that coal and iron ore are in Ohio today. Flint from Ohio has been found from the Atlantic seaboard to Louisiana. Flint was so important, in fact, that it has become the state gem of Ohio.

Located near Newark, the Moundbuilders State Memorial and Ohio Indian Art Museum tell about the Hopewell Indian civilization, which is most remembered because of large earthworks that were constructed there. Exhibits show the artistic achievements of these prehistoric cultures that lived in the area from around 10,000 BC to AD 1,600. The Octagon Earthworks and Wright Earthworks are also located near Newark.

Cultural

The Historic National Road in Ohio hosts a rich tradition of culture. Museums, festivals, and other cultural facilities offer a chance to both explore more of the National Road's history and seek diversions from it. Outstanding performing arts venues are well represented along the Byway. In addition to these cultural features, the eastern section of the Byway is known for its selection of traditional and modern crafts.

Historical

The history of the Historic National Road in Ohio highlights the importance of this road in terms of development and settlement that it brought to the Ohio area. The history of the construction of the National Road is significant because it serves as an example of larger events that were transpiring in America simultaneously. Early pioneer settlement gave way to railroads, and finally the automobile became the most frequent traveler along the National Road.

Natural

While traveling the Historic National Road in Ohio, you are treated to a diverse Byway that traverses steep wooded hills and valleys in the east and gently rolling farmland in the west. This diversity of natural features offers refreshing and contrasting views along the Byway. The changing landscape determined how the National Road was constructed, as well as the types of livelihoods settlers engaged in throughout the history of the road.

Recreational

A tremendous network of large state parks, regional metropolitan parks, local parks, and privately run facilities provides a bountiful array of outdoor recreational facilities that give you a chance to enjoy the natural beauty of the area. For the most part, the state parks are located on the eastern half of the Byway, and over 50,000 acres of state parks, forests, and wildlife areas are easily accessible from the Ohio Historic National Road. Along portions of the Byway, you can hike, camp, fish, hunt, and picnic while relishing the various species of local flora and fauna.

Scenic

The Historic National Road in Ohio is full of variation and diversity. Changing topography and landscapes provide scenic views for travelers of the Byway, from hilly ridges to long, unbroken views of the horizon. Small towns, unique and historic architecture, and stone bridges all provide scenes from the past. Farms, unspoiled scenery, and large urban landscapes give you a sense of the great diversity of this Byway.

see page A13 for color map

THINGS TO SEE AND DO

Driving along the Historic National Road will certainly keep your senses engaged, but if you yearn to get out of the car and stretch your legs, or if you'd like to make a mini-vacation out of your trip, check out these attractions along the route.

BUCK CREEK STATE PARK. *1901 Buck Creek Ln, Springfield (45502). Phone 937/322-5284.* A 4,030-acre park with swimming, lifeguard, bathhouse (open Memorial Day-Labor Day), fishing, boating (launch, ramp), hiking, snowmobile trails, picnicking, concession, camping, and cabins. Standard fees. Open daily.

COSI COLUMBUS, OHIO'S CENTER OF SCIENCE AND INDUSTRY. *333 W Broad St, Columbus (43215). Phone 614/228-2674. cosi.org.* Hands-on museum includes exhibits, programs, and demonstrations. Battelle Planetarium shows (open daily). Coal Mine, Hi-Tech Showcase, Free Enterprise Area, Foucault pendulum, Solar Front Exhibit Area, Computer Experience, Street of Yesteryear, Weather Station, KIDSPACE, and FAMILIESPACE. Open daily. **$$$**

DAVID CRABILL HOUSE. *818 N Fountain Ave, Springfield (45504). Phone 937/399-1245.* Built by Clark County pioneer David Crabill in 1826; restored. Period rooms, log barn, smokehouse. Maintained by the Clark County Historical Society. Open Tues-Fri. **$**

DILLON STATE PARK. *5265 Dillon Hills Dr, Zanesville (43830). Phone 740/453-4377.* A 7,690-acre park with swimming, boating (ramps, rentals), picnicking (shelter), concession, camping, and cabins (by reservation). Open daily. **FREE**

FLINT RIDGE STATE MEMORIAL. *7091 Brownsville Rd SE, Newark (43799). Phone 740/787-2476.* Prehistoric Native American flint quarry; trails for the disabled and the visually impaired; picnic area. Museum (open Memorial Day-Labor Day, Wed-Sun; after Labor Day-Oct, weekends only). Park (open Apr-Oct). **$**

FORT HILL STATE MEMORIAL. *13614 Fort Hill Rd, Hillsboro (45133). Phone toll-free 800/283-8905.* This is the site of a prehistoric Native American hilltop earth and stone enclosure. The identity of its builders has not been determined, but implements found in the vicinity point to the Hopewell people. A 2,000-foot trail leads to the ancient earthworks. Picnic area and shelterhouse. Open daily. **FREE**

GERMAN VILLAGE. *588 S 3rd St, Columbus (43215). Phone 614/221-8888. www.germanvillage.org.* Historic district restored as an old-world village with shops, old homes, and gardens; authentic foods. Bus tour available. Open daily. **FREE**

MOUNDBUILDERS STATE MEMORIAL. *65 Messimer Dr, Unit 2, Newark (43055). Phone toll-free 800/600-7174.* The Great Circle, 66 acres, has walls from 8 to 14 feet high with burial mounds in the center. Museum containing Hopewell artifacts is open Memorial Day-Labor Day, Wed-Sun; after Labor Day-Oct, weekends only. Park open Apr-Oct. **$**

★ **NATIONAL ROAD-ZANE GREY MUSEUM.** *8850 E Pike, Zanesville (43767). Phone 740/872-3143.* A 136-foot diorama traces the history of the National Road from Maryland to Illinois; display of vehicles that once traveled the road; Zane Grey memorabilia, reconstructed craft shops, antique art pottery exhibit. Open Mar-Apr and Oct-Nov, Wed-Sun; May-Sept, daily. **$$**

★ **NEWARK EARTHWORKS.** *S 21st St and OH 79, Newark (43055). Phone toll-free 800/600-7174. www.ohiohistory.org.* The group of earthworks here was originally one of the most extensive of its kind in the country, covering an area of more than 4 square miles. The Hopewell used their geometric enclosures for social, religious, and ceremonial purposes. Remaining portions of the

Ohio

✹ The Historic National Road

Newark group are Octagon Earthworks and Wright Earthworks, with many artifacts of pottery, beadwork, copper, bone, and shell exhibited at the nearby Moundbuilders State Museum.

OCTAGON EARTHWORKS. *N 30th St and Parkview, Newark (43055). Phone toll-free 800/600-7174.* The octagon-shaped enclosure encircles 50 acres that includes small mounds and is joined by parallel walls to a circular embankment enclosing 20 acres. **FREE**

OHIO CERAMIC CENTER. *7327 Ceramic Rd, Roseville (43777). Phone 740/697-7021; toll-free 800/752-2604.* Extensive displays of pottery are housed in five buildings. Exhibits include primitive stoneware and area pottery. Demonstrations of pottery-making during pottery festival (weekend in mid-July). Open daily. **$**

✪ **OHIO HISTORICAL CENTER.** *1982 Velma Ave, Columbus (43211). Phone 614/297-2300 www.ohiohistory.org.* Modern architectural design contrasts with the age-old themes of Ohio's prehistoric culture, natural history, and cultural history. Exhibits include an archaeology mall with computer interactive displays and life-size dioramas; a natural history mall with a mastodon skeleton and a demonstration laboratory; and a history mall with transportation, communication, and lifestyle exhibits. Ohio archives and historical library open Wed, Thurs, Sat. Museum open Tues-Sun; closed Jan 1, Thanksgiving, Dec 25. **$$**

OHIO VILLAGE. *1982 Velma Ave, Columbus (43211). Phone 614/297-2300.* Reconstruction of a rural 1860s Ohio community with one-room schoolhouse, town hall, general store, hotel, farmhouse, barn, doctor's house, and office. Costumed guides. Open Memorial Day-Oct, Sat-Sun. **$$**

PARK OF ROSES. *Acton and High sts, Columbus (43214).* This park contains over 10,000 rose bushes representing 350 varieties. Picnic facilities. Rose festival (early June). Musical programs Sun evenings in summer. Open daily. **FREE**

PENNSYLVANIA HOUSE. *1311 W Main St, Springfield (45504). Phone 937/322-7668.* Built as a tavern and stagecoach stop on the National Pike, this house includes period furnishings, pioneer artifacts, and button, quilt, and doll collections. Open the first Sun afternoon of each month; also by appointment; closed Easter and late Dec-Feb. **$$**

SANTA MARIA REPLICA. *Battelle Riverfront Park, Marconi Blvd and Broad St, Columbus (43215). Phone 614/645-8760.* A full-scale, museum-quality replica of Christopher Columbus's flagship, the *Santa Maria*. Costumed guides offer tours of the upper and lower decks. Visitors learn of life as a sailor on voyages in the late 1400s. Open Apr-Jan, Tues-Sun; closed holidays. **$**

SERPENT MOUND STATE MEMORIAL. *3850 St Rte 73, Pebbles (45660) Phone 937/587-2796; toll-free 800/752-2757.* The largest and most remarkable serpent effigy earthworks in North America. Built between 800 BC and AD 100 of stone and yellow clay, it curls like an enormous snake for 1,335 feet. An oval earthwall represents the serpent's open mouth. In the 61-acre area are an observation tower, a scenic gorge, a museum, and picnicking facilities. Site (open all year); museum (open Apr-Oct, daily; Nov-Mar hours vary, so phone ahead). **$$**

THE WILDS. *14000 International Rd, Cumberland (43732). Phone 740/638-5030. www.thewilds.org.* A 9,154-acre conservation center dedicated to increasing the population of endangered species. Open May-Oct, daily. **$$$**

ZANESVILLE ART CENTER. *620 Military Rd, Zanesville (43701). Phone 740/452-0741. www.zanesvilleartcenter.org.* American, European, and Asian art; children's art; early Midwestern glass and ceramics; photographs; special programs; and gallery tours. Open Tues-Sun; closed holidays. **FREE**

PLACES TO STAY

If you choose to include an overnight stay in your trip along this All-American Road, Mobil Travel Guide recommends the following lodgings.

★★ **ADAM'S MARK.** *50 N 3rd St, Columbus (43215). Phone 614/228-5050. www.adamsmark .com.* 415 rooms, 21 story. Check-out noon. Valet parking $15. TV; cable (premium). Heated pool; whirlpool. Restaurant, bar. Room service. Convention facilities. Business services available. In-room modem link. Coin laundry. Exercise equipment; sauna. $

★ **BEST WESTERN SUITES.** *1133 Evans Way Ct, Columbus (43228). Phone 614/870-2378. www.bestwestern.com.* 66 suites, 2 story. Complimentary continental breakfast. Check-out noon. TV; cable (premium). VCR (movies). In-room modem link. Laundry services. Exercise equipment, sauna. Indoor pool; whirlpool. ¢

★ **FAIRFIELD INN BY MARRIOTT.** *1870 W 1st St, Springfield (45504). Phone 937/323-9554. www.fairfieldinn.com.* Located across the street from the Marketplace shops, this hotel offers guests personal and attentive service along with well-appointed guest rooms. 124 rooms, 6 story. Check-out noon. TV; cable (premium). VCR available. In-room modem link. Restaurant, bar. Luxury level. ¢

★ **SPRINGFIELD INN.** *100 S Fountain Ave, Springfield (45502). Phone 937/322-3600.* 63 rooms, 3 story. Complimentary continental breakfast. Check-out noon. TV; cable (premium). VCR available. Some refrigerators. Microwave in suites. Restaurant adjacent. Health club privileges. Game room. Indoor pool; whirlpool. Business services. ¢

★ **KNIGHTS INN.** *51260 E National Rd, St. Clairsville (43950). Phone 740/695-5038. www.knightsinn.com.* 104 rooms, 16 kitchen units. Pet accepted, some restrictions. Check-out noon. TV; cable (premium), VCR available (movies). Pool. Restaurant nearby. Business services available. In-room modem link. Some in-room whirlpools; microwaves available. ¢

★ **SUPER 8.** *550 E National Rd, Vandalia (45377). Phone 937/898-7636. www.super8.com.* 94 rooms, 3 story. Check-out noon. TV; cable (premium). Pool. ¢

★★★ **WORTHINGTON INN.** *649 High St, Worthington (43085). Phone 614/885-2600.* 26 rooms, 3 story. Complimentary full breakfast. Check-out noon, check-in 3 pm. TV. In-room modem link. Dining room, bar. Room service. Concierge service. Renovated Victorian inn. $$

★ **AMERIHOST INN.** *230 Scenic Crest Dr, Zanesville (43701). Phone 740/454-9332. www.amerihostinn.com.* 60 rooms, 2 story. Complimentary continental breakfast. Check-out noon. TV; cable (premium). Restaurant adjacent. Business services available. In-room modem link. Exercise equipment; sauna. Indoor pool; whirlpool. In-room whirlpool, refrigerator, microwaves in suites. ¢

Ohio

❈ The Historic National Road

★★ **HOLIDAY INN.** *4645 East Pike, Zanesville (43701). Phone 740/453-0771. www.holiday-inn.com.* 130 rooms, 2 story. Pet accepted. Check-out noon. TV; cable (premium). Indoor pool; whirlpool, poolside service. Playground. Restaurant, bars. Room service. Coin laundry. Business services available. In-room modem link. Bellhops. Sundries. In-house fitness room; sauna. Refrigerators, microwaves available. ¢
🅧 D ⬚ ⬚ SC ⬚

PLACES TO EAT

A long day of driving is sure to make you hungry. At the end of your journey, take a table at one of the following restaurants.

★ **BEARS DEN.** ☺ *13320 East Pike, Cambridge (43725). Phone 740/432-5285.* American menu. Closed Sun. Dinner. Elegant rotisserie home cooking in a rustic setting. $

★ **PLAZA RESTAURANT.** ☺ *1038 Wheeling Ave, Cambridge (43725). Phone 740/432-7997. www.plazarestaurant.com.* Indian menu. Closed Sun. Dinner. Homemade curries, pastry, and garam masala. $

★★ **BEXLEY'S MONK.** *2232 E Main St, Columbus (43209). Phone 614/239-6665.* Eclectic, seafood menu. Closed major holidays. Lunch, dinner. Bar. Entertainment. Reservations accepted. $$$
D

★ **KATZINGER'S.** *475 S 3rd St, Columbus (43215). Phone 614/228-3354.* Continental menu. Closed Easter, Thanksgiving, Dec 25. Breakfast, lunch, dinner. Children's menu. Outdoor seating. Totally nonsmoking. $$
D

★ **OLD MOHAWK.** *821 Mohawk St, Columbus (43206). Phone 614/444-7204.* Closed some major holidays. Lunch, dinner. Bar. Building from the 1800s was once a grocery and tavern; exposed brick walls. $

★★★ **MORTON'S OF CHICAGO.** *2 Nationwide Plz, Columbus (43215). Phone 614/464-4442.* For fresh lobster and steaks, put Morton's on your list. Professional service and a clubby setting offer a truly satisfying dining experience. Closed major holidays. Dinner. Bar. Reservations accepted. Valet parking available. $$$
D

★★ **CASEY'S.** *2205 Park Rd, Springfield (45504). Phone 937/322-0397.* American menu. Closed Sun, major holidays. Dinner. Bar. $$
D

★★ **KLOSTERMAN'S DERR ROAD INN.** *4343 Derr Rd, Springfield (45503). Phone 937/399-0822.* Continental menu. Closed most holidays. Lunch, dinner. Bar. Children's menu. $$
D

★★ **MARIA ADORNETTO.** *953 Market St, Zanesville (43702). Phone 740/453-0643.* Italian menu. Closed Sun, major holidays. Lunch, dinner. Bar. Contemporary dining room in a converted home. $$

★★ **OLD MARKET HOUSE INN.** *424 Market St, Zanesville (43701). Phone 740/454-2555.* Italian, American menu. Closed Sun, major holidays. Dinner. Bar. $$
D

Hells Canyon Scenic Byway

❋ OREGON

Quick Facts

LENGTH: 218 miles.

TIME TO ALLOW: 8 hours.

BEST TIME TO DRIVE: Late May to October, when you see spectacular snow-capped mountains, lush green hills, and wildflowers in bloom. High season is in July and August.

BYWAY TRAVEL INFORMATION: Eastern Oregon Visitor's Association: 541/856-3272; Byway travel and tourism Web site: www.eova.com.

SPECIAL CONSIDERATIONS: You won't find any services beyond Joseph, so make sure you have plenty of gas before leaving Baker City or La Grande. Before starting out, take notice of the travel times as well as mileage between stops and keep your fuel tank as full as possible. Be prepared for temperatures that vary as much as 50 degrees as the day wears on.

RESTRICTIONS: Wallowa Mountain Loop USFS Road 39, between Joseph and Halfway, is closed from November through February due to heavy snow.

BICYCLE/PEDESTRIAN FACILITIES: Distances between destinations make pedestrian activity impractical along much of the Byway, except along Highway 351 around Wallowa Lake. Most of the local pedestrian activity occurs in the communities along the Byway, where you find sidewalks and crosswalks.

Leave the fast pace and fenced-in views of Interstate 84 and follow the contours of the land into slower times and wilder places. Travel this 218-mile journey from river's edge to mountaintop and down to valley floor. Have lunch overlooking a Wild & Scenic River. Share a canyon road with a cattle drive. Pass through lush valleys rimmed by the snow-tipped Wallowa Mountains. Savor the scent of pine on the fresh mountain air. Enjoy panoramic views of rugged basalt cliffs and grassy open ridges. Stand next to the majestic Snake River as it begins its tumbling course through North America's deepest canyon. Place your hand in the weathered track of a wagon wheel. Hear the wind rushing through the forest. This is a journey you won't forget.

The route of the Hells Canyon Scenic Byway is a loop that encircles the Wallowa Mountains, intersecting with Interstate 84 at La Grande and Baker City. Small towns scattered along the drive offer visitor services. The entire route is on a paved highway, but plan ahead: you'll find stretches of more than 80 miles without gas stations and with few services. A segment of the Byway between Joseph and Halfway closes due to snow in winter but allows access to winter recreation areas, offering a different kind of northeast Oregon adventure.

THE BYWAY STORY

The Hells Canyon Scenic Byway tells archaeological, cultural, historical, natural, recreational, and scenic stories that make it a unique and treasured Byway.

Oregon

Hells Canyon Scenic Byway

Archaeological

Extremes in the land have dictated the course of the area's natural and cultural history. Relatively mild winters and abundant wildlife drew people to the canyon over 7,000 years ago. Archeological evidence, ranging from rock art to winter "pithouse" villages, can be found in the Snake River corridor. Pictographs and petroglyphs are scattered along the river where Native Americans spent their winters. Please use care when viewing these sites; these national treasures have stood the test of time and will be enjoyed long into the future.

Cultural

On the map, northeastern Oregon looks far removed from metropolitan area amenities. However, you may be surprised by the availability of arts and culture. Musical events along the Byway range from old-time fiddling to blues to Beethoven. Plays, concerts, and living-history productions can be enjoyed daily in Baker City. The small town of Joseph has earned a national reputation for its bronze foundries and galleries. Some of the nation's most highly acclaimed artists cast their bronzes at one of the four area foundries or show their work in one of the many galleries that line the town's picturesque main street. Eastern Oregon University, located in La Grande, offers theatrical productions and concerts, including a full season of music from the Grande Ronde Symphony Orchestra. The Historic Elgin Opera House in Elgin is also a crowd pleaser for concerts, movies, and plays.

Historical

For many centuries, the Grande Ronde Valley was used seasonally by Native Americans. Covered largely by wetlands, the beautiful valley was lush with grass and alive with game. Herds of elk summered in the surrounding high country and wintered in the milder valley. Mule deer, pronghorn antelope, and big-horn sheep browsed the hills and meadows. This bountiful scene was a neutral meeting place for members of the Umatilla, Yakima, Shoshone, Cayuse, and Bannock nations, who came to enjoy the hot springs, hunt, graze their horses, and gather plants for food. The picturesque Wallowa Valley was the beloved home of the Nez Perce Indians. By winter of 1877, settlement conflicts drove young Chief Joseph to make a harrowing attempt to reach Canada with a group of 250 men, women, and children. They struggled to within 24 miles of safety before being captured at Montana and sent to reservations.

This area remains a significant religious and cultural center for the Nez Perce, Umatilla, and Cayuse Indians. Every fall, when leaving the valley to winter in the milder climate along the Columbia plateau, these early residents lit huge fires in the valleys, burning off old grass and allowing for healthy regrowth in the spring.

Natural

Millions of years ago, the Wallowa Mountains formed the coast of what would eventually be called Oregon. Uplifted layers of limestone on the peaks harbor fossilized shells that once sat at the bottom of the ocean. Eons of volcanic action and faulting pushed the masses of rock upward while new land formed to the west. The Coast Range, Cascade Mountains, and upland desert of central Oregon now separate the Wallowas from the ocean by hundreds of miles. Flows of plateau basalt, batholiths of granite, and layers of shale were buckled and folded to form the mountain range. Raging rivers and gigantic glaciers carved the peaks and canyons. In short, nature took a long time to sculpt the dramatic beauty you see along the Byway.

Recreational

Recreational opportunities along the Hells Canyon Scenic Byway are seemingly endless and range from tranquil to thrilling. Four distinct seasons alter the scenery and determine the activities.

In spring, warm sunshine carpets the hills with green grass and colorful wildflowers. The landscape becomes a patchwork quilt with fields of freshly plowed soil, sprouting crops, and blossoming fruit trees. It's a great time for sightseeing from a car or on a bike. Watch the meadows for frisky new calves and wobbly foals. Along the streams, willows, dogwood, and mock orange create a changing palette of yellows, pinks, and vibrant greens. Fish for steelhead or trout on the Grande Ronde, Minam, Wallowa, and Imnaha rivers. Take a thrilling raft or jet boat ride through the Class III and IV rapids on the Snake River or float the waters of the Grande Ronde and Minam rivers.

Summer bursts with energy. Warm, dry weather and lots of sunshine make the outdoors impossible to resist. Microclimates at different elevations and aspects mean you can always find a cooler or hotter spot within miles. The Wallowa-Whitman National Forest, along with county and state parks departments, operates numerous campgrounds, trail systems, viewpoints, and picnic facilities along or near the route. Hike or mountain bike into the high country. Cast a fishing line on several of the rivers and streams and at Wallowa Lake. Hire a private outfitter to experience horseback riding and pack trips, rafting, parasailing, or jet boat adventures. Cycle the back roads or mountain trails for the amazing views. Watch hang gliders and hot air balloonists catch the breeze high above the Wallowa and Grande Ronde valleys.

In autumn, cooler temperatures and shorter days turn tamarack (western larch) needles to gold and leaves to jewel tones of yellow, orange, and red. Canadian geese are on the move, filling the air with melancholy calls. Hunt for deer, elk, bear, cougar, and bighorn sheep or use them as photo opportunities. Fall is also the time for cattle drives, harvesting, and blue-sky days crisp with the smell of winter. Catch the small-town spirit by watching a high school football game in splendid, scenic surroundings—visitors are always welcome.

Winter's dry, powdery snow opens area ski resorts and turns backcountry side trips and hiking trails into a giant playground for adventurers on skis, snowmobiles, and snowshoes. The FS Road 39 section of the Byway between Joseph and Halfway is closed to auto and truck traffic in winter, when it becomes an especially popular route for snowmobilers. It connects into much larger networks providing access to hundreds of miles of groomed trails in the region. Enjoy winter raptor viewing in Minam and Hells canyons, a horse-drawn sleigh ride in Joseph, or ice fishing on Wallowa Lake. Near the Byway, ride a horse-drawn wagon through a herd of Rocky Mountain elk at the Elkhorn Elk Feeding Site and find out about the majestic animal's history in the area. By day, surround yourself with spectacular scenery topped with fresh white snow. By night, relax before a crackling fire in cozy lodgings.

Scenic

Travel the Hells Canyon Scenic Byway and see much of the majesty and mystery of the West within a 218-mile corridor. The magnificent

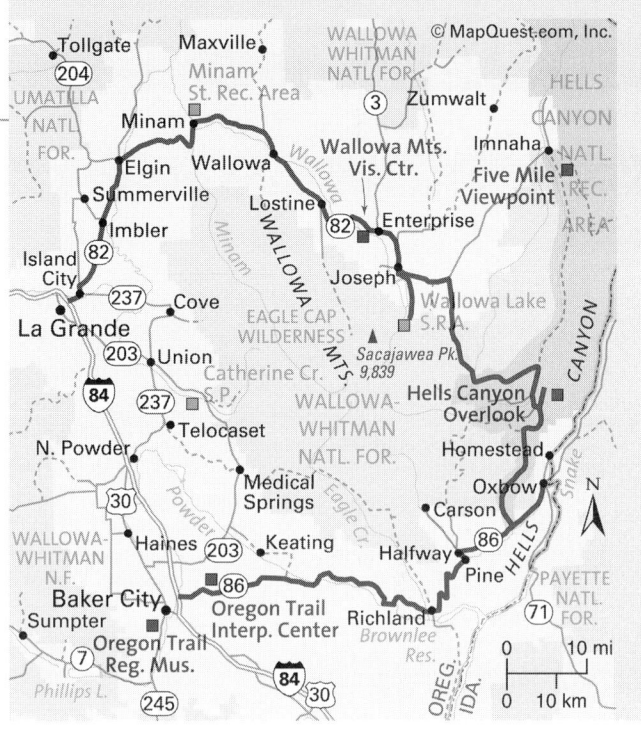

see page A21 for color map

Oregon

✽ Hells Canyon Scenic Byway

Snake River twists and churns over boulders and past towering cliffs. Pungent sagebrush and bunch grasses cover the flats and crouch at the feet of dramatic rock formations. Sparkling streams tumble through thick forests of pine and mixed conifers. Lush valleys lie at the feet of magnificent mountain ranges with peaks that tower to nearly 10,000 feet. Fields of hay, wheat, grass, mint, and canola color the valley floor. Cattle, sheep, and horses graze on a menu of sweet clover and timothy. Historic barns and houses bring human warmth and scale to the dramatic scenery.

HIGHLIGHTS

- Start your summer outdoors tour at about midday so you can go to the **Wallowa Mountains Visitor Center** (about half a mile northwest of Enterprise) to get current and detailed information about camps and hikes in the area. Spend the night camping in the Wallowa Mountains or beside the Imnaha River.

- Visit **Wallowa Lake** (about 6 miles south of Joseph) and relax for a few hours of swimming, fishing, boating, or hiking. You can also take a tram from here to the peak of Mount Howard and enjoy wonderful views.

- Next, visit the **Hell's Canyon Overlook.** The overlook is about 30 miles along the Byway from the lake. This is a staggering view, 5,400 feet above the canyon floor.

- In Copperfield (about 15 miles south of the Overlook), secure a jet boat tour on the **Snake River.** You can also rent rafts and such here. After a few hours of enjoying the Snake, end your day at the **Hole-in-the-Wall Slide.** The geographically intriguing slide is about 30 miles west on the Byway from Copperfield.

THINGS TO SEE AND DO

Driving along the Hells Canyon Scenic Byway will certainly keep your senses engaged, but if you yearn to get out of the car and stretch your legs, or if you'd like to make a mini-vacation out of your trip, check out these attractions along the route.

ANTHONY LAKES SKI AREA. *47500 Anthony Lake Hwy North Powder, Baker City (97814). Phone 541/856-3277 www.anthonylakes.com.* Triple chairlift, Pomalift; patrol, school, rentals; nursery; day lodge, cafeteria, concession area, bar. Longest run 1 1/2 miles; vertical drop 900 feet. Fishing, hiking, cabin rentals, store (open in summer). Cross-country trails. Open mid-Nov-mid-Apr, Thurs-Sun. $$$$

✪ HELLS CANYON NATIONAL RECREATION AREA. *612 SW 2nd St, Enterprise (97828). Phone 541/426-5546. www.fs.fed.edu/hellscanyon/.* Created by the Snake River at the Idaho/Oregon border, Hells Canyon is the deepest river-carved gorge in North America—1 1/2 miles from Idaho's He Devil Mountain (elevation 9,393 feet) to the Snake River at Granite Creek (elevation 1,408 feet). An overlook at Hat Point, southeast of Imnaha, is a fire lookout. The recreation area includes parts of the Wallowa-Whitman National Forest. Activities include float trips, jet boat tours, boat trips into the canyon from the Hells Canyon Dam, backpacking, and horseback riding. Some developed campgrounds; much of the area is undeveloped, and some is designated wilderness. Be sure to inquire about road conditions before planning a trip; some roads are rough and open for a limited season.

NATIONAL HISTORIC OREGON TRAIL VISITOR CENTER. *Hwy 86, Baker City (97814). Phone toll-free 800/523-1235. www.nps.gov/oreg/oreg.htm.* Built and operated by the Bureau of Land Management, this center was built as a monument to emigrants who journeyed on the Oregon Trail. It is highly regarded for the quality of exhibits and the commanding view from its hilltop location. Exhibits, living history presentations, and multimedia displays. Open daily; closed Jan 1, Dec 25. $$$

ALL-AMERICAN ROADS

OREGON TRAIL REGIONAL MUSEUM. *2490 Grove St, Baker City (97814). Phone toll-free 800/523-1235.* This museum houses one of the most outstanding collections of rocks, minerals, and semiprecious stones in the West. Also an elaborate sea-life display, wildlife display, period clothing, and artifacts of early Baker County. Open late Mar-Oct, daily. **$**

SUMPTER VALLEY RAILWAY. *OR 7, Baker City (97814). Phone toll-free 800/523-1235. www.srvy.com.* Restored gear-driven Heisler steam locomotive and two observation cars travel 7 miles on a narrow-gauge track through a wildlife game habitat area where beavers, muskrats, geese, waterfowl, herons, and other animals may be seen. Also passes through the Sumpter mining district, location of the Sumpter Dredge that brought up more than $10 million in gold between 1913 and 1954 from as far down as 20 feet. Open May-Sept, Sat, Sun, holidays. **$$**

VALLEY BRONZE OF OREGON. *307 W Alder St, Joseph (98746). Phone 541/432-7445. www.valleybronze.com.* This company produces finished castings of bronze, fine and sterling silver, and stainless steel. The showroom displays finished pieces. Tours of the foundry depart from the showroom (by reservation). Open May-Nov, daily; rest of year, by appointment. **$$**

WALLOWA LAKE STATE PARK. *72214 Marina Ln, Joseph (97846). Phone 541/432-4185; toll-free 800/452-5687. www.oregonstateparks.org.* The park has 201 forested acres in an alpine setting formed by a glacier at the base of the rugged Wallowa Mountains. Swimming, water sport equipment rentals, fishing, boating (dock, motor rentals); picnicking, concession, improved tent and trailer sites (dump station). Park at the edge of the Eagle Cap wilderness area; hiking and riding trails begin here. Horse stables are nearby.

WALLOWA-WHITMAN NATIONAL FOREST. *47794 Oregon Hwy 244, Baker City (97814). Phone 541/523-6391. www.fs.fed.us/r6/w-w/.* More than 2 million acres include the 14,000-acre North Fork John Day Wilderness; 7,000-acre Monument Rock Wilderness; 358,461-acre Eagle Cap Wilderness; and 215,500-acre Hells Canyon Wilderness. Snowcapped peaks, Minam River; alpine meadows, rare wildflowers; Buckhorn Lookout; Anthony Lake and Phillips Lake. Stream and lake trout fishing; elk, deer, and bear hunting; float and jet boat trips; saddle and pack trips. Picnic area. Camping. **$**

PLACES TO STAY

If you choose to include an overnight stay in your trip along this All-American Road, Mobil Travel Guide recommends the following lodgings.

★★ **ELDORADO INN.** *695 Campbell St, Baker City (97814). Phone 541/523-6494.* 56 rooms, 2 story. Pet accepted; $2/day. Check-out noon. TV; VCR available. Indoor pool. Restaurant open 24 hours. Business services available. Refrigerators available. **¢**

Oregon

Hells Canyon Scenic Byway

★ **RODEWAY INN.** *810 Campbell St, Baker City (97814). Phone 541/523-2242. www.rodewayinn .com.* 54 rooms, 2 story. Pet accepted; $2/day. Complimentary continental breakfast. Check-out noon. TV. Pool privileges. Restaurant nearby. Meeting rooms. Some refrigerators. ¢

★★ **CHANDLERS BED, BREAD, AND TRAIL INN.** *700 S Main St, Joseph (97846). Phone 541/432-9765; toll-free 800/452-3781. www.eoni.com/~chanbbti.* 5 rooms, 2 share bath, 2 story. No A/C. No room phones. Children over 11 years only. Complimentary full breakfast. Check-out 11 am, check-in 2 pm. Whirlpool. Downhill, cross-country ski 6 miles. Picnic tables. Cedar and log interiors with high vaulted ceilings. Outdoor gazebo. Totally nonsmoking. ¢

★ **INDIAN LODGE MOTEL.** *201 S Main, Joseph (97846). Phone 541/432-2651; toll-free 888/286-5484.* 16 rooms. TV; cable (premium). Pet accepted; $5-$10. Check-out 11 am. Restaurant nearby. Lake 1 mile. ¢

★ **HOWARD JOHNSON EXPRESS INN.** *2612 Island Ave, La Grande (97850). Phone 541/963-7195; toll-free 800/446-4656. www.hojo.com.* 146 rooms, 2 story. Pet accepted. Complimentary continental breakfast. Check-out noon. TV; cable (premium). Outdoor pool; whirlpool. Restaurant adjacent open 24 hours. Free laundry. Meeting rooms. Business services available. In-house fitness room; sauna. Refrigerators. Private patios, balconies. ¢

★ **ROYAL MOTOR INN.** *1510 Adams Ave, La Grande (97850). Phone 541/963-4154. www.royal-motor-inn.com.* 43 rooms, 2 story. Check-out 11 am. TV; cable (premium). Restaurant nearby. ¢

★★ **STANG MANOR BED & BREAKFAST.** *1612 Walnut St, La Grande (97850). Phone 541/963-2400; toll-free 888/2UNWIND. www.stangmanor.com.* 4 rooms, 2 story. No A/C. Children over 10 years only. Complimentary full breakfast. Check-out 11 am, check-in 3 pm. TV in some rooms, living room; VCR available. Totally nonsmoking. $

PLACES TO EAT

A long day of driving is sure to make you hungry. At the end of your journey, take a table at one of the following restaurants.

★★ **GEISER GRILL.** *1966 Main St, Baker City (97814). Phone toll-free 866/826-3850.* American menu. Breakfast, lunch, dinner. Located in the Geiser Grand Hotel with the largest stained-glass ceiling in the West. $$

★★ **THE PHONE COMPANY.** *1926 First St, Baker City (97814). Phone 541/523-7997.* American menu. Closed Monday. Lunch, dinner. Upscale restaurant located in a classic 1910 building that once housed the local telephone company. Known for local originality. $$

★★ **FOLEY STATION.** *1011 Adams, La Grande (97850). Phone 541/963-7473.* American menu. Closed Mon. Breakfast, lunch, dinner. Chef-owned restaurant known for eclectic breakfasts. $$

★★ **TEN DEPOT STREET.** *10 Depot St, La Grande (97850). Phone 541/963-8766.* American menu. Closed Sun. Lunch, dinner. Innovative cuisine in a turn-of-the-century brick two-flat with antique furnishings. $$

★ **WILDFLOWER BAKERY.** *600 N Main St, Joseph (97846). Phone 541/432-7225.* American menu. Closed Thurs, Fri, Sat. Breakfast, lunch. Organic baked goods, breakfast items, and sandwiches in a small, out-of-the-way building. $

Historic Columbia River Highway
✹ OREGON

Quick Facts

LENGTH: 70 miles.

TIME TO ALLOW: 3 to 5 hours.

BEST TIME TO DRIVE: Mid-week sees the fewest crowds along the Byway. Fall has the best weather; spring provides the best time to view the waterfalls. High season is April through September.

BYWAY TRAVEL INFORMATION: US Forest Service—Columbia River Gorge National Scenic Area: 541/386-2333; Byway local Web site: www.odot.state.or.us/hcrh.

SPECIAL CONSIDERATIONS: Some attractions are closed during the winter months. Also, the Byway is narrow and winding, so you may want to consider traveling in a car instead of an RV.

RESTRICTIONS: The Multnomah Falls Lodge is open daily throughout the year. The Vista House is open from April through September.

BICYCLE/PEDESTRIAN FACILITIES: You can bike fairly safely on this highway because of the relatively low volume of automobiles. You'll also find plenty of trails around the Byway on which you can bike. Most notably, portions of the Historic Columbia River Highway that were abandoned during the construction of I-84 are being restored as multi-use trails. Numerous other trailheads are located along the Byway as well. These trails have a good range of length and difficulty, ranging from flat, paved trails to high mountain trails.

The Historic Columbia River Highway (HCRH) is exquisite: drive through the Columbia River Gorge for nearly 50 miles and sweep past majestic waterfalls, including Multnomah Falls, the most visited natural site in Oregon. This Byway also travels through a spectacular river canyon that you often view from the tops of cliffs over 900 feet above the river. During the spring, you experience magnificent wildflower displays, including many plants that exist only in this area.

This is the first scenic highway in the United States to gain the distinction of National Historic Landmark. (To give you an idea of what this means, less than 3 percent of the sites on the National Register of Historic Places become Landmarks.) The construction of this highway was considered one of the greatest engineering feats of the modern age. Its engineer, Samuel C. Lancaster, did "not [want] to mar what God had put there." It was designed in 1913-1914 to take advantage of the many waterfalls and other beautiful spots.

Make sure you travel both the well-known western section of the Byway from Troutdale to Dodson as well as the less-traveled eastern section from Mosier to The Dalles. The difference in vegetation zones and views between the two sections is amazing.

THE BYWAY STORY

The Historic Columbia River Highway tells historical, natural, recreational, and scenic stories that make it a unique and treasured Byway.

Historical
The HCRH has many nationally significant historic features on the National Register of

Oregon

✻ Historic Columbia River Highway

Historic Places—one of which is the highway itself. It is also a National Historic Civil Engineering Landmark that includes 23 unique bridges. The historic district includes not only the highway, but also the Portland Women's Forum State Scenic Viewpoint, Crown Point and Vista House, Multnomah Falls Lodge and Recreation Site, Eagle Creek Recreation Area, and several other waterfall areas.

Natural

The Columbia River Gorge is a spectacular river canyon, 80 miles long and up to 4,000 feet deep, cutting the only sea-level route through the Cascade Mountain Range. The Gorge includes 16 endemic plant species (those that exist only within the Gorge) and over 150 rare plant species. Bald eagles, peregrine falcons, Snake River salmon, and Larch Mountain salamanders also reside here. Wildflower tours of the Historic Columbia River Highway are common in the spring.

Recreational

Recreational facilities in the Columbia River Gorge National Scenic Area are also of national significance, including the three major highways (Historic Columbia River Highway, I-84, and Washington State Route 14) that are used extensively for pleasure driving. The highways provide access to many hiking trails, windsurfing sites, and the Mount Hood Railroad, a scenic and historic passenger and freight route up the Hood River Valley.

Scenic

The HCRH leaves the Sandy River and climbs to the top of the cliffs, offering spectacular views of the landscape. The Byway was designed in 1913-1914 to take advantage of the many waterfalls and other attractive sites along the route. The corridor contains some of the most dramatic views available anywhere in the country, including the Columbia River, with basalt cliffs and canyon walls; Multnomah Falls, a 620-foot, two-tiered waterfall that is the most visited natural attraction in the state of Oregon; the largest aggregation of high waterfalls outside of Yosemite, including Multnomah Falls, Horsetail Falls, Latourell Falls, Bridal Veil Falls, and Wahkeena Falls, plus numerous small falls; and giant basalt cliffs and monoliths, including Beacon Rock, Rooster Rock, Crown Point (a National Natural Landmark), Oneonta Bluff, and others.

HIGHLIGHTS

Start your must-see tour in Troutdale, the western entry point to the Historic Columbia River Highway. The attractive setting, unique shopping district, and convenient distance from the interstate make this small town a perfect start to your tour of the highway.

- Drive east. The first stop along the tour is **Sandy River.** An old iron bridge crosses the river at this point. Cross and enjoy. You can even take a side trip to the left to visit Lewis and Clark Park, but be sure to return to the Byway to continue your journey east.

- If you want a stunning scenic vista, you must stop at **Portland Women's Forum State Scenic Viewpoint.** It is located about 10 minutes from Troutdale (milepost 10.3).

- **Crown Point** and historic **Vista House** is next, about a mile farther east (milepost 11.5). Take a stroll around the point (carefully—the road curves around the building here) and enjoy yet another wonderful view of the river and the **Columbia River Gorge.**

- Scattered throughout the next few miles are many waterfalls, each with its own history and qualities. **Latourell Falls, Shepherd's Dell, Wahkeena Falls,** and **Bridal Veil Falls** each whet your appetite for the most visited waterfall on the Byway: **Multnomah Falls.** This beautiful double-cascade falls more than 650 feet. Stop and take the hike up to the bridge, crossing the waterfall for an up-close view.

see page A22 for color map

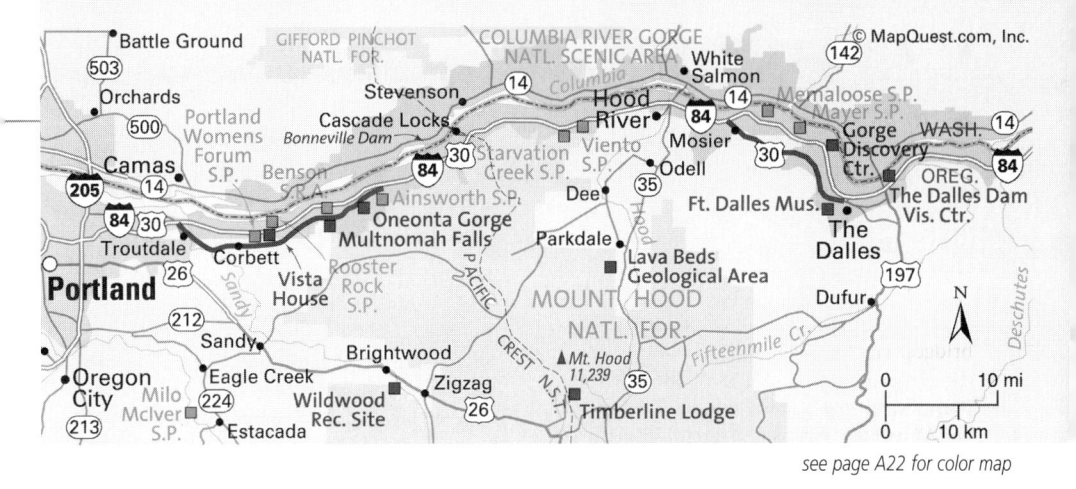

- Back on the highway, you shortly encounter **Oneonta Gorge.** This narrow canyon and its associated stream is a cool, dark, and shady hike. To enjoy it fully, follow the path to its river crossing, take off your shoes, and wade in the chilly stream.

- Continuing east, you rejoin the interstate for a while. The **Bridge of the Gods at Cascade Locks** connects Oregon to Washington.

- The city of **Hood River,** at the confluence of the Hood River and the Columbia River, is the windsurfing capital of the world. Stop and watch expert windsurfers from the riverside or from vantage points at hotels and viewpoints along the river. Or visit the **downtown historic district** and stop by the **Hood River County Museum.**

- Take time to leave your car now and walk a portion of the Historic Columbia River Highway between Hood River and Mosier that has been converted to a **state trail.** Remnants of the original auto highway and railings may still be seen. Or, if you continue in your car along the main highway instead, look for tunnels and roadbed high above you—a visible clue to a tremendous engineering feat.

- As you leave the rain forest of the Gorge and enter the drier, wide rolling plains west of Rowena and The Dalles, stop a moment at the **Memaloose Overlook** near the **Tom McCall Preserve.** Below you, the highway twists in the hairpin turns of the **Rowena Loops.** This engineering achievement remains remarkable even by today's standards.

- After you navigate the switchbacks of the Rowena Loops, catch your breath with a stop at the **Gorge Discovery Center** and **Wasco County Museum.** Opened in 1997, this museum offers interpretive exhibits about the human and natural history of the Columbia River Gorge.

- End your trip on the Historic Columbia River Highway at **The Dalles.** You can view the nearby **Dalles Lock and Dam** or tour the **historic district** of this city.

THINGS TO SEE AND DO

Driving along the Historic Columbia River Highway will certainly keep your senses engaged, but if you yearn to get out of the car and stretch your legs, or if you'd like to make a mini-vacation out of your trip, check out these attractions along the route.

BONNEVILLE LOCK AND DAM. *Cascade Locks (97014). Phone 541/374-8820.* The dam consists of three parts: one spillway and two powerhouses. It has an overall length of 3,463 feet and extends across the Columbia River to Washington. It was a major hydroelectric project of the US Army Corps of Engineers. On the Oregon side is a five-story visitor center with underwater windows into the fish ladders and new navigation lock with viewing facilities. There are audiovisual presentations and tours of fish ladders and the original powerhouse. The state salmon hatchery is adjacent. Fishing (salmon and sturgeon ponds); picnicking. Open June-Sept, daily or by appointment; closed Jan 1, Thanksgiving, Dec 25. **FREE**

COLUMBIA GORGE. *Port of Cascade Locks, Hood River (97031). Phone 541/374-8427. www.sternwheeler.com.* This sternwheeler makes daytime excursions, sunset dinner and brunch

181

Oregon

✻ Historic Columbia River Highway

cruises, harbor tours, and special holiday cruises. Reservations are required except for daily excursions from mid-June through Sept.

◘ COLUMBIA GORGE DISCOVERY CENTER. *5000 Discovery Dr, The Dalles (97058). Phone 541/296-8600. www.gorgediscover.org.* This building, at over 26,000 square feet, is the official interpretive center for the Columbia River Gorge National Scenic Area. Hands-on and electronic exhibits detail the volcanic upheavals and raging floods that created the Gorge, describe the history and importance of the river, and look to the Gorge's future. There are also Early Explorers, Steamboats and Trains, and Industry and Stewardship exhibits. Guided tours, seminars, classes, and workshops (some fees). Library and collections (by appointment). Café. Open daily; closed Jan 1, Thanksgiving, Dec 25. **$$$**

THE DALLES DAM AND RESERVOIR. *Exit 88, The Dalles (97058). Phone 541/296-1181.* Two-mile train tour with views of a historic navigation canal, visitor center, petroglyphs, and fish ladder facilities. Open Memorial Day-Labor Day, daily; Apr-May and Oct-Mar, Wed-Sun. **FREE**

◘ MOUNT HOOD NATIONAL FOREST. *65000 E US 26, Welches (97067). Phone 503/522-7674; toll-free 888/622-4822. www.fs.fed.us/r6/mthood/.* Mount Hood (11,235 feet) is the natural focal point of this large forest (over 1 million acres) with headquarters in Sandy. Its white-crowned top, the highest point in Oregon, can be seen for miles on a clear day. It is also popular with skiers, who know it has some of the best slopes in the Northwest. There are five winter sports areas. Throughout the year, however, you can take advantage of the surrounding forest facilities for camping (1,600 camp and picnic sites), hunting, fishing, swimming, mountain climbing, golfing, horseback riding, hiking, and tobogganing. The Columbia Gorge cuts through the Cascades here. You have your choice of nine routes to the summit, which has fumed and smoked several times since the volcanic peak was discovered. Only experienced climbers should try the ascent, and then only with a guide.

MOUNT HOOD SCENIC RAILROAD. *110 Railroad Ave, Hood River (97031). Phone 541/386-3556; toll-free 800/872-4661 (reservations). www.mthoodrr.com.* This historic railroad (built in 1906) offers 44-mile round-trip excursions. Dinner, brunch, and murder mystery excursions are available. Open Apr-Dec; schedule varies.

PANORAMA POINT. *Hwy 35 S and E Side Rd, Hood River (97031). Phone toll-free 800/366-3530.* Observation point for Hood River Valley and Mount Hood.

PLACES TO STAY

If you choose to include an overnight stay in your trip along this All-American Road, Mobil Travel Guide recommends the following lodgings.

★★ BEST WESTERN HOOD RIVER INN. *1108 E Marina Way, Hood River (97031). Phone 541/386-2200; toll-free 800/828-7873. www.hoodriverinn.com.* 149 rooms, 2-3 story. Pet accepted. Check-out noon. TV; cable (premium). Outdoor pool. Restaurant, bar; entertainment. Room service. Coin laundry. Business services available. In-room modem link. Private patios. Beach access; windsurfing. In the Columbia River Gorge. **¢**

★★★ **COLUMBIA GORGE HOTEL.** 4000 Westcliff Dr, Hood River (97031). Phone 541/386-5566; toll-free 800/345-1921. www.columbiagorgehotel.com. Nestled in the Columbia Gorge National Scenic Area, trees and mountain peaks will adorn your views from this hotel featuring a waterfall and beautiful gardens. For the outdoorsy, there is windsurfing, skiing, and fishing. 40 rooms, 3 story. Pet accepted; $15. Complimentary full breakfast. Check-out noon. TV; VCR available. Restaurant, bar. Business services available. Free train station transportation. Health club privileges. Restored building (1920s) with formal gardens. Jazz Age atmosphere. $$

★ **RIVERVIEW LODGE.** 1505 Oak St, Hood River (97031). Phone 541/386-8719; toll-free 800/789-9568. www.riverviewforyou.com. 20 rooms, 2 kitchen units, 2 story. Check-out 11 am. TV; cable (premium). Restaurant nearby. Business services available. Indoor pool; whirlpool. Refrigerators, microwaves. Some balconies. ¢

★★★ **DOLCE SKAMANIA LODGE.** 1131 SW Skamania Lodge Way, Stevenson (98648). Phone 509/427-7700; toll-free 800/221-7117. www.dolce.com/skamania/. With remarkable design, ultimate comfort, and a setting that will leave you breathless, this spectacular mountain resort is a must-see. Guests bask in the glory of the surrounding beauty. 195 rooms, 4 story. Check-out noon. TV. Indoor pool; whirlpool. Playground. Restaurant, bar. Room service. Meeting rooms. Business center. In-room modem link. Bellhops. Sundries. Tennis. Mountain bike rentals. 18-hole golf, pro, greens fee $40, putting green, driving range. In-house fitness room; sauna. Massage. Game room. Lawn games. Refrigerators. Some balconies. $

★★ **BEST WESTERN RIVER CITY INN.** 112 W 2nd St, The Dalles (97058). Phone 541/296-9107; toll-free 800/935-2378. www.bestwestern.com. 65 rooms, 2-4 story. Pet accepted; $5. Check-out 11 am. TV; cable (premium). Outdoor pool. Restaurant, bar. Room service. Meeting rooms. Business services available. In-room modem link. Health club privileges. Some refrigerators. ¢

★ **INN AT THE DALLES.** 3550 SE Frontage Rd, The Dalles (97058). Phone 541/296-1167. 45 rooms, 4 kitchen units. Pet accepted. Check-out 11 am. TV. Indoor pool. Restaurant nearby. Business services available. Free airport transportation. View of the Columbia River, Mount Hood, and The Dalles Dam. ¢

★★ **QUALITY INN COLUMBIA RIVER GORGE.** 2114 W 6th St, The Dalles (97058). Phone 541/298-5161; toll-free 800/848-9378. www.qualityinn.com. 85 rooms, 2 story, 16 kitchen units. Pet accepted; $2. Check-out 11 am. TV. Outdoor pool; whirlpool. Restaurant. Coin laundry. Meeting rooms. Business services available. In-room modem link. Health club privileges. Some fireplaces. ¢

★★ **INN OF THE WHITE SALMON.** 172 W Jewett Blvd, White Salmon (98672). Phone 509/493-2335; toll-free 800/972-5226. www.innofthewhitesalmon.com. 16 rooms, 5 suites, 2 story. Pet accepted. Complimentary full breakfast. Check-out noon, check-in 3 pm. TV. Restaurant nearby. European-style inn built in 1937; antique décor, original art. $

Oregon

❋ *Historic Columbia River Highway*

PLACES TO EAT

A long day of driving is sure to make you hungry. At the end of your journey, take a table at one of the following restaurants.

★★ **MULTNOMAH FALLS LODGE.** *50000 Historic Columbia River Hwy, Bridal Veil (97010). Phone 503/695-2376. www.multnomahfallslodge.com.* American menu. Breakfast, lunch, dinner. Elegant dining room with scenic views. **$**

★ **COUSIN'S.** *2115 W 6th St, The Dalles (97058). Phone 541/298-2771.* American menu. Closed Dec 25. Breakfast, lunch, dinner. Bar. Children's menu. Frontier motif. **$-$$**
D

★ **WINDSEEKER.** *1535 Barge Way Rd, The Dalles (97058). Phone 541/298-7171.* American menu. Breakfast, lunch, dinner. Small supper club-style restaurant featuring contemporary American and Pan-Asian cuisine. **$**

★ **WINDY RIVER RESTAURANT.** *315 E 3rd St, The Dalles (97058). Phone 541/296-2028.* American menu. Closed Sun. Lunch, dinner. Highly regarded locally, this restaurant focuses on pasta and seafood. **$**

★★★ **COLUMBIA GORGE DINING ROOM.** *4000 Westcliff Dr, Hood River (97031). Phone 541/386-5566. www.columbiagorgehotel.com.* American menu. Breakfast, lunch, dinner. Restored 1920s hotel dining room with scenic views of the Columbia River Gorge. **$$**

★ **WILDFLOWER CAFÉ.** *904 2nd Ave, Mosier (97040). Phone 541/478-0111.* American menu. Breakfast, lunch, dinner. Excellent pancakes; live music on weekends. **$**

★★ **BLACK RABBIT.** *2126 SW Halsey, Troutdale (97060). Phone 503/492-3086.* Specializes in fresh Northwestern cuisine. Breakfast, lunch, dinner. Bar. Children's menu. Outdoor seating. Reservations accepted. Totally nonsmoking. **$$**
D

Pacific Coast Scenic Byway
❈ OREGON

Quick Facts

LENGTH: 363 miles.

TIME TO ALLOW: 10 to 12 hours.

BEST TIME TO DRIVE: Spring to fall.

BYWAY TRAVEL INFORMATION: Oregon Coast Visitor's Association Oregon Tourism Commission: 503/986-0000.

SPECIAL CONSIDERATIONS: Services may be several miles apart or closed at night. Slides and floods caused by extreme weather conditions sometimes temporarily disrupt access. With the ocean providing year-round air-conditioning, temperatures are comfortably in the 60s and 70s in the summer and rarely drop below freezing in the winter. Be prepared for fog, drizzle, or rain showers any time of year, but mainly in the winter and spring. Steady breezes are common most of the year. However, winter storms occasionally bring gusts above 50 mph. At the Oregon Dunes National Recreation Area, temperatures are at their highest and winds are at their lowest during the early fall. Be prepared for rapidly changing weather conditions.

BICYCLE/PEDESTRIAN FACILITIES: This Byway is designated by the Oregon Department of Transportation as a state bike route. Signage and stripes are provided for the bike route and pedestrian crossings. Bicycling on the Oregon Coast Bike Route is considered to be the most exciting way to explore the scenery along this Byway.

This Byway trots along the full length of the Oregon coast. The northern end starts in the shadow of the impressive Astoria-Megler Bridge, where the mouth of the Columbia River gapes wide (Astoria is the oldest US settlement west of the Rockies). Shining beaches and temperate rain forests govern the following dozens of miles. Parallelling the Lewis and Clark Trail, the route stops by attractive places, such as the resort town of Seaside, famous for its 2-mile beachfront promenade, and the busy Garibaldi fishing port on Tillamook Bay.

The southern portion of the Byway changes a little because it is dominated by rugged cliffs, farms, and sandy beaches. This segment maintains some of the most photographed areas in Oregon; photographers often capture Siletz and Depoe Bays, the colorful Oregon skies, lots of dairy land, and the city of Tillamook (the producer of the famous brand of cheese).

THE BYWAY STORY

The Pacific Coast Scenic Byway tells archaeological, cultural, historical, natural, recreational, and scenic stories that make it a unique and treasured Byway.

Archaeological

The relics and structures located in this area indicate that people have lived and prospered here for several millennia. This Byway's archaeological residue fits into two main categories: relics of a native people that reveal an Eden-like past (such as ancient campsites) and evidences of the activities of a more recent people. Of the ancient people, scientists have found remnants of spears, knives, and other hunting equipment.

Oregon

✽ Pacific Coast Scenic Byway

Discoveries of bones near campsites indicate the type of food these people ate: fish, large animals (elk and deer), and some birds. The people were largely industrious and thrived in this area for thousands of years.

The sites from a more recent people are mostly historic bridges and lighthouses such as Yaquina Head's 125-year-old lighthouse, the 125-foot Astoria Column in Astoria, and the occasional shipwreck, such as the one known as *Peter Iredale* at Fort Stevens State Park. Some of these impressive structures still stand as landmarks to help guide travelers, while others function as attractions for tourists.

Cultural

Appreciate this area more by taking part in everyday activities to familiarize yourself with the area's culture. For instance, go to Lincoln City to soar a colorful kite alongside the locals; after that, visit some of Lincoln City's many art galleries. Another popular destination is Bandon, a charming town famous for its lighthouse, its giant seastacks, its cheese factory, and the cranberry harvest.

You might stop in Tillamook and see Oregon's largest cheese factory for a taste-testing tour: something residents like to do every now and then. This impressive factory has been around for over 100 years. It boasts of continuing to use the time-tested recipe that has made its cheese famous. Other areas of note include North Bend and Coos Bay, cities that compose the coast's largest urban area; here, you find cultural activities galore, such as fantastic symphonies, art galleries, and restaurants.

Historical

The gorgeous and rich Oregon coast has drawn and sustained native people for centuries, and it has done likewise for sightseers and settlers ever since Lewis and Clark highly acclaimed the area. Each new wave of people who came to live around the route added a new facet of culture and history to it and left their mark through historical and archaeological remains.

These remains, shadows of past, are waiting in places like Astoria. Other important historical sites on the Byway include Fort Clatsop National Memorial, a life-size replica of Lewis and Clark's 1805-1806 winter outpost; historic Battle Rock Park in Port Orford, one of Oregon's oldest incorporated towns; and Yaquina Head's lighthouse, a testament to the area's historical shipping industry. The area's history is also evidenced in the many Victorian homes that scale the hillside, the 1883 Flavel House, and the shipwreck of the *Peter Iredale* at Fort Stevens State Park.

Natural

The Byway runs along the coastline, bringing highway travelers to the sea and away again, winding by estuarine marshes, clinging to exposed seaside cliffs, passing through gentle agricultural valleys, and brushing against wind-sculpted dunes. Travelers encounter the scenic splendor of sea-stack rock formations that are eroding under constant surf, as well as a plethora of unusual plants and animals that provide natural wonder.

The highest waterfall in the Coast Range is an easy side trip from the Byway. To find this waterfall, go 7 miles south of Tillamook, and then watch for a small sign to Munson Creek Falls. Follow the narrow road 1 1/2 miles to the parking area. A short stroll takes you to the base of this 266-foot cataract.

Many travelers enjoy watching water wildlife along this Byway. Waysides and state parks along the coast make excellent vantage points for watching gray whales that migrate between December and May.

Recreational

Beaches along the Byway are open to public use. In addition, many state parks run the length of the Byway and provide public access and protection to beaches. An abundance of public campsites, motel rooms, beach houses, and eateries along the Byway corridor ensure a delightful extended stay along Oregon's Pacific Coast Scenic Byway.

Florence is the gateway to the Oregon Dunes National Recreation Area, a 47-mile sandbox with areas designated for bird-watching and dune riding. Honeyman State Park is a popular place to water-ski and camp. As you travel on through the dunes, take a side trip to the Dean Creek Elk Viewing Area at Reedsport. The Oregon Dunes National Recreation Area has more than 31,000 acres. Visitors can camp, arrange a tour, take an exhilarating off-highway vehicle ride, or just walk along tranquil lakes, forest trails, and beaches.

Tucked in among some of the highest coastal dunes in the world, you'll find plenty of fishing and boating opportunities in small communities like Winchester Bay and Lakeside. The dunes end near the cities of North Bend and Coos Bay, the coast's largest urban area. As Oregon's deepest natural harbor, Coos Bay has long been a major shipping port for the timber industry and a haven for sport-fishing enthusiasts.

Depoe Bay also offers fishing and whale-watching excursions from the world's smallest navigable harbor.

Flying large, beautiful kites is a common practice all along the coast, but is especially popular in Lincoln City, which was recognized by *KiteLines* magazine as the best place to fly a kite in North America. Annual spring and fall kite festivals draw kite enthusiasts from all over. Get out your kite and watch with the crowds as the delicate crafts are lofted up into the sky by the strong coastal winds.

Scenic

Keep your camera handy so that you can capture the coast's most photographed seascape, Cape Foulweather and the churning waves at Devil's Punch Bowl. The superb scenery continues through Waldport and Yachats to the Cape Perpetua Scenic Area. Here, you can watch the waves rush in and out of Devil's Churn, or you can hike on trails high above it. As the rugged cliffs give way to graceful sand dunes, you'll arrive in Florence, a city that explodes with wild rhododendrons in the spring. The drive into

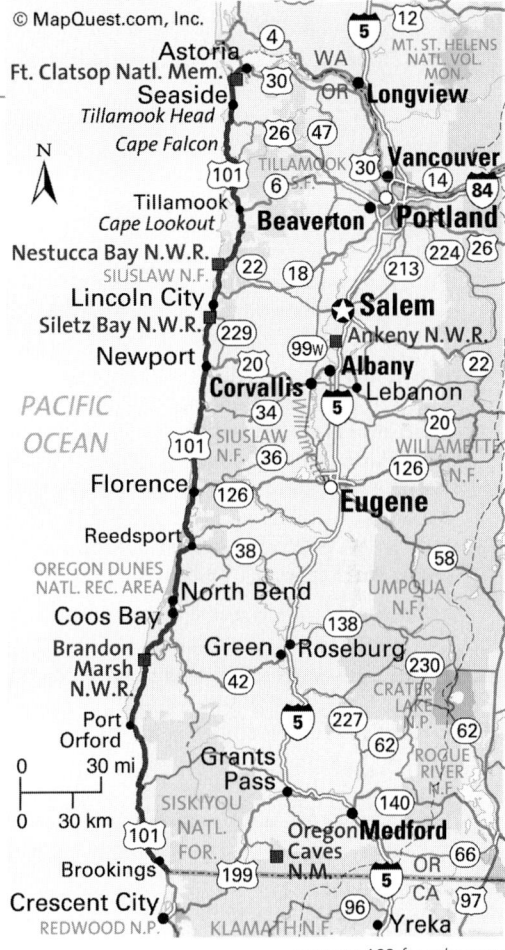

see page A23 for color map

Brookings saves some of the best scenery for last. For example, Samuel Boardman State Park shows off 9 miles of rocky viewpoints and quiet beaches at the base of the Siskiyou Mountains. After crossing the crystal blue Chetco River, the Pacific Coast Scenic Byway ends in redwood country at the California border.

HIGHLIGHTS

Take the Pacific Coast Highway's must-see tour:

- **Astoria:** You will pass through Long Beach and go on to the city of Astoria, the oldest American settlement west of the Rockies. Astoria offers more points of historical interest than any other place on the Oregon coast.

- **Fort Clatsop National Memorial:** For a glimpse into life on one of the most important expeditions in the nation's history, travel 3 miles east on Alternate (Old) 101 to Fort

Oregon

✽ *Pacific Coast Scenic Byway*

Clatsop Road and follow signs to the memorial. It is operated by the National Park Service on the site where the Lewis and Clark Expedition spent the winter of 1805-1806.

- **Seaside:** You reach the city of Seaside, which was Oregon's first seashore resort. The Turnaround there is the location of the statue designating the end of the Lewis and Clark Trail. At the south end of the Promenade, you will find the Lewis and Clark Salt Cairn, where members of the expedition made salt from seawater.

- **Cannon Beach:** The site of the famous annual Sandcastle Building Contest in early June. The beach was named for a cannon washed ashore in 1846 after the wreck of the schooner *Shark*.

- **Lincoln County:** Lincoln County has miles of ocean beaches known for fine agates and other minerals, ocean cruises, and whale-watching trips out of Depoe Bay and Newport. Lincoln City also has Oregon's first factory outlet shopping center.

- **Yaquina Bay Lighthouse:** The lighthouse houses a museum and is open during scheduled hours.

- **Devil's Churn:** The basalt that forms the shore here is penetrated by a split in the rock that narrows to a few feet before finally disappearing into the cliff. Fascinating in summer, it is awe-inspiring during winter storms and is an excellent spot for photographers.

- **Cape Perpetua Viewpoint:** Just south of Devils Churn you'll find a road going inland. At the branch in the road, turn left and continue climbing sharply to the Cape Perpetua Viewpoint. There is a fine view of the coast both north and south.

- **Heceta Head Lighthouse State Scenic Viewpoint (formerly Devil's Elbow State Park):** This pretty little cove is the place to see Heceta Head Lighthouse up close. Just walk up the trail to the former assistant lighthouse keeper's home, Heceta House, and continue on to the lighthouse.

- **Sea Lion Caves:** These natural caves are home to Steller sea lions.

- **Florence:** There are many delightful shops, restaurants, and galleries in this town near the Siuslaw River.

- **Oregon Dunes National Recreation Area (NRA):** The Oregon Dunes NRA extends from Florence to North Bend with many access points off of the Byway.

- **Umpqua River:** The Umpqua River Bridge is one of the historic coast bridges. The Umpqua is one of the major rivers in Oregon and is navigable by fairly large vessels upstream as far as Scottsburg.

- **Cape Blanco:** Five miles west of the Byway, Cape Blanco was discovered by the Spanish explorer Martin de Aguilar in 1603. The lighthouse is located at the westernmost point in Oregon.

- **Prehistoric Gardens:** In the rain forest atmosphere of the Oregon coast, the developers of Prehistoric Gardens have created life-sized replicas of dinosaurs.

THINGS TO SEE AND DO

Driving along the Pacific Coast Scenic Byway will certainly keep your senses engaged, but if you yearn to get out of the car and stretch your legs, or if you'd like to make a mini-vacation out of your trip, check out these attractions along the route.

ALDER HOUSE II. *611 Immonen Rd, Lincoln City (97367). www.alderhouse.com.* Set in a grove of alder trees, this is the oldest glass-blowing studio in Oregon. Watch molten glass drawn from a furnace and shaped into pieces of traditional or modern design. Open mid-Mar-Nov; daily. **FREE**

AZALEA PARK. *Hwy 101 and North Bank Chetco River Rd, Brookings (97415). Phone 541/469-2021; toll-free 800/535-9469. www.brookingsor.com/playing/azaleapark.shtml.* A 36-acre city park with five varieties of large native azaleas, some blooming twice a year. Observation point. Hiking. Picnicking.

C&M STABLES. *90241 Hwy 101, Florence (97439). Phone 541/997-7540. www.touroregon.com/horses/.* Experience the spectacular scenery of Oregon's coast on horseback. Beach (1 1/2 to 2 hours), dune trail (1 to 1 1/2 hours), sunset (2 hours, with or without a meal), and coast range (1/2-day or all-day) rides. Must be 8 years or older. Open daily; closed Thanksgiving, Dec 25. **$$$$**

CAPE ARAGO. *Coos Bay (97420). Phone 541/888-8867. www.oregonstateparks.org/park_94.php.* This 134-acre promontory juts 1/2 mile into the ocean. Two beaches, fishing; hiking (on the Oregon Coast Trail), picnicking. Observation point (whale and seal watching).

CAPE BLANCO STATE PARK. *91814 Cape Blanco Rd, Port Orford (97465). Phone 541/332-6774. www.oregonstateparks.org/park_62.php.* A 1,880-acre park, once a ranch owned by the hard-working Hughes family, affords marvelous views of the Cape Blanco Lighthouse and boasts the historic Hughes house, hiking trails, beach access, and a campground. River access for boats. Picnicking. Horse camp, horse trails, rustic cabins. Improved campsites.

CAPE LOOKOUT STATE PARK. *13000 Whiskey Creek Rd, Tillamook (97141). Phone 503/842-4981. www.oregonstateparks.org/park_186.php.* A 1,974-acre park with a virgin spruce forest and observation point. One of most primitive ocean shore areas in the state. Hiking trail to the end of the cape. Picnicking. Tent and trailer sites (dump station). Open daily.

CAPE SEBASTIAN STATE PARK. *Gold Beach (97444). Phone 541/469-2021. www.oregonstateparks.org/park_73.php.* Approximately 1,143 acres of open and forested land. Cape Sebastian is a precipitous headland, rising more than 700 feet above tide with a view of many miles of coastline. 1.5-mile trail to the tip of the cape; beach access. A short roadside through the forest area is marked by wild azaleas, rhododendrons, and blue ceanothus in season. Trails; no rest rooms or water. Open daily.

CARL G. WASHBURNE MEMORIAL. *93111 Hwy 101, Florence (97439). Phone 541/547-3416. www.oregonstateparks.org/park_123.php.* This 1,089-acre park is a good area for the study of botany. Two-mile-long beach, swimming, fishing, clamming, hiking, picnicking, tent and trailer campsites with access to beach. Elk may be seen in campgrounds and nearby meadows. Open daily.

CHINOOK WINDS CASINO & CONVENTION CENTER. *1777 NW 44th St, Lincoln City (97367). Phone 541/996-5825; toll-free 888/CHINOOK. www.chinookwindscasino.com.* About 80 miles south of the Washington border on the scenic Oregon coast, Chinook Winds is the largest convention facility between Seattle and San Francisco. With more than 1,200 machines and tables, the modern casino has all the requisite games—slots, blackjack, keno, poker, roulette, craps, and even bingo—with a betting limit of $500. The cavernous showroom sees regular performances by classic rock bands, country artists, and comedians, many of them household

Oregon

✹ *Pacific Coast Scenic Byway*

names. There are also three restaurants (an upscale room, a buffet, and a deli), a lounge, and childcare services and an arcade for the kids, but no hotel rooms. (There are plenty of the latter in Lincoln City, however.) Best of all, the casino's beachfront location is serene. Hours vary.

COLUMBIA RIVER MARITIME MUSEUM. *1792 Marine Dr, Astoria (97213). Phone 503/325-2323. www.crmm.org.* Rare maritime artifacts and memorabilia of the Columbia River, its tributaries, and the Northwest coast. *Columbia, Lightship 604* at moorage in Maritime Park. Fishing industry, discovery and exploration, steamship, shipwreck, navigation, and steamboat exhibits. Coast Guard and Navy exhibits. Open daily; closed Thanksgiving, Dec 25. $$

DEAN CREEK ELK VIEWING AREA. *3 miles E on OR 38, Reedsport (97467). Phone 541/756-0100.* Area has 440 acres of pasture and bottomland where Roosevelt elk (Oregon's largest land mammal) and other wildlife can be viewed. Interpretive center. No hunting. Open daily. **FREE**

DEVIL'S ELBOW. *84505 Hwy 101, Florence (97439). Phone 541/997-3641.* A 545-acre park. Ocean beach, fishing; hiking, picnicking. Observation point. Open daily. $

DEVIL'S PUNCH BOWL. *Newport (97365). Phone 541/265-9278.* An 8-acre park noted for its bowl-shaped rock formation that fills at high tide; ocean-carved caves, marine gardens. Beach. Trails. Picnicking. Observation point. Open daily. **FREE**

ECOLA STATE PARK. *Ecola Rd, Cannon Beach (97110). Phone 503/861-1671. www.oregonstateparks.org/park_188.php.* The end of the trail for Lewis and Clark expedition. A 1,303-acre park with 6 miles of ocean frontage, sea lion and bird rookeries on rocks and offshore islands, and the Tillamook Lighthouse. Beaches, fishing; hiking (on the Oregon Coast Trail), picnicking at Ecola Point. Whale-watching at observation point. Open daily. $

FLAVEL HOUSE. *441 8th St, Astoria (97103). Phone 503/325-2203. www.oldoregon.com/Pages/Havel.htm.* Built by Captain George Flavel, pilot and shipping man; outstanding example of Queen Anne architecture (1883-1887). Restored Victorian home houses antique furnishings and fine art; collection of 19th- and 20th-century toys. Carriage house, museum store, orientation film. Open daily; closed holidays. $$

✪ **FORT CLATSOP NATIONAL MEMORIAL.** *Cannon Beach (97110). Phone 503/861-2471. www.nps.gov/focl/.* This site marks the western extremity of the territory explored by Meriwether Lewis and William Clark in their expedition of 1804-1806. The fort is a reconstruction of their 1805-1806 winter quarters. The original fort was built here because of its excellent elk hunting grounds, its easy access to ocean salt, its protection from the westerly coastal storms, and the availability of fresh water. The expedition set out on May 14, 1804, to seek "the most direct and practicable water communication across this continent" under orders from President Thomas Jefferson. The first winter was spent near Bismarck, North Dakota. In April 1805, the party, then numbering 33, resumed the journey. On November 15, they had their first view of the ocean from a point near McGowan, Washington. The company left Fort Clatsop on March 23, 1806, on their return trip and returned to St. Louis on September 23 of the same year. The Lewis and Clark Expedition was one of the greatest explorations in the history of the United States, and its journals depict one of the most fascinating chapters in the annals of the American frontier. The visitor center has museum exhibits and provides audiovisual programs. The canoe landing has replicas of dugout canoes of that period. Ranger talks and living history demonstrations are presented mid-June-Labor Day. Open daily; closed Dec 25. $

FORT STEVENS STATE PARK. *10 miles W of Astoria, in Hammond (97121). Phone 503/861-1671; toll-free 800/452-5687. www.oregonstateparks.org/park_179.php.* A 3,763-acre park adjacent to an old Civil War fort. Wreck of the *Peter Iredale* (1906) is on the ocean shore. Fort Stevens is the only military post in the lower 48 states to be fired upon by foreign forces since 1812. On June 21, 1942, a Japanese submarine fired several shells from its 5-inch gun; only one hit land. Visitor center and self-guided tour at the Old Fort Stevens Military Complex. Ocean beach, lake swimming, fishing, clamming on beach, boating (dock, ramp); bicycling, picnicking at Coffenbury Lake. Improved tent and trailer sites. Dump station. Open daily. **$**

HARRIS BEACH. *1655 Hwy 101 N, Brookings (97415). Phone 541/469-2021.* A 171-acre park with scenic rock cliffs along the ocean. Ocean beach, fishing; hiking trails, observation point, picnicking, improved tent and trailer campsites (dump station).

HATFIELD MARINE SCIENCE CENTER OF OREGON STATE UNIVERSITY. *2030 S Marine Science Dr, Newport (97365). Phone 541/867-0100. hmsc.oregonstate.edu.* Conducts research on oceanography, fisheries, water quality, marine science education, and marine biology; research vessel *Wecoma*; nature trail; aquarium-museum; films; special programs in summer. Winter and spring gray whale programs. Braille text and other aids for the hearing and visually impaired. Open daily; closed Dec 25. **DONATION**

HECETA HEAD LIGHTHOUSE. *92072 Hwy 101 South, Yachats (97498). Phone 541/547-3696. www.hecetalighthouse.com.* A picturesque beacon set high on a rugged cliff. Heceta Head Lighthouse (1894) is one of the most photographed beacons in the United States. **$**

JERRY'S ROGUE RIVER JET BOAT TRIPS. *Port of Gold Beach Boat Basin, Gold Beach (97444). Phone 541/247-4571; toll-free 800/451-3645. www.roguejets.com.* A six-hour (64-mile) round-trip into wilderness area; two-hour lunch or dinner stop at Agness. Also eight-hour (104-mile) and six-hour (80-mile) round-trip whitewater excursions. Rogue River Museum and Gift Shop (open all year). Open May-Oct, daily. **$$$$**

JESSIE M. HONEYMAN MEMORIAL. *84505 Hwy 101, Florence (97439). Phone 541/997-3641. www.oregonstateparks.org/park_134.php.* This park has 522 coastal acres with wooded lakes and sand dunes, an abundance of rhododendrons, and an excellent beach. Swimming, water-skiing, fishing, boat dock and ramps; hiking, picnicking, improved camping, tent and trailer sites (dump station). Open daily. **$**

MAIL BOAT WHITEWATER TRIPS. *94294 Rougeriver Rd, Gold Beach (97444) Phone 541/247-7033; toll-free 800/458-3511. www.mailboat.com.* A 104-mile round-trip by jet boat into wilderness and whitewater of the upper Rogue River. Narrated 7 1/2-hour trip. Open mid-May-mid-Oct, daily. Also 80-mile round-trip to the middle Rogue River. Narrated 6 3/4-hour trip departs twice daily. Open mid-June-Sept. Reservations advised for all trips. **$$$$**

MARINE DISCOVERY TOURS. *345 SW Bay Blvd, Newport (97365). Phone 541/265-6200; toll-free 800/903-2628. www.marinediscovery.com.* Whale-watching and river cruises. Hands-on activities. Hours vary seasonally; closed Dec 25. **$$$$**

OFFICIAL ROGUE RIVER MAIL BOAT HYDRO-JET TRIPS. *94294 N Bank Rogue River Rd, Gold Beach (97444). Phone 541/247-7033; toll-free 800/458-3511.* A 64-mile round-trip by jet boat up the wild and scenic Rogue River; two-hour lunch stop at Agness. Open May-Oct, daily. Reservations advised. **$$$$**

Oregon

✱ Pacific Coast Scenic Byway

OREGON COAST AQUARIUM. *2820 SE Ferry Slip Rd, Newport (97365). Phone 541/867-3474. www.aquarium.org.* The aquarium houses 15,000 animals representing 500 species in unique habitats. Open daily; closed Dec 25. $$$

★ **OREGON DUNES NATIONAL RECREATION AREA.** *855 Hwy 101, Reedsport (97467). Phone 541/271-3611. www.fs.fed.us/r6/siuslaw/odnra.htm.* Large coastal sand dunes, forests, and wetlands comprise this 32,000-acre area in Siuslaw National Forest. Beachcombing; fishing; boating. Hiking, horseback riding, off-road vehicle areas. Picnicking. Camping (fee; some campgrounds closed Oct-May). Visitor center and headquarters in Reedsport at US 101 and OR 38. Open daily.

OSWALD WEST STATE PARK. *9500 Sandpiper Ln, Nehalem (97131). Phone 503/368-5943; toll-free 800/551-6949. www.oregonstateparks.org/park_195.php.* A 2,474-acre park with outstanding coastal headland; towering cliffs; low dunes; rain forest with massive spruce and cedar trees; road winds 700 feet above sea level and 1,000 feet below the peak of Neahkahnie Mountain. Surfing (at nearby Short Sands Beach), fishing; hiking trails (on the Oregon Coast Trail), picnicking, primitive campgrounds accessible only by 1/4-mile foot trail.

SADDLE MOUNTAIN STATE PARK. *Seaside (97138). Phone 503/368-5154 or 503/436-2844. www.oregonstateparks.org/park_197.php.* A 2,922-acre park with a trail to a 3,283-foot summit, one of the highest in the Coastal Range. Hiking. Picnicking. Primitive campsites. Open daily.

SALMON HARBOR. *100 Ork Rock Rd, Winchester Bay (97103). Phone 541/271-3407.* Excellent boat basin for charter boats and pleasure and fishing craft. Fishing for silver and chinook salmon in the ocean, a short run from the mouth of the Umpqua River. Open May-Sept, daily; rest of year, Mon-Fri.

SAND DUNES FRONTIER. *83960 Hwy 101, Florence (97439). Phone 541/997-3544. sanddunesfrontier.com.* Excursions aboard 20-passenger dune buggies or drive-yourself Odysseys; miniature golf; flower garden. Open daily. $$$$

★ **SEA LION CAVES.** *91560 Hwy 101 N, Florence (97439). Phone 541/547-3111. www.sealioncaves.com.* Descend 208 feet under a basaltic headland into a cavern (1,500 feet long); home of wild sea lions. These mammals (up to 12 feet long) are generally seen on rocky ledges outside the cave in spring and summer and inside the cave in fall and winter. Self-guided tours; light jacket and comfortable shoes suggested. Open daily; closed Dec 25. $$

SEASIDE AQUARIUM. *200 N Prom, Seaside (97138). Phone 503/738-6211. www.seasideaquarium.com.* Deep-sea life and trained seals; seal feeding (fee). Open Mar-Nov, daily; rest of year, Wed-Sun; closed Thanksgiving, Dec 24-25. $$$

SHORE ACRES. *89814 Cape Arago Hwy, Coos Bay (97420) Phone 541/888-3732 or -8867. www.oregonstateparks.org/park_97.php.* Former grand estate of Coos Bay lumberman, noted for its unusual botanical and Japanese gardens and spectacular ocean views (743 acres). Ocean beach; hiking (on the Oregon Coast Trail), picnicking.

SIUSLAW PIONEER MUSEUM. *85294 US 101S, Florence (97439). Phone 541/997-7884. www.florencechamber.com/RecAtt_PioneerM.html.* Exhibits preserve the history of the area; impressive display of artifacts and items from early settlers and Native Americans. Library room; extensive genealogy records; hundreds of old photographs. Open Jan-Nov, Tues-Sun; closed holidays. $

SUNSET BAY. *Coos Bay (97420). Phone 541/888-4902; toll-free 800/551-6949. www.oregonstateparks.org/park_100.php.* A 395-acre park with swimming beach on sheltered bay, fishing; hiking, picnicking, tent and trailer sites. Observation point.

ALL-AMERICAN ROADS

TILLAMOOK COUNTY PIONEER MUSEUM. *2106 2nd St, Tillamook (97141). Phone 503/842-4553. www.tcpm.org.* Possessions of early settlers, replica of a pioneer home and barn, blacksmith shop, logging displays, war relics, relics from Tillamook Naval Air Station and Blimp Base, minerals, guns, books, vehicles, natural history and wildlife exhibits that include nine dioramas; "great-grandma's kitchen." Open daily; closed Thanksgiving, Dec 25. **$$**

UMPQUA LIGHTHOUSE STATE PARK. *460 Lighthouse Rd, Reedsport (97467). Phone 541/271-4118. www.oregonstateparks.org/park_121.php.* This 450-acre park touches the mouth of the Umpqua River, borders the Umpqua Lighthouse Reservation, and skirts the ocean shore for more than 2 miles, with sand dunes rising 500 feet (the highest in the United States). Noted for its marvelous seasonal display of rhododendrons. Swimming; fishing. Hiking; trail to beach and around Lake Marie. Picnicking. Tent and trailer sites. Whale-watching area.

YAQUINA HEAD. *Lighthouse Dr and Hwy 101, Newport (97365). Phone 541/574-3100. www.yaquinalights.org/yhead.html.* The lighthouse here is a popular spot for whale-watching and fully accessible tidal pool viewing. Also an interpretive center.

PLACES TO STAY

If you choose to include an overnight stay in your trip along this All-American Road, Mobil Travel Guide recommends the following lodgings.

★ **ASTORIA DUNES MOTEL.** *288 W Marine Dr, Astoria (97103). Phone 503/325-7111; toll-free 800/441-3319. astoriadunes.qwestdex.com.* 58 rooms, 18 A/C, 2-3 story. No elevator. Check-out 11 am. TV; cable (premium). Indoor pool; whirlpool. Restaurant nearby. Coin laundry. Business services available. Some refrigerators. Opposite river. ¢

★ **SPRINDRIFT MOTOR INN.** *1215 Chetco Ave, Brookings (97415). Phone 541/469-5345; toll-free 800/292-1171.* 35 rooms, 2 story. Check-out 11 am. TV; cable (premium). Restaurant opposite. Business services available. Refrigerators. ¢

★ **BEST WESTERN HOLIDAY MOTEL.** *411 N Bayshore Dr, Coos Bay (97420). Phone 541/269-5111. www.bestwestern.com.* 77 rooms, 2 story. Check-out noon. TV; cable (premium). Laundry services. In-house fitness room. Indoor pool, whirlpool. ¢

★★ **RED LION HOTEL COOS BAY.** *1313 N Bayshore Dr, Coos Bay (97420). Phone 541/267-4141; toll-free 800/359-4827. www.redlion.com.* 143 rooms, 1-2 story. Pet accepted, some restrictions. Check-out noon. TV; cable (premium). Pool. Restaurant, bar; entertainment Fri, Sat. Room service. Guest laundry. Meeting rooms. Business services available. In-room modem link. Free airport transportation. In-house fitness room. Refrigerators, microwaves available. On Coos Bay. ¢

★ **BEST WESTERN PIER POINT INN.** *85625 Hwy 101, Florence (97439). 541/997-7191; toll-free 800/528-1234. www.bestwestern.com.* 55 rooms, 3 story. Complimentary continental breakfast. Check-out 11 am. TV; cable (premium). Sauna. Whirlpool. Overlooks the Siuslaw River. **$**

★★★ **THE WESTIN SALISHAN LODGE AND GOLF RESORT.** *7760 Hwy 101 N, Gleneden Beach (97388). Phone 541/764-2371; toll-free 800/452-2300. www.salishan.com.* This lodge offers guests the option of a view of the forest, the golf course, or the bay. The lodge provides private access to the beach, a pool, a sauna, a fitness center, and an on-site wine cellar. 205 rooms, 2-3 story. Pet accepted, some restrictions; $25. Check-out noon. TV; cable (premium), VCR

Oregon

✻ Pacific Coast Scenic Byway

available. Indoor pool; whirlpool, hydrotherapy pool. Restaurants, bar; entertainment weekends. Room service. Meeting rooms. Business services available. Bellhops. Shopping mall. Indoor/outdoor lighted tennis, pro. 18-hole golf, greens fee $35-$50, pro, putting greens, covered driving range. Self-guided nature trail. In-house fitness room, sauna. Massage. Game room. Refrigerators. Art gallery. Library. $

★★★ **TU TU' TUN LODGE.** *96550 N Bank Rogue, Gold Beach (97444). Phone 541/247-6664; toll-free 800/864-6357. www.tututun.com.* Enjoy the stone fireplace, the library, or the intimate bar in the main lodge of this rustic hideaway. Here guests are welcomed with fresh flowers in each room. There's also a four-hole pitch-and-putt course and horseshoe courts. 16 rooms, 2 suites, 1 garden house. Check-out 11 am, check-in 3 pm. Outdoor pool. Complimentary hors d'oeuvres. Dining room open May-Oct (public by reservation): breakfast 7:30-9:30 am, lunch sitting (registered guests only) 1 pm; dinner sitting 7 pm. Bar. Business center. In-room modem link. Free airport transportation. Dock; guides, whitewater boat trips. Private patios, balconies. Library. $

★ **COHO INN.** *1635 NW Harbor Ave, Lincoln City (97367). Phone 541/994-3684; toll-free 800/848-7006. www.thecohoinn.com.* 50 rooms, 31 kitchen units, 3 story. No A/C. No elevator. Pet accepted, some restrictions; $6. Check-out 11 am. TV; cable (premium). Some fireplaces. Sauna. Whirlpool. $

★★ **SHILO INN OCEANFRONT RESORT.** *1501 NW 40th Pl, Lincoln City (97367). Phone 541/994-3655; toll-free 800/222-2244. www.shiloinns.com.* 247 rooms, 3-4 story. Pet accepted, some restrictions; $10/day. Check-out noon. TV; cable (premium), VCR available. Indoor pool; whirlpool. Restaurant adjacent.

Bar. Room service. Coin laundry. Meeting rooms. Business center. Free airport transportation. In-house fitness room, sauna. Health club privileges. Refrigerators, microwaves; some bathroom phones. Picnic tables. On beach. $

★ **WHALER MOTEL.** *155 SW Elizabeth St, Newport (97365). Phone 541/265-9261; toll-free 800/433-9444. www.whalernewport.com.* 73 rooms, 3 story. No elevator. Check-out noon. TV; cable (premium). Indoor pool; whirlpool. Complimentary continental breakfast, refreshments, newspaper. Restaurant nearby. Coin laundry. In-house fitness room. Free airport transportation. Some refrigerators, microwaves, wet bars. Balconies. Ocean view. $

★ **BAY BRIDGE MOTEL.** *33 Coast Hwy, North Bend (97459). Phone 541/756-3151; toll-free 800/557-3156.* 16 rooms, 3 kitchen units. Pet accepted, some restrictions; $5/day. Check-out 11 am. TV. Restaurant nearby. Some refrigerators. On Pacific Bay. ¢

★ **ANCHOR BAY INN.** *1821 Hwy 101, Reedsport (97467). Phone 541/271-2149; toll-free 800/767-1821.* 21 rooms, 4 kitchen suites, 2 story. Pet accepted, some restrictions; $5/day. Check-out 10 am. TV; cable (premium), VCR available. Outdoor pool. Complimentary continental breakfast. Restaurant nearby. Coin laundry. Business services available. Some refrigerators, microwaves. ¢

★ **EBB TIDE MOTEL.** *300 N Prom, Seaside (97138). Phone 503/738-8371; toll-free 800/468-6232. www.ebbtide.citysearch.com.* 99 rooms, 48 kitchen units, 3-4 story. No A/C. Check-out noon. TV; cable (premium), VCR available. In-room modem link. In-house fitness room, sauna. Indoor pool, whirlpool. On beach. ¢

ALL-AMERICAN ROADS

★★★ **GILBERT INN BED & BREAKFAST.** *341 Beach Dr, Seaside (97138). Phone 503/738-9770; toll-free 800/410-9770. www.gilbertinn.com.* This Queen Anne Victorian home was built in 1892 and features a large fireplace in the parlor and a rich and warm atmosphere. It is located near shops, restaurants, beaches, and other attractions. 10 rooms, 1 suite, 3 story. No A/C. Closed Jan. Complimentary breakfast. Check-out 11 am, check-in 3-11 pm. TV. Free airport transportation. Totally nonsmoking. $

★★ **MARCLAIR INN.** *11 Main Ave, Tillamook (97141). Phone 503/842-7571; toll-free 800/331-6857. www.marclairinn.com.* 47 rooms, 6 kitchen units, 1-2 story, no A/C. Check-out 11 am. TV. Restaurant. Sauna. Heated pool, whirlpool. Sun deck. ¢

★★ **SHILO INN SUITES.** *1609 E Harbor Dr, Warrenton (97146). Phone 503/861-2181; toll-free 800/221-2244. www.shiloinns.com.* 63 rooms, 4 story, 11 kitchen units. Pet accepted; $10. Check-out noon. TV; cable (premium), VCR (movies). Indoor pool; whirlpool. Restaurant, bar. Room service. Coin laundry. Meeting rooms. Business services available. Sundries. Free airport transportation. In-house fitness room, sauna. Refrigerators, microwaves, wet bars. ¢

PLACES TO EAT

A long day of driving is sure to make you hungry. At the end of your journey, take a table at one of the following restaurants.

★★ **T. PAUL'S URBAN CAFÉ.** *1119 Commercial St, Astoria (97103). Phone 503/338-5133. www.tpaulsurbancafe.com.* American menu. Closed Sun. Lunch, dinner. Located on the north coast in the heart of Astoria, featuring eclectic local cuisine, regional wines, and microbrew beers. $

★★ **PIER 11 FEED STORE.** *77 11th St, Astoria (97103). Phone 503/325-0279.* Specializes in seafood, steak. Closed Thanksgiving, Dec 25. Breakfast, lunch, dinner. Bar. Reservations accepted. Old feed store on pier (late 1800s); natural beamed ceilings. $$
D

★★ **SHIP INN.** *1 2nd St, Astoria (97103). Phone 503/325-0033.* Specializes in Cornish and chicken pasties, seafood. Closed major holidays. Lunch, dinner. Bar. $$
D

★★ **SILVER SALMON GRILLE.** *1105 Commercial St, Astoria (97103). Phone 503/338-6640. www.silversalmongrille.com.* American, seafood menu. Lunch, dinner. Located on the beautiful Oregon coast in a 1924 commercial building; renovated interior featuring an abundance of regional specialties. $$

★★ **LORD BENNETT'S.** *1695 Beach Loop Dr, Bandon (97411). Phone 541/347-3663.* Come relish this restaurant's spectacular Pacific Ocean view and fresh, straightforward preparations of pasta, beef, pork, veal, chicken, and seafood. The atmosphere is refined but casual, with a slightly nautical feel, and the adjacent lounge offers great cocktails and live entertainment. Closed Dec 25, Jan. Lunch, dinner, Sun brunch. Bar. Children's menu. Casual attire. $$
D

★★ **PORTSIDE.** *8001 Kingfisher Rd, Charleston (97420). Phone 541/888-5544.* Seafood menu. Lunch, dinner. Bar. Entertainment Fri-Sun. Children's menu. Outdoor seating. $$
D

★★ **CLAWSON WINDWARD INN.** *3757 Hwy 101 N, Florence (97439). Phone 541/997-8243.* American menu. Closed Dec 25. Breakfast, lunch, dinner. Bar. Children's menu. $$
D SC

195

Oregon

❋ *Pacific Coast Scenic Byway*

★★ **THE DINING ROOM AT SALISHAN.** *7760 N Hwy 101, Glenedon Beach (97388). Phone 541/764-2371. www.salishan.com.* American menu. Breakfast, lunch, dinner. American regional menu with beautiful views of the Westin Salishan Golf Resort. $$$

★★ **NOR'WESTER SEAFOOD.** *10 Harbor Way, Gold Beach (97444). Phone 541/247-2333.* Seafood, steak menu. Closed Dec, Jan. Dinner. Bar. Children's menu. Casual attire. $$ D

★★★ **BAY HOUSE.** *5911 SW Highway 101, Lincoln City (97367). Phone 541/996-3222. www.bayhouserestaurant.com.* American menu. Dinner. Romantic dining room at the south end of the city, overlooking Siletz Bay. $$$

★ **DORY COVE.** *5819 Logan Rd, Lincoln City (97367). Phone 541/994-5180.* Seafood menu. Lunch, dinner. Children's menu. $$ D SC

★ **WHALE'S TALE.** *152 SW Bay Blvd, Newport (97365). Phone 541/265-8660.* Seafood menu. Closed Dec 24-25; Jan 2-Feb 14; Wed in spring, fall, winter. Breakfast, lunch, dinner. Children's menu. $$

★★ **HILLTOP HOUSE.** *166 N Bay Dr, North Bend (97459). Phone 541/756-4160.* Continental menu. Lunch, dinner. $$ D

★ **CAMP 18.** *42362 Hwy 26, Seaside (97138). Phone 503/755-1818.* American menu. Closed Dec 25. Breakfast, lunch, dinner, Sun brunch. Bar. Children's menu. $$ D

★★ **DOOGER'S SEAFOOD & GRILL.** *505 Broadway, Seaside (97138). Phone 503/738-3773.* Specializes in seafood, steak. Lunch, dinner. Children's menu. Totally nonsmoking. $$ D

Volcanic Legacy Scenic Byway
❋ OREGON
Part of a multistate Byway; see also CA.

Quick Facts

LENGTH: 140 miles.

TIME TO ALLOW: 5 to 7 hours.

BEST TIME TO DRIVE: Spring to fall; summer is the high season.

BYWAY TRAVEL INFORMATION: Klamath County Department of Tourism: 800/445-6728; Byway local Web sites: www.sova.org/volcanic and www.volcaniclegacy.net.

SPECIAL CONSIDERATIONS: The portion of the route from the south rim of Crater Lake to the North Park Entrance, including Rim Drive, is closed from mid-October to mid-June each year due to snow. The opening of Rim Drive each year is a locally celebrated event that signals the beginning of summer. Views of Crater Lake are available year-round at the south rim near the visitor facilities. The route generally provides safe winter access.

RESTRICTIONS: The Byway from the Oregon/California border to Crater Lake National Park is open year-round. In Crater Lake National Park, the Byway from the south rim of Crater Lake to the North Park Entrance (including the Rim Drive) is closed from mid-October to mid-June.

BICYCLE/PEDESTRIAN FACILITIES: Portions of this Byway are well suited for bicycle travel and pedestrian use (to some extent). The Westside Road (County 531) and the southern portion of Oregon Highway 140 have generous shoulder bikeways and gentle grades. The shared road/bikeways in the Fort Klamath area, the climb to Crater Lake, and the Rim Drive are all popular with touring cyclists. The US Highway 97 segment also has paved shoulders, but it is less desirable for biking due to heavy truck traffic. The northern portion of Oregon Highway 140 over Doak Mountain to the Westside Road needs reconstruction to add bikeway shoulders to safely accommodate bike travel.

This diverse Byway follows the brims of lakes, diverse wetlands, scenic ranches, thriving croplands, and forests full of bald eagles. It passes brilliant Crater Lake National Park and historic Crater Lake Lodge. It also threads its way through volcanic landscapes, craggy mountain reaches, and high-desert wetlands.

As the Byway passes the 90,000-surface-acre Upper Klamath Lake, you can see over 1 million birds during peak migrations in the fall. The Klamath Basin is the largest freshwater ecosystem west of the Great Lakes. Six national wildlife refuges in these wetlands were favorite fishing spots of President Roosevelt.

You can also visit the same Pelican Bay where John Muir (naturalist, writer, conservationist, and founder of the Sierra Club) wrote *The Story of My Boyhood and Youth* in 1908.

THE BYWAY STORY

The Volcanic Legacy Scenic Byway tells archaeological, cultural, historical, natural, recreational, and scenic stories that make it a unique and treasured Byway.

Archaeological

This Byway was (and still is) littered with ancient Native American artifacts. Most of the artifacts that have been discovered along this route and are displayed among the 100,000 artifacts in the Byway's own Favell Museum of Western Art and Indian Artifacts. This museum focuses on the area's Native American tribes but also spotlights tribes across the country. It covers 12,000 years of history in its collections of basketry, beadwork, stone tools, and pottery.

Oregon
✻ Volcanic Legacy Scenic Byway

Cultural

The Klamath tribes (more specifically, the Klamaths, Modocs, and Yahooskin) are an integral part of the communities along the Byway because they lived here before anyone can remember. Also, the determination and grit they have demonstrated to survive the changes of years, famine, and new settlers have affected positively the attitudes of other groups who have lived in the area, including the groups who caused their setbacks.

The Klamath tribes have worked hard to maintain their own culture in spite of circumstances. When the tribes were forced to reservations in the 1860s, they turned to cattle ranching and made a profitable living. And even though the tribes were not federally recognized for about 30 years and had to work without supplemental human services or their reservation land, they have sustained the economy of Klamath County for decades; they contribute $12 million per year to the Klamath County economy. They have also instituted training schools to make their enterprises more competitive.

Historical

This Byway's past dwells in some of its historic buildings. By visiting these buildings, you can learn about the significant historical forces and events that shaped the area. For instance, logging was a major part of the early 20th century, and you can get a feel for the area's logging history at Collier State Park and Logging Museum. Through displays featuring actual equipment and other related items, the incredibly difficult life of a lumberjack is told.

Fort Klamath also tells an important story of early settlement. The fort was built in 1863 to protect Oregon Trail pioneers and southern emigrant trains from the nearby Modoc and Klamath tribes who were inclined to attack on occasion. Two notable events happened at this fort: one was when Captain Jack, a Modoc leader who figured centrally in the war of 1872-1873, was executed at the fort along with three other Modoc warriors in late 1873 (their graves are at the fort); the second was when the fort played an important part in the working out of the 1864 Council Grove peace treaty.

Crater Lake Lodge's historical guest register shows what a popular vacation spot Crater Lake has always been: it has hosted important visitors, such as First Lady Eleanor Roosevelt and author Jack London. It is listed on the National Register of Historic Places.

Natural

This Byway sustains masses of wildlife in its several wildlife refuge areas, bulky mountains, and unique geological formations. Six national wildlife refuges have been established in the area: Lower Klamath, Tule Lake, Clear Lake, Bear Valley, Upper Klamath, and Klamath Marsh. These refuges are diverse; they include freshwater marshes, open waters, grassy meadows, coniferous forests, sagebrush, juniper grasslands, agricultural lands, rock cliffs, and slopes. Over 100 different species have been identified in the refuges. In the spring, more than 1 million birds retreat here. This number is added to in the summer, as ducks and Canadian geese join the throng. In the fall, the birds (ducks, geese, swans, and green-winged teal) number in the millions. In addition, the Klamath Basin is home to the largest concentration of wintering bald eagles in the lower 48 states.

Crater Lake, Oregon's only national park, is not only a place for wildlife to refuge, but is also one of the nation's favorite places to retreat. The deepest lake in the United States, it was formed inside the collapsed peak of an ancient volcano, Mount Mazama, that erupted 8,000 years ago. The eruptions were 42 times greater than those of Mount St. Helens in 1980, and the ash spewed over eight states and three Canadian provinces. One of the finest and most accessible examples of a young caldera (a certain kind of volcanic crater) in the world, Crater Lake is recognized worldwide as a scenic wonder.

Recreational

You can do just about anything outdoorsy on the Volcanic Legacy Scenic Byway. In the summer, you can fish, camp, visit a horse and cattle ranch, whitewater raft, or hike. You can also tour the scenic shores of the Upper Klamath Canoe Trail by canoe. Crater Lake National Park is especially good for camping, hiking, and RV camping. Lake of the Woods is popular for any kind of summer activity and is also great for winter activities, such as cross-country skiing (although cross-country skiing is exceptional in many other areas along the Byway as well). Willamette Ski Lodge and Diamond Lake Resort are particularly good for downhill skiing.

Scenic

The Volcanic Legacy Scenic Byway is visually diverse: it starts out as 140 miles of craggy volcanic landscape, switches to the high desert, and then transforms to the wetland habitats of the Klamath Basin. Even though these scenes are varied, you'll feel the same surge of grandeur and affection as you experience the croplands' expanse, birds in flight at Upper Klamath Lake, the Wild & Scenic Klamath River, views of the majestic Mount Shasta, and wetlands and rising forests.

HIGHLIGHTS

When traveling the Byway from north to south, consider following this scenic-viewpoints tour. If you're starting from the south, simply read this list from the bottom up:

- **Crater Lake National Park:** Located 65 miles north of Klamath Falls on Highways 97 and 62. Here are the world-renowned views you've seen on postcards and in magazines. Many viewpoints are accessible by wheelchair; some are found at the ends of hiking trails.

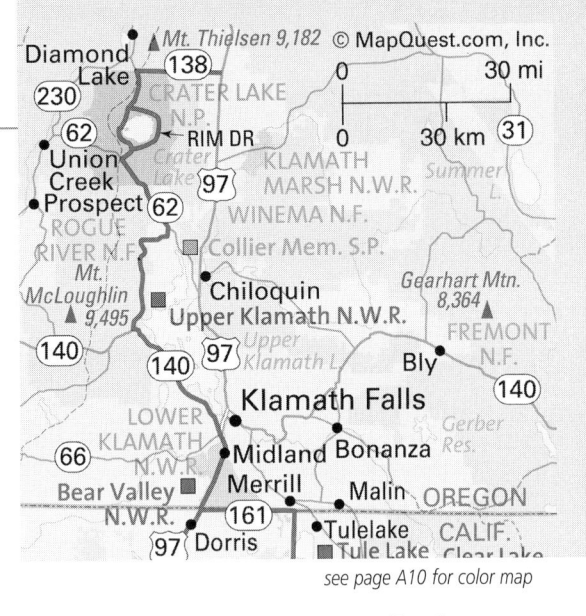

- **Ouxkanee overlook:** A short drive off Highway 97 leads to a picnic area with a stunning overlook of the Williamson River valley and the surrounding landscape. Scan the horizon as far as Mount Shasta in northern California.

- **Pelican Butte:** The summit offers breathtaking views of Upper Klamath Lake and Sky Lakes Wilderness. Old-growth timber lines the narrow, rough road to the top, which takes about an hour and is accessible only by high-clearance vehicle and by foot.

- **Calimus Butte:** This historic, cupola-style lookout was built by the Bureau of Indian Affairs in 1920 and overlooks the scene of the 48-square-mile Lone Pine fire in 1992, as well as Klamath Marsh and Sprague River Valley. Accessible by high-clearance vehicle only.

- **Herd Peak:** A gravel road off Highway 97 leads to Herd Peak, where a fire lookout is staffed during the summer months and is open to the public. The summit offers breathtaking views of Mount Shasta and the surrounding area.

- **Walker Mountain:** On a clear day, the view from the fire lookout extends from Mount Jefferson in central Oregon to Mount Shasta in northern California. There, you're surrounded by a sea of forest land. Accessible by high-clearance vehicle only.

Oregon

✽ Volcanic Legacy Scenic Byway

THINGS TO SEE AND DO

Driving along the Volcanic Legacy Scenic Byway will certainly keep your senses engaged, but if you yearn to get out of the car and stretch your legs, or if you'd like to make a mini-vacation out of your trip, check out these attractions along the route.

COLLIER MEMORIAL STATE PARK AND LOGGING MUSEUM. *46000 Hwy 97, Klamath Falls (97601). Phone 541/783-2471. www.collierloggingmuseum.org.* A 655-acre park located at the confluence of Spring Creek and Williamson River, Collier offers an open-air historic logging museum with displays of tools, machines, and engines; various types of furnished 1800s-era pioneer cabins; and a gift shop. Fishing; hiking, picnicking. Tent and trailer campsites (hookups, dump station). Open daily.

✪ CRATER LAKE NATIONAL PARK. *Klamath Falls (97601). Phone 541/594-2211. www.nps.gov/cr/a/.* One of Crater Lake's former names, Lake Majesty, probably comes closest to describing the feeling visitors get from the deep blue waters in the caldera of dormant Mount Mazama. More than 7,700 years ago, following climactic eruptions, this volcano collapsed and formed a deep basin. Rain and snow accumulated in the empty caldera, forming the deepest lake in the United States (1,932 feet). Surrounded by 25 miles of jagged rim rock, the 21-square-mile lake is broken only by Wizard and Phantom Ship islands. Entering by road from any direction brings you to the 33-mile Rim Drive (open July to mid-Oct or until the first snow), leading to all observation points, park headquarters, and a visitor center at Rim Village (open June-Sept, daily). The park can be explored on foot or by car following spurs and trails extending from Rim Drive: the Watchman Peak is reached by a trail almost 1 mile long that takes hikers 1,800 feet above the lake with a full view in all directions; Mount Shasta in California, 105 miles away, is visible on clear days. Six miles farther on Rim Drive, going clockwise, is the start of a 2 1/2-mile hiking trail, 1,230 feet to Mount Scott, soaring 8,926 feet, the highest point in the park. In winter, the south and west entrance roads are kept clear in spite of the annual 45-foot snowfall; the north entrance road and Rim Drive are closed from mid-Oct-June, depending on snow conditions. Depending on snow, the campground (fee) is open from late June-mid-Oct. Mazama, at the junction of the south and west entrance drives, has a camp store, fireplaces, showers, laundry facilities, toilets, water, and tables; no reservations. The wildlife includes black bears—keep your distance and never feed them. You may also see deer, golden-mantled ground squirrels, marmots, and coyotes. Do not feed any wildlife in park. $$$

FAVELL MUSEUM OF WESTERN ART AND NATIVE AMERICAN ARTIFACTS. *125 W Main, Klamath Falls (97601). Phone 541/882-9996; toll-free 800/762-9096. www.favellmuseum.com.* Contemporary Western art; working miniature gun collection; extensive display of Native American artifacts. Also art and print sales galleries. Gift shop. Open Tues-Sat. $$

KLAMATH COUNTY MUSEUM. *1451 Main St, Klamath Falls (97601). Phone 541/883-4208.* Local geology, history, wildlife, and Native American displays; research library has books on history, natural history, and anthropology of the Pacific Northwest. Open Tues-Sat; closed holidays. $

MIGRATORY BIRD REFUGE. *4009 Hill Rd Tulelake CA (96134). Phone 530/667-2231.* Located in both California and Oregon, the six national wildlife refuges in the Kalmath Basin are a major stopover on the Pacific Flyway. Upper Klamath and Klamath Marsh refuges lie to the north, and Lower Klamath, Bear Valley, Tule Lake, and Clear Lake lie to the south of the city. A visitor center with exhibits stands at refuge headquarters in Tule Lake, California. Open daily. Waterfowl (Mar-Apr, Oct-Nov); bald eagles (Dec-Mar); migratory birds (Mar-Apr); waterfowl and colonial bird nesting (summer). **FREE**

WINEMA NATIONAL FOREST. *2819 Dahlia, Klamath Falls (97601). Phone 541/883-6714. www.fs.fed.us/r6/winema/.* This forest (more than 1 million acres) includes former reservation lands of the Klamath Tribe, high country of Sky Lakes, portions of Pacific Crest National Scenic Trail, and several recreation areas (Lake of the Woods, Recreation Creek, Mountain Lakes Wilderness, and Mount Theilson Wilderness). Swimming, boating; picnicking, camping (some areas free). $$

PLACES TO STAY

If you choose to include an overnight stay in your trip along this All-American Road, Mobil Travel Guide recommends the following lodgings.

★ **BEST WESTERN OLYMPIC INN.** *2627 S 6th St, Klamath Falls (97603). Phone 541/882-9665; toll-free 800/600-9665. www.bestwestern.com.* 71 rooms, 3 story. Complimentary continental breakfast. Check-out 11 am. TV; cable (premium). In-room modem link. In-house fitness room. Outdoor pool, whirlpool. ¢

★ **CIMARRON MOTOR INN.** *3060 S 6th St, Klamath Falls (97603). Phone 541/882-4601; toll-free 800/742-2648.* 163 rooms, 2 story. Pet accepted; $5. Check-out noon. TV; cable (premium). Outdoor pool. Continental breakfast. Restaurant adjacent open 24 hours. Meeting room. Business services available. ¢

★★ **QUALITY INN KLAMATH FALLS.** *100 Main St, Klamath Falls (97601). Phone 541/882-4666; toll-free 800/732-2025. www.qualityinn.com.* 80 rooms, 4 suites, 2 story. Pet accepted, some restrictions. Check-out noon. TV; cable (premium). Outdoor pool. Complimentary continental breakfast. Restaurant adjacent. Coin laundry. Meeting rooms. Business services available. In-room modem link. Some in-room whirlpools, microwaves. ¢

★★ **SHILO INN SUITES HOTEL.** *2500 Almond St, Klamath Falls (97601). Phone 541/885-7980; toll-free 800/222-2244. www.shiloinns.com.* 143 suites, 4 story. Pet accepted, some restrictions; $7. Check-out noon. TV; cable (premium), VCR (movies). Complimentary continental breakfast. Restaurant, bar. Room service. Meeting rooms. Business center. In-room modem link. Bellhops. Valet service. Sundries. Coin laundry. Free airport transportation. In-house fitness room, sauna. Health club privileges. Indoor pool; whirlpool. Bathroom phones, refrigerators, microwaves, wet bars. $

PLACES TO EAT

A long day of driving is sure to make you hungry. At the end of your journey, try the following restaurant.

★★ **FIORELLA'S.** *6139 Simmer Ave, Klamath Falls (97603). Phone 541/882-1878.* Northern Italian menu. Closed Sun, Mon; Dec 25. Dinner. Bar. Children's menu. Reservations accepted. $$

The Historic National Road

PENNSYLVANIA

Part of a multistate Byway; see also IL, IN, MD, OH, WV.

Quick Facts

LENGTH: 90 miles.

TIME TO ALLOW: 2 hours to 1 day.

BEST TIME TO DRIVE: The colors of fall make it a great time to travel the National Road.

BYWAY TRAVEL INFORMATION: Byway local Web sites: www.nationalroadpa.org and www.dcnr.state.pa.us/recreation/heritage/nationalroad.htm.

BICYCLE/PEDESTRIAN FACILITIES: Transportation along the National Road is predominantly automobile or tour bus. No pedestrian facilities exist along the road itself; however, numerous areas just off the road are friendly to bike and pedestrian travel.

As America entered the 19th century, the young nation faced one of its first challenges: how to link the people and cities along the Eastern seaboard to those on the frontiers west of the Allegheny Mountains. Settlers moving west faced perils aggravated by the lack of a well-defined roadway. And easterners were unable to take advantage of the abundant produce and goods from the western frontier without a road to transport them over the Alleghenies. The solution was the National Road, America's first interstate highway, and the only one constructed entirely with federal funds.

Construction began in 1811, and by 1818, the road stretched from Cumberland, Maryland, to what is now Wheeling, West Virginia. In time, the National Road ran the whole way to Vandalia, Illinois, a distance of 600 miles. The story of the National Road is a human tale of how Native American pathways became the settlers' lifeline and eventually a major artery, allowing the east-to-west interchange of the nation's commerce. It is the story of visionaries, mercenaries, common people, and most uncommon acts. The history of the National Road is high drama that deserves to be told, relived, and imparted to future generations.

For three decades, the history, influence, and heritage of the National Road has been celebrated at the annual National Road Festival, held on the third weekend each May. The festival features memorable festivities and a wagon train that comes into town—quite a sight to see.

Pennsylvania

❋ *The Historic National Road*

THE BYWAY STORY

The National Historic Road tells cultural, historical, natural, and scenic stories that make it a unique and treasured Byway.

Cultural

The National Road was developed from existing Native American pathways and, by the 1840s, was the busiest transportation route in America. Over its miles lumbered stagecoaches, Conestoga wagons with hopeful settlers, and freight wagons pulled by braces of mules, along with peddlers, caravans, carriages, foot travelers, and mounted riders. In response to demand, inns, hostels, taverns, and retail trade sprang up to serve the many who traveled the road. Today, reminders of National Road history are still visible along this corridor, designed as one of Pennsylvania's heritage parks to preserve and interpret history throughout the region.

Historical

The first cries for a "national road" were heard before there was even a nation. Such a road would facilitate settlement and help the budding nation expand in order to survive and flourish. Economic considerations weighed heavily in favor of a national road, which would be a two-way street, allowing farmers and traders in the west to send their production east in exchange for manufactures goods and other essential of life. By the end of the 18th century, there was a growing consensus that a national road was needed. In May 1820, Congress appropriated funds to lay out the road from Wheeling to the Mississippi. Construction in Ohio did not commence until 1825. Indiana's route was surveyed in 1827, with construction beginning in 1829. By 1834, the road extended across the entire state, albeit in various stages of completeness. The road began to inch across Illinois in the early 1830s, but shortages of funds and national will, plus local squabbles about its destination, caused it to end in Vandalia rather than on the shore of the Mississippi River.

The major engineering marvels associated with the National Road may have been the bridges that carried it across rivers and streams. The bridges came in a wide variety of styles and types and were made of stone, wood, iron, and, later, steel. They were the wonder of their day, and bridge-building did much to advance engineering knowledge in America before the Civil War. One bridge style often associated with the road was the S-type. Contrary to the popular, misguided opinion of the day, the bridges were not the product of the fevered, whiskey-inspired imagination of an engineer, but were built that way because it was easier to construct them in that configuration than as a straight span at that time. As the bridges indicate, an amazing variety of skills were needed to build the road: surveyors laid out the path; engineers oversaw construction; carpenters framed bridges; and masons cut and worked stones for bridges and milestones.

Initial cost estimates for the National Road were $6,000 per mile, but, like many other government projects, this estimate proved optimistic. Portions of the road through the hilly sections of Pennsylvania cost $9,000 to $13,000 per mile. Expenditures were sometimes lower as the road stretched across the flatlands of western Indiana and eastern Illinois.

Natural

One hundred eighty years ago, the National Road was a lifeline, bringing people and prosperity to the regions of the country removed from the eastern coast. First a Native American trail cutting through the mountains and valleys, and then a primitive wagon trail to the first federal highway, the National Road is surrounded by the views of history. You'll see pristine hardwood forests blanketing rolling hills, vintage homes and barns, historic farmlands, orchards, and hunting grounds. The view laid out along your route is a blended cacophony of sights and sounds that cannot be described, only experienced.

see page A13 for color map

Scenic

The scenic qualities of the Historic National Road can be described as a rich tapestry that changes with the seasons. Obvious reference can be made to the beauty of the budding leaves in the vast mountain woodlands, and the lush green look of the trees and fields in summer, or the vibrant colors of autumn. Some of the real beauty, however, arrives with winter, with the starkness of the woods and barren trees. It is then that the whole landscape reveals itself to the visitor, seeing further into the viewshed to the ruts of the original trails, the traces of the Historic National Road and buildings nestled therein.

One of the most amazing sights along the road occurs just after you climb the Summit Mountain traveling west from Farmington and Chalk Hill at the Historic Summit Inn. Just over the crest of that "hill," your eyes fall onto a vast, endless valley, with rolling hills and a lushness that makes you believe you have found the promised land. This breathtaking view beckons you to imagine the sense of jubilation pioneers must have felt after struggling to cross the Appalachians, realizing that the mountains were behind them as they began their final, steep descent down the western side.

THINGS TO SEE AND DO

Driving along the Historic National Road will certainly keep your senses engaged, but if you yearn to get out of the car and stretch your legs, or if you'd like to make a mini-vacation out of your trip, check out these attractions along the route.

BRADDOCK'S GRAVE. *200 Caverns Park Rd, Farmington (15437). Phone 724/329-5512. www.nps.gov/fone/braddock.htm/.* Granite monument marks the burial place of British General Edward Braddock, who was wounded in battle with French and Native American forces on July 9, 1755, and died four days later.

DAVID BRADFORD HOUSE. *175 S Main St, Washington (15301). Phone 724/222-3604. www.bradfordhouse.org.* Restored frontier home (1788) of a leader of the Whiskey Rebellion. Open May-mid-Dec, Wed-Sat, limited hours, also Sun afternoons.

★ **FALLINGWATER.** *PA 381 S, Mill Run (15464). Phone 724/329-8501. www.wpconline.org/fallingwaterhome.htm.* One of the most famous structures of the 20th century, Fallingwater, designed by Frank Lloyd Wright in 1936, is cantilevered on three levels over a waterfall. The interior features Wright-designed furniture, textiles, and lighting, as well as sculpture by modern masters. Extensive grounds are heavily wooded and planted with rhododendron, which blooms in early July. Visitor center with self-guided orientation program; concession; gift shop. Guided tours from mid-Mar through Nov, Tues-Sun; winter, Sat-Sun. No children under 6; child-care center. No pets. Reservations required. $$$

FORT NECESSITY NATIONAL BATTLEFIELD. *1 Washington Pkwy, Farmington (15437). Phone 724/329-5512. www.nps.gov/fone/.* (1754) The site of Washington's first major battle and the opening battle of the French and Indian War (1754). This land was known as the Great Meadows. A portion was later purchased by Washington, who owned it until his death. A replica of the original fort was built on the site following an archaeological survey in 1953. Picnic area is open mid-spring-late fall. $$

FRIENDSHIP HILL NATIONAL HISTORIC SITE. *15 miles S on US 119 to PA 166, Uniontown (15401).) Phone 724/329-5512; 724/725-9190. www.nps.gov/frhi/.* Preserves the restored home of Albert Gallatin, a Swiss immigrant who served his adopted country, in public and private life, for nearly seven decades. Gallatin made significant contributions in the fields of finance, politics, diplomacy, and scholarship. He is best known as the treasury secretary

Pennsylvania

✤ *The Historic National Road*

under Jefferson and Madison. Exhibits, audio-visual program, and audio tour provide info on Albert Gallatin. Open daily; closed Dec 25. **FREE**

JUMONVILLE GLEN. *200 Caverns Park Rd, Uniontown (15401).* Site of a skirmish between British and French forces that led to the battle at Fort Necessity. Open mid-Apr-mid-Oct.

LAUREL CAVERNS. *200 Caverns Park Rd, Farmington (15437). Phone 724/438-3003; toll-free 800/515-4150. www.laurelcaverns.com.* Colored lighting; unusual formations. Indoor miniature golf. Repelling (fee). Guided tours. Exploring trips. Open May-Oct, daily. **$$$$**

LEMOYNE HOUSE. *49 E Maiden St, Washington (15301). Phone 724/225-6740. www.wchspa.org.* Abolitionist's home, built by the LeMoyne family (1812), was a stop on the underground railroad; period furnishings, paintings, library; gardens; museum shop. Administered by the Washington County Historical Society. Open Jan-Feb, Tues-Fri; Mar-Dec, Tues-Sat. **$$**

MEADOWCROFT MUSEUM OF RURAL LIFE. *401 Meadowcroft Rd, Avella (15312). Phone 724/587-3412. www.meadowcroftmuseum.org.* A 200-acre outdoor museum complex that preserves the history of life on the land in western Pennsylvania. General store, restored log houses, one-room schoolhouse, blacksmith shop, and archaeology exhibit. Open May-Oct, Wed-Sun. **$$**

OHIOPYLE STATE PARK. *Dinner Bell Rd, Ohiopyle (15470). Phone 724/329-8591.* Approximately 18,700 acres of overlooks, waterfalls. Fishing, hunting; whitewater boating. Hiking, bicycling. Cross-country skiing, snowmobiling, sledding. Picnicking, playground, snack bar. Tent and trailer sites. Nature center, interpretive program.

PENNSYLVANIA TROLLEY MUSEUM. *1 Museum Rd, Washington (15301). Phone 724/228-9256; toll-free 877/PA-TROLLEY. www.pa-trolley.org.* Museum displays include more than 35 trolley cars dating from 1894. Scenic trolley ride; car barn and trolley-restoration shop; visitor center and gift shop with exhibit, video presentation, and picnic area. Open June-Aug, daily; Apr-May and Sept-Dec, weekends. **$$$**

PLACES TO STAY

If you choose to include an overnight stay in your trip along this All-American Road, Mobil Travel Guide recommends the following lodgings.

★★ **LODGE AT CHALK HILL.** *Rte 40E, Chalk Hill (15421). Phone 724/438-0168.* 60 units, 6 suites, 6 kitchen units. Pet accepted, some restrictions; $10. Complimentary continental breakfast. Check-out noon. TV; cable (premium), VCR available. Balconies. Restaurant opposite. Picnic tables. Business services. ¢

★★★★ **NEMACOLIN WOODLANDS RESORT.** *1001 Lafayette Dr, Farmington (15437). Phone 724/329-8555.* 220 rooms, 60 condo units (1-2 bedroom), 4 and 5 story. AP, MAP available. Check-out noon, check-in 3 pm. TV; cable (premium), VCR available. In-room modem link. Balconies. Microwaves in condos. Bathroom phones, minibars; many refrigerators. Valet services, laundry facilities in condos. Dining room. Snack bar. Bar; entertainment. Room service 24 hours. Supervised children's activities, ages 4-12. Playground. Exercise room, massage, sauna. Social director. Sports director. Game room, recreation room. Four pools, two indoor; whirlpools, poolside service, lifeguard. Miniature golf. Two 18-hole golf courses, greens fee (includes cart) $69-$109. Lighted tennis, pro. Downhill, cross-country ski on site. Picnics. Lawn games. Bicycle rentals. Boats. Hiking. Sleighing, tobogganing. Business services, convention facilities. Concierge. Situated on 1,250 acres with seven lakes; landing strip. Equestrian center; surrey rides all year. $$

★★★ **INNE AT WATSON'S CHOICE.** *234 Balsinger Rd, Uniontown (15401). Phone 724/437-4999.* This charming inn is guaranteed to relax the mind and delight the senses. Experience the romance and charm from a bygone era while enjoying all the luxuries of today. Guests will find the service to be warm and friendly and the guest rooms to be uniquely appointed, each with its own theme. A particular favorite is the Flower Garden Room, furnished in a charming country Victorian décor with views of the scenic rolling fields and lush wooded acres. 7 rooms, shower only, 2 story. Weekends, holidays 2-day minimum. Adults only. Complimentary full breakfast. Check-out 11 am, check-in after 3 pm. TV in common room; cable (premium), VCR available (movies). Many fireplaces. Guest laundry. Golf privileges. Downhill, cross-country ski 10 miles. Picnic tables. Concierge service. Built in 1820; German architecture. Totally nonsmoking. $

★ **ECONO LODGE WASHINGTON.** *1385 W Chestnut St, Washington (15301). Phone 724/222-6500. www.econolodge.com.* 62 rooms, 1-2 story. Check-out 11 am. TV; cable (premium). Complimentary continental breakfast. Restaurant adjacent open 24 hours. Business services available. Bellhops. Airport transportation. Picnic tables. ¢

PLACES TO EAT

A long day of driving is sure to make you hungry. At the end of your journey, take a table at one of the following restaurants.

★★★ **CHEZ GERARD FRENCH RESTAURANT.** *1187 Highway 40 E, Hopwood (15445). Phone 724/437-9001. www.chezgerard.net.* French menu. Closed Tues. Lunch, dinner. Authentic French cuisine in a turn-of-the-century farmhouse. $$

★★ **SUN PORCH.** *US 40E, Hopwood (15445). Phone 724/439-5734.* Specializes in fresh seafood, beef, poultry. Closed Mon; Dec 24-25. Lunch, dinner. Children's menu. Many plants; atmosphere of a country garden. $

★★★ **COAL BARON.** *7606 National Pike, Uniontown (15401). Phone 724/439-0111.* Continental menu. Closed Mon; Dec 24-25. Lunch, dinner. Bar. Children's menu. Jacket required. Valet parking available. $$

Natchez Trace Parkway
❋ TENNESSEE
Part of a multistate Byway; see also AL, MS.

Quick Facts

LENGTH: 84 miles.

TIME TO ALLOW: 2 days.

BEST TIME TO DRIVE: Summer is the best time to see the lush vegetation along the Byway, late March-April for spring flowers, and September-October for fall colors. However, the Natchez Pilgrimage during March to October is an excellent time to visit many of Natchez's antebellum homes. The high season is in March and April.

BYWAY TRAVEL INFORMATION: Natchez Trace Parkway: 800/305-7417; Byway local Web site: www.nps.gov/natr.

SPECIAL CONSIDERATIONS: Be alert for animals on the parkway, as well as copperheads, cottonmouths, and rattlesnakes. Fire ants can inflict painful bites, so do not disturb their mounds. Poison ivy grows throughout the area. All natural, historical, and archaeological objects must be left undisturbed. Also, the Natchez Trace Parkway is a designated bike route, so please watch for bikers. You'll find one service station on the parkway (and it's located in the Mississippi portion of the Natchez Trace), but gas, food, and lodging are available in the communities near the parkway. Plan ahead for these amenities because of the relatively rural setting of most of the parkway. Also, the roadway is not illuminated.

RESTRICTIONS: The speed limit along this Byway is 50 mph. Commercial trucking is not allowed, and tent and trailer camping is allowed at designated campgrounds only.

BICYCLE/PEDESTRIAN FACILITIES: The Natchez Trace Parkway is popular among bicyclists—both for distance touring and for local riders out for a day of fresh air. Pedestrian facilities along the parkway consist of separate hiking/nature/horse trails.

The Natchez Trace Parkway tells the story of people on the move, the story of the age-old need to get from one place to another. It is a story of Natchez, Chickasaw, and Choctaw tribes following traditional ways of life; of French and Spanish people venturing into a new world; and of people building a new nation.

At first, the Trace was probably a series of hunters' paths that slowly came together to form a trail that led from the Mississippi River over the low hills into the Tennessee Valley. By 1785, Ohio River Valley farmers searching for markets had begun floating their crops and products down the rivers to Natchez or New Orleans. Because they sold their flatboats for lumber, returning home meant either riding or walking. The trail from Natchez offered the most direct route for them to follow.

The parklands along the Trace preserve important examples of our nation's natural and cultural heritage. Since the late 1930s, the National Park Service has been constructing a modern parkway that closely follows the course of the original Trace. Today, the parkway gives present-day travelers an unhurried route from Natchez, Mississippi, to Nashville, Tennessee. It is a subtle driving experience. Motorists and bicyclists alike enjoy the scenery, from the rock-studded hills of Tennessee, past the cotton fields of Alabama, to the flat and meandering southern extremes shaded by trees and Spanish moss. The Natchez Trace Parkway winds along 445 scenic miles through three states, including Alabama, Mississippi, and Tennessee.

The Alabama segment of the Natchez Trace Parkway is the middle leg of a Byway that covers the entire length of the Natchez Trace. The Old Trace is still closely followed by the parkway, which is preserved and administered

Tennessee

✻ Natchez Trace Parkway

by the National Park Service. A lovely tree-lined drive through woods and fields, the Byway offers a wealth of early pioneer history at well-maintained historic sites like Colbert Ferry Park, Freedom Hills, and Buzzard Roast Springs.

THE BYWAY STORY

The Natchez Trace Parkway tells archaeological, cultural, historical, natural, recreational, and scenic stories that make it a unique and treasured Byway.

Archaeological

Archaeological sites on the Natchez Trace date from the Paleo-Indian period (12,000 BC–8,000 BC) through historic Natchez, Choctaw, and Chickasaw settlements (AD 1540–1837). Campsites, village sites, stone quarry sites, rock shelters, shell heaps, and burial sites are among the archaeological treasures along the Trace. The most visually obvious are burial and ceremonial earthen mounds associated with the Woodland and Mississippian periods. The Mississippians were highly skilled farmers and artists who may have traded with people from as far away as Mexico and Central America. They established elaborate political systems and lived in large permanent towns that were often fortified with stockades.

Cultural

The cultural aspects of the Natchez Trace can be seen in its heritage. From rough frontier towns on the edge of Indian Territory to the rise of Southern comforts, the people who live along the Trace embody its rich culture. Southern traditions and hospitality are apparent as you meander through the heart of Dixie. From Natchez to Memphis, you'll enjoy the people you meet along the Natchez Trace.

Because the Natchez Trace is a long Byway, take an extra day or two to fully appreciate Southern living. On your extended stay, take in one of the many opportunities for cultural entertainment. These range from concerts by community bands to performances by small stage theater troops. Spend a night at the opera or attend some of the special events on the Byway. Just be sure to keep your camera handy for some good ol' Southern memories.

Historical

The Natchez Trace Parkway was established to commemorate the historical significance of the Old Natchez Trace as a primitive trail that stretched some 500 miles through the wilderness from Natchez, Mississippi, to Nashville, Tennessee. Although generally thought of as one trail, the Old Natchez Trace was actually a number of closely parallel routes. The Trace probably evolved from the repeated use of meandering game trails by the earliest human inhabitants. Over time, these paths were gradually linked and used for transportation, communication, and trade, first by Indians and later by European explorers, American traders, and others.

History has witnessed several phases in the development of the Natchez Trace, each with a distinct origin and purpose. The first phase was an Indian trail, actually known as the Chickasaw Trace by residents of Fort Nashborough (now present-day Nashville, Tennessee). Heading to the southwest from Nashville, the Chickasaw Trace led to the Chickasaw Nation, near present-day Tupelo, Mississippi. From there, other trails led southwest through country controlled by the Choctaw Nation and onward to Natchez. The southern portion of this trail appeared on 18th-century British maps as the "Path to the Choctaw Nation."

Word spread among the early white settlers that it was possible to travel by foot between Nashville and Natchez through the Indian nations. Traffic increased along this "Boatman's Trail," with men returning home to the north after selling cargo and flatboats at Natchez or

New Orleans. Added usage caused discontent to grow due to the harsh conditions of this new route. In 1806, Thomas Jefferson directed the Postmaster General to oversee a route improvement project. Unfortunately, funds for maintenance weren't included in the appropriation. Complaints concerning conditions on the rugged wilderness trail flooded in as river trade boomed along with the increasing population.

However, before improvements were ever made, the need for them diminished. After his victory at the Battle of New Orleans in 1815, Andrew Jackson marched his troops home along the Trace—an event that signaled not only the war's end, but also the decline of the Natchez Trace's importance as a transportation corridor. By 1820, steamboats were common on the Mississippi River, making upriver travel easy. Boatmen now chose to return home by water rather than by the overland route.

Not until the years following 1820, when much of the route fell into disuse, was it referred to as the "Natchez Trace." Speculation is that those who had experienced hardships and adventure on the Natchez Road spoke of it more glamorously as the "Natchez Trace" when reminiscing about it. By the 1830s, this term had replaced "Natchez Road."

Natural

The Natchez Trace Parkway encompasses a diversity of natural resources. From Natchez, Mississippi, to Nashville, Tennessee, the motor road cuts through six major forest types and eight major watersheds. The parkway ranges from 70 to 1,100 feet in elevation and covers a distance of 445 miles, resulting in a variety of habitats.

Within the park, approximately 800 species of plants help to support 57 species of mammals, 216 species of birds, 57 species of reptiles, 36 species of amphibians, and a variety of other vertebrates and invertebrates. Three of these species are classified as endangered and include the southern bald eagle, the red-cockaded woodpecker, and the gray bat; three more are classified as threatened and include the Bayou darter, the slackwater darter, and the ringed sawback turtle. In addition, four state protected species that have been identified in Tennessee include goldenseal, Tennessee yellow-eyed grass, yellow honeysuckle, and Indian plantain.

From Alabama, the parkway traverses primarily oak and hickory dominated forests on Tennessee's Highland Rim, where it reaches its highest elevation of 1,100 feet above sea level. The parkway terminus at Pasquo is on the eastern edge of the Nashville Basin, which was historically similar to the open bluegrass region of Kentucky.

The more fertile farmlands along the 445-mile-long parkway are devoted to the production of milo, soybeans, corn, wheat,

see page A5 for color map

Tennessee

✤ Natchez Trace Parkway

and cotton, while the marginal agricultural lands are used primarily for the grazing of cattle and horses. Some of the more common wildlife along the entire length of the parkway includes white-tailed deer, turkeys, bobcats, raccoons, opossums, foxes, coyotes, and field and forest dwelling songbirds.

Recreational

You can find numerous opportunities for recreation along the Natchez Trace Parkway. By far the most popular is simply enjoying the historic and natural beauty, which abounds all along the parkway. Take in one of the many museums located throughout the Byway or take a walk among the dogwoods. The Byway has many historic battlefields, allowing you the chance to stretch your legs and reminisce about the past. Pack a picnic and see the many Southern mansions along the route or hunt for souvenirs in one of the many quaint shops along the way.

At least ten months of fine weather each year and a combination of natural resources, including lakes, woodlands, and wildlife, make outdoor recreation along the Trace favorable. Hunting is excellent along the Natchez Trace, as are golfing, bicycling, jogging, swimming, tennis, baseball, football, soccer, and other sports. If you're a fisherman, take advantage of the many rivers located throughout the Byway and wet your line.

Scenic

As the interstate highway of its time, the Natchez Trace entertained travelers along its well-trod path with its picturesque views of the surrounding countryside. You can enjoy these same wonders today. From blossoming flowers and trees to historical Native American earthen mounds, the Natchez Trace offers scenic vistas at every turn. By winding through six major forest types and eight major watersheds, you are afforded the opportunity to see a variety of habitats and wildlife; the changing seasons enhance the scenic qualities of the Natchez Trace.

HIGHLIGHTS

The Tennessee section of the Natchez Trace Parkway includes these points of interest between mile 428 and mile 350. If you're traveling in the other direction, simply read this list from the bottom up.

- **Mile 427.6—Garrison Creek:** Named for a nearby 1801-1802 US Army post, this area is a trailhead for horseback riders and hikers.
- **Mile 423.9—Tennessee Valley Divide:** When Tennessee was admitted to the Union in 1796, this watershed was the boundary between the United States to the north and the Chickasaw Nation to the south.
- **Mlle 404.7—Jackson Falls:** Named for Andrew Jackson, the falls are on the intermittent Jackson Branch that empties into Duck River.
- **Mile 401.4—Tobacco Farm:** Exhibits at the farm and barn explain tobacco growing. A 2-mile drive along the Old Trace begins here.
- **Mile 400.2—Sheboss Place:** This is the site of one of the stands that once served travelers on the Trace.

- **Mile 397.3—Old Trace:** Here the Trace marked the boundaries of the Chickasaw lands ceded to the United States in 1805 and 1816.
- **Mile 385.9—Meriwether Lewis:** A campground, picnic area, rest rooms, ranger station, and the grave of Meriwether Lewis, of Lewis and Clark fame, are all here.
- **Mile 382.8—Metal Ford:** Travelers crossed the Buffalo River here; an ironworks and McLish's Stand were located nearby.
- **Mile 381.8—Napier Mine:** This open pit was worked during the 19th century.
- **Mile 363.0—Sweetwater Branch nature trail:** A clear, fast-flowing stream parallels the route of this 20-minute walk; wildflowers are brilliant in season.
- **Mile 352.9—McGlamery Stand:** The nearby village still bears the name of the stand that has long since disappeared.
- **Mile 350.5—Sunken Trace:** Here are three sections of the original road that show how the route was relocated to avoid mudholes.

THINGS TO SEE AND DO

Driving along the Natchez Trace Parkway will certainly keep your senses engaged, but if you yearn to get out of the car and stretch your legs, or if you'd like to make a mini-vacation out of your trip, check out these attractions along the route.

THE ATHENAEUM. *808 Athenaeum St, Columbia (38401). Phone 931/381-4822. www.athenaeumrectory.com.* Buildings of Moorish design (1835-1837) were used as a girls' school after 1852; during the Civil War the rectory became the headquarters of Union Generals Negeley and Schofield. Open Feb-Dec, Tues-Sun; fall tour Sept. **$$**

DAVY CROCKETT BIRTHPLACE STATE PARK. *3 miles E off US 11E, Greeneville (37743). Phone 423/257-2167 or -2168.* A 100-acre site overlooking the Nolichuckey River serves as a memorial to Crockett—humorist, bear hunter, congressman, and hero of the Alamo. A small monument marks his birthplace; nearby is a replica of the log cabin in which Crockett was born in 1786. Swimming pool (fee). Picnicking. Camping (hook-ups). Museum and visitor center (open Mon-Fri, or by appointment). Park open daily.

JAMES K. POLK ANCESTRAL HOME. *301 W 7th St, Columbia (38401). Phone 931/388-2354. www.jamespolk.com.* Built by Samuel Polk, father of the president, in 1816, the Federal-style house is furnished with family possessions, including furniture and portraits used at the White House. Gardens link the house to the adjacent 1818 building owned by the president's sisters. Visitor center. Open daily; closed Jan 1, Thanksgiving, Dec 24-25. **$$**

⭐ **SHILOH NATIONAL MILITARY PARK.** *10 miles SW of Savannah on TN 22, Savannah (38372). Phone 901/689-5696. www.nps.gov/shil/.* Bitter, bloody Shiloh was the first major Civil War battle in the West and one of the fiercest in history. In two days, April 6 and 7, 1862, nearly 24,000 men were killed, wounded, or missing. The South's failure to destroy Grant's army opened the way for the attack on and siege of Vicksburg, Mississippi. It was a costly battle for the North as well. General Grant's Army of the Tennessee, numbering almost 40,000, was camped near Pittsburg Landing and Shiloh Church, waiting for the Army of the Ohio under General Don Carlos Buell to attack the Confederates who, they thought, were near Corinth, Mississippi, 20 miles south. But the Southern General Albert Sidney Johnston surprised Grant with an attack at dawn on April 6. Although General Johnston was mortally wounded on the first day, the Southerners successfully pushed the Union Army back and nearly captured their supply base at Pittsburg Landing. On the second day, however, the Northerners, reinforced by the 17,918-man Army of the Ohio, counterattacked and forced the Confederates to retreat toward Corinth.

Tennessee

✻ *Natchez Trace Parkway*

At Shiloh, one of the first tent field hospitals ever established helped save the lives of many Union and Confederate soldiers. Among the men who fought this dreadful battle were John Wesley Powell, who lost an arm but later went down the Colorado River by boat and became head of the US Geological Survey; James A. Garfield, 20th president of the United States; Ambrose Bierce, famous satirist and short story writer; and Henry Morton Stanley, who later uttered the famous phrase, "Dr. Livingstone, I presume." Open daily; closed Dec 25. $

PLACES TO STAY

If you choose to include an overnight stay in your trip along this All-American Road, Mobil Travel Guide recommends the following lodgings.

★ **DAYS INN.** *1504 Nashville Hwy, Columbia (38401). Phone 931/381-3297. www.daysinn.com.* 54 rooms, 2 story. Complimentary continental breakfast. Check-out 11 am. TV; cable (premium), VCR available. Pool. Restaurant nearby. Meeting room. Business services available. ¢

★ **HONORS INN & CONVENTION CENTER.** *1208 Nashville Hwy, Columbia (38401). Phone 931/388-2720.* 155 rooms, 2 story. Pet accepted. Check-out noon. TV; cable (premium), VCR available. Restaurant, bar. Room service. Pool. Meeting rooms. ¢

★ **EAST HILLS BED & BREAKFAST INN.** *100 East Hill Terrace, Dickson (37055). Phone 615/441-9428. www.easthillsbb.com.* 7 rooms, 1 story. This inn was originally built by the owner's father in the early 1940s and features complete seclusion. Five of the rooms have private bathrooms. $

★★ **THE INN AT WALKING HORSE FARM.** *1490 Lewisburg Pike, Franklin (37064). Phone 615/790-2076.* 4 rooms, 1 story. Set on 40 acres of rolling pastureland, with eight walking horses. Guests are welcome to bring their own horses; boarding, meals, and grooming are available. $$

★ **A HOMEPLACE BED & BREAKFAST.** *7826 Nolensville Rd, Nolensville (37135). Phone 615/776-5181.* 3 rooms, 1 story. A pre-Civil War-era home, hidden in dense forests. Each room has a canopy bed and fireplace. $

PLACES TO EAT

A long day of driving is sure to make you hungry. At the end of your journey, take a table at one of the following restaurants.

★ **RANCH HOUSE.** *900 Riverside Dr, Columbia (38401). Phone 931/381-2268.* Closed Sun, Mon. Dinner. Children's menu. Reservations accepted Mon-Thurs. $$

★★ **THE OLE LAMPLIGHTER.** *1000 Riverside Dr, Columbia (38401). Phone 931/381-3837.* Specializes in steak, seafood. Closed some major holidays; also the first week of July. Reservations accepted. Dinner. Bar. Children's menu. Rustic log building at the river. $$$

★★★ **ARTHUR'S.** *1001 Broadway, Nashville (37203). Phone 615/255-1494. www.arthursrestaurant.com.* French menu. Dinner. Upscale restaurant located in the Union Station Hotel, featuring high ceilings, ornate fixtures, and cozy banquettes. Only a seven-course, prix fixe dinner is offered. $$$

★★★ **CAPITOL GRILLE.** *231 6th Ave N, Nashville (37219). Phone 615/345-7116. www.westinhermitage.com.* Southern menu. Breakfast, lunch, dinner. Located in the historic Hermitage Hotel. Eclectic menu changes weekly. Reservations required. $$$

★★ **DRUNKEN FISH.** *123 2nd Ave, Nashville (37201). Phone 615/254-5550.* Eclectic/International menu. Closed Sat-Sun. Lunch. Seafood-oriented cuisine in a clubby atmosphere. $$

★ **KOTO SUSHI BAR.** *137 7th Ave N, Nashville (37203). Phone 615/255-8122.* Sushi menu. Closed Sun. Lunch, dinner. Authentic Japanese cuisine with an impressive display of live fish. $

★★★ **MERCHANTS RESTAURANT.** *401 Broadway, Nashville (37203). Phone 615/254-1892. www.merchantsrestaurant.com.* American menu. Lunch, dinner. Upscale restaurant located in a 19th-century building, serving classic American food. $$$

★★★ **THE PALM.** *140 5th Ave S, Nashville (37203). Phone 615/742-7256.* Steak menu. Lunch, dinner. Legendary steakhouse decorated with caricatures of local luminaries. The portions are very large, with family-style sharing encouraged. $

★ **TOWN HOUSE TEA ROOM AND RESTAURANT.** *165 8th Ave N, Nashville (37203). Phone 615/254-1277.* American menu. Closed Sat-Sun. Breakfast, lunch. Located in a historic 24-room mansion built in the 1840s. $

★★★★ **THE WILD BOAR.** *2014 Broadway, Nashville (37203). Phone 615/329-1313.* A restaurant named The Wild Boar might not immediately bring to mind an upscale dining experience marked by stellar service and haute modern cuisine, but in Nashville, that's precisely what you'll get. The just slightly over-the-top restaurant is ornately decorated with brocade banquettes, tapestry wall hangings, medieval flags, swords, and animal heads. The contemporary American menu is as extravagant as the décor, with creations that often include the likes of black truffles and caviar. Each sumptuous and intensely flavored dish is assembled from seasonal ingredients and prepared with a gallant mix of Tennessee style and French technique. An impressive wine list is on hand for those in the mood to pair dinner with a selection or two from the extensive wine cellar. American menu. Closed Sun. Dinner. Extravagant contemporary American cuisine with regional Southern influences in a medieval setting. $$$

A Journey Through Time Scenic Byway
HIGHWAY 12 ❈ UTAH

Quick Facts

LENGTH: 124 miles.

TIME TO ALLOW: 1 to 3 days.

BEST TIME TO DRIVE: Spring is the best time of year to explore the lands surrounding Route 12. High season comes during the summer, when travelers are visiting Bryce Canyon and Capitol Reef. A dry climate with lots of sunny days is normal for this area of the country. Winter is the off-season, yet many travelers find this area to be a wonderland—Highway 12 is open and maintained year-round.

BYWAY TRAVEL INFORMATION: Garfield County Travel Council: 800/444-6689; Byway travel and tourism Web site: www.brycecanyoncountry.com.

SPECIAL CONSIDERATIONS: Weather can change quickly; thunderstorms are common during the summer. Several stretches are quite isolated and rugged. Several stretches of this road are 12 percent grades. The road climbs to 8,000 feet as it crosses Boulder Mountain. The road rises and falls in steep switchbacks through Escalante Canyons and Boulder Mountain. You'll find several short tunnels in the Red Canyon area. The Aquarius Plateau/Boulder Mountain segment receives heavy accumulations of winter snow and may be temporarily closed during heavy snowstorms. However, the road is plowed to allow year-round access.

RESTRICTIONS: This road is maintained all year. The Hogsback is high, narrow, and can be windy. High-profile vehicles should be prepared.

BICYCLE/PEDESTRIAN FACILITIES: Highway 12 offers a paved bicycle path that allows cyclists to pedal through Red Canyon. Other places along the Byway are suitable for cyclists, although places like the Hogsback have little shoulder space for cyclists.

As you drive the Byway that connects Bryce Canyon Park and Capitol Reef National Park, you are treated to enticing views and stops, along with a kaleidoscope of color. Byway towns in between offer a flavor of a simple life in the middle of a fantastic wilderness. Historic stops and pullouts provide stories for the curious Byway traveler. Ancient ruins and artwork can also be found throughout the canyons and rock faces that line this Byway.

At nearly every turn, you have an opportunity to get out of the car and stretch. But stretching is only the beginning. Hiking, horseback riding, and traveling by ATV are all irresistible activities that allow you to explore the back roads and trails of the area. As you continue through this wonderland of sculpted color, the urge to explore it firsthand is irresistible.

THE BYWAY STORY

Highway 12 tells archaeological, cultural, historical, natural, recreational, and scenic stories that make it a unique and treasured Byway.

Archaeological

Driving this road through some of Utah's most unusual landscapes, the climate and the topography seem all too fantastic for human beings to dwell there. Nevertheless, evidence of ancient civilization is around every corner and within every crevasse of the canyons along Highway 12. The Anasazi, Fremont, and Utes all left their mark on the rugged and challenging land. Their occupation has been preserved in the sandstone of the plateaus and under the sands and soils of the valleys. A thousand years ago, these people made a home of this unique landscape and left evidence of their habitation for visitors, travelers, and archaeologists to see.

Utah

HIGHWAY 12 ❋ A Journey Through Time Scenic Byway

Not only was their survival in this wilderness commendable, but the structures that the Anasazi left behind astound travelers and archaeologists alike. As you drive along the base of cliffs and canyons on Highway 12, alcoves high in the rocks hold ancient stone granaries where this hunting and gathering culture would store the food they had collected. The granaries reside in grooves within the cliff side and consist of rocks stacked like bricks with a small hole in the center near the bottom of the structure. Today, we can only guess how the people of so long ago would reach these heights.

Farther along the Byway, a remarkable display of an excavated Anasazi village is located on the Byway in the community of Boulder. The Anasazi Village State Park Visitor Center is located at the site of a village that once held 200 people. Walls of homes and structures of pit-houses are displayed there as examples of the way these people once lived. Only a few of the structures have been uncovered. The rest remain buried in the ground that surrounds the walkways that take visitors on a tour of the past. Signs of life from so many centuries ago captivate travelers.

One of the most riveting scenes on the Byway is an occasional glimpse of a petroglyph or pictograph. Some of the most impressive examples of this rock art can be seen at Capitol Reef as images of ancient people and animals line the red rock face of nearby Highway 24 and the Fremont River. Pictures and figures were etched on these stone walls all along the Byway and remain as a memorial to this vanished culture. Many of these pictures remain unknown and undiscovered to be found by an alert explorer. While hiking in the mountains of Highway 12, visitors are compelled to treat these drawings and carvings with an utmost solemnity. These pictures of the past are somehow related to us today, and to disturb them is to cause a breach in the connections of these two great periods.

Cultural

Embedded in the rocky precipices of Highway 12 is a conglomeration of cultures—past and present. Over the ages, travelers moving into the area built a home for themselves, incorporating ideas and methods of survival perfected by preceding cultures. The culture that permeates the Byway today is made up of people who hold a deep respect for their predecessors, and towns of the past are now a haven for both travelers and residents on the Byway. Find their heritage and their future in the many festivals and favorite spots all along the Byway.

The cultures of the Fremont Indians and the Anasazi vanished before any cultures surviving today could know them. However, their archaeological remains and artwork enable modern-day experts and visitors to speculate about what these people must have been like. These cultures had a belief system of legends and histories that explained the landforms that surrounded them. One thing is certain: the cultures of the Anasazi, Fremont, and Paiute revered the land of Highway 12 as a special land. Today's cultures feel the same. Preserving the land and celebrating its natural beauty are common goals for the people who live in communities along the Byway.

Before there was a bridge between the cultures of the future and the past, there was a culture of growth and development. Mormon pioneers established communities over a century ago whose presence today has brought a new collection of stories and histories to tell the story of the Byway. The communities that visitors will observe display the classical elements of a Mormon settlement. People would gather in a town and spread their farms all around the town. This way, an agricultural people developed and preserved a sense of community. This strong sense of community still exists today, and you are invited to partake of it. Thus influences of past cultures are a force that preserves the rural culture of today and passes its spirit onto the travelers who pass this way.

Historical

Visitors find a piece of history around every corner along the Journey Through Time. Before Highway 12 became a Scenic Byway, it was a passageway for native tribes, explorers, and pioneers. Their legacy is left behind in the names of prominent places like Powell Point and in places like the historic town of Escalante. Many of the sacred places of the Fremont and Anasazi have been lost and forgotten, but the history that these people left behind is archaeology now. Through the influences of the explorers and the pioneers, lands along the Byway reflect the history of the west to build upon an archaeological and geological history.

The first explorers were Spanish and claimed the land for Spain in 1776. The name of the town Escalante comes from one of the priests who was on the expedition, Silvestre Velez de Escalante. John Wesley Powell more thoroughly explored the land nearly 100 years later in 1869 on a treacherous journey where he lost several of his company. Nearby Lake Powell and Powell Point are now two landmarks that carry his name. By the time he explored the area, Mormon pioneers had already begun to inhabit the region in an attempt to make the desert bloom.

The town of Panguitch was the first place the pioneers attempted to settle. Because of conflicts with the native tribes, they abandoned the settlement until 1871. A string of other towns along the Byway retain a western town appearance with wood storefronts, stone walls, and old fashioned architecture. In Tropic, visit Ebenezer Bryce's cabin. This rancher/farmer began to utilize the landscape at the mouth of what is now known as Bryce Canyon, one of Utah's most fantastic national parks. The town of Boulder was the last town on the Byway to receive mail by mule. This fertile mountainside is still covered with wooden pioneer fences and old-fashioned barns.

see page A24 for color map

Natural

Landforms along the Highway 12 Scenic Byway inspire visitors with awe and curiosity for the powers of nature. Desertscapes have been preserved to become masterpieces of art that has been tempered with time. Their alluring shapes and curves have a story that begins millions of years ago. That story continues today with the thriving forests and wildlife that live along the Byway. Drive the Highway 12 Byway and tour a land carved by water and wind. Layers of rock stacked like giant pancakes pick at the imaginations of travelers. Why is the stone here so colorful? How can the rock formations maintain such unusual shapes? The answers are embedded in layers of color within plateaus and canyon walls that have been decorated with trees and wildlife.

Red Rock Canyon, Bryce Canyon, and Kodachrome Basin offer some of the strangest geological sites that travelers will ever see. The walls of Bryce Canyon are lined with singular, human-like pinnacles that protrude from the rock. So many of them in succession make the canyon look like a crowded stadium. The irregular shapes of the rocks in Bryce Canyon were formed when ancient rivers carved exposed

Utah

HIGHWAY 12 ❈ *A Journey Through Time Scenic Byway*

layers of the earth. The meandering of these rivers must have been erratic, for there are thousands of paths through the pinnacles at Bryce Canyon. Red Rock Canyon displays a range of orange and red colors in the rock. Take a hike to discover all the natural arches there. In Kodachrome Basin, evidence of another natural wonder from millions of years ago is in the strange pinnacles of stone. This used to be a geyser basin not unlike the kind found in Yellowstone National Park today. Geologists believe that the towers of stone there are actually fossilized geysers. Their vivid colors are evident from a distance.

Recreational

When Utah's visiting outdoor recreationists get tired of Utah's national parks and other well-known recreation areas, they come to A Journey Through Time Scenic Byway for supreme recreational experiences. Some of the most captivating hikes in Utah are located just off the Byway in the slot canyons of the Grand Staircase or near one of the Byway's state parks. Red Canyon and its accompanying canyons offer trails for hikers, bikers, horseback riders, and ATV enthusiasts. Be ready for an adventure on the slickrock when you travel Highway 12. With trails, backways, and paths, an exciting ride is ahead whether you are on or off the Byway.

Scenic

Spanning a route of more than 120 miles, Utah's Highway 12 Scenic Byway travels through some of the most diverse and ruggedly beautiful landscapes in the country. The surrounding red rock formations, slickrock canyons, pine and aspen forests, alpine mountains, national and state parks, and quaint rural towns all contribute in making Highway 12 a unique route well worth traveling.

Highway 12 travels from west to east through Garfield County, the home of three national parks, three state parks, and one national recreation area. At the junction of Highway 89, the Byway quickly bisects the beautiful red rock formations of Dixie National Forest's Red Canyon and continues eastward.

Hiking trails, campgrounds, and side roads along the way provide numerous opportunities to further explore the area. Highway 12 ends in Wayne County. The town of Torrey is near the junction, and travelers can take the short drive east along Highway 24 to Capitol Reef National Park, thus adding to the Highway 12 experience.

THINGS TO SEE AND DO

Driving along Highway 12 will certainly keep your senses engaged, but if you yearn to get out of the car and stretch your legs, or if you'd like to make a mini-vacation out of your trip, check out these attractions along the route.

ANASAZI INDIAN VILLAGE STATE PARK. 60 N Highway 12, Boulder (84716). Phone 435/335-7308. This partially excavated village, believed to have been occupied from AD 1050-1200, is one of the largest ancient communities west of the Colorado River. Fremont and Kayenta Anasazi occupied the area. Picnicking. Museum. Open daily; closed Jan 1, Thanksgiving, Dec 25. $

★ **BRYCE CANYON NATIONAL PARK.** *UT 63, Panguitch (84764). Phone 435/676-8585. www.nps.gov/brca/.* Bryce Canyon is a 56-square-mile area of colorful, fantastic cliffs created by millions of years of erosion. Towering rocks worn to odd, sculptured shapes stand grouped in striking sequences. The Paiute, who once lived nearby, called this "the place where red rocks stand like men in a bowl-shaped canyon." Although termed a canyon, Bryce is actually a series of breaks in 12 large amphitheaters—some plunging as deep as 1,000 feet into the multicolored limestone. The formations appear to change color as the sunlight strikes from different angles and seem incandescent in the late afternoon. The famous Pink Cliffs were carved from the Claron Formation; shades of red, orange, white, gray, purple, brown, and soft yellow appear in the strata. Park Road follows 17 miles along the eastern edge of the Paunsaugunt Plateau, where the natural amphitheaters are spread out below; plateaus covered with evergreens and valleys filled with sagebrush stretch away into the distance. The visitor center at the entrance station has complete information about the park, including orientation shows, geologic displays, and detailed maps. Open daily; closed Jan 1, Thanksgiving, Dec 25. Lodging is available Apr-Oct. **$$**

★ **CAPITOL REEF NATIONAL PARK.** *10 miles E of Richfield on UT 119, then 65 miles SE on UT 24, Loa (84747). Phone 435/425-3791. www.nps.gov/care/.* Capitol Reef, at an elevation ranging from 3,900-8,800 feet, is composed of red sandstone cliffs capped with domes of white sandstone. Located in the heart of Utah's slickrock country, the park is actually a 100-mile section of the Waterpocket Fold, an upthrust of sedimentary rock created during the formation of the Rocky Mountains. Pockets in the rocks collect thousands of gallons of water each time it rains. Capitol Reef was so named because the rocks formed a natural barrier to pioneer travel, and the white sandstone domes resemble the dome of the US Capitol. From AD 700-1350, this 378-square-mile area was the home of an ancient people who grew corn along the Fremont River. Petroglyphs can be seen on some of the sandstone walls. A schoolhouse, farmhouse, and orchards, established by early Mormon settlers, are open to the public in season. The park can be approached from either the east or the west via UT 24, a paved road. A visitor center is located about 7 miles from the west boundary and 8 miles from the east. A 25-mile round-trip scenic drive, some parts unpaved, starts from this point. There are evening programs and guided walks (Memorial Day-Labor Day; free). Three campgrounds are available. Open daily; closed Dec 25. **$**

DIXIE NATIONAL FOREST. *82 N and 100 E, Cedar City (84720). Phone 435/865-3200.* Camping, picnicking, hiking, mountain biking, winter sports. Open daily. **FREE**

ESCALANTE STATE PARK. *UT 12, Escalante (84736). Phone 435/826-4466.* Petrified forest; mineralized wood, and dinosaur bones. Swimming, fishing, boating (ramps) at reservoir; hiking, bird-watching, picnicking, camping (fee; rest rooms, showers, dump station). Open daily. **$$**

PANGUITCH LAKE. *Within Dixie National Forest, Cedar City (84720). Phone 435/676-2649.* This 8,000-foot-high lake, which fills a large volcanic basin, is your chance to fish while on the Byway. Resorts, public campgrounds (developed sites, fee), ice fishing, snowmobiling, cross-country skiing.

PAUNSAGAUNT WILDLIFE MUSEUM. *50 E Center St, Panguitch (84759). Phone 435/676-2500. www.brycecanyonwildlifemuseum.com.* More than 400 North American animals in their natural habitats can be viewed here. Also catch sight of exotic game animals from Africa, India, and Europe. Open May-Oct, daily. **$**

Utah

HIGHWAY 12 ✻ A Journey Through Time Scenic Byway

PLACES TO STAY

If you choose to include an overnight stay in your trip along this All-American Road, Mobil Travel Guide recommends the following lodgings.

★★ **BRYCE CANYON LODGE.** *1 Bryce Canyon Lodge, Bryce Canyon (84717). Phone 435/834-5361.* 114 units in cabins, motel. Closed Dec-Mar. Check-out 11 am, check-in 4 pm. Restaurant. Coin laundry. Bellhops. Sundries. Trail rides on mules, horses available. Private patios, balconies. Original 1925 building. **$**
D ✦ ⛷

★★ **BRYCE CANYON PINES MOTEL.** *Hwy 12, Panguitch (84764). Phone 435/834-5441.* 50 rooms, 1-2 story. Check-out 11 am, check-in 2 pm. TV. Heated pool. Restaurant. Some fireplaces, balconies. Early American décor. **$**
D SC ⛷

PLACES TO EAT

A long day of driving is sure to make you hungry. At the end of your journey, try the following restaurant.

★ **FOSTER'S STEAK HOUSE.** *UT 12, Bryce Canyon National Park (84764). Phone 435/834-5227.* Steak menu. Breakfast, lunch, dinner. Children's menu. Specializes in prime rib. Salad bar. Bakery adjacent. **$$**
D

Chinook Scenic Byway
❋ WASHINGTON

Quick Facts

LENGTH: 85 miles.

TIME TO ALLOW: 1 1/2 to 2 hours.

BEST TIME TO DRIVE: Late May to late October, when the entire route is open.

BYWAY TRAVEL INFORMATION: Enumclaw Chamber of Commerce: 360/825-7666; Yakima Valley Visitor and Convention Center: 800/221-0751; Mount Rainier Visitor Information: 360/569-2211; Washington State Tourism Division: 800/544-1800, ext. 036; Byway local Web site: www.chinookscenicbyway.org.

SPECIAL CONSIDERATIONS: The park segment of the road is typically closed during the winter. However, the road is open on the northwest side of Mount Rainier National Park (milepost 57.6) and on the east side of Morse Creek (milepost 74.97). Mount Rainier National Park is open year-round, but only the Nisqually to Paradise road stays open. The east and west road segments outside of the park are open in the winter for recreational use. Also, tour buses are accommodated along the parkway under a permit system.

RESTRICTIONS: Autumn and spring access along the Byway is weather dependent. The typical opening dates for Cayuse and Chinook passes are May 2 and May 26, respectively. Closing dates for these same areas are normally December 6 and December 14.

BICYCLE/PEDESTRIAN FACILITIES: This Byway is popular for bicycling. In addition, the number of mountain bike routes off the Byway has increased yearly. Each year brings the annual Ride Around Mount Rainier in One Day (RAMROD) bicycle event, which is limited to 750 people.

The Chinook Scenic Byway (also known as the Mather Memorial Parkway) is possibly the most scenic route crossing the Cascade Mountain Range, and it is the most accessible road for viewing Mount Rainier. Mount Rainier National Park (which the Byway travels through) was established in 1890, and the Mather Parkway was established in 1931. Because of its national park status, all features in the park are protected.

The route has a uniquely varied landscape. Traveling east, the route climbs through a closed canopy of Douglas fir. At Chinook Pass, the roadway descends dramatically through the Wenatchee National Forest and along the American River. The road also passes the unique basalt flows of the Columbia Plateau. The Byway ends near the fertile agricultural valleys of Yakima County.

THE BYWAY STORY

The Chinook Scenic Byway tells archaeological, historical, natural, recreational, and scenic stories that make it a unique and treasured Byway.

Archaeological

Even though only about 2 percent of the park has been systematically surveyed for archaeological remains, it has 79 known sites in the park, of which 62 have been fully documented and recorded.

One prehistoric site dates to between 2,300 and 4,500 years ago. Sites just outside of the park hint at much earlier occupation, perhaps as much as 8,000 years, but most prehistoric archaeological sites are about 1,000 years old.

Washington

❋ *Chinook Scenic Byway*

Later, the area was used on a seasonal basis by lowland tribes for hunting and gathering, and for spiritual and ceremonial events. A few sites were hunting camps (killing and butchering sites), where cedar bark was stripped from trees, rock shelters created, and stone for tools procured.

In more modern centuries, five principal Native American tribes (specifically, the Nisqually, Puyallup, Muckleshoot, Yakama, and Taidnapam) came to the park in the summer and early fall to hunt and to collect resources. These tribes continued to come even after the park was officially designated in 1899. Sites that were used by these tribes are littered with broken weapon points.

Sites from European settlements in the late 19th and early 20th centuries confirm mining, recreation, and early park development. Specifically, sites reveal old campsites, trash dumps, collapsed structures, mine shafts, and other debris.

Historical

Part of this Byway has a unique historic designation: that of a National Historic Landmark District. This district, called the Mount Rainier National Historic Landmark District, was designated so because it is one of the nation's finest collections of "national park rustic" architecture, both in the park's road system and in its historically developed areas.

In the 1920s, the park developed a plan—the Mount Rainier National Park's Master Plan—that was unusual at the time and is historically significant because it was the first and most complete national park plan developed by the National Park Service Landscape Division.

Natural

This Byway's wide range of plants and animals live relatively undisturbed and can, therefore, exist in greater abundance (some 50 species of mammals and 130 species of birds live here) and can attain greater longevity. For example, some high-elevation coniferous stands are over 500 years old. Some of the highest alpine stands are up to 1,000 years old.

In addition, extraordinary geological processes have created this magnificent and unique landscape: Rainier's 25 glaciers form the largest single-peak glacier system in the United States outside of Alaska; the glacier-carved canyon of the Rainier fork of the American River is geologically rare; and mountain parks (lush subalpine meadows encircling the mountain between 5,000 and 7,000 feet) are without parallel in the Cascades or Pacific volcano system.

Mount Rainier has four main glaciers: Nisqually Glacier, Cowlitz-Ingraham Glacier, Emmons Glacier, and Carbon Glacier. Nisqually Glacier is one of the most accessible glaciers on Mount Rainier. It can easily be seen from Nisqually and Glacier Vistas, located less than 1 mile from the Paradise Visitor Center. Emmons Glacier has a surface area of 4.3 square miles, the largest area of any glacier in the contiguous United States. Carbon Glacier is best viewed from a 4-mile trail from Ipsut Creek Campground on the north side of Mount Rainier. This glacier has the greatest measured thickness (700 feet) and volume (0.2 cubic miles) of any glacier in the contiguous United States. Because of the weather patterns in recent years, all of these glaciers are slowly retreating.

Along the Byway and in your forages into Mount Rainier National Park, you can see four distinct life, or vegetation, zones. They are the lowland forest, montane zone, subalpine zone, and alpine zone. Each zone is filled with varied and splendid wildlife and flora.

In the lowland forest zone, a canopy of stately giants allow little sunlight to filter down to the forest floor. Deer browse in the shadows of western hemlock and western red cedar, among others. Hawks and owls perch in the trees waiting for prey to scurry across the shady floor. Bald eagles also thrive in these forests, diving down to grab fish from the water with their talons.

see page A25 for color map

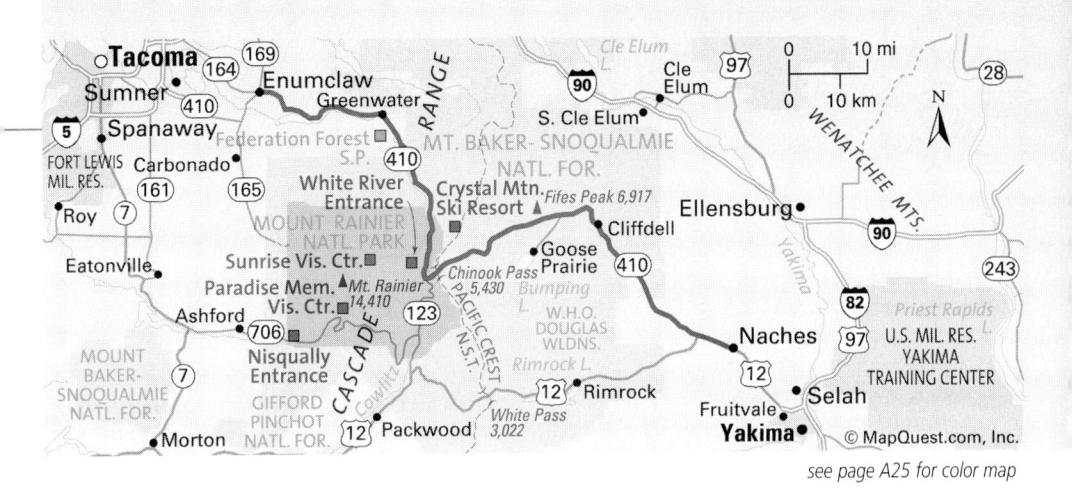

The montane zone is a bit farther up the mountainside and a little wetter and colder. The delicate and elusive calypso orchid blooms here in the spring, and patches of huckleberry bushes abound. Black bears, who really like huckleberries, are one of this area's large predators, although you'll probably never encounter a black bear.

The subalpine zone is typified by tree "islands" mixed with open meadows. The snow lasts longer among the sheltering trees of this zone. By late July, a rainbow of wildflowers carpets the meadow. These flowers include white avalanche lilies, yellow marsh marigolds, purple lupine, magenta paintbrush, and plumed bear grass. Glacier lilies and snowbed buttercups bloom at the treeline. A special feature in the subalpine zone are the krummholzes, trees that are strikingly twisted and stunted due to the severe winds and snow. Trees only 3 feet in height may be centuries old. The last and highest zone is the alpine zone. It is found above the timberline and is a world of extremes. On a summer day, the sun can shine warm and bright, but in just moments clouds can bring a sudden snow or lightning storm. During storms, the wind knifes across the tundra because there are no trees to break up the wind. Consequently, most alpine plants grow to be only a few inches high.

Recreational

The area surrounding the Chinook Scenic Byway is rife with recreational activities. Any time of year affords a combination of beautiful scenery and fun things to do. A visit in summer offers great opportunities for fishing, hunting, hiking, biking, and rafting. Summer is not the only time to experience the beauty, however. Mount Rainier and its surrounding area is one of the snowiest places on Earth. In 1972, Paradise received 94 feet of snow, a world record. Naturally, snow sports also abound. Skiing and snowshoeing are the most popular, and plenty of snow-laden slopes and meadows provide remarkable experiences. Although people come here continuously throughout the year, solitude is only a moment away. With over 200 hiking and horse trails, 20 mountain biking trails, 50 Nordic ski trails, six designated wildlife/bird viewing areas, and 24 campgrounds with over 500 campsites, you can still find quiet among nature's majesty.

Spectacular scenery meets the eye with every turn of the Byway, and every stop along the way offers an interesting trail to try out. The grade and length of the trails vary, offering the perfect hike for every person. Many visitors love to hike trails in Mount Rainier National Park. Biking provides a great way to bring you into direct contact with more of the serene area of the Byway a little more quickly than hiking. The Byway itself is equipped to handle bicyclers. The shoulders along the road are paved varying from 2 to 8 feet.

Scenic

Chinook Scenic Byway takes you through picturesque mountain towns and historical sites and guides you past Mount Rainier, "the shining jewel of the Northwest." The Byway's scenic properties are manifested largely in one of the world's greatest mountains, 14,411-foot Mount Rainier. Rainier is the tallest volcano in the 48 contiguous states and is the largest mountain in the Cascade chain of volcanoes

Washington

✻ Chinook Scenic Byway

extending from California to the Canadian border. At the numerous developed viewpoints along the roadside, you can enjoy the deep shadowy forests, misty waterfalls, sparkling streams, towering peaks, and snowy rocky ridges that are all a part of Mount Rainier's wonder. Stands of old-growth Douglas fir found in few other places are available at every turn.

A short distance from SR 410 is the road to Sunrise, the highest point in the park accessible by car. The road to Sunrise winds through forests of cedar, fir, and hemlock, offering glimpses of the four dormant volcanoes, including Mounts Baker and Adams. Mount Rainier rises above alpine meadows profuse with delicate wildflowers to the rocky summit of Little Tahoma Peak visible to the left. Snap a few photographs: Mount Rainier's mountain meadows with their clear icy lakes are among the most visited and photographed areas of the national park. From Sunrise, the views of Emmons Glacier, the largest on Mount Rainier, are breathtaking.

HIGHLIGHTS

Beginning near Naches and traveling northwest on the Byway, you enter the Mount Rainier National Forest a few miles outside of the town of Cliffdell. This national park is known for its scenic, recreational, and natural resources.

After passing through Cliffdell, the road continues for a short space to the Builder Cave National Recreation Trail and Norse Peak, both known for their scenic beauty and recreational value. Here, the road changes to a southwesterly course, enters the Mount Rainier National Park, and passes through old-growth environments that surround Fife Peak. Union Creek Waterfall is also located in this area. Edgar Rock Chinook Pass Historic CCC Work Camp is located at Chinook Pass, where the parkway resumes its northwestern direction. Tipsoo Lake is on the eastern side of the parkway shortly after the pass, followed by the Chinook Pass Overlook and Crystal Mountain Ski Resort.

Leaving the Mount Rainier National Park, the parkway continues through the national forest to the Skookum Flats National Recreation Trail found at the edge of the forest. A popular viewpoint for Mount Rainier is also located here. The parkway travels through the town of Greenwater and the Federation Forest State Park before continuing on to Enumclaw, where the parkway ends.

THINGS TO SEE AND DO

Driving along the Chinook Scenic Byway will certainly keep your senses engaged, but if you yearn to get out of the car and stretch your legs, or if you'd like to make a mini-vacation out of your trip, check out these attractions along the route.

FEDERATION FOREST STATE PARK, *49201 Hwy 410 E, Enumclaw (98022). Phone 360/663-2207. www.parks.wa.gov/parks/.* Approximately 620 acres of old-growth timber make up the Federation Forest State Park. The Catherine Montgomery Interpretive Center displays exhibits on the state's seven life zones. Three

ALL-AMERICAN ROADS

interpretive trails, hiking trails, and part of the Naches Trail, one of the first pioneer trails between eastern Washington and Puget Sound. Fishing; hiking, picnicking. **FREE**

FLAMING GEYSER STATE PARK. *23700 SE Flaming Geyser Rd, Auburn (98002). Phone 253/931-3930. www.parks.wa.gov/parks/.* Two geysers (actually old test holes for coal) are in the park, one burning about 6 inches high and the other bubbling methane gas through a spring. Fishing, boating, rafting; hiking, picnicking, playground. Abundant wildlife, wildflowers. No camping. Open daily.

GREEN RIVER GORGE CONSERVATION AREA. *29500 SE Green River Gorge, Enumclaw (98022).* This conservation area protects a unique 12-mile corridor of the Green River, which cuts through unusual rock areas, many with fossils. Views of present-day forces of stream erosion through caves and smooth canyon walls. **FREE**

★ MOUNT RAINIER NATIONAL PARK. *Tahoma Woods, Star Rte, Ashford (98304). Phone 360/569-2211. www.nps.gov/mora.* Majestic Mount Rainier, towering 14,411 feet above sea level and 8,000 feet above the Cascade Range of western Washington, is one of America's outstanding tourist attractions. More than 2 million people visit this 378-square-mile park each year to picnic, hike, camp, climb mountains, or simply admire the spectacular scenery along the many miles of roadways. The park's various "life zones," which change at different elevations, support a wide array of plant and animal life. Douglas fir, red cedar, and Western hemlock, some rising 200 feet into the air, thrive in the old-growth forests. In the summer, the subalpine meadows come alive with brilliant, multicolored wildflowers. Mountain goats, chipmunks, and marmots are favorites among visitors, but deer, elk, bears, mountain lions, and other animals can also be seen here.

Mount Rainier is the largest volcano in the Cascade Range, which extends from Mount Garibaldi in southwestern British Columbia to Lassen Peak in northern California. The eruption of Mount St. Helens in 1980 gives a clue to the violent history of these volcanoes. Eruptions occurred at Mount Rainier as recently as the mid-1800s. Even today, steam emissions often form caves in the summit ice cap and usually melt the snow along the rims of the twin craters. A young volcano by geologic standards, Mount Rainier was once a fairly symmetrical mountain rising about 16,000 feet above sea level. But glaciers and further volcanic activity shaped the mountain into an irregular mass of rock. The sculpting action of the ice gave each face of the mountain its own distinctive profile. The glaciation continues today, as Mount Rainier supports the largest glacier system in the contiguous United States, with 35 square miles of ice and 26 named glaciers. The glaciers are the source of the many streams in the park, as well as several rivers in the Pacific Northwest. The meltwaters also nourish the various plants and animals throughout the region.

Winters at Mount Rainier are legendary. Moist air masses moving eastward across the Pacific Ocean are intercepted by the mountain. As a result, some areas on the mountain commonly receive 50 or more feet of snow each winter. Yet the park's transformation from winter wonderland to summer playground is almost magical. Beginning in June or July, the weather becomes warm and clear, although the mountain is occasionally shrouded in clouds. The snow at the lower elevations then disappears, meltwaters fill stream valleys and cascade over cliffs, wildflowers blanket the meadows, and visitors descend on the park for its many recreational activities.

You are offered several entrances to the park. The roads from the Nisqually entrance to Paradise and from the southeast boundary to Ohanapecosh are usually open year-round but

Washington

❋ *Chinook Scenic Byway*

may be closed temporarily during the winter. Following the first heavy snow, around Nov 1, all other roads are closed until May or June. $$

MUD MOUNTAIN DAM. *WA 410, Enumclaw (98022). Phone 360/825-3211.* One of the world's highest earth-core and rock-fill dams.

PLACES TO STAY

If you choose to include an overnight stay in your trip along this All-American Road, Mobil Travel Guide recommends the following lodgings.

★★ **ALEXANDER'S COUNTRY INN.** *37515 WA 706E, Ashford (98304). Phone 360/569-2300. www.alexanderscountryinn.com.* 12 rooms, 7 with shower only, 2 guest houses, 3 story. No A/C. No room phones. Complimentary full breakfast; evening refreshments. Check-out 11 am, check-in 3 pm. Restaurant. Built in 1912. Totally nonsmoking. ¢

★ **THE NISQUALLY LODGE.** *31609 WA 706, Ashford (98304). Phone 360/569-8804; toll-free 888/674-3554. www.escapetothemountains.com.* 24 rooms, 2 story. Complimentary continental breakfast. Check-out 11 am. TV; VCR available. Restaurant. Whirlpool. Totally nonsmoking. ¢

★★ **PARADISE INN.** *PO Box 108, Ashford (98304). Phone 360/569-2275. www.guestservices.com/rainier.* 117 rooms, 95 with bath, 2-4 story. No A/C. No elevator. No room phones. Closed early Oct-late May. Check-out 11 am. Restaurant, bar. Business services available. Bellhops. Sundries. Naturalist programs nightly. Shake-shingle mountain lodge built with on-site timber in 1916. Totally nonsmoking. $

★★ **BEST WESTERN PARK CENTER HOTEL.** *1000 Griffin Ave, Enumclaw (98022). Phone 360/825-4490; toll-free 800/780-7234. www.bestwestern.com.* 40 rooms, 2 story. Pet accepted; $10. Check-out 11 am. TV. Restaurant, bar. Room service. Meeting rooms. Business services available. In-room modem link. In-house fitness room. Whirlpool. Some refrigerators, microwaves. Picnic tables. ¢

★ **APPLE COUNTRY BED & BREAKFAST.** *524 Okanagon Ave, Wenatchee (98801). Phone 509/664-0400. www.applecountryinn.com.* 5 rooms, 2 story. One of the first homes built (in 1920) in the Okanogan Heights addition in Wenatchee. $

PLACES TO EAT

A long day of driving is sure to make you hungry. At the end of your journey, try the following restaurant.

★★ **ALEXANDER'S COUNTRY INN.** *37515 SR 706E, Ashford (98304). Phone 360/569-2300. www.alexanderscountryinn.com.* Closed weekdays mid-Oct-mid-Apr. Breakfast, lunch, dinner. Children's menu. Reservations accepted. $$

The Historic National Road
✤ WEST VIRGINIA
Part of a multistate Byway; see also IL, IN, MD, OH, PA.

Quick Facts

LENGTH: 16 miles.

TIME TO ALLOW: Less than 1 hour.

BEST TIME TO DRIVE: The Byway is open all year, but many feel it is best to drive during the summer, the high season, when more cultural activities are taking place.

BYWAY TRAVEL INFORMATION: Wheeling Convention and Visitors Bureau: 800/828-3097.

BICYCLE/PEDESTRIAN FACILITIES: A paved trail is available for bikers and pedestrians along most of the Byway.

West Virginia's National Historic Road takes you on a trip through history. In 1863, West Virginia developed into a new state—the only state to successfully break off from another. The building where the Restored Government of Virginia was established is located along the Byway—many important decisions and debates regarding the Civil War took place in this building. You can tour this historic site that has been painstakingly preserved and beautifully restored.

The Historic National Road boasts many impressive museums and art galleries. One of the most popular museums along the Byway is the Kruger Street Toy and Train Museum, where the annual Marx Toy Convention is held. The Byway also features restored mansions, such as the Oglebay Institute Mansion Museum. This 16-mile attraction offers a high level of historic aesthetics and cleanliness. On almost every spot along this Byway, you see historic buildings and bridges, not to mention beautiful scenery. To make this route even more accommodating, you find bike paths and paved trails through most of the Byway's highlights.

THE BYWAY STORY

The Historic National Road tells cultural, historical, recreational, and scenic stories that make it a unique and treasured Byway.

Cultural

The cultural qualities of the Historic National Road are many in number and offer diverse experiences. Two of perhaps the most meaningful include music (particularly Jamboree USA) and religion.

W. Virginia

✻ The Historic National Road

The Capitol Music Hall, located next to the famous Wheeling Suspension Bridge, is home to both Jamboree USA and the Wheeling Symphony Orchestra. The Jamboree is the longest-running live radio program in America's history. Since 1933, famous artists from all over the nation have come to perform to an eager audience and have their show aired live over the radio each Saturday night. It was founded with the idea of promoting the regional country music that is dear to the South. When the Jamboree first began, fans drove hundreds of miles for this weekly event. This tradition continues today, as many still drive great distances to participate in the yeehawin' fun.

Religion has played a powerful role in shaping the communities along the Byway. Places of worship dot this area, some with beautiful aesthetics and architecture. Churches along the route tell the story of the great diversity of those who traveled the road and settled along the nation's first interstate. You can view beautiful cemeteries near the churches with many unique monuments and headstones indicative of the artistry of earlier eras.

Historical

Without question, the historic qualities here are the richest attribute this Byway has to offer. With two national historic landmarks, numerous designated historic districts, and National Register structures, the Historic National Road had a great impact on not only West Virginia's past, but on America's, too. From Monument Place, the oldest home standing in Wheeling, to the Elm Grove Stone Arch Bridge, the oldest stone bridge in the state, the Byway is steeped in history.

The National Road Corridor Historic District consists of a variety of homes built by Wheeling's wealthy industrial class. It also includes Wheeling Park, Greenwood Cemetery, and Mt. Calvary Cemetery. In 1888, farms outside the city began to be developed as "suburbia." The Woodsdale-Edgewood Neighborhood Historic District is a result of this type of development. The district contains many high-style houses, such as Queen Anne, Colonial Revival, and Shingle styles. As the route descends Wheeling Hill into the city of Wheeling, you enter the North Wheeling Historic District. Ebenezer Zane, the founder of Wheeling, laid out the Victorian district in 1792. The houses include a variety of simple Federal townhouses offset with the high styles of Italianate, Queen Anne, Second Empire, and Classical Revival architecture.

The Wheeling Suspension Bridge crosses the Ohio River to Wheeling Island. The engineering marvel spans 1,010 feet and was the first bridge to cross the Ohio River. Designed by Charles Ellet, Jr., it was the longest single span in the United States at the time of its completion in 1849. You cross the bridge to get to Wheeling Island, one of the largest inhabited river islands in the country. The Wheeling Island Historic District includes a diverse collection of lavish 19th-century residential homes.

Recreational

Why do over a million people come each year to the city of Wheeling to watch dogs? Simple. They come to view and bet on some of the world's fastest canines in the races. This popular event is usually open every day all year long.

Visitors go to Wheeling Downs to watch the races in person. These sleek thoroughbreds give quite a show as they thunder along the tracks at speeds of up to 40 miles per hour. Here at the Downs, people can enjoy the luxury of attending the races while eating at a fine diner that overlooks the track. Each of the tables also has tabletop televisions that relay the race and broadcast any replays and results. Many have found the restaurant's service, coupled with the excitement of the live races, an invigorating experience not easily forgotten.

Scenic

Time almost stands still while looking down on the city of Wheeling from Mt. Wood Overlook. Looking carefully, you can spot old, restored Victorian homes, as well as other important buildings in the nation's history. This vantage point, resting on top of Wheeling Hill, also overlooks the mighty Ohio River. It's at these heights that the observer starts to appreciate the accomplishment of the early Americans who constructed the single-spanned Wheeling Bridge across this wide river. At the time of its completion in the early 1800s, this was the longest single-spanned bridge in the world. As you continue to gaze in the area around Wheeling, more sights become visible. Ancient deciduous forests surround the city and small streams make their way to the grand Ohio. Maple trees thrive here, and some of the locals harvest the syrup. The area is a saturated green during the warm months and a calm white during the winter ones.

THINGS TO SEE AND DO

Driving along the Historic National Road will certainly keep your senses engaged, but if you yearn to get out of the car and stretch your legs, or if you'd like to make a mini-vacation out of your trip, check out these attractions along the route.

THE ARTISAN CENTER. *1400 Main St, Wheeling (26003). Phone 304/233-4555. www.artisan.center.com.* Restored 1860s Victorian warehouse houses River City Ale Works, West Virginia's largest brewpub. "Made in Wheeling" crafts and exhibits; artisan demonstrations. Open daily.

GRAVE CREEK MOUND STATE PARK. *801 Jefferson Ave, Moundsville (26041). Phone 304/843-1410.* Features the nation's largest prehistoric Adena burial mound—79 feet high, 900 feet around, and 50 feet across the top. Some excavating was done in 1838; exhibits in the Delf Norona Museum and Cultural Center. Open daily.

JAMBOREE USA. *1015 Main St, Wheeling (26003). Phone 304/234-0050; toll-free 800/624-5456. www.jamboreeusa.com.* Live country music shows presented by WWVA Radio since 1933. Open Sat. $$$$

KRUGER STREET TOY & TRAIN MUSEUM. *144 Kruger St, Wheeling (26003). Phone 304/242-8133. www.toyandtrain.com.* Collection of antique toys, games, and playthings in a restored Victorian-era schoolhouse. Open daily 10 am-6 pm. $$

OGLEBAY INSTITUTE MANSION MUSEUM. *Inside Oglebay Park, Wheeling (26003). Phone 304/242-7272. www.oionline.com.* The original section of this Greek Revival home was built in 1844, and additions were made in 1856. Sold to Cleveland industrialist Earl Oglebay in 1900, it was transformed into the present Neoclassical Revival style. $$

OGLEBAY RESORT PARK. *WV 88, Wheeling (26003). Phone 304/243-4000; toll-free 800/624-6988.* A 1,650-acre municipal park. Indoor and outdoor swimming pools, fishing, paddle boating on three-acre Schenk Lake; three 18-hole golf courses, miniature golf, tennis courts, picnicking, restaurant, snack shop, cabins, lodge. Train ride; 65-acre Good Children's Zoo (fee) with animals in natural habitat. Benedum Natural Science Theater; garden center; arboretum with 4 miles of walking paths; greenhouses; observatory.

WEST VIRGINIA INDEPENDENCE HALL-CUSTOM HOUSE. *1801 National Rd, Wheeling (26003). Phone 304/238-1300.* Site of a meeting (1859) at which Virginia's secession from the Union was declared unlawful and the independent state of West Virginia was created. The building, used as a post office, custom office, and federal court until 1912, has been restored. It now houses exhibits and events relating to the state's cultural heritage, including an interpretive film and rooms with period furniture. Open Mar-Dec, daily; rest of year, Mon-Sat; closed state holidays. $$

W. Virginia

❄ The Historic National Road

WHEELING PARK. *1801 National Rd, Wheeling (26003). Phone 304/242-3770.* Approximately 400 acres. Swimming pool, water slide, boating on Good Lake; golf, miniature golf, indoor/outdoor tennis, ice skating (rentals), picnicking, playground, refreshment area with video screen and lighted dance floor. Aviary. Fees for activities. Open daily; some facilities seasonal.

PLACES TO STAY

If you choose to include an overnight stay in your trip along this All-American Road, Mobil Travel Guide recommends the following lodgings.

★★ **BEST WESTERN WHEELING INN.** *949 Main St, Wheeling (26003). Phone 304/233-8500. www.bestwestern.com.* 82 rooms, 4 story. Pet accepted; $10. Complimentary continental breakfast. Check-out 11 am. TV; cable (premium). In-room modem link. Restaurant, bar. Exercise equipment, sauna. ¢

★ **HAMPTON INN.** *795 National Rd, Wheeling (26003). Phone 304/233-0440. www.hamptoninn.com.* 104 rooms, 5 story. Complimentary continental breakfast. Check-out noon. TV; cable (premium), VCR available. In-room modem link. Restaurant adjacent, bar. Room service. Exercise equipment. $

★★★ **OGLEBAY CONFERENCE CENTER.** *Oglebay Park, Wheeling (26003). Phone 304/243-4000.* 261 rooms, 2 story. Pet accepted. Check-out 11 am, check-in 3 pm. TV; cable (premium), VCR available (movies). In-room modem link. Fireplaces. Dining room. Snack bar. Lounge. Supervised children's activities (June-Aug), ages 6-14. Exercise equipment. Massage. Game room. Two pools, one indoor; wading pool, whirlpool, poolside service. Golf. Lighted tennis courts. Downhill ski 1/2 mile. Lawn games. Paddleboats. Fishing. Valet parking available. Airport transportation. Business center. Children's zoo. Mansion museum, garden center. Stables. Rustic setting in Oglebay Park. $

PLACES TO EAT

A long day of driving is sure to make you hungry. At the end of your journey, try the following restaurant

★★★ **ERNIE'S ESQUIRE.** *1055 E Bethlehem Blvd I 470 Exit 2, Wheeling (26003). Phone 304/242-2800.* A local landmark for nearly 50 years, this fine-dining restaurant serves a wide variety of options to suit any palate. Closed Dec 25. Lunch, dinner, Sun brunch, late night. Bar. Entertainment Fri, Sat. Children's menu. Casual attire. Valet parking available. $$

Beartooth Scenic Byway

❈ WYOMING

Part of a multistate Byway; see also MT.

Quick Facts

LENGTH: 69 miles.

TIME TO ALLOW: 3 hours.

BEST TIME TO DRIVE: Early summer mornings.

BYWAY TRAVEL INFORMATION: Shoshone National Forest: 307/527-6921.

SPECIAL CONSIDERATIONS: The alpine climate is rigorous, and severe weather conditions can occur any month of the year. Even during the summer, temperatures range from the 70s on sunny days to below freezing during sudden snowstorms.

RESTRICTIONS: The entire length of the Byway is open from Memorial Day weekend through about mid-October. Snow closes sections of the route during the winter. Check with the local ranger district offices before planning a trip in May or September, because occasional snowstorms can occur during these months.

BICYCLE/PEDESTRIAN FACILITIES: A growing number of visitors experience the Byway and its surrounding areas by bicycle and on foot. You'll find hundreds of miles of designated trails that are easily accessible from the Byway. Although the Byway can be biked from end to end, stretches of the route require cautious travel.

The Beartooth Highway is one of the most spectacular national forest routes on this continent. To many, it is known as "the most beautiful highway in America." From its beginning at the border of the Custer National Forest to its terminus near the northeast entrance to Yellowstone National Park, the Beartooth Highway (US 212) offers you the ultimate high-country experience as it travels through the Custer, Shoshone, and Gallatin national forests.

Since its completion in 1936, the highway has provided millions of visitors a rare opportunity to see the transition from a lush forest ecosystem to alpine tundra in the space of just a few miles. The Beartooth area is one of the highest and most rugged areas in the lower 48 states, with 20 peaks reaching over 12,000 feet in elevation. Glaciers are found on the north flank of nearly every mountain peak that is over 11,500 feet high in these mountains.

Recreational opportunities are abundant in the area traversed by the Byway. You can cross-country ski in June and July, hike across broad plateaus, and view and photograph wildlife like Rocky Mountain goats, moose, black bears, grizzly bears, marmots, and mule deer. You can also take a guided horseback trip, fish for trout in the streams and lakes adjacent to the Byway, and camp in the 12 national forest campgrounds in the area. Even when the highway is formally closed to automobiles, snowmobilers can travel the route and enjoy a spectacular winter wonderland.

Wyoming

❃ Beartooth Scenic Byway

THE BYWAY STORY

The Beartooth Scenic Byway tells historical, natural, recreational, and scenic stories that make it a unique and treasured Byway.

Historical

The first recorded travel across the Beartooth Pass area occurred in 1882, when General Sheridan, with a force of 129 soldiers and scouts, 104 horses, and 157 mules, pioneered and marked a route across the mountains from Cooke City to Billings. A year later, a packer named Van Dyke modified the trail and located a route off the Beartooth Plateau into Rock Creek and Red Lodge. Van Dyke's trail was the only direct route between Red Lodge and Cooke City until the Beartooth Highway was constructed in 1934 and 1935. Remnants of Van Dyke's trail are visible from the Rock Creek Overlook parking lot, appearing as a Z on the mountain between the highway switchbacks about 1/4 mile south of the parking lot.

Doctor Siegfriet and other visionaries from the Bearcreek and Red Lodge communities foresaw, in the early 1900s, the value of a scenic route over the mountains to connect to Yellowstone Park. These men spent many years promoting the construction of a road over the mountains, and even began the construction of a road with hand tools and horse-drawn implements. Other routes were surveyed in the 1920-1925 period, and in 1931, President Hoover signed the "Park Approach Act," which was the forerunner to the funding of the road you now know as the Beartooth Highway. This highway was first opened to public travel on June 12, 1936. The Beartooth Highway was classified as a National Forest Scenic Byway on February 8, 1989.

Natural

A variety of theories exist on the formation of the Beartooth Mountains, but geologists generally agree that the mountains resulted from an uplifting of an Archean block of metamorphic rocks that were eroded, flooded with volcanic lava on the southwest corner, and covered with glaciers. Seventy million years of formation went into making this section of the Rocky Mountains.

The Palisades that stretch along the Beartooth Front were first sedimentary rocks originally deposited as flat-lying beds in an ancient sea. Thrust skyward, they have become conspicuous spires. Pilot and Index Peaks are the remainders of an extensive volcanic field that came into existence 50 million years ago.

Changes are continuing in the present. Yellowstone Park has been an active volcanic center for more than 15 million years. Erosional forces are still at work. Glaciers have shaped the mountains into the range it is today. The glaciers edged their ways down just 10,000 years ago. Younger rocks are the sources of coal that was exploited by the early settlers of Red Lodge.

The Stillwater Complex, a body of igneous magma formed along the northern edge of the mountain range 2.7 million years ago, is one of the rarest and least understood geologic occurrences in the world. It is the site of the only source of the platinum group metals in the Western Hemisphere, mined by Stillwater Mining Company of Nye, Montana.

Recreational

Recreational opportunities are abundant in the area traversed by the Beartooth National Scenic Byway. Cross-country ski on the snowfields in June and July. Play in the snow, hike across the broad plateaus and Forest Service trails (some of which are National Recreation Trails), camp, picnic, and fish for trout in the streams and lakes adjacent to the highway. You can also view wildflowers, view and photograph wildlife (moose, Rocky Mountain goats, mule deer, black bears, grizzly bears, marmots, and pikas), visit a guest ranch, or take a guided horseback trip from Cooke City. Also, you can bicycle, downhill ski on the headwalls, and photograph nature at its finest. Even when the highway is formally closed to automobiles, snowmobilers may travel the route in a spectacular winter wonderland.

see page A17 for color map

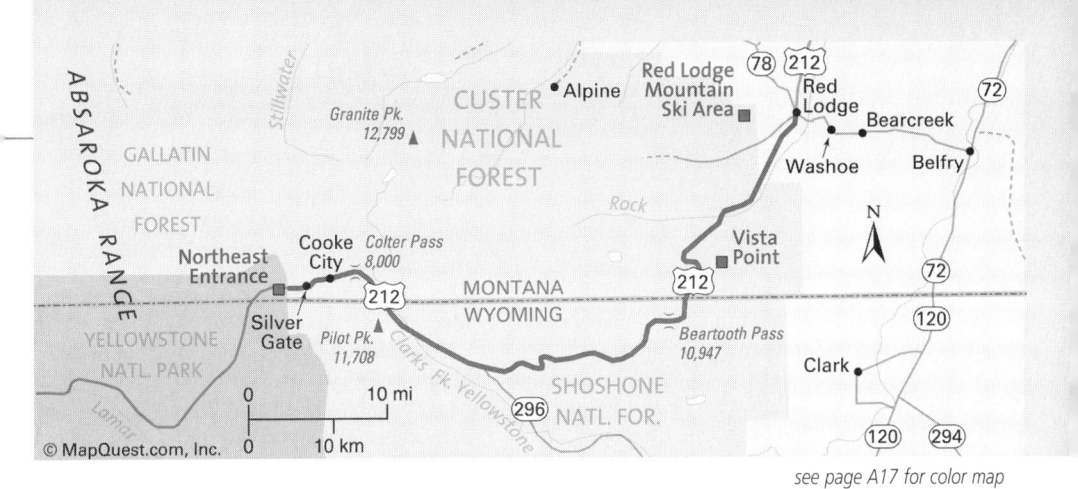

If you enjoy skiing, each summer in June and July the Red Lodge International Ski Race Camp is conducted on the north side of the East Summit on the Twin Lakes Headwall. This camp, not open to the public for skiing, is for aspiring Olympic-caliber skiers and provides a terrific viewing opportunity.

Scenic

The spire known as the Bears Tooth was carved in the shape of a large tooth by glacial ice gnawing inward and downward against a single high part of a rocky crest. Beartooth Butte is a remnant of sedimentary deposits that once covered the entire Beartooth Plateau. The red-stained rock outcrop near the top of Beartooth Butte was a stream channel some 375 million years ago, so fossils are found in abundance in the rocks of Beartooth Butte.

These treeless areas, near or above the timberline, generally are areas that cannot grow trees. Vegetation is often small, low-growing, and compact—characteristics that are vital to the survival of the plants at this elevation. Wildflowers, often as tiny as a quarter-inch across, create a literal carpet of color during the 45-day or shorter growing season.

On the other hand, the common flowers found below the timberline in wet meadows are Indian paintbrush, monkeyflower, senecio, and buttercups; in drier areas are lupine, beardstongue, arrowleaf balsamroot, and forget-me-nots. The colors and the flowers change weekly as the growing season progresses, but mid-July is generally the optimum for wildflower displays.

Wildlife in the Beartooth country varies from the largest American land mammal, the moose, to the shrew, which is the smallest land mammal. Other animals commonly seen along the highway are mule deer, white-tailed deer, elk, marmots (rock chucks), and pine squirrels. Bighorn sheep, Rocky Mountain goats, black bears, and grizzly bears are residents of the area, but none is seen often. Birds include the golden eagle, raven, Clarks nutcracker, Stellars jay, robin, mountain bluebird, finch, hawk, and falcon. Watch for the water ouzel darting in and out of—and walking along the bottoms of—streams.

The snowbanks often remain until August near Beartooth Pass, and remnants of some drifts may remain all summer. A pink color often appears on the snow later in the summer, which is caused by the decay of a microscopic plant that grows on the surface of the snowbank. When the plant dies, it turns red and colors the snow pink.

HIGHLIGHTS

Consider using the following itinerary as you travel the Beartooth Scenic Byway.

- As you come into Red Lodge from the north on US 212, the **Beartooth Plateau** looms over the surrounding prairie foothills as a hulking mass of black, rounded mountains. The plateau, an immense block of metamorphic rock, was heaved up through the Earth's crust about 50 million years ago. Much later, an enormous ice cap smoothed its surface and flowed down into the plateau's side canyons, hollowing them into spacious U-shaped valleys.

Wyoming

❋ Beartooth Scenic Byway

- **Red Lodge** is an 1880s coal mining and ranching town lined with turn-of-the-century redbrick storefronts and hotels that cater mainly to skiers and visitors to Yellowstone. Visit the **Beartooth Nature Center,** at the north end of Red Lodge, which exhibits native wildlife.

- The road follows **Rock Creek** into the mountains, winding through grassy hills that soon give way to heavily forested mountains. Rocky outcrops interrupt evergreen forests, and an occasional spire juts over the trees. About 13 miles from Red Lodge, the road climbs away from the creek, and suddenly the vista opens up toward the 1,800-foot cliffs that bend around the head of the valley in a tight semicircle.

- After 5 miles of dramatic switchbacks, stop at the **Vista Point scenic overlook.** Here, at 9,200 feet, a short path leads to the tip of a promontory with phenomenal views across Rock Creek Canyon to the high, rolling country of the **Beartooth Plateau.** Signs brief you on the geology, plants, and animals of the area. As you continue on US 212, the trees give out entirely, and you begin crossing a landscape of low, rounded hills covered with grasses, sedges, and lavish wildflowers in summer. Soon, the road cuts back to the rim of the canyon, and from the narrow turnouts, you can see a chain of glacial lakes, including Twin Lakes, 1,000 feet below. Even in July, enough snow accumulates against the headwall here to draw skiers.

- As you pass the ski lift, the **Absaroka Range** breaks over the southwest horizon in a row of jagged volcanic peaks. Wildflower meadows lead to the west summit of **Beartooth Pass,** at an exalted 10,947 feet. From the pass, you descend to a landscape where scattered islands of pine and spruce eke out a living amid knobs of granite and fields of wildflowers. Hundreds of tiny ponds and several small lakes shimmer in glaciated depressions. As you approach the turnoff for Island Lake Campground, two prominent spires of the Absaroka Range swing into view: 11,708-foot Pilot Peak and 11,313-foot Index Peak. Beyond this point, you descend to a forest of lodgepole and whitebark pines toward 10,514-foot Beartooth Butte. Soon, you pass Beartooth Lake, a great picnic spot nestled against the butte's 1,500-foot cliffs.

- When the road breaks out of the trees, look to the left across a deep canyon to see Beartooth Falls cascading through the forest. In another mile, follow the gravel road to **Clay Butte Lookout,** a fire tower with a smashing view of some of Montana's highest mountains.

- Watch for deer, moose, and elk in the meadows as the road moves down the flank of the plateau to the **Pilot & Index Overlook.** You're looking at the northeastern edge of the Absaroka Range, an eroded mass of lava, ash, and mudflows that began forming 50 million years ago.

- Continue 5 1/2 miles to an unmarked bridge over **Lake Creek** and take the short path back to a powerful waterfall thundering through a narrow chasm. A completely different sort of cascade fans out over a broad ramp of granite in the trees above **Crazy Creek Campground,** 2 1/2 miles farther.

- From here, the road picks up the **Clarks Fork River** and follows it through what is left of a centuries-old forest, much of which fell victim to the great Yellowstone fires of 1988. Soon, the road passes through the tiny tourist crossroads of **Cooke City,** begun as a 19th-century mining camp. In 1877, the Nez Perce Indians retreated through this area on their way to Canada. Four miles beyond, the drive ends at the northeast entrance to Yellowstone National Park.

THINGS TO SEE AND DO

Driving along the Beartooth Scenic Byway will certainly keep your senses engaged, but if you yearn to get out of the car and stretch your legs, or if you'd like to make a mini-vacation out of your trip, check out these attractions along the route.

SHOSHONE NATIONAL FOREST. *808 Meadow Lane Ave, Cody (82414). Phone 307/527-6241. www.fs.fed.us/r2/shoshone/.* This 2,466,586-acre area is one of the largest in the national forest system. The Fitzpatrick, Popo Agie, North Absaroka, Washakie, and a portion of the Absaroka-Beartooth wilderness areas all lie within its boundaries. Includes outstanding lakes, streams, big-game herds, mountains, and some of the largest glaciers in the continental United States. Fishing; hunting. Camping.

✪ YELLOWSTONE NATIONAL PARK. *NE Entrance Rd and Grand Loop Rd, Cody (82190). Phone 307/344-2109. www.nps.gov/yell/.* In 1872, the US Congress set aside more than 3,000 square miles of wilderness in the Wyoming Territory, establishing the world's first national park. More than a century later, Yellowstone boasts a marvelous list of sights, attractions, and facilities: a large freshwater lake, the highest in the nation (7,733 feet); a waterfall almost twice as high as Niagara; a dramatic, 1,200-foot-deep river canyon; and the world's most famous geyser, Old Faithful.

Most of the park has been left in its natural state, preserving the area's beauty and delicate ecological balance. Yellowstone is one of the world's most successful wildlife sanctuaries. Within its boundaries live a variety of species, including grizzly and black bears, elk, deer, pronghorn, and bison—these are wild animals that may look friendly but should not be approached.

The Norris Geyser Basin is 21 miles south of Mammoth Hot Springs. The hottest thermal basin in the world provides a multitude of displays; springs, geysers, mud pots, and steam vents hiss, bubble, and erupt in a showcase of thermal forces at work. The visitor center has self-explanatory exhibits and dioramas (open June-Labor Day, daily). A self-guided trail (2 1/2 miles) offers views of the Porcelain and Back basins from boardwalks (open mid-June-Labor Day). The Museum of the National Park Ranger is also nearby. The area includes more than 1,100 miles of marked foot trails. Some areas may be closed for resource management purposes; inquire at one of the visitor centers in the area before hiking in the backcountry. Guided tours of the wilderness can be made on horseback; horse rentals are available at Mammoth Hot Springs, Roosevelt, and Canyon Village.

Recreational vehicle campsites are available by reservation at Fishing Bridge RV Park (contact TW Recreational Services, Inc, at 307/344-7901 for general information or 307/344-7311 for reservations). During July and August, demand often exceeds supply and many sites are occupied by mid-morning. Overnight vehicle camping or stopping outside designated campgrounds is not permitted. Reservations are required for Bridge Bay, Canyon, Madison, Grant Village, as well as Fishing Bridge RV Park. There are seven additional National Park Service campgrounds at Yellowstone; these are operated on a first-come, first-served basis, so arrive early to secure the site of your choice. Campfires are prohibited except in designated areas or by special permit obtained at ranger

Wyoming

❋ *Beartooth Scenic Byway*

stations. Backcountry camping is available by permit only, no more than 48 hours in advance, in person, at ranger stations. Backcountry sites can be reserved for a $15 fee.

Fishing in Yellowstone National Park requires a permit. Rowboats, powerboats, and tackle may be rented at Bridge Bay Marina. Permits are also required for all vessels and must be obtained in person at any of the following locations: South Entrance, Bridge Bay Marina, Mammoth Visitor Center, Grant Village Visitor Center, Lake Ranger Station, and Lewis Lake Campground. Information centers near Yellowstone Lake are located at Fishing Bridge and Grant Village (both open Memorial Day-Labor Day, daily).

At several locations, there are visitor centers, general stores for provisions, service stations, tent and trailer sites, hotels, and lodges. Bus tours run through the park from mid-June to Labor Day (contact Xanterra Parks and Resorts at 307/344-7311).

PLACES TO STAY

If you choose to include an overnight stay in your trip along this All-American Road, Mobil Travel Guide recommends the following lodgings.

★★★ **LAKE YELLOWSTONE HOTEL.** *Yellowstone National Park (82190). Phone 307/344-7311.* This beautiful retreat overlooking Yellowstone Lake was built in 1891. 194 rooms. No A/C. Closed late Sept-late May. Check-out 11 am. Restaurant, bar. $

★ **MAMMOTH HOT SPRINGS HOTEL AND CABINS.** *PO Box 165, Yellowstone National Park (82190). Phone 307/344-7311.* 97 rooms, 69 baths, 4 story, 126 cabins. No A/C. Closed Oct-Nov and Mar-Apr. Check-out 11 am. Bar. Cross-country ski on site. $

★★ **OLD FAITHFUL INN.** *PO Box 165, Yellowstone National Park (82190). Phone 307/344-7311.* 325 rooms, 246 with bath, 1-4 story. No A/C. Closed mid-Oct-Apr. Check-out 11 am. Restaurant, bar. Many room phones. Historic log structure (1904). Some rooms have a view of Old Faithful. $

PLACES TO EAT

A long day of driving is sure to make you hungry. At the end of your journey, try the following restaurant.

★★ **LAKE YELLOWSTONE DINING ROOM.** *Yellowstone National Park (82190). Phone 307/344-7311.* Closed Oct-May. Breakfast, lunch, dinner. Bar. Children's menu. Totally nonsmoking. $$

NOTES

NOTES

NOTES

NOTES

NOTES

NOTES

NOTES

NOTES